Product
Strategy for
High-Technology
Companies

Product Strategy for High-Technology Companies

Accelerating Your Business to Web Speed

Michael E. McGrath

Second Edit

McG ll

New York   San Francisco   Washington, D.C.   Aucklan otá
Caracas   Lisbon   London   Madrid   Mexico C an
Montreal   New Delhi   San Juan ore
Sydney   Tok nto

Library of Congress Cataloging-in-Publication Data

McGrath, Michael E.
    Product strategy for high technology companies / by Michael E. McGrath.—2nd ed.
       p. cm.
    ISBN 0-07-136246-0
    1. Strategic planning. 2. Product management. 3. High technology
industries—Management. 4. Industrial management. I. Title.
HD30.28.M3837 2000
658.4'012—dc21

00-055928

McGraw-Hill

A Division of The McGraw-Hill Companies

1 2 3 4 5 6 7 8 9 0   DOC/DOC   0 6 5 4 3 2 1 0

0-07-136246-0

he sponsoring editor for this book was Catherine Schwent, the editing supervisor
is Ruth W. Mannino, and the production supervisor was Charles Annis.
was set in Palatino by Victoria Khavkina of McGraw-Hill's desktop composition
it in cooperation with Spring Point Publishing Services.

nted and bound by R. R. Donnelley & Sons Company.

publication is designed to provide accurate and authoritative information in regard to
ubject matter covered. It is sold with the understanding that neither the author nor the
isher is engaged in rendering legal, accounting, or other professional service. If legal
e or other expert assistance is required, the services of a competent professional person
d be sought.

       —From a Declaration of Principles jointly adopted by a Committee of
       the American Bar Association and a Committee of Publishers

To Molly McGrath

Contents

13. Growth through Acquisitions   287

14. Growth through New Ventures   305

15. Growth through Innovation   321

Preface

Managing a high-technology company is a little like participating in an adventure story. It is fast-paced, exciting, surprising, and dangerous. The right moves can lead to tremendous success. The wrong moves can result in disaster. Nobody is really sure what lies ahead, but those with vision, insight, and a strategy can succeed. They can survive mistakes, but only if they are nimble enough to adjust in time.

As with all adventures, high-technology product strategy is not an adventure for the faint of heart. Nor is it for those who do not clearly know what they are doing. To be successful—perhaps even to survive—a company must master product strategy and skillfully navigate through competitive challenges, or the adventure will go astray. History shows that it is the proper development, application, and management of product strategy that separates enduring success from failure.

One of the great adventurers of our time, Bill Gates, started Microsoft in 1975 at age 19 and expanded it to a $20 billion software giant in 25 years by skillfully applying product strategy to new, rapidly emerging markets. Microsoft's expansion strategy leveraged its core competencies, enabling it to expand from early computer languages to operating systems, applications, and other related products. Microsoft continually differentiated its products to achieve competitive advantage. Windows provided clear ease-of-use advantages. Microsoft Office provided an integrated suite of products that was difficult for competitors to copy.

Although it took longer, 3M followed a similar expansion strategy to develop more than 50,000 products and over $13 billion in revenue by 1992. Building on technical competencies in disciplines such as adhesives, bonding, abrasives, and materials, the company continuously expanded into new product platforms.

In high technology, innovation can create new markets and fuel growth. Intel, for example, identified a product opportunity for the microprocessor in 1969, while solving the problem of a calculator circuit. It used this innovation to build a $29 billion business.

Developing new technology provides companies the opportunity to distinguish their products. Apple Computer successfully applied "vectors of differentiation" (see Chapter 7) in its product strategy to distinguish its products from those of other early personal computer companies. Its Macintosh computers are a classic example of product differentiation, and its differentiation strategy for the PowerBook product line resulted in first-year sales of more than $1 billion.

High-technology product strategy cannot be static. Companies need to adapt their product strategy as the market and competition shifts. Compaq Computer's strategy of product differentiation succeeded, while other computer companies failed. It used first-to-market strategies to introduce a portable computer in 1982 and the first Intel 386-based systems in 1986. Then it stumbled as low-cost competitors, such as Dell, began to steal market share. On the brink of disaster in 1991, Compaq reacted in time by adopting a price-based product strategy, supported by competencies in low-cost operations. By 1993, it was the most successful personal computer company. In 1996, however, Compaq embraced a more ambitious vision, and by 1998 it was in trouble again. Growth stopped, and it lost $2.7 billion.

In high-technology markets, new technology can also replace older technology, destroying existing markets in the process. In the mid-1970s, Wang abandoned the calculator market and introduced the first screen-based word processor. This fueled Wang's growth to $3 billion in revenue and 31,000 employees by 1988, but then personal computers displaced special-purpose word-processing systems, and Wang responded too slowly and with the wrong strategy. It filed for bankruptcy in 1992, reducing employment to approximately 6,000 in 1993. Had Wang adjusted differently to changing technology, it might have become one of the most successful application software companies by now.

Failure like Wang's is common for high-technology companies. For example, in 1970 minicomputers were the hot technology: More than 90 companies entered this market; 60 of these were new ventures founded to make minicomputers. By 1990, most of the new minicomputer companies were out of business and most of the companies that entered the minicomputer market had withdrawn from it.

Product strategy success and failure frequently occur in the same company. IBM had a knack for this, demonstrating numerous examples of each during the 1980s. In one business segment alone—personal computers—it built a dominant position, failed to capitalize on this position, and then lost out to competitors because its product strategy failed. Yet in 1993, IBM changed its personal computer product strategy and strengthened its competitive position.

Product strategy in high-technology companies presents many unique challenges not faced by companies in other industries. These challenges make product strategy in this sector both more critical and more difficult. It is more critical because continual technological change forces more frequent strategic decisions. If a high-technology company stops to rest on its laurels, a change in technology can cause it to fall hopelessly behind. If a company moves quickly, it can use changing technology to achieve competitive advantage. Product strategy is much more difficult to implement in high-technology companies, because technology is complex; it advances rapidly, changing competitive advantages in the process. Product and market life cycles are short. Markets with short life cycles mature rapidly, and competitive advantages shift throughout these life cycles. It is this combination—the criticality and the difficulty of product strategy—that makes it exciting. Those who are good at it succeed in the adventure; those who are not, fail.

There were several reasons I decided to say "yes" when McGraw Hill asked for a second edition of this book. Product strategy has become increasingly important in the six years since the first edition of this book, intensifying people's interest in the topic and the adventure. Then, too, the world has changed much in the past decade. I found I wanted to add fresh examples to reflect the current "state of the art." There were also a few new product strategy topics that called out for more in-depth coverage, including product strategy in new ventures and acquisitions, as well as other growth strategies.

Pittiglio Rabin Todd & McGrath (PRTM) has grown several times larger in the last six years, and over that time we have worked with many high-technology companies to improve their product strategy. I wanted to reflect some of that extensive body of experience in this revised edition, including a description of two very important frameworks used by PRTM consultants: The Core Strategic Vision (CSV) Framework and the Market Platform Plan (MPP) Framework.

This revised edition contains a lot of new material that will hopefully make it interesting not just to new readers, but also to those who read the first edition. There are five new chapters and dozens of new examples and case studies. All chapters have been revised, some of them extensively.

Although this book was written primarily for executives in high-technology companies, much of it applies to companies in other industries as well. The impact of technology, especially the Internet, is becoming more pervasive; every company is turning into a high-technology company in some way.

This book reflects more than my own experience and knowledge. It reflects the collective experience and knowledge of PRTM as a whole. For that reason, I've chosen to use the first person plural "we" throughout the book. The "we" represents the hundreds of PRTM consultants and directors who have worked to help high-tech companies of all sizes throughout the world produce better products faster, and now on Internet time.

In the preface to the original edition, I mentioned that this book might be of interest to investors in high-technology companies. At one of my many speeches on this topic, someone from the audience challenged me to "put my money where my mouth is and invest in some of these companies that I wrote about." I did. Over the next three years, each of these investments multiplied four to eight times, and my wife and I set up the McGrath Charitable Foundation with the proceeds. For those looking for investment recommendations in this revised edition, I want to remind you that while a good product strategy is a good indication of potential success, this success is only one aspect of a good investment. The other is the valuation at the time of the investment.

This edition is organized into four parts each with a common theme. The first part covers somewhat complex material that provides the appropriate conceptual foundation for the remaining chapters. In our consulting at PRTM, we've found that the Core Strategic Vision (CSV) and the CSV framework have proven to be an important starting point, not only for product strategy but also for business strategy. The concepts underlying platform strategy, product line strategy, and their implementation using the MPP framework have become accepted as a critical element of product strategy. The Expansion Framework in Chapter 6 continues to be a primary path to growth. Because of the importance of this material, I've expanded this part of the book considerably and added many new examples.

Part 2 includes all of the chapters on competitive strategy that were in the original edition. Each of the five chapters has been revised to include new examples to illustrate competitive strategy, and I've added some new material related to competitive strategies of Internet companies.

Part 3 specifically focuses on growth strategies. It includes three new chapters, as well as a revision of the chapter on innovation. In this section I build upon the previous material in the book and show how to use this to accelerate growth. This section also shows how product strategy is applied to new ventures and acquisitions.

In the fourth and final part, I summarize the process of product strategy. This is a central theme to the book: Product strategy is a process, and the better the process, the better the strategy.

Michael E. McGrath

Acknowledgments

As in the original edition, many people have contributed to this revised edition. As always, the direct and indirect contributions of PRTM's clients have been extremely important. Working with many of the best companies in the high-technology industry, PRTM has the opportunity to tackle some of the most challenging problems and opportunities, and push the envelope of management practice. The incessant desire of our clients for excellence continues to inspire us to look for better management practices.

Since the first edition of this book, consulting in product strategy has become a mainstay of PRTM's consulting practice. This edition reflects the extensive experience by the PRTM consulting staff in numerous product strategy consulting engagements to help advance the "state of the art" of product strategy. It's impossible to thank all of the individuals, since PRTM's team approach blends all experiences collectively. Nevertheless, I'd like to mention the contribution of these individuals: Bob Rabin, Cindy Akiyama, and Mark Strom; Mike Anthony, John Riggs, Rob Franco, and Mark Deck; Dean Gilmore, Craig Divino, Tom Godward, John Harris, and Anand Iyer; and Daryoush Larizadeh, Tavor White, and Doug Billings.

As in the original edition, I'd also like to recognize the writers and editors of the popular business press and the World Wide Web whose efforts usually go unrecognized. In doing the research for both the original edition and this revised edition, I read thousands of their articles, which contributed to the examples and overall perspectives in this book. This gave me an appreciation for the contributions they make to business management.

I'd like to also give a special thanks to freelance writer/editor Rhonda Keith for her help in copyediting the manuscript; my assistant, Beth Reed, for her help throughout the process; Cynthia Sherman, manager of PRTM's graphics services group, for her construction of the charts; and the associate editor of our quarterly magazine, *PRTM's Insight*, Michael Lecky, for his writing of the introductions to the four parts of the book. I was encouraged greatly by McGraw-Hill editors Catherine Schwent and Ruth Mannino. I'm especially indebted to PRTM's corporate communications director, Victoria Cooper, who gave up her weekends and nights to restructure the manuscript during the last six weeks of this project. The final work clearly reflects her unique talent, and her inspiration at the end of this project was essential to its completion.

Finally, I want to thank my family, especially my wife, Diane, and my youngest daughter, Molly, for giving me up for the many, many nights, weekends, and holidays I worked on this revised edition. We trust it is, as they say in publishing, "a contribution to the literature."

PART 1

Framework for Product Strategy

There are two approaches to travel. Pick a destination and proceed toward it, or wander off in any direction at all. Both approaches will take you someplace. If your motive is to travel for the sake of travel, then any direction will do. But if you have someplace specific in mind, you will need to plan your route. No technology organization exists for the sake of existing. Each is created with some intention in mind: to offer some product, service, or combination of the two. But an intention isn't a strategy any more than a chosen destination is a map to that destination. So then: Where does product strategy begin?

Part 1 describes the foundations of a product strategy. The keystone is what we call a *core strategic vision* (CSV). It has nothing to do with receiving premonitions or gazing off into the horizon. A CSV is the answer to three absolutely basic questions: Where do we want to go? How will we get there? And why do we think we will be successful? But *core* doesn't mean unalterable. High-tech business history is littered with the wrecks of fabled companies that clung to the core visions of their technologies, business environments, and markets, despite overwhelming evidence that their visions were obsolete. Citing a wealth of case examples, Part 1 looks at strategic vision from various angles: what it is, how it guides product strategy, what it can accomplish in its best forms, and the destruction it can wreak in its most misguided forms. It examines the challenges of aligning the core strategic vision with product strategy in the blended context of opportunities and limitations in order to create a "vector of differentiation" between the company's products and those of competitors. Part 1 also describes product platform strategy and its transformation into product line strategy. It concludes by explaining the role of technological leverage in expanding into new technology markets.

1
Strategy Requires Vision

*Product strategy begins with a strategic vision that states
where a company wants to go, how it will get there,
and why it will be successful.*

As in *Alice in Wonderland*, if a company does not have any vision of where it wants to go, then any product strategy is likely to take it somewhere. The problem is, the company, like Alice, may not be happy with "some-where" once it gets there. Product strategy is like a roadmap, and like a roadmap it's useful only when you know where you are and where you want to go. What we call a core strategic vision (CSV) provides the destination and the general direction from where you currently stand. It supplies the context for product strategy and guides those developing the product strategy by telling them where the company wants to go, how it expects to get there, and why it believes it can be successful.

> **Product strategy is like a roadmap, and like a roadmap it's useful only when you know where you are and where you want to go.**

While knowing where you want to go appears obvious, too many companies operate as though they are blind or as though their strategic vision has deteriorated. In fact, most business failures can be traced to such deficiencies. In this chapter, we examine ways that companies learn to see clearly so they can act effectively. Sometimes it's helpful to know what's not working, before you can understand what will work.

Developing a core strategic vision is not a static process. When Ken Olsen founded Digital Equipment, his original vision of a "minicomputer" in the 1950s led to the creation of a new market. He developed the first small, low-cost computer and introduced a keyboard and video screen that interacted directly with the computer. Likewise, An Wang turned his vision of word processing systems into reality.

Unfortunately, in both of these cases, the founders' vision became shortsighted. They didn't foresee how the continued evolution of information technology would change their industry, and when change did occur, they didn't change their vision of where they wanted to go. As a result, their companies stayed where they were, while the rest of their industry changed. For Digital Equipment and for Wang, as well as for many others like them, the status quo proved to be fatal. Conversely, those companies that articulate a core strategic vision know where they want to go, how they will get there, and why they will get there successfully. They are confident that they will be successful, and they move decisively. There is no confusion about what to do or how to do it. They determine their product strategies to achieve their visions and then execute these strategies.

Some of the biggest successes in industrial history were created by people with exceptional vision. Joseph Wilson saw copying machines in Chester Carlson's xerography. Tom Watson saw the future in computing. Bob Noyce saw the potential of microprocessors. Henry Ford envisioned a process that would put a car in every garage. And Bill Gates saw better than anyone else that the explosion in microprocessors would open vast opportunities for computer software.

Even these visionaries, however, could not always see clearly into the future. Tom Watson turned down Carlson's xerography because he did not see future opportunity for it. Henry Ford did not see the need for more than one color or model of automobile. Bill Gates's early vision for the future of computing underestimated the Internet revolution.

We put the word *core* in front of strategic vision advisedly, because we want to emphasize that we are referring to the essence of strategic vision. In this chapter we discuss the advantages of a core strategic vision and the necessary ingredients for a successful one. We also discuss who is responsible for a company's CSV. Success in achieving an effective core strategic vision requires competence in conceiving future opportunity and directing product strategy toward that future.

Impaired Vision

There are many types of vision that companies employ to power their strategies, but most of them fall short of core strategic vision. Before examining the characteristics of a CSV, let's look at some of those other types of vision and why they fail to serve strategy as well.

Tunnel Vision

A company can take a very narrow view of the future and not see threats or opportunities outside of its narrow focus. This narrow focus can help the company excel where it is concentrating, but its peripheral vision may be diminished; as a result, it doesn't see the impact of a new technology with better potential, the possibility of a new industry standard that could change the market, or emerging competition coming at the market from a new perspective.

Tunnel vision is particularly fatal to high-technology companies. In the late 1970s, Adam Osborne was considered by many to be a visionary of the fledgling microcomputer industry. He published his views on its technology and markets in books and magazine articles. In 1981, he introduced the Osborne 1, a portable computer with bundled software that sold for $1,795. His vision was a computer for the masses—not the best computer, but one that was adequate and priced to sell in volume. He saw himself as the Henry Ford of the new microcomputer industry.

The Osborne 1 proved to be a hit. Sales took off; in 1982 Osborne Computer was one of the fastest-growing companies in American history, and Osborne predicted that his company would reach $1 billion in sales by 1984. But Osborne's tunnel vision reinforced his self-perception that he could do no wrong, and he failed to see the looming impact of changes taking place in the industry.

In 1981, IBM, which Osborne had repeatedly put down as an obsolete company, introduced its PC based on a 16-bit microprocessor that was faster than Osborne's 8-bit microprocessor. Osborne predicted that "IBM will soon be out of the business completely."[1] However, the DOS operating system developed by Microsoft made Osborne's CP/M operating system obsolete. IBM's computer screens and disk drives were superior to those of the Osborne 1. Other companies, such as Compaq Computer, improved on Osborne's original strategy by making portable computers that were IBM-compatible. Sales of Osborne computers dropped precipitously in 1983, and by September the company had to lay off almost all of its employees. Soon after, it filed for Chapter 11 bankruptcy.

IBM's Bill Lowe also suffered from tunnel vision when he maintained an IBM-centric view of the future. In 1985, he gave Microsoft the rights to sell the jointly developed DOS operating system to other manufacturers in return for IBM's free use of it on IBM PCs. IBM, after all, had 80 percent of the DOS market. Microsoft's Bill Gates saw that this would change. By 1992, IBM's share of the market dropped to 20 percent, and IBM had given away its share of a $2 billion market for PC operating systems.[2] It would spend over a billion dollars developing a competitive operating system, called OS/2 and later renamed WARP. But this offering was too late to make a difference.

Blindness

Some companies appear to be blind or at least sleepwalking. They just keep moving along contentedly until they hit a wall without ever seeing it coming. Because they lacked a vision to show them what was ahead, they were blind to what would or could happen. Companies can be strategically blind for different reasons. Some companies just don't seem to have any strategic vision. Maybe they think it isn't very important, or perhaps they just forget about it. Actually, this is not as outlandish as it seems. Without any deliberate process for evaluating a core strategic vision, it's all too easy for executives in a company to neglect it. They may have the best intentions and know that it's something they need to get to, but other things keep getting in the way. As we discuss throughout this book, a company needs to have a deliberate process to give creation of strategic vision sufficient priority.

Other strategically blind companies may think they have a strategic vision, but what they really have is a statement of how they would like to feel, not where they are going. It's as if someone said he or she wanted to be where it is warm and the sun always shines, instead of figuring out where that is and how to plan to get there.

Prime Computer is a classic example. It stated in 1988 that it had a "clear goal: to make money for its customers, and through that, for its owners." That "clear" goal was too vague and too general. Some within Prime may have had a more specific vision of where they thought the company should go, but theirs was not the company's vision. Prime was a cash-starved company with few core competencies in a market that was deteriorating. If any company needed a core strategic vision it was Prime. Eventually, it went bankrupt and spun off its only real technology of value, the Computervision business it had previously acquired.

A company may have a vision of its future, but this vision might have a blind spot—typically an issue or assumption about which it is markedly ignorant. For example, one company making advanced composite materials failed to acknowledge the advantages of an alternative technology. A competitor was able to see those advantages and won in the market.

Bachman Information Systems is an example of a company with a blind spot. It achieved meteoric growth and went public through the success of its mainframe-oriented software. Ranked nineteenth among *Inc.* magazine's fastest-growing companies in 1992, it grew from $13 million in 1990 to $48 million in 1992. Bachman failed to see the changes that were taking place in the mainframe market, though. Revenue collapsed in 1993 as PC-based client-server computing began to replace mainframe computing.

The trend had been visible to others for several years, but Bachman didn't see it. "I should have had my periscope up faster and seen this happen," was how CEO Arnold Kraft acknowledged his lack of vision. Former employees believed that the company's close ties to IBM, which was a stockholder and joint developer, blinded the company to the shift to distributed computing.[3] This example illustrates how easily a company can develop a blind spot by unconsciously assuming that a critical factor that determines its success is unchangeable.

Some companies are virtually blind because they see things in so many different ways that their vision is blurred. Dozens of incompatible visions may be scattered throughout the company. Individuals may have beliefs about where they think the company should go, but there is no collective vision. There is no visionary leadership. One major electronics conglomerate gave up on developing a strategic vision, and its CEO stated that it was going to be "customer led." This resulted in each business unit and division working on so many different products that repetition, duplication, and wasted development dollars became a way of life. It doesn't take long to get in trouble when leadership lacks a sharply focused vision.

Since they don't know where to go, blind companies typically try to go in multiple directions. They launch many initiatives but are unable to make the tough decisions necessary to select a strategy and set priorities. As a result, resources are overallocated, and product development activities tend to drift. Frustration results, but this is just a symptom of the malaise: The cause is lack of strategic vision.

Shortsightedness

Some companies, on the other hand, tend to be too shortsighted, not seeing far enough into the future. They may be very good at the immediate tactical issues of management, but they don't see opportunities in time to take advantage of them, or threats in time to defend against them. Technological leaders are most vulnerable to shortsightedness. They are so tied to their own technological advantages that they underestimate those of others. Ironically, some of the biggest success stories in history happened when industry leaders were too shortsighted to see future product opportunities based on new technologies. Kodak, for example, was not interested in Edwin Land's instant-camera invention in 1947, so Land founded Polaroid Corporation.

Another shortsighted company was Ampex Corporation, which invented the video tape recorder (VTR) in 1956. Even at an initial price of $50,000, the VTR became a big success with broadcasting companies. Ampex had a strong patent position and actively improved the VTR product with solid-state circuitry and color capability. But it did not have a sufficiently clear vision of the possibilities for the VTR in the consumer market, choosing instead to focus on the broadcast market and to diversify outside of VTRs. As a result, Ampex lost the opportunity to be a participant, or possibly even the leader, in the multi-billion-dollar consumer VCR market.

Shortsightedness is most critical when technological discontinuities are on the horizon. Technological discontinuities appear when the improvement of one technology begins to diminish, and another technology takes its place. DuPont was successful in introducing nylon cord tire technology to displace rayon in the 1960s. Later, however, it did not see the technological discontinuity coming when polyester fiber technology proved to be superior to nylon, and it lost out to Celanese.

Hallucination

Sometimes a company looks into the future and sees an exciting opportunity that turns out to be as illusory as a mirage. High-technology companies frequently try to create products for new markets that don't yet exist, and sometimes these new markets fail to appear.

In 1980, SOLVation, Inc., envisioned the emergence of PC-based information systems for small businesses. It saw a market opportunity even larger than the $10 billion systems market for computing in midsized companies. As part of its vision, SOLVation saw low-cost customized application software, online support, and total turnkey solutions for specific industries, all at 5 percent of the price of minicomputer-based information systems.

To implement its vision, SOLVation pioneered the development of several new technologies. Innovative online support systems enabled SOLVation support staff to operate customer computers remotely in order to tutor customers or diagnose problems. It created software application generators using large, powerful computers to develop and customize software for individual customers. Finally, it configured turnkey systems with complete applications software for small accounting firms, advertising agencies, and manufacturers. SOLVation sold its systems at a competitive price on three computers: one of the first multiuser systems; IBM PCs; and, through a joint venture with Sony, the Sony personal computer.

Four years and $16 million later, SOLVation failed. Its vision turned out to be a mirage, because the market it envisioned never emerged. Instead, small businesses were content to use Lotus 1-2-3 spreadsheets as their introduction to computers. Even 10 years later, the market for customized computer applications in small business was not significant.[4]

Strategic hallucination is a particular problem for new ventures that are trying to establish an entirely new market. They have a vision of the future, but sometimes it never really materializes. Today, at the beginning of the twenty-first century, the Internet is creating new visions of the future. Numerous start-ups are trying to capitalize on these visions. Some will succeed, but for all too many their visions will turn out to be hallucinations.

Exceptional Vision

There are also effective types of vision. Those who possess superior vision are able to see product strategy opportunities ahead of others.

20/20 Vision

20/20 vision represents the average capability for anticipating what lies ahead. With 20/20 vision, a company can see sufficiently far into the future to decide where it wants to go and how it will get there, incorporating an understanding of technological trends and market opportunities. Usually this is sufficient—as long as the competition doesn't have better vision.

Understanding technological trends requires focusing on technologies critical to the company's product strategy. To do this, a company needs to identify its key technologies. Valid Logic saw the coming trend in open systems and adapted its circuit-board design software to work with the UNIX operating system. Mentor Graphics, its leading competitor, stayed with the Apollo proprietary closed operating platform and did not convert to UNIX until four years later. This cost Mentor significant market share.

Sometimes even with 20/20 vision, it may be difficult for a company to formulate an appropriate core strategic vision. IBM faced this in 1984 with its PC business. It couldn't quite see how to avoid becoming a commodity business. Bill Gates saw how IBM could do it, and he even shared that vision with IBM CEO John Akers in 1984. Gates's strategic vision was for IBM to use its semiconductor expertise to differentiate its microprocessors from those that Intel was making available to IBM's competitors, the clone manufacturers. Then IBM could produce operating system improvements to take advantage of the special features it built into its chips.[5] But Akers ignored Gates's advice, and IBM failed to achieve any unique competitive advantages in the PC business.

Peripheral Vision

A company with peripheral vision is more aware of surrounding technologies, emerging trends, and potential opportunities than many companies that have not honed their peripheral vision. It sees opportunities to leverage its technologies and skills into new markets. It sees trends in unrelated technologies that can threaten its product platforms and market position. Wang, for instance, did not have sufficient peripheral vision to see the personal computer surge coming at it from the side. Its vision focused on minicomputers and stand-alone word processing systems. Had Wang seen the PC trend, it could have considered the opportunity to extend its software capability to PCs.

Foresighted Vision

By seeing ahead, foresighted companies are able to take advantage of opportunities and parry threats that others have not yet seen. They can get the jump on competitors by developing new product platforms and solidifying skills that will be needed in the future. Bill Gates at Microsoft, for example, saw how quickly microprocessors would emerge and understood the need for graphical user interfaces. Seeing how the combination would create new software opportunities, he was able to shape product strategies more advanced than those of competitors.

Intel has shown this foresightedness. It was able to anticipate that computer users would need increasing processing power, even as others believed that current processing power was more than sufficient. Intel acknowledged the validity of Moore's Law, and saw that semiconductor technology would double processing power every 18 months.[6] As a result of this foresightedness, Intel unrelentingly developed improved microprocessors, making its own products obsolete every couple of years and dominating the market.

Core Strategic Vision

It's easy to see with hindsight why some visions proved untrue. While we can learn from the past, we can also learn from looking at the components of successful strategic visions. There are several characteristics of the type of vision that can lead to successful product strategy.

Focus

A good core strategic vision is sufficiently focused. A broad vision is too general, sounding more like a mission statement than a real strategic vision. Here is a typical example of a "vision" that could be used in any company at any time—exactly like a mission statement from the Dilbert Mission Statement Generator (http://www.dilbert.com):

> *A good core strategic vision is sufficiently focused.*

> Our strategy is to develop products that truly fulfill customer needs by exploiting our skills and abilities to the maximum level in order to provide a maximum profit to our shareholders. We will do this with high-quality products that provide a substantial competitive advantage. And while achieving this, we will be supportive of our community and our employees.

This does not provide any direction at all for product strategy, or for any other strategy. It could be applied to any type of business: supercomputers, soap, or insurance. Yet it is typical of a company that confuses general goals or a mission statement with a core strategic vision. Compare that vision statement with the following from Compaq Computer in 1993:

> We want to be the leading supplier of PCs and PC servers in all customer segments worldwide. We intend to accomplish this goal by leading the industry in developing new products, pricing competitively, controlling costs, supporting customers, and expanding distribution. Compaq understands the dynamics of the industry and is poised to move decisively to exploit new opportunities.

Compaq's core strategic vision provided the necessary focus for shifting its product strategy directly to PCs and PC servers in all market segments throughout the world. This aim is sufficiently specific, but not too limiting, since it provides opportunity for expansion into several markets.

Clarity

If a core strategic vision is too ambiguous, then there is a danger that different managers within the company will have different interpretations, and execution of the vision will not be aligned. Some additional explanation or interpretation might be required in order to clarify the vision.

A brief strategic vision statement is preferable—if it works. If not, then it should be expanded for clarification. But don't confuse length of a strategic vision with clarity. In our experience, lengthy strategic vision statements tend to be less clear.

Completeness

A good core strategic vision must be complete. We have found that completeness means that the vision can answer three questions:

- Where do we want to go?
- How will we get there?
- Why will we be successful?

Let's discuss them one by one. Although it seems obvious to state that the core strategic vision needs to describe where the company wants to go, we've reviewed too many visions that fail to answer this question. The desired destination needs to be as specific as possible, without restricting the company too much. "We aim to take advantage of growth opportunities" doesn't answer the question; nor does it provide direction on where product strategy should be headed. It's a little like telling friends that you will meet them in a restaurant somewhere in New York City sometime next week.

On the other hand, statements such as "We aim to provide manual diagnostic tests for tuberculosis" limit the company to a single product line. This may be appropriate if the company has no desire to expand into other markets, but it is too restrictive otherwise.

The key to answering the question "Where do we want to go?" is in finding the right balance between short-term objectives and longer-term opportunities. Compaq achieved that balance in 1993: "We want to be the leading provider of PCs and PC servers in all customer segments worldwide." Another very successful company, Intel, also knew where it was going in the mid-1990s. It wanted to dominate the ever-increasing market for microprocessors and related devices. Wal-Mart is an example outside the high-technology industry. It wanted to be the largest, most successful discount store chain in the world.

The following—Compaq's core strategic vision in 1993—is a good example of a vision that clearly states where a company wants to go:

> We want to be one of the top three companies providing computer-based tools for improving programmer productivity. These tools will take advantage of increasing computer power to provide ease of use.

The first part of the vision describes in reasonably specific terms where this company wants to go—what it wants to achieve—while not restricting it to a specific type of tool. Products could include tools for automated design, systems analysis, or object-oriented programming. The vision also stresses the market focus—software productivity. This provides a common theme for new products stated in terms of customer value. Notice that the vision intentionally omits any restriction of computer platform. "UNIX software development tools" would be an entirely different vision. The vision stated here provides strategic flexibility regarding computer platforms.

The second question that a core strategic vision needs to answer is how the company expects to get where it wants to go. The Compaq vision statement did a very good job of describing how it would get there: by having a better product development process than its competitors, by competing strongly with a price-based strategy, by managing costs effectively, and by having good customer support. Here again, there's value in being specific without being too restrictive. "By taking advantage of the new 386 microprocessor," for example, would be a limited vision. It describes how to get there for now, but it does not provide any guidance on what to do next.

Intel also clearly knew how it would get to where it wanted to go. It would take advantage of Moore's Law. In addition, Intel would create new users and uses for microprocessors. Wal-Mart would get to where it wanted by establishing discount stores with a wide array of merchandise at a low price with friendly service.

The "how" ingredient needs to be robust enough to last beyond the next product, as is illustrated by the middle part of our example vision statement: "These tools will take advantage of increasing computer power." This vision provides the direction to develop these productivity tools. Computer power is increasing rapidly, and the company intends to take advantage of this trend in its products. When combined with the initial ingredient of the vision, this defines the opportunity: Increasing computer power will provide new uses, perhaps new markets, for software productivity tools.

The third question—why will we be successful?—usually is based on a unique value provided to the customer. This ingredient of the vision is the basis of a competitive strategy. For a company competing on price, the core strategic vision would include something like "by being the price leader and low-cost producer." For a company using a strategy of differentiation, the vision would provide direction for that differentiation.

Compaq's vision provides direction for its future success: because it will understand the dynamics of the industry. While this is not very specific, it's probably appropriate for an industry with a rapidly changing technology. The vision also indicates that Compaq expects to manage these changes in technology better than its competitors. This provides direction for expected performance.

The basis for competitive advantage needs to be reasonably specific. "Our products will use appropriate technologies to fulfill customer needs and provide the highest quality" does not instill a great deal of confidence that the company really knows how it will be successful.

Intel clearly knew why it would be successful: by continually improving microprocessor designs faster than competitors, by building state-of-the-art microprocessors in large quantities, and by setting industry standards. And it did all that in the 1990s. Wal-Mart intended to create the most efficient and sophisticated distribution system and to institutionalize friendly service. Note the emphasis on its intent to institutionalize friendly service. This set it apart from others who merely paid lip service to it.

The last part of our example company's core strategic vision, to provide ease of use, declares that feature as the company's differentiating characteristic for each of its markets. All product platforms and individual products will be positioned on "ease of use," and the company will segment the market based on this vector.

Feasibility

It's all too easy for a company to get carried away and define a core strategic vision that is impossible. It looks good on paper, and company executives are hopeful that they will be able to "carry it off." But, in fact, a CSV is only as good as its ability to be implemented. Creating an effective core strategic vision is not the end product of product strategy; it's only the beginning. Here is an interesting example of this problem in a well-known company. The CEO of a major software company had a clear vision of the future for his company. He knew that the company had to change. It had to develop a lower-cost platform to fend off competition and expand into a growing market segment. However, he had no idea how to execute his vision through platform strategy. Nothing happened. Out of frustration, he wrote a 53-page memo to all the employees outlining his vision, including, incredibly, a strategy for a competitor to defeat the company. Needless to say, that did not work either.

The problem was not disagreement with the CEO's vision. Everyone agreed with it, and shared his frustration. The problem was that the company did not understand product strategy and did not have a process for linking the CEO's vision to new products.

Who's Responsible for Vision?

Our hapless CEO is a good example of another recurring problem at high-tech companies: the question of who is responsible for the strategic vision. Is it the board of directors, the CEO, or the executive team?

After six months on the job, Lou Gerstner, CEO of IBM in 1993, was pressured to give his vision for IBM. He was not far off when he said, "Our mission is to be the most successful information technology company in the world. ...OK, you wanted a vision statement. Fine, we got it, now let's go back to work."[7] As time went on, it became apparent that Gerstner was really formulating a core strategic vision for IBM as a whole that focused on e-business. He had realized that it was premature to disclose this vision until it was sufficiently defined, and that would take some time. It was not immediately clear how the e-business market opportunity would unfold and what the best role was for IBM. Gerstner began to position IBM to take advantage of this opportunity, but couldn't immediately articulate a vision that would have credibility. If he had described it prematurely it would have been attacked, for, at best, the vision would have been only partially formulated.

The responsibility for a business unit's core strategic vision rests clearly with the CEO or general manager of that unit. We specify business unit, because, in a large, diversified business, different units are likely to have different strategies and different visions guiding them. Successful companies are led by CEOs who are skilled at formulating and communicating an effective core strategic vision. There are really very few exceptions to this rule. There is also a high correlation in failed companies to

> *The responsibility for a business unit's core strategic vision rests clearly with the CEO or general manager of that unit.*

CEOs who lacked this skill or simply ignored strategic vision. This doesn't mean that every CEO needs to be a visionary. He or she may simply need to tap into the visionary skills of others either inside or outside the company. But the CEO needs to make sure that the core strategic vision is the best possible.

Sometimes a CEO's philosophy can serve as the basis for a core strategic vision of product strategy. For example, T. J. Rogers of Cypress Semiconductor has never left anyone in the dark about what he thinks, and his philosophy is clear: "If it doesn't make for faster circuits, happier customers, or more motivated employees, we don't spend a nickel on it." While this does not provide a complete vision, it certainly is clear philosophy, which fulfills many of the purposes of a strategic vision.

A CEO can and should expand on the company's vision and explain it from time to time in presentations to employees, at strategy sessions, and in annual reports. The brief vision statement becomes the theme for more in-depth explanations. These explanations may vary as the circumstances change, since visions often need to be reinterpreted over time. Vision is a living thing.

The CEO should turn to the executive team for help in developing the core strategic vision. It is a mistake to develop a vision in a vacuum. We have found that the executive team of a business collaboratively develops the most effective core strategic vision with its CEO. Each member contributes different views and usually argues certain aspects of the vision. Friendly debate helps ensure wider support for implementation. One word of caution, however. Executive consensus does not mean a political compromise, where everybody gets a little of what he or she wants. This is certainly a recipe for disaster.

What happens if the CEO doesn't or can't formulate a successful strategic vision? The company's board of directors needs to step up. If the directors are not satisfied with the CSV created by the CEO and his or her executive team, then it's the board's job to redirect or replace the CEO. This is the primary job entrusted to the board by a company's shareholders.

When Change in Vision Is Called For

Even successful core strategic visions eventually become obsolete. They need to change as technology, competition, and customer expectations change. Sticking to an obsolete vision for too long is almost always the reason that once-successful companies fail. At the other extreme, changing a vision too frequently is disruptive: "Gee, I changed my mind again. I guess everything that you have done is wasted; let's try going in this direction for a while." This does not instill confidence in leadership. But knowing when and how to change a core strategic vision is perhaps the most important skill of CEOs who are successful over the long term.

> *Sticking to an obsolete vision for too long is almost always the reason that once-successful companies fail.*

A core strategic vision can be changed in several ways. It can be clarified, as the company moves closer to achieving its original vision. It can evolve, as the company learns more about itself and its markets. Technology may change enough that the original vision is no longer exciting or profitable. Whatever the reason, eventually all high-technology companies—all companies, given enough time—need to change their vision.

Need for Clarification

A clarification of core strategic vision is not a change in direction. It is merely a matter of bringing the vision more clearly into focus so the company can better achieve it. Typically, with a clarification, one element will change slightly, but the general direction remains the same.

Need for Evolution

Core strategic visions also evolve. If they evolve properly, companies can adjust the where, how, or why, while still maintaining momentum. Companies try to change direction deliberately, but the change should not be too abrupt. Bill Foster's strategic vision for Stratus Computer evolved as the company's market and competition changed. Initially, the company's vision was "fault-tolerant" computing, or what was sometimes called redundant computing. Later, it became "high availability." This adjustment was made because computer hardware redundancy became less important, while high-availability software architecture became more important.

By 1992, Stratus's vision evolved into "continuous availability." This evolution was necessary to crystallize the difference between its products and general-purpose computers that were incorporating aspects of fault resiliency or high availability. The distinction between "high" and "continuous" was essential to the evolution of the vision. By 1993, Stratus's vision was to be "the leading supplier of comprehensive solutions, where availability is a critical need." Solutions included computer software as well as hardware, and led to a continued evolution of the company's vision to be a leading provider of total computer systems for the communications industry, which required high-availability systems.

While Xerox had focused on significant tactical objectives, increasing quality to improve its performance in the marketplace, as it entered the 1990s it became more strategically focused. It developed a single-minded vision of the future: to be "The Document Company." It believed that despite, or possibly because of, changing technology, the need for document-based office productivity would increase. Xerox then focused all its research, product development, and marketing on achieving this vision. It diminished or eliminated nonrelated activities and got out of the financial services business.

As part of the evolution of its vision, Xerox not only embraced digital technology as an alternative to its patented light-lens technology; but it was also a leader in the transition. By steadily and deliberately evolving its vision, it was able to direct itself to an entirely new product strategy based on digital technology, color products, and total systems. This is a rare accomplishment.

Obsolescence

A company needs to change its vision when that vision becomes obsolete, preferably before an obsolete vision gets it into trouble. Changing the vision turns the company in an entirely new direction; because of this, the change can be traumatic. Conner Peripherals is a case in point. It set the growth record for a new company, exceeding $100 million in revenue for its first year. It achieved this success by introducing increased capacity and performance in its disk drives, which were sold to personal computer manufacturers, such as Compaq. The Conner vision was narrowly focused on advanced-technology disk drives custom designed for PC manufacturers. These were developed around a philosophy of "sell–design–build," which guaranteed high-volume sales for customized products. But this vision ran out of gas and could no longer provide Conner with the growth it wanted.

In 1992, Conner Peripherals embraced a new vision to transform itself into a "leading supplier of total storage solutions for the computer industry by providing a comprehensive offering of disk drives, tape drives, storage management software, and value-added distribution." By diversifying across many related businesses, Conner hoped to take advantage of the individual growth curves of these new product platforms. Sometimes this is called the phoenix strategy: A new company rises from the ashes of a previous company. For example, EMC was originally a subcontractor for cables and subassemblies, but it saw little future in this business. Instead, it concentrated on new opportunities in RAID (redundant arrays of independent disks) drives and created a tremendously successful business.

How Vision Guides Strategy

An effective core strategic vision provides the necessary starting point for successful product strategy in the following ways.

1. *It establishes a framework for product platform strategy.* Generally, it's the core strategic vision that initiates high-level activities to replace or add a new product platform. Without a strategic vision, platform strategy is unguided; a company may be at a loss to decide when to launch development of a new product platform. One company's dilemma illustrates this problem:

"I think we need to develop a new product platform," the VP of engineering told the CEO as they discussed the upcoming R&D budget.

"What kind of platform?" the CEO asked.

"I don't know. Who's supposed to identify these?"

"Tom, the VP of marketing, is—I think," replied the CEO.

"He's entirely focused on selling current *products*. He doesn't think strategically."

"New platforms are driven by technology. What new platforms can be created by emerging technology?" the CEO asked.

"There are hundreds."

"We need to find out how other high-technology companies solve this problem."

In another example, a minicomputer company sent a team offsite to conceptualize its next generation of products. With virtually no direction from top management, the team spent two months being creative, "pushing the envelope" of technology. It came back with a de facto mainframe product concept that was a complete departure from the company's direction into a smaller, more competitive system. The proposal was rejected, and the team was directed to start again from scratch, but this time it was guided by a clearer divisional product vision.

A core strategic vision can also be the trigger mechanism to launch expansion into new markets. If it shows that a company cannot achieve its desired growth for its current product platforms and markets, then the CSV initiates exploration of opportunities to expand into new markets.

2. *It focuses the efforts of those responsible for identifying new product opportunities.* The core strategic vision indicates the direction in which product strategy teams should look for new opportunities. With a strategic vision, they begin to consider more appropriate opportunities almost subconsciously, because they know generally where to look. Without a vision, they come up with diverse ideas for new products that may not be consistent with the company's strengths or direction. While potentially creative, myriad infeasible opportunities distract a company and dilute scarce resources, since the critical mass required for success cannot be manifested.

For example, one consumer electronics company pursued an opportunity in broadcasting because someone thought it would be interesting. This opportunity appeared easier than it turned out to be. After investing significant time and money to initiate development, the company finally realized that the opportunity did not fit its strategic direction or competencies. The company deceived itself because it had little experience and "didn't know what it didn't know." In the meantime, it neglected other opportunities that could have better taken advantage of its skills. Its competitors focused on these opportunities and benefited from the company's distraction.

3. *It aligns other strategies and initiatives.* A core strategic vision is the primary point of strategic alignment. As we shall see in the next chapter, it's where strategic alignment begins. Strategic alignment is important for effec-

tive execution. Every critical function, process, and activity must be aligned, especially if a company wants to change strategic direction. If not aligned, different functions and initiatives in the company go in different directions and usually don't get very far. In today's rapidly changing world, a company cannot take too long to change direction. It doesn't have several years to align individual functional strategies and strategic initiatives.

4. *It guides product development.* The people working directly on new products are more successful if they know where the company is going and how it expects to get there. They are able to make design decisions consistent with a clear strategic vision. If that vision is communicated effectively, designers don't need management to review their work to see if it is consistent. A core strategic vision also helps align product development across similar projects, allowing better linking of individual products. Then, everyone is working in the same direction, guided by the same vision.

If those developing products do not understand the company's vision, they must guess at it or make it up themselves. When they make it up as part of product design, organization responsibilities are inverted. We've seen this too many times: The product developers determine the company's strategic vision because the CEO and senior staff are too busy fighting fires and making detailed product design decisions.

5. *It guides technology strategy.* A core strategic vision helps set the general agenda for technology development. It suggests the core competencies that will enable a company to succeed. Xerox, for example, invented a dry-processing film called VerdeFilm to replace the traditional darkroom chemical-processing technique.

> **A core strategic vision suggests the core competencies that will enable a company to succeed.**

The film was targeted for image setters and scanners in the $2 billion printing industry because it could print only one color at a time. While use of this technology in full-color 35mm consumer film application was feasible, it was not consistent with Xerox's vision. Hardy Sonnenburg, head of the Xerox lab that developed the new film, said, "To produce such a film does not fit in with our corporate profile, which is in the document business."[8]

6. *It sets expectations for customers, employees, and investors.* Various groups help a company achieve its vision. Employees contribute by their effort. Investors provide the necessary financial support. Customers join the company on its journey by buying its products. A core strategic vision is the best way to communicate to each of these groups where the company is going. If the groups believe in the vision, they will enthusiasti-

cally support the company. If they do not, they may abandon it. Without a vision, their support is likely to be unpredictable.

An effective core strategic vision can motivate people to work not just smarter but also harder. If the engineers have confidence that management knows where the company is going and has a good vision of the future, they will put in the extra effort to ensure that the company gets there with new products at the right time. Nothing helps motivate a product development team better than a crisp, well-thought-out strategic vision. If a development team lacks confidence in a company's vision, it is difficult to keep the members committed.

The dilemma is how to communicate the core strategic vision. If a company tells everyone its strategic vision, competitors might learn about it. This points out one of the differences between core strategic vision and product strategy. The vision does not describe specific details. While it can be of some help to competitors, it is not specific competitive intelligence.

Core Strategic Vision in Action

The three core strategic vision case studies that follow are all from the computer industry. At one time, each of the three companies achieved success with a deft core strategic vision, but had to adjust when the vision no longer worked. As the case studies show, they all found the adjustment to be difficult.

There are some interesting similarities in these examples. They all emphasize the point that the success of any strategic vision is transitory. Eventually it needs to change, yet most companies seem to be surprised by the need for change. In addition, in all these examples, the core strategic vision changed only when the company changed its CEO; the fate of the company rested with the success of that new CEO's vision. This also underscores the difficulty and pain associated with changing direction. It may be almost impossible for the same leader who successfully led the company in one direction to abruptly change direction and vision.

Digital Equipment Corporation: Wandering Without a Vision

When originally founded more than 40 years ago, Digital Equipment had a clear strategic vision. Ken Olsen's bold pioneering vision for the development and manufacturing of minicomputers created an entirely new market that brought the power of computing directly to users at their own locations, away from dependence on large, unresponsive corporate data centers. At the same time, Digital made the power of computer automation affordable to midsize companies for the first time. For two decades, Digital's strategic vision was tremendously successful. By the 1970s, some believed Digital to be the heir apparent to IBM as the computer giant of the future.

As the 1980s unfolded, however, Digital's strategic vision developed a blind spot. While Digital was obviously aware of the advent of personal computers and the shift toward open standards instead of proprietary computing systems, it failed to comprehend the implications of these trends on its core strategic vision. Digital didn't adjust its vision or create a new vision, even after it became clear that the original vision was no longer viable. By the early 1990s, Digital was adrift without any vision at all, and this was reflected in nine years of stagnant revenue (see Figure 1-1) and approximately $4 billion of losses over that period.

Bob Palmer was promoted from within to replace Ken Olsen, but under his leadership as chairman, CEO, and president for most of the 1990s, Digital still lacked an effective strategic vision. Palmer, however, thought he had one. In 1996 he stated that he spent considerable time and energy defining Digital's strategy for the future and came up with the following:[9]

- To help our customers create more value for their customers and shareholders.

- To build cooperative, mutually beneficial relationships with our partners.

- To create a rewarding environment for our employees.

Figure 1-1   With no strategic vision, Digital Equipment drifted from 1989 to 1997, with virtually no growth.

- To achieve long-term, sustainable growth and profitability for Digital and increased value for shareholders.

This, of course, does not constitute a strategic vision. It is little more than wishful thinking. Palmer's statements did not describe where he saw Digital going; they could have been applied to any business. Nor did they describe how Digital would get where it wanted to go or how it would be successful.

Without a core strategic vision, Digital wandered off in every direction, developing all kinds of new products. Many of these were technically interesting, but did not have much potential. Digital was the first to introduce home theater-quality audio into its PCs, something that few customers cared about. It invested more to develop proprietary operating systems, including Digital UNIX, even though the industry was moving toward Windows. It developed Mediplex software so that an Alpha server could combine video, audio, and text.

Digital continued developing computers in just about any variation possible, from the HiNote Ultra Laptop PC to a fault-tolerant VAX. In between, it developed mainframe computers (VAX 9000) and many different types of PCs, including the DECpc LP series, Pentium-based PCs, the VAXstation 2000, the MicroVAX, DECtp, and Alpha systems that ran Windows NT.

In the networking area, Digital developed a number of interesting products, such as LAN to enterprise software, PATHWORKS, and GIGAswitch/FDDI. It developed the enVISN architecture for building interactive network applications and small tool products such as Mobilizer for Windows.

To an outside observer, it appeared that Digital was desperately trying to find anything at all that might work. With the depth of its technical skills and some of these early innovations, Digital had an opportunity to be an early leader in the networking marketplace and could have rivaled companies such as Cisco, if only it had stepped back and refocused its strategic vision on the emerging communications market, possibly creating an autonomous communications business unit. But it didn't.

Digital also had some exciting computer technology, but it couldn't exploit it effectively without a vision. With the 64-bit Alpha system, Digital had the fastest microprocessors and computer systems on the market. Alpha workstations set a new standard for price/performance, in fact. But Digital did not have a vision that could be achieved by this product advantage. Nor could the advantage become the basis for Digital's strategic vision, since it did not hold enough opportunity to support the entire company.

Digital even created some interesting Internet products. Of these, AltaVista was the most successful. Yet, here again, it didn't fit into any vision, and Digital couldn't exploit it to its fullest.

Digital became desperate to maintain its revenue base—even at a loss. The only solution it saw was to offer a product line that used Intel-based processors instead of its own. The company sold these through independent distribution and retail channels at low prices, since it didn't have the appropriate sales channel. Although it built a multi-billion-dollar business on the surface, Digital was adding no real value in this new business. It was only assembling computers from components sold by other companies and relying on someone else to sell them. At the same time, Digital continued to maintain its own microprocessor manufacturing and its own sales force, and continued to develop its own operating system.

To make matters worse, Digital had too many employees for a very long time. Even at its high point in the late 1980s, Digital had almost twice as many employees as it needed. When things began to fall apart, the problem changed from an inefficiency to a crisis. Digital decided to use its excess employees to expand its service business. It created the Digital Multi-Vendor Customer Services Division, expanding its services in systems integration to include the support of more than 14,000 products from more than 1,300 vendors. Digital also added desktop support of other companies' products. It supported more than a million users of Microsoft Exchange in 1997.

A cynic could have described Digital's strategic vision during the 1990s as follows:

> Try to find a way to maintain revenue and find something for all of these employees to do, in any way at any cost. Invest R&D in anything that is interesting and keep investing in operating systems, computer systems, and microprocessor technology even if the future for them is questionable.

Although Digital was actively involved in creating alliances, without any vision there was no clear purpose for them. Instead of using alliances as a way to achieve a vision, Bob Palmer saw them as a strategic vision. In 1996 he said, "We introduced a clear and forward-looking corporate strategy in which I have a lot of confidence. It builds on our historic strengths and on opportunities for significant growth. We formed strategic alliances with industry leaders." He then went on to describe the alliances as the strategy.[10] However, Palmer confused activity with vision. Without any vision, there is really no reason for alliances.

By 1997, Palmer began talking about another vision, one in which he saw Digital as the undisputed leader in Web-based enterprise computing.[11] This could have been the basis for a successful strategic vision a few years earlier, but by that time it was too late; Palmer couldn't realign Digital's strategies to his new vision. By 1998, Digital Equipment essentially died by selling off its assets. It sold its chip-making business to Intel for $700 million and its network products to Cabletron Systems for $430 million. It had previously disposed of its relational database software, storage, and system management software businesses. Compaq Computer bought what remained in 1998.

To be fair, Digital was in a very difficult position by the late 1980s. The changes in technology and the market's acceptance of that technology had made its earlier vision totally ineffective. Changing to a new vision would have been very difficult for any company, but especially for Digital. It was highly vertically integrated. It made its own proprietary microprocessors. It developed its own proprietary operating systems. It provided a full line of computer systems, and it sold them through its own sales force. Most of these core competencies would be of diminished value under any new vision.

"If only..." is a tough pill for many Digital alumni to swallow. Here is what a winning vision might have looked like in the early 1990s with the benefit of hindsight:

> Digital recognizes the profound changes in its industry and the need to change strategic direction. Accordingly, we will migrate all our computer systems, microprocessor technology, and operating systems to support industry standards, eventually becoming leaders in advancing these technologies. We will leverage our technical capabilities to create a new business around communications and networking. Finally, we will integrate these, as well as our Internet software products, around the emergence of the Internet as the platform of the future. We know that this change will be difficult, but we believe that we have unique technical capabilities and resources to take advantage of these new opportunities better than anyone else.

In many ways Digital was like a frog in gradually boiling water. If you drop a frog into already boiling water, it will jump right out, but if you put the frog into cool water and then start to boil it, the frog will not notice that the water is heating up until it is too late. One of the likely reasons that Digital did not change its strategy in the late 1980s was that it was so successful: In 1988, it grew 22 percent and made an operat-

> *One of the challenges of changing a core strategic vision is to change it while your business is still strong.*

ing income of $1.6 billion. This is one of the challenges of changing a core strategic vision: to change it while your business is still strong.

The responsibility for the core strategic vision falls on the CEO. Although it's all too easy to place the blame on Bob Palmer, he was like the frog in water beginning to boil. Digital could have benefited from a new leader, someone who would have immediately seen the need to change quickly and define a new strategic vision. The ultimate responsibility for making this change falls upon the board of directors.

Compaq Computer: Changing Its CEO to Change Its Vision

When it created the first industry-standard portable computer in 1983, Compaq Computer had a crystal-clear core strategic vision: having the best portable computers. Its very name expressed this vision. And the vision worked quickly and exceptionally well. Compaq set the record for the highest first-year revenue of a start-up company ($111 million), as it did again in 1984 with second-year revenue of $329 million.

Compaq's vision evolved in 1988 to being the best at incorporating leading-edge, high-performance technology into personal computers. This was a wonderful evolution: Not only was the new vision a consistent extension of the original vision, it also provided Compaq with a much larger market opportunity. Revenue increased over the next two years from $2.1 billion to $3.6 billion, as seen in Figure 1-2.

But in 1991 everything began to unravel for Compaq. Its core strategic vision no longer worked. Revenue declined from $3.6 billion to $3.3 billion, and the company was barely profitable. Despite clear signs of prob-

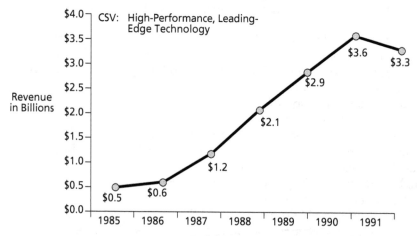

Figure 1-2   As Compaq's vision evolved to a high-performance, cutting-edge provider between 1985 and 1990, its revenues grew.

lems, its CEO and founder, Rod Canion, continued stubbornly to hold onto his vision for the company.

Unlike the Digital example, in which the board of directors seemed to be asleep, Compaq's board of directors intervened quickly in 1992 by replacing Canion as CEO. The new CEO, Eckhard Pfeiffer, immediately issued a new strategic vision and moved aggressively to implement it. Compaq's new strategic vision, described earlier in this chapter, was based on trying to achieve leadership in PCs and servers by pricing products aggressively and controlling costs. To quantify his vision, Pfeiffer set the goal of being number one in the PC market by 1996.

Compaq changed its strategies to align them with its new vision. It immediately developed a low-cost platform strategy that replaced its higher-cost platforms. Manufacturing costs were reduced dramatically by shortening cycle time and reducing overhead. Selling and administrative costs were cut in half. Since its new vision was not based on leading-edge technology, Compaq slashed its R&D investment from 6 to 2 percent of revenue.

Throughout the company, a new emphasis was placed on productivity. With the implementation of these new strategies, Compaq was able to aggressively price its computers while still being more profitable than its competitors. Its revenue per employee increased to $872,000, almost 40 percent higher than that of its nearest competitor.

Compaq continued to pursue its new strategic vision with remarkable results. Revenue more than tripled from $3.3 billion in 1991 to $10.9 billion three years later. Compaq achieved its goal of becoming number one in the PC market by 1994, two years earlier than expected! Even more impressive was Compaq's ability to achieve exceptional profitability in the cost-competitive PC business; 1994 profits increased 88 percent to $867 million, by far the best in the industry.

So what does a company do once it achieves its vision? Compaq's core strategic vision clearly described where it wanted to go, and it got there even earlier than expected. It could keep moving forward on this vision or a version of it, if such a strategy provided sufficient opportunity for growth. Or it could change its vision. In 1995, Compaq opted to change its vision, perhaps because continuing with the original vision didn't seem very exciting. By 1996 it was clearly headed in a new direction with another very ambitious goal:

> Compaq wants to be one of the top three global computer companies in the world by 2000. It will achieve this goal by becoming the global leader in providing industry standard solutions to businesses, from start-up companies to multinational corporations. Compaq can be successful by leveraging the competitive advantages we've used to become a world leader in PCs, by providing total solutions, by invest-

ing in new strategic markets and products, by promoting the Compaq brand name, and through solid partnerships.

As this vision reflected, Pfeiffer believed there was even greater potential ahead for Compaq. The new vision extended Compaq into much larger markets and held the promise of more growth. It clearly stated where Compaq wanted to go, and even how it expected to get there: by providing industry-standard solutions. However, the answer to why it would be successful was weak. Even without the benefit of hindsight, it was clear at the time that Compaq might not be able to get where it wanted to go. The competencies that helped make it so successful in PCs would not help it become successful in providing enterprise solutions. Relying on its brand name, investments, and partnerships was a clear danger sign that Compaq did not have a clear strategy for providing those solutions.

Compaq faltered as it pursued this vision. Growth began to slow and profits stagnated, as seen in Figure 1-3: 1998 revenue was relatively flat, and Compaq lost $2.7 billion. In 1999, Dell overtook Compaq as the leader in the PC industry with the largest market share.

In trying to achieve its vision, Compaq made several acquisitions, including Tandem Computer in August 1997 for $3 billion and Digital Equipment in January 1998 for $8.4 billion. In announcing the Digital acquisition, Pfeiffer stated: "We want to do it all, and we want to do it now."[12] In acquiring Digital, Compaq gained a large global customer base, an enterprise-focused sales force, and a large support organization, but it also acquired all of Digital's problems.

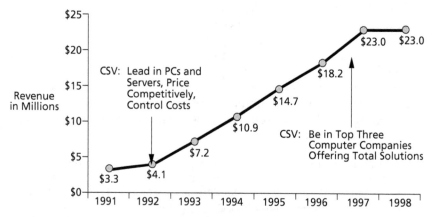

Figure 1-3   When Compaq switched its vision to providing enterprise solutions, in 1996, it faltered.

Robert Sterns, who was chief strategist at Compaq until he left in 1998, saw the Digital acquisition as a mistake. "In his [Pfeiffer's] quest for bigness, he lost an understanding of the customer, and built what I call empty market share—large but not profitable."[13]

On April 18, 1999, the Compaq board again did what it needed to do when its CEO led the company in the wrong direction: It fired him. On July 22, 1999, Michael Capellas was named the new CEO. By the end of 1999, his strategic vision for Compaq was still unclear; it sounded more like an e-business variation of the vision than a redirection:

> We will secure Compaq's destiny as the information technology leader. As the Internet transforms business, we have the powerful solutions and range of products necessary to maximize eBusiness benefits for our customers. Compaq's Internet portfolio covers the full spectrum of products and services our customers will demand as eBusiness proliferates. We occupy the enterprise space with a full range of high-availability server technology. We power an enormous installed base of customers to meet their mission-critical requirements. Each of our three business groups, supported by a global sales and marketing force and effective supply chain, is focused clearly on its defined customer base. Business needs are moving rapidly toward Compaq's strengths. This company has transformed the information technology industry before, and we will do it again.[14]

Interestingly, Dell Computer continued to follow successfully a vision that was essentially the same as Compaq's 1992 vision. Dell continued to excel in the PC market by providing low-priced PCs; however, Dell was able to reduce its cost structure even more than Compaq by using the Internet to take customer orders and configure them on the production line to customer requirements.

The Compaq example demonstrates the important role that the board of directors plays in making sure that a company has an effective core strategic vision. Compaq has always had its positions of chairman and CEO held by different people. Ben Rosen has served as the chairman of Compaq since its inception, overseeing three CEOs during that time. The Compaq board of directors takes it responsibilities seriously and acts decisively when needed.

Apple Computer: Confusing Strategy with Vision

Apple Computer was founded in 1976 by Steve Jobs and others. Like most start-ups of that era, Apple pursued a rather narrow vision: Make some money by selling computer components assembled into an Apple I motherboard. After the success of the Apple II and failures of the Apple III and the Lisa, Apple settled into a successful strategic vision that took shape around the Macintosh computer. Its vision was to create a business with the theme of a computer "for the rest of us," with ease of use as a clear basis for differentiation.

This was a very successful vision. Apple knew where it was going. It was building a large, successful company by making personal computers really usable to the masses, not just sophisticated users. And Apple knew clearly how it would get there. It would focus on ease of use. At that time, it was difficult to install personal computers, it was frustrating to get applications to work properly, and the user interface was intimidating. Apple knew why it would succeed. It would focus its development strategy on solving all these problems, and it could charge a premium for it.

This core strategic vision was not only clear, it was also strongly aligned with all of Apple's strategies.

This core strategic vision was not only clear; it was also strongly aligned with all of Apple's strategies. The Macintosh operating system was revolutionary in ease of use. Apple also introduced the mouse to make it easier to navigate the computer screen. Apple developed printers and custom software so that users could simply plug in the printer and run it. (The printer interface was a major stumbling block with most PCs at that time.) The Macintosh came with application software for word processing and a drawing program that were unique at that time.

Apple also developed software that made it easy to hook up Macintoshes in a network. Everything that Apple did supported the ease-of-use "vector of differentiation" (see Chapter 7) articulated in its simple core strategic vision.

Then along came John Sculley, replacing Jobs as CEO of Apple in 1983. Initially, he was very successful. But by 1985, Jobs and Sculley were having major disagreements, ending in Steve Jobs resigning from Apple to pursue a new venture.

Apple continued to prosper for the next decade. Even though there was no formal Apple core strategic vision, the implied vision surrounding the Macintosh carried Apple for a long time. Interestingly, Apple was perceived as a company that didn't need any formal vision because its innovative culture would simply carry on into the future no matter what lay ahead. Actually, the reverse was true. Apple had an innovative culture because it had a very clear, very successful strategic vision based on the Macintosh ease-of-use theme. So when this core strategic vision failed to carry Apple, the company began to fail.

Under John Sculley, Apple didn't pay attention to its core strategic vision. Instead, Sculley focused on what he knew best from his days at Pepsi: building a brand name through advertising and public relations. In fact, he sometimes referred to brand as the strategy: "I had a very consistent strategy with Apple that never changed. Using my marketing experience, I wanted to build a great brand through advertising and public relations."[15] This was all fizz—Apple was without a strategic vision under Sculley, and it could not decide whether to pursue a strategy of market share leadership or of premium pricing. Apple had no basis for formulating product platform strategy. While it invested a tremendous amount in R&D, without a vision or platform strategy, the effort was largely wasted. Most of the products it developed never came to market or failed soon after release.

At one time Apple tried to establish a shared vision of the future with a series of internal meetings and conferences called New Enterprise. But even after a lot of time and money were invested in this effort, nothing materialized. If anything, awareness was heightened of a strategic disconnect between Sculley and his management team owing to a lack of vision. Instead of a core strategic vision, in 1992 Apple set the following strategies:[16]

Market Share Strategies
- Reduce the time it takes to bring products to market.
- Lower prices on Macintosh products to attract more customers.
- Broaden the Macintosh family.

Enterprise Computing Strategy
- Establish Apple as a key player in client-server computing.
- Work with partners to provide better ways to integrate Macintosh into large enterprise networks.

Emerging Technologies Strategy
- Move Macintosh to RISC (reduced instruction set computing) technology.
- Take a leadership role in emerging technologies.

Although on the surface these objectives may look like the details of a core strategic vision, it's now clear that there wasn't any vision behind them. These were simply reasonable objectives, more tactical than strategic, unrelated to any vision.

Sculley made a major mistake in 1990 when he declared himself to be Apple's chief technology officer, despite a lack of technical experience. He took away any strong technical voice in a period of technology transition, during which he fell in love with the Newton product platform (which later failed).

Under John Sculley, Apple's share of the personal computer market declined from 20 percent to approximately 8 percent. In June 1993, he was replaced as CEO by Michael Spindler, then president and COO. Spindler, in turn, was replaced in February 1996 by Gil Amelio, who lasted 500 days. Apple's revenue peaked in 1995 and then began to decline precipitously as sales of the Macintosh declined. As a result, Apple suffered $2 billion in losses in 1996 and 1997.

Steve Jobs returned to Apple, first as interim CEO, then at the beginning of 2000 as permanent CEO. He appears to be reestablishing a strategic vision for the company. The problem with Apple wasn't that its core strategic vision was no longer applicable. The company slipped because it gave up on its vision. Granted, other PC manufacturers and Microsoft Windows caught up on ease of use, and application software support of Windows made the Macintosh less competitive. But essentially the same core strategic vision could have been robust enough to lead Apple into the future. Here is a possible scenario, one that again with hindsight could have been written in 1992:

> Apple continues to be committed to making computing more available to the masses through ease of use, but will deliver this in several ways. We will redesign the Macintosh operating system to run on Intel-based computers, compatible with a large range of applications software. At the same time, we will continue to exploit ease of use with the Macintosh integrated hardware/software system in emerging areas such as the Internet.

If this had been the case, Apple might have gone on to develop a viable operating system competitive with Windows on Intel-based PCs and exploit the Internet browser before

This is what a core strategic vision is all about—making sure you think about where you want to go.

Netscape got a foothold. While this scenario didn't happen, it was possible. Apple had the market position, inclination to ease of use, and technology to do it. It just didn't think to do it. This is what a core strategic vision is all about—making sure you think about where you want to go.

Notes

1. Phil Patton, "Champion of the Adequate," *Audacity,* Spring 1993.
2. Paul Carroll, *Big Blues: The Unmaking of IBM* (Crown Publishers, 1993), p. 90.

3. Maria Shao, "Bachman Information Systems Recasts Itself After Crash," *The Boston Globe*, May 2, 1993.

4. The author confesses to being the architect of the SOLVation vision as the company's CEO.

5. Paul Carroll, *Big Blues: The Unmaking of IBM* (Crown Publishers, 1993), p. 111.

6. In 1965, Gordon Moore was preparing a speech and made a memorable observation. When he started to graph data about the growth in memory chip performance, he realized there was a striking trend. Each new chip contained roughly twice as much capacity as its predecessor, and each chip was released within 18 to 24 months of the previous chip. If this trend continued, he reasoned, computing power would rise exponentially over relatively brief periods of time. Moore's observation, now known as Moore's Law, described a trend that has continued and is still remarkably accurate. It is the basis for many planners' performance forecasts. In 26 years the number of transistors on a chip has increased more than 3,200 times—from 2,300 on the Intel 4004 in 1971 to 7.5 million on the Pentium II processor.

7. Judith H. Dubrzynski, "An Exclusive Account of Lou Gerstner's First Six Months," *Business Week*, October 4, 1993.

8. Christopher Lloyd, "Film Developers Without Chemicals," *The Sunday London Times*, November 7, 1993.

9. Digital Equipment, 1995 Annual Report.

10. Digital Equipment, 1996 Annual Report.

11. Digital Equipment, 1997 Annual Report.

12. "Can Compaq Catch Up?" *Business Week*, May 3, 1999.

13. "Ekhard's Gone but the PC Rocks On," *Fortune*, May 24, 1999.

14. Compaq Computer Web site, July 22, 1999.

15. Jim Carlton, *Apple: The Inside Story of Intrigue, Egomania, and Business Blunders* (Random House, 1997), p. 75.

16. Apple Computer, 1992 Annual Report.

2
Aligning Vision and Strategy

The Core Strategic Vision Framework broadly establishes strategic alignment within both constraining and enabling boundaries. Without such alignment, a vision will not get translated into strategy.

When we introduced the concept of core strategic vision (CSV) five years ago, it was enthusiastically embraced by many companies. It was unlike the SWOT (strength-weakness-opportunity-threat) analysis used by many firms at that time, because it was more proactive. Traditionally, when applying SWOT, a business would analyze its strengths and weaknesses, identify potential opportunities and threats, and then combine these to produce an overall strategic picture. It could then decide to correct its weaknesses and leverage its strengths to take advantage of opportunities and reduce threats. In application, SWOT was primarily an evolutionary approach that identified small steps of annual incremental improvement. It did not create dramatic improvements.

Today, most companies can't afford to evolve incrementally.

Although strategic frameworks such as SWOT may have been sufficient for the competitive environment of the 1970s through the 1990s, they are not adequate for the fast-moving technology-driven industries of the twenty-first century. Today, most companies can't afford to evolve incrementally. They don't want simply to go where their strengths and their opportunities lead them. They want to exert more control over their destiny, and they want to get where they're going as quickly as possible.

Many companies wonder how they can make their core strategic vision workable and translate it into strategic actions. We have found that the framework explored in this part of the book helps. It drives the decisions necessary to shape an effective core strategic vision and to identify the strategies required to implement it—by defining the conditions and constraints that shape the vision. Using the CSV Boundary Framework helps companies answer their core strategic questions: Where are we going? How will we get there? Why will we be successful?

The CSV Boundary Framework

The CSV Boundary Framework has two very important purposes. First, it makes sure the strategic vision is achievable. A good CSV may be aggressive and it may be a stretch to accomplish, but it shouldn't be impossible or even unrealistic. A realistic CSV is aligned with the company's strategies, as well as the outside world—market, competition, technology trends, and so on. The Boundary Framework thoroughly evaluates how well the CSV keeps to this alignment.

Second, the framework identifies strategic changes necessary to achieve the vision. This makes it proactive. The resulting CSV, in conjunction with these strategic initiatives, tells the company how it will get where it wants to go and defines the strategies to get there.

Figure 2-1 illustrates the CSV Boundary Framework and its six conditions. The preliminary core strategic vision is placed in the center of the framework and is then evaluated for consistency with each of the boundary conditions. The region inside the boundary conditions defines what a company wants to be; the region outside the boundary conditions defines what it is not, and what it does not want to be.

- Core competencies (value chain)
- Financial plan (economic model)
- Business charter
- Technology trends/strategy
- Product strategy
- Market trends/competitive strategy

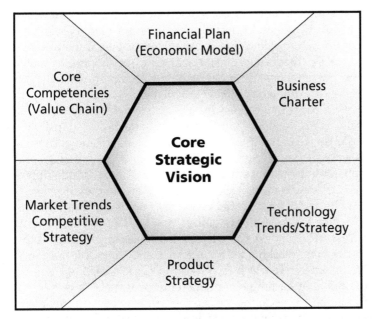

Figure 2-1 The Core Strategic Vision Framework has six "boundaries" that must be expanded or contracted to provide strategic alignment.

The purpose of these boundary conditions is not to restrict a vision, but to align it with a variety of factors and open it up to new possibilities. Boundary conditions represent different edges that shape the vision—external factors such as technology, market trends, and competitive position, as well as internal considerations such as a company's business charter, core competencies, and financial goals.

Every company has a core strategic vision (CSV), whether it has identified it as such or not.

Every company has a core strategic vision (CSV), whether it has identified it as such or not.

Every company has a core strategic vision (CSV), whether it has identified it as such or not. The vision may just be too broad and therefore meaningless, or it could be ambiguous. In some cases a company may have numerous visions without a consensus on any one. Since the CSV Boundary Framework discussed in this chapter starts with a company's current vision, it's necessary to define at least a "straw man" CSV as a starting point. Only then can the framework be used to align that vision with a strategy. A vision can be defined in several ways. Interviews with executives and selected managers can identify a shared vision, if there is one, and determine the range of visions, if there is not. Sometimes a broadly distributed questionnaire can be helpful. In many cases, published documents and formal planning documents describe the actual vision, even if a different vision is articulated.

The scope of a CSV is determined by the scope of the organization it covers. Typically, every business unit with profit and loss responsibility has its own CSV. Usually, the CSV spans multiple markets and addresses the trade-offs across these markets. But if the scope is too broad, a CSV may not be coherent. If the scope is too narrow, then there is little difference between a CSV and a market platform plan (see Chapter 5).

The best way to construct an initial vision is to use the three questions provided in Chapter 1: Where are we going? How will we get there? Why will we be successful? Let's take Cisco Systems as an example. Cisco is the worldwide leader in networking for the Internet, and, since this market is exploding, it's an attractive place to go—or, in Cisco's case, to remain. Cisco has identified three target markets: enterprise networks, service providers, and small to medium-size businesses. It expects to maintain worldwide leadership by providing end-to-end network solutions in each of these markets. And it expects to be successful primarily by being the technology leader. So Cisco's CSV can be stated as:

> Cisco expects to continue to be the worldwide leader in networking for the rapidly growing Internet market, especially for enterprise networks, service providers, and small to medium-size businesses. It expects to maintain this leadership position by providing end-to-end network solutions using its competitive advantage of being the technology leader. Technology leadership in this rapidly changing environment will be maintained aggressively by development, acquisition of technology, and alliances.

By looking at your vision as inclusive and exclusive of certain conditions that you either impose (internal facing) or accept (external facing), you can align your strategies with the realities of your company's "condition" at any given time. The framework helps you test your vision against these boundaries and identify inconsistencies and contradictions. It helps you understand how to reshape your vision or alter your boundaries until you gain alignment and therefore avoid trying to achieve the impossible.

A boundary condition defines the border between where a company wants to go and where it doesn't want to go, between external trends that are incorporated into its core strategic vision and those that are excluded. It defines the border between what current capabilities a company can leverage going forward and what the company needs to do differently to be successful. It's important to understand how boundaries either constrain or enable your vision.

Some boundary conditions push on your strategic vision to stay within them or call for eliminating the constraint. You can do something about certain constraints, whereas you might not be able to do anything but accept others. Here are some examples:

- If a multidivision company defines the scope of business activities for its divisions in a CSV, this charter constrains the CSV, unless or until the company modifies the division's charter.

- Once a company has determined its core competencies, the success of its CSV is constrained by these competencies. It is unrealistic to expect a CSV requiring new core competencies to be successful without strategies for developing these new competencies.

- A CSV is constrained by limitations of financial resources. For example, a CSV calling for higher R&D investments than planned would require that the current constraint be lifted.

- Boundary conditions include external trends. An emerging technology could threaten the potential of a company's CSV and become a constraint to the success of that vision. Similarly, a market trend that is inconsistent with the CSV becomes a boundary to the success of that vision.

Boundary constraints are not always a bad thing. They can keep the core strategic vision realistic. However, sometimes, removing constraints can make the CSV *more* realistic. This process of identifying and initiating actions to remove constraints is a critical step in strategic alignment. Changing a boundary condition to remove a constraint typically requires a strategic initiative. For example, an aggressive CSV might be inconsistent with the potential of a company's current product platforms. To remove this constraint, the company needs to explore the possibilities of developing a new product platform, potentially to expand into new markets. This is how the CSV guides product platform strategy (see Chapter 3) and triggers efforts for a new product platform.

Unlike constraints, boundary enablers don't require alignment of the CSV and a boundary condition; instead, they create possibilities by expanding the vision. The CSV can then take advantage of these possibilities, or it can pass them up. Here are some examples of boundary enablers:

- When a company has some strong core competencies, it can consider a strategic vision that takes advantage of those competencies. It need not use them, but it does need to address what to do with such competencies if it doesn't use them.

- A financial boundary enables work in the opposite direction of constraints. Frequently, companies need to expand their core strategic vision to meet their goals for expected revenue and profit growth. If the current CSV does not have the potential of achieving new goals, it must be expanded.

- An emerging technology may enable a company to expand its CSV in order to achieve a competitive advantage or enter a new market. Again, the company may or may not choose to incorporate this new technology into its core strategic vision.

- If a market trend creates a new opportunity, then a company can expand its CSV to take advantage of it.

In most cases, a company can't take advantage of all these enabling or expansive conditions, but it's important not to overlook them. In other cases, alignment means explicitly deciding *not* to take advantage of a boundary condition. Core competencies frequently fall into this category. Eventually, a company may determine through its CSV that it no longer needs a particular core competency. Options include eliminating the capability, spinning it off into a new business, or selling it outright. In any of these cases, it is better for that company to make a clear decision and communicate it, rather than let the organization continue to invest in improving a core competency that is no longer needed to achieve its vision.

As we have said, six boundary conditions shape the CSV. There can be more or fewer than six boundaries; however, in our experience, this number of conditions seems to work in most cases. Sometimes different boundary conditions are defined, or they are grouped differently. In some cases, when three internal boundary conditions and three external boundary conditions are used, most internal actions are initiated by the core competency boundary. Changes in product platform strategy, for example, are initiated through this boundary instead of a separate product strategy boundary.

Strategies and trends are not only aligned with the CSV; they are also aligned with one another through the CSV. So the CSV Boundary Framework broadly establishes strategic alignment. Without such alignment, a company tends to follow inconsistent strategies. Strategies need to be integrated for maximum effectiveness; if they are not, they can actually work against one another.

One company strategically invested in a new technology that its research staff passionately believed would dramatically change all of its products. At the same time, however, its development organization was busy perfecting and launching a new product platform based on an alternative technology. Once the company released new products based on this alternative technology, it was committed to support the technology in the marketplace; it couldn't apply the other new technology despite its superiority and its availability. Even the alternative of licensing that new superior technology was not possible, since the company didn't want the more advanced technology to be used by competitors.

Another company was actively implementing a strategy of low-cost, high-volume manufacturing by building a supply chain optimized to that goal. But its product strategy was to shift toward more complex, high-value, customized systems. Its optimized (for low-cost, high-volume) supply chain put it at a disadvantage when these new products were launched.

The layperson usually diagnoses these problems as resulting from "a failure to communicate." While that's certainly true, it's unrealistic for complex organizations to expect to communicate complicated strategic alignments without a formal process. The CSV Boundary Framework is the basis for this process.

Strategic alignment is both vertical and horizontal: vertical to set priorities within each strategy, and horizontal to achieve a fit across all strategies. The CSV Boundary Framework provides horizontal alignment through the process of fitting the CSV within the boundary conditions. It prompts vertical alignment by defining what strategic changes need to be initiated.

The point is, no matter how many "boundaries" you choose, they need to be defined and then aligned with the core strategic vision. Let's look at each of the six standard boundary conditions in turn.

Aligning Financial Plans/Economic Model

In the first chapter we talk about the frustration of companies that define a qualitative vision of where they want to go and then don't like it when they get there. In most cases, financial goals characterize where a company wants to go. This first boundary condition addresses the financial aspects of this problem by testing the alignment of a company's CSV to its financial goals, typically expressed in terms of revenue growth, profitability, and investment

Typically, financial goals are defined in the company's long-term financial plan, although they could simply be stated as financial goals. The most important financial goals are revenue growth and profitability. Profitability is the result of several different cost elements, so other financial measures such as gross margin, R&D investment, and selling expense may also be important. Some companies may have a financial objective that restricts their cash requirements.

The primary test of this boundary condition is to see if the CSV can achieve the financial objectives. Surprisingly, many companies fail this test. When they state their core strategic vision explicitly and then model it economically, they find that even if the vision is fully achieved, it will fall short of their more ambitious financial goals. Or they may find that their financial objectives will be achieved only if the CSV is achieved fully: Partial achievement would be devastating, for there is no margin for error.

There can be several underlying reasons for this disconnection. The company's market growth and its projected share of market may not yield the revenue growth expected, or the economics of the business could be changed by the CSV. For example, one company with a dominant market share for a well-established product redefined its CSV to take advantage of a new technology and the emerging preference by its customers for products using this technology. Its new CSV was shaped primarily, then, by technology and customer trends. But there was a major disconnect between the CSV and the company's financial goal, which was to grow 20 percent per year. The new products would generate less revenue per customer. So even if the company achieved its vision and dominated the revised market, its revenue would be cut almost in half.

How can a company be surprised by a gap that big? In this case, the company's new vision changed the economic model of its business, but the company didn't understand or quantify the impact until it applied the rigorous analysis of the CSV Boundary Framework. The way to align this boundary is by creating an economic model of the CSV. In most cases the economic model is not simply a forecasted income statement. It's a high-level model of the critical elements of the CSV expressed in financial terms.

The test for this boundary condition is not deterministic. The outcome can't be predicted precisely, because all the factors that will determine that outcome can't be reliably predicted. But they *can* be modeled. By developing an economic model of the CSV, a company can understand the range of potential outcomes under different assumptions. Thus the model can provide some level of probability that the CSV will achieve financial goals with different levels of success.

Aligning Market Trends

Market trends can be threats or opportunities. A change in direction or a new market trend can affect the core strategic vision several ways:

- It can change the size of market opportunities.
- It can change the importance of satisfying different customer needs.

- It can change the relative importance of buying behavior and customer retention.
- It can change elements of the supply chain.

Two companies can look at the same market at the same time and see two very different trends. A fascinating example is how Boeing and Airbus in 1999 each saw the future of the long-range travel market. Both companies anticipated growth in passenger travel and similar sales of new aircraft; however, each envisioned very different patterns of travel.

Airbus reasoned that the number of passengers traveling between the world's biggest and busiest airports would grow faster than airport capacity. It believed that a new generation of giant planes would be required to serve this market, so it began developing the A-3XX, which would carry more than 650 passengers and travel more than 8,800 miles before refueling. It would be more like a cruise ship than an airplane and was expected to cost more than $12 billion to develop.

Boeing had an opposite vision. It envisioned airlines moving toward point-to-point service between smaller cities, with passengers preferring more moderately sized planes. As a result, it planned a 747S-Stretch version of its existing 747 platform, which would carry approximately 500 passengers and be expected to travel approximately 8,600 miles before refueling. The key difference with Airbus has been a much more modest investment—of approximately $2 billion.[1]

Emerging high-technology markets present unique challenges to defining a CSV. New markets frequently emerge in unpredictable ways, so the CSV may need to be more flexible or reevaluated more frequently. Open Market, Inc., suffered from this challenge. As a pioneer and leader in the e-commerce software market with a 31 percent share, Open Market initially focused on the complex software for large Web sites and then on software for electronic catalogs. But these weren't the segments that emerged most quickly. The segment enjoying most rapid growth was software for building less complex electronic storefronts. As a result, by 1999, Open Market lost its momentum and had a difficult time achieving its vision of continuing to be a leader in e-commerce software.[2]

Market segmentation may show how the CSV needs to be shaped for each segment. As Cisco validated its CSV, it reconfirmed that all three of its major market segments were interested in end-to-end solutions, even though the specific elements of those solutions varied by market. In 1998, Cisco heard its customers correctly: Businesses in the enterprise market wanted to begin incorporating voice into their networks. Service providers wanted to deliver broadband capabilities and integrated data, voice, and video networking solutions. The small to medium-sized business market wanted a variety of integrated products and also wanted them easily available through two-tier distribution.

One word of caution: Don't automatically rely on customers to define the market trend boundary. Sometimes they are wrong, and this incorrect input could distort the CSV. Bob Metcalfe, founder of 3Com, shares this example. In 1982, 3Com was the leader in Ethernet cards for multibus-compatible computers, and customers wanted 3Com to develop a next-generation card. Although 3Com heard this input loud and clear, it did not heed it; instead, it redirected its strategic vision to develop an Ethernet card, EtherLink, for the new IBM PC. Today, there are no multibus computers left, but 3Com ships more than 20 million EtherLink cards per year.[3]

> *Don't automatically rely on customers to define the market trend boundary. Sometimes they are wrong, and this incorrect input could distort the CSV.*

A company's position in the marketplace relative to its competitors also shapes its vision, particularly *how* it expects to be successful. Will the vector of differentiation (see Chapter 7) implied in a company's vision enable it to successfully differentiate its products and services against competitors? A company will anticipate how its competitors will compete and assess their likelihood of success.

Finally, a company needs to keep an eye on the possibility of competition from unexpected sources. This was once a challenge unique to technology-based companies, but with the pervasive impact of e-commerce, it's occurring in many more industries.

Aligning Technology Trends/Strategy

Technology trends can be threats or opportunities, depending on whether they are incorporated successfully into the CSV. To thoroughly understand the impact of technology trends on its CSV, a company needs to identify the future roadmap of key technologies, emerging technologies that could affect the vision in the future, and unrelated technologies that could possibly create substitute products.

As we will discuss later in more detail, Xerox's vision of being the most successful document company was threatened by an emerging technology trend. It was one of the world's best companies in commercializing the technologies of light-lens copying, but the emergence of digital technologies threatened to displace these systems. Fortunately, Xerox's CSV was effective enough to identify this technology threat, and the company was agile enough to change its vision and launch a product strategy to develop new product platforms based on digital technologies.

Cisco takes an interesting approach to maintaining technology leadership. Its vision calls for end-to-end solutions and technical leadership, but in the late 1990s Cisco simply didn't have the resources or time to develop all the technologies necessary to accomplish this ambitious vision. Cisco was confronted with an inconsistent boundary condition. Instead of changing its vision, it opted to acquire the technology it needed. By the end of 1998 Cisco had made 25 acquisitions, and in 1999 it made another 65. These were mostly small companies with advanced technology that would help it maintain its technical leadership.

Technology trends are important not only for how they influence product technologies but also for how they affect the value chain. Dell Computer provides an excellent example. In 1996, Dell decided to apply Internet technology to its customer order process, which gave it a cost advantage. Inventory was lowered by 80 percent, and operating costs were reduced. Dell was able to compete on price and still make a profit.

Major disruptive technologies broadly affect many industries, both directly and indirectly. For instance, the advent of railroads not only changed transportation, it also changed manufacturing and trade, and stimulated innovation in many areas. The introduction of the telephone created new industries and enabled new management approaches as well as changes in communications. As in the case of other major disruptive technologies—such as the internal combustion engine, electric power, and television—the invention of plastics and microelectronics has had sweeping effects. Today, the Internet is a broad disruptive technology that affects the CSV of almost all companies, not just high-technology companies.

Broad disruptive technologies must be considered in the technology boundary condition. Companies must understand how these trends can affect their CSV. The advent of the Internet has caused almost every company to reassess and alter its CSV; successful companies have reacted more quickly to this trend.

Aligning Product Strategy

The current capabilities of a company's products limit its CSV, to some degree. A company may not be able to expand or change its CSV without also revising its product strategy, particularly its platform strategy (see Chapters 3 and 5).

This alignment begins by defining the capabilities of current products as well as the product strategy going forward. Are they sufficient to achieve the CSV? If not, changes need to be made to the product strategy to support the vision, or the vision must be adjusted to fit within this constraint. Most often, it's the product strategy that needs to change, and the changes are generally of two types. The first type comes from the need to develop a new generation of product to replace current products. We refer to this as a product platform replacement or a next-generation platform, since it requires development of a new platform. Such a change is necessary if the current product capabilities are not expected to be competitive enough to achieve the vision, or if new capabilities are needed to expand the current market or markets. With this type of product strategy change, there is an implicit assumption that the current market or markets are sufficient to achieve the CSV, an assumption that would have been made during the evaluation of the market trend/competitive strategy boundary.

As we discuss earlier, Xerox realized that digital technology was a threat to its vision, so it changed its product strategy to develop a new generation of copiers and printers based on digital technology. As expected, this new generation of products began to replace light-lens copiers. Some companies, such as Intel, have institutionalized next-generation product platform development into their product strategies. They don't need to change their vision; constant regeneration of new product platforms is already part of their vision, as well as the basis for their product strategy.

The second type of product strategy change comes from the need to develop a new product platform to expand into a new market. If the current market does not provide sufficient opportunity to achieve the CSV, then growth can be achieved only by expanding into new markets. A medical device manufacturer dominated its primary market with a market share greater than 85 percent, and had little opportunity for either expanding the size of the market or increasing market share. As a result of its CSV boundary analysis, the company realized that it needed to expand into a new market to grow, so it launched a combined development and acquisition strategy to create products for a related market for test products. Here again, companies that set objectives of rapid growth build expansion into new markets into their CSV and product strategy; Microsoft is an obvious example.

In our experience, many companies find that defining a new, more aggressive product strategy to achieve their CSV throws them out of financial alignment. They can't afford the R&D necessary to fund their new product strategy. At this point, they face strategic decision making and need to make critical trade-offs in their strategy.

Aligning the Business Charter

A company's business charter is essentially what everyone thinks the company is and what it isn't. To some extent a company is defined by its mission, culture, values, and history. For a business unit within a multi-division company, the charter may actually be delineated formally as well as informally. The business charter boundary enables a company to focus its initial CSV where it is expected. This constraint keeps the CSV from bouncing around too much and dispersing a company's focus. In a way, Cisco's practice of acquiring companies became a part of its business charter. It made acquisitions and the integration of acquired companies a normal business practice.

The business charter may restrict the vision to "doing what's expected," but when the vision doesn't fit within other constraints, this boundary condition should be reconsidered. Doing so encourages out-of-the-box thinking: What else can we do? How can we expand and grow the business in new ways? Explicitly recognizing this boundary condition enables a company to deliberately decide to expand its charter rather than leaving a gap. A company can evaluate alternatives before deciding on the most appropriate change, and anticipate the implications of that change.

The medical device manufacturer discussed above was a division within a broader company. When it decided to grow by expanding into a new market, it defined a CSV that was outside of its charter. So the division's general manager went to the CEO, described the process they had gone through, and explained why it was necessary to expand the division's charter. The CEO was impressed by the thoroughness of the thinking and immediately approved the change in the division's business charter. Interestingly, other divisions without a thorough CSV approach were not able to get similar changes approved.

Aligning Core Competencies/Value Chain

A core competency is a critical skill or unique expertise that enables a business to provide a superior value to its customers that's difficult for competitors to emulate. The core competencies a company possesses form the CSV boundary condition in this realm; the core competencies it doesn't have are outside this boundary.

When a company's revised CSV requires new core competencies, it pushes the boundary condition out. Compaq Computer's successful CSV change in 1991 is an example. When Compaq's CSV was based on being the first to incorporate high-performance, leading-edge technology into its products, then its core competencies of rapid product development and excellent technical skills were critical to its success. However, when Compaq changed its CSV to lead in PCs and servers by pricing competitively and controlling costs, it needed to develop new core competencies. Compaq used its technical skills to design low-priced PCs, and it developed core competencies in low-cost manufacturing. It also cut selling and administrative costs in half. Since Compaq no longer needed to maintain a deep technical competency, it reduced R&D spending from 6 percent to 2 percent of revenue. Making these changes successfully realigned Compaq's core competencies with its new CSV.

If a company's CSV takes advantage of its core competencies, then its vision is aligned with its core competencies. If its CSV doesn't use a core competency, then it no longer needs to cultivate that competency. Such was the case with a company that was one of the best in the world at manufacturing simple products at very high volumes. When it changed its CSV to replace these products with more complex, assembled products, it discarded one of its most significant competitive advantages. When a company changes its CSV and no longer has a need for some of its core competencies, it must decide how to dispose of them. In some cases, it can simply let a competency atrophy. If the company has a unique competency in a technology it no longer needs, it can stop investing in that technology.

However, when a competency involves employees and facilities that are no longer needed with the new CSV, a company may want to sell these in order to get some value for them. Take Qualcomm, Inc., as an example. By 1999, it had built a $4 billion mobile telecommunications business, but it changed its CSV to focus on becoming the wireless industry's best research lab. With this new vision, it no longer needed a competency in manufacturing products based on its technology. Instead, Qualcomm decided to license its technology and design computer chips, outsourcing the manufacturing. Its vision was to become the Intel or Microsoft of the wireless industry. So it sold off its wireless network division early in 1999 and later sold its cellular telephone business.[4]

The CSV Boundary
Framework in Action:
Company ABC[5] Case Study

Company ABC, a manufacturer of computer peripherals (and a disguised PRTM case), had flat sales for the last five years, despite the growth of its market and strong revenue gains by competitors. Like an airplane without a flight plan, this company was flying in circles and rapidly running out of fuel. Most of its revenue and profits came from older products based on stale technology, and its image and brand were tightly linked to those increasingly outdated offerings. The company had aspirations of moving up market with better-performing, higher-priced products and a new brand positioning, but it had no flight plan for getting there. It was beginning to realize that there is a big difference between aspirations and a core strategic vision.

Looking to 2002 and beyond, the management team wanted to establish a clear strategic vision that was challenging, yet compatible and consistent with the organization's capabilities. To accomplish this goal, the management team used the CSV Boundary Framework to evaluate various core strategic visions against the boundary conditions. When there was an inconsistency with a boundary condition, the team worked to determine how that boundary condition might be changed, or how the core strategic vision in question might be changed or disqualified from consideration.

Forming a New CSV   As a result of thoroughly applying the CSV Boundary Framework, Company ABC formed a new CSV:

> Company ABC will become known for its attention to customer needs with "print on paper" products and complementary supporting solutions. We will focus on business markets, including vertical and specialty markets. We will pursue a leadership position by leveraging our competitive advantages in color and monochrome technology. Our channels, buyers, and end users will view Company ABC as the supplier of choice in terms of customer satisfaction and value.

Financial Plan Alignment   As a privately held company, ABC was not under the same pressures as a publicly held company to increase profits and shareholder value. The financial focus of the management team was on unit growth and revenue. For each of the core strategic vision alternatives under consideration, Company ABC assessed its ability to reach revenue goals while managing investment, profits, and cash flow at a level that could sustain its desired growth rate.

With sales operations in both developed and undeveloped countries, the company also wanted to clearly delineate the revenue contribution of each geographic concern in support of the overall objectives. Given these boundary conditions, the management team augmented its core strategic vision with a set of high-level financial goals:

> Company ABC's revenue will be $1.2 to $1.5 billion by 2002 with a margin structure that allows for investment in its brand. Developing countries will contribute 20 percent of total annual revenue by 2002.

Business Charter Alignment   The business charter of Company ABC had been informal and not clearly understood by its workforce. In the past, the company had explored business opportunities that went beyond its traditional computer peripherals business, but mostly more or less randomly, as opportunities presented themselves, and with limited communication to the workforce as to overall goals or objectives. Now, for each of the core strategic vision alternatives, members of the management team weighed their growth goals against the market opportunities represented by their core business, and their capabilities for extracting value from new business opportunities. They concluded that the growth opportunities in existing markets were sufficient to realize their financial plan, but also elected to clarify their business charter by highlighting the new focus on business markets and print-on-paper products.

Market Trends/Competitive Strategy Alignment   Members of the management team analyzed market conditions and their competitive landscape. Given the relatively small size of the company, they were particularly concerned with the breadth and depth of the competition and their brand name domination. All of their competitors were vying for leadership positions in color and multifunction product categories. There was also an observable move toward increasing customer value beyond the traditional hardware-related experience through software and Internet-enabled delivery vehicles. Within the channels, a dramatic transition was under way toward digital products and services. The management team members carefully considered this "gold rush" toward the digital realm as they selected and refined their core strategic vision.

Technology Trends/Strategy Alignment   The management team of Company ABC spotted dramatic changes on the horizon from several different technological directions. The team was particularly concerned about the encroachment of ink-jet technology on laser-based printing technology. Ink-jet printing devices were reaching higher performance levels and fast becoming a mainstream alternative to the company's primary printing technology. The management team was also paying careful attention to the apparent convergence of digital peripherals. High-end digital copiers and networked multifunction products were threatening to move down market, as substitutes for a multitude of middle-market fax machines and printers resident on local area networks. With the pervasive use of e-mail, multimedia applications, and the Internet, business documents were becoming increasingly complex, with a higher percentage of their content in color, and a majority of the document life cycle shifting to digital. The result was a stronger demand for device interoperability and network-related services. These factors and trends weighed heavily on the management team's selection of a core strategic vision and more specifically, on its chartering of product strategy teams.

Product Strategy Alignment   Serving its current market, Company ABC had product platforms that supported monochrome and color, networked and stand-alone, and low- to middle-market products, including form printers, line printers, page printers, and fax machines. Given the convergence of digital peripherals, the pressure from below by advances in ink-jet technology, and the threat from above from digital copier manufacturers, Company ABC believed its highest priority for product strategy and subsequent development was in multifunction products for the office. With a potential advantage in its color printing technology, the management team also recognized a significant opportunity to sell its products to peripheral and PC manufacturers for resale under their own brand names. The company didn't have any explicit plans in place to address this OEM (original equipment manufacturer) market. With these two issues at play, ABC began to implement its core strategic vision by initiating the following strategic actions:

> To reach our goals, product strategy initiatives will be chartered for multifunction products for business markets in the Americas. In addition, a team will be chartered to assess OEM opportunities, define the company's OEM strategy, and develop an implementation plan.

Core Competencies (Value Chain) Alignment   With a long history of developing and manufacturing printers, team members believed the company had specific competitive advantages in printer architecture and paper handling. While their current product set was becoming increasingly outdated, they believed they still possessed a strong brand image for product durability and reliability. They also believed their corporate culture fostered a uniquely strong commitment, both to the company's objectives and to the satisfaction of its customers. In order to achieve any of the core strategic visions they were considering, team members did, however, recognize the need for improved management practices in alliance management, product planning, and product development. With these considerations in mind, the management team elected to implement the core strategic vision by establishing the following new objectives:

> Company ABC will leverage and invest in the development of the following capabilities and core competencies:
>
> - Harness our printing technology and architecture to support a leadership position in color.
> - Build upon the company's brand image, promoting broader brand awareness for its new offerings.

- Focus on "customer value creation," including end-user feedback in product planning and development, and establishment of a leadership position in customer satisfaction.
- Develop an approach for effectively managing the strategic alliances and partnerships required for sourcing technologies and delivering timely solutions.
- Attract and retain highly motivated, competent employees, committed to the company's goals and highly effective at achieving results with and through others.

Results   The exercise using the CSV Boundary Framework provided Company ABC with a new strategic direction that promised to significantly increase sales and profits. By following the new core strategic vision, the company was expected to more than double its revenue in five years. Moreover, this CSV was credible, and the company's strategies and strategic initiatives were aligned around it. Employees clearly understood the company's direction and observed immediate action by executive and senior management in support of realizing the CSV.

Notes

1. *The Wall Street Journal*, November 3, 1999. Note that these different visions are still being pursued.
2. *Business Week*, "E.BIZ: Where Is It Now? Open Markets Fall," November 1, 1999.
3. Bob Metcalfe, "Innovation Is a Flower, Innovation Is a Weed," *Technology Review*, November–December 1999.
4. *Business Week*, December 6, 1999, pp. 96–98.
5. The case was originally published by John Riggs in PRTM's *Insight*, Spring 1999.

3

Building the Foundation: Product Platform Strategy

A product platform is a collection of common elements,
particularly the underlying technology elements, implemented across
a range of products. It is primarily a definition for planning,
decision making, and strategic thinking.

Product platform strategy is the foundation of product strategy, especial-ly in high-technology companies that have multiple products related by common technology. It defines the cost structure, capabilities, and differ-entiation of the resulting products. By separating product platform strat-egy from product line and individual product strategy, a company can concentrate on its most important strategic issues.

A product platform is not a product. It is a collection of the common elements, especially the underlying defining technology, implemented across a range of products. In general, a platform is the lowest common denominator of relevant technology in a set of products or a product line. These common elements are not necessarily complete in the sense that they are something that could be sold to a customer. A product platform is primarily a definition for planning, decision making, and strategic thinking.

Product failures in high-tech companies frequently can be traced to an incomplete product platform strategy, in which a company may have missed or ignored critical ingredients of the strategy or may have made some bad choices. Many companies simply do not have product platform strategies. They rely on their product strategy to carry a weight it cannot bear. In this chapter, we explore the differences between platform and product strategy and why it's so important to have platform strategy in place *before* developing product line strategy.

The nature of product platforms varies widely across industries and product applications. For example, the product platform for a personal computer consists of the microprocessor combined with its operating system, such as the Apple Macintosh or the Intel/Windows platform, along with the packaging, power supply, computer memory, disk drives, monitors, and interfaces. The operating system combined with the type of microprocessor are what we refer to as the defining technology of the platform. Individual products from this platform are defined by variations in microprocessor speed and configurations of other platform elements, such as the amount of memory, size of disk drive, and type of monitor.

In an application software product, the platform comprises the architecture (such as mainframe, client/server, desktop, or Web-based), input/output, and application functionality. These determine how the resulting products can be used and what computer hardware is required. The individual features and functions of the applications are configured to the specific products.

A product platform can also be a core chemical compound combined with the manufacturing process for producing a range of products from this compound. It could be a unique resin that produces high-temperature materials of varying strength depending on the fibers used. In life sciences, a platform could be a base chemistry used in a range of immunodiagnostic tests, or it could be a delivery vehicle for a class of drugs.[1]

A product platform provides the foundation for a number of related products, typically a product line. Figure 3-1 illustrates how new products are built over time on a common platform. While all products are unique in some way, they are related by the common characteristics of the product platform. Platform A was developed with a number of related products in mind. Product 1 was the first product to use this platform, and it was targeted at the midrange market segment in price and performance. Product 2 and Product 3, which implemented the platform at lower and higher price/performance levels, respectively, followed it. Products 3A, 3B, 3C, and 3D were international variations of Product 3 that incorporated country-specific modifications. Finally, Product 4 was

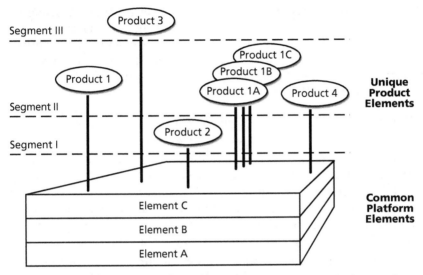

Figure 3-1 New products are built over time on a common platform and are related through common elements.

developed toward the end of the platform life cycle. It was a low-cost product developed to sustain the life of the platform a little longer.

The definition and sequence of specific products derived from a platform constitute a product line strategy (see Chapter 4).

Ingredients of Platform Strategy

Successful product platform strategy can be the biggest determinant of success, especially for high-technology companies. All other aspects of product strategy are enabled and constrained by the platform. In our experience, several ingredients are necessary for successful platform strategy.

1. *The underlying elements of the platform are clearly understood.* A product platform consists of a number of elements—frequently, although not always, related to technology. Some of these elements are configured differently to make different products from the platform. Each element has different characteristics, requiring a company to understand how they fit together, how they may change over time, and how they differ from competitors' platforms.

Often, it's all too easy to oversimplify a product platform and fail to really understand its elements. Take Amazon.com, for example. To say that it's simply a way of ordering discounted books and other products over the Internet fails to show an understanding for Amazon's product platform. There are several important elements to Amazon's platform that are spread across all the products that use it:

- The one-click online ordering process makes placing an order so convenient that it gives Amazon an advantage over competitors.

- Extensive information is provided about products, especially books. Information such as the book contents, book reviews, customer ratings, and rankings based on sales enables the customer to make informed decisions. In some ways, this extensive information more than offsets the advantage of going to a store, seeing the physical product, buying it, and taking it home without having to wait for delivery.

- Related services, such as wish lists, purchase circles, discussion boards, and the ability to browse by age or interest, provide real value to customers beyond the sale, and many of these services create an Amazon community.

- The distribution network purposely built to handle e-commerce is also a critical part of the Amazon product platform.

When you understand the Amazon product platform more deeply, it shows values that extend far beyond low-cost distribution.

> *The choice of a defining technology in platform strategy is perhaps the most critical strategic decision that a high-technology company makes.*

A company makes its choice of underlying technology when it defines the elements of a new product platform. Since this decision is frequently irreversible, the choice of a defining technology in platform strategy is perhaps the most critical strategic decision that a high-technology company makes. The technology underlying a product platform defines the potential and limits of its performance and frames its cost structure. Frequently, making the decision about what the defining technology of a product platform will be is difficult.

2. *The platform's defining technology is clearly distinguishable from other platform elements.* In any product platform, one element above all others usually defines the real nature of that platform. It defines the platform's capabilities and limitations. It defines the unique characteristic of all products developed from that platform. The life cycle of the platform is usually dependent on the continuing strength of that element. We refer to this as

the *defining technology*. While several technologies may be necessary to create a successful product, the defining technology is most critical.

The defining technology is also the key to understanding a product platform. Typically, the defining technology of a platform differentiates the products that are based on that platform. The Macintosh platform, for example, is differentiated by its easy-to-use graphical interface. The Motorola 68000 microprocessor and the Mac's electronic architecture are an integral part of the Macintosh product platform, but they are supporting rather than defining technologies. Without its graphical operating system, the Macintosh platform would not have any significant distinguishing characteristics. It would still have been a platform, but would not have been very successful.

Its graphical operating system defining technology provided the Macintosh with its differentiating advantage, but it also had limitations. The Macintosh operating system was incompatible with much of the available applications software.

Advanced composite materials combine multiple materials, such as fillers, resins, and reinforcing materials, in order to achieve specific performance characteristics. The underlying platform of these composite products is the material that provides the critical characteristic. For example, DuPont's Kevlar 49 is a prepreg material (a reinforcement or carrier material that has been preimpregnated with a liquid resin) that provides composite materials with the characteristics of light weight and high tensile strength. It is combined with other materials for different composite applications, such as aircraft structural components and sports equipment; when combined with low-shear-strength polyester, it forms bulletproof armor products.

The inability to understand the defining technology of a platform dooms a platform strategy to failure. When Steve Jobs started Next

> ***The inability to understand the defining technology of a platform dooms a platform strategy to failure.***

Computer, he intended to produce a computer that he felt was clearly differentiated from others. But Jobs failed to understand the defining technology of his product platform. Next's workstations—the Cube and the Nextstation—were sleek boxes with advanced microelectronics technology and innovative disk storage. Yet these factors were not the defining technology of Next's workstations. Experts estimate that fewer than 50,000 Next workstations were sold, and most of those were purchased because of Next's operating system.[2]

Ironically, this operating system, NextStep, was acquired almost by accident. NextStep incorporated object-oriented programming, which significantly improved programmer productivity. It was based on software called Mach, developed at Carnegie Mellon University. Jobs did not select the operating system because of this differentiation, but rather because it enabled other programmers to write applications software faster, thereby helping Next sell more workstations.

By early 1993, Next finally recognized its defining technology and began to sell an effectively differentiated product: its software. NextStep 486 ran on other computers—namely, Intel 486-based systems—and was offered as an alternative to other operating systems. To implement this shift in its product strategy, Next Computer closed its manufacturing facility and cut its employee rolls by half.

For personal computers and workstations, the defining technology of the product platform is not the computer hardware; it is the operating system, which drives the microprocessor and interfaces with the user.

The defining technology is not always obvious. For example, the major product line of a medical products company was biological sample collection devices. The platform for these devices incorporated several technologies, including chemical reagents, the design and shape of the device, the gas mixture within the device, and the manufacturing process to produce high-quality devices. However, the *defining* technology was the material used to make the device. The properties of this material determined the performance of the device, its cost, and its shelf life. The material also determined its susceptibility to breakage, which was important because of the fear of infectious disease.

Wang Laboratories is a clear case of a company that failed to understand its defining technology. In the late 1970s, Wang had established a dominant position in word processing systems: Most large companies were using Wang word processors to increase their typing productivity. With the arrival of the PC, however, special-purpose word processing equipment became too limited and too expensive. Wang failed to apply this new technology, because it didn't understand that the defining technology of its word processing platform was its software, not its hardware.

What if Wang had understood its defining technology and converted its word processing software to work on IBM and Apple PCs? Most likely it would have become the dominant word processing application, since it was already the standard that most people used. Perhaps today Wang would be a large software company, as successful as Microsoft, if it had been able to leverage this initial advantage in software.[3]

Why did Wang make this fatal mistake? It wasn't because the executives were stupid or didn't understand technology. Quite the contrary was true. With Wang, it was simply a matter of determining which technology was really the defining technology; the obvious technology is not always the defining technology.

Sometimes the defining technology is identified, but the challenge is selecting the best alternative technology for a product platform. In 1993, there were three alternative supercomputing architectures: vector-based machines, massively parallel processor systems, and workstation clusters. Each offered advantages and differing performance characteristics, but one would likely emerge as the most successful supercomputing platform.

Traditionally, supercomputing platforms were vector-based, using a small number of very fast, custom-built processors. Writing software for this technology was reasonably straightforward; as a result, a large amount of application software was available. Cray Research, Cray Computer, Fujitsu, NEC, Hitachi, Convex, and IBM used this product platform. By 1992, sales of supercomputers with vector-based platforms exceeded $1.3 billion, but the trend was declining. The underlying architecture of this technology was reaching its limits, and performance improvements were becoming more difficult.

Parallel processor platforms incorporate relatively inexpensive microprocessors—hundreds or even thousands—linked together in a coordinated system. This technology provides the advantage of scalability: the ability to increase or decrease performance by adding or subtracting microprocessors. It also benefits from the cost advantage of microprocessors made in extremely high volume for the personal computer market. The limitation of this technology is the difficulty of writing software to break a computing problem into hundreds of pieces so that each microprocessor handles a manageable piece. Intel, Thinking Machines, Kendall Square Research, nCube, MasPar, and NCR Teradata used this technology for their product platforms in 1993. IBM and Cray Research were developing platforms using this technology in addition to their vector-based platforms.

With workstation cluster technology, groups of workstations and servers create the computer power equivalent to a parallel processor platform. This approach faced a similar, but even more difficult, challenge of segmenting and distributing computing tasks. Its advantage was lower cost and flexibility for use outside of supercomputing. Traditional workstation companies such as Silicon Graphics, Hewlett-Packard, Convex, and Sun Microsystems competed in supercomputing using this technology, as did IBM and Cray Research.

3. *The platform's unique differentiation provides a sustainable competitive advantage.* A product's unique differentiation is implemented primarily through the underlying product platform, not the individual products from that platform. The differentiation in a product platform provides the constant theme woven throughout the product line built upon it, with individual products providing variations on the theme.

A product platform could be based on materials that have unique properties. For example, products made from the Kevlar 49 platform have some clearly differentiated characteristics. They are 20 percent to 35 percent lighter than traditional metal products. They have higher tensile strength, which provides the stiffness desired in skis, tennis rackets, and golf clubs. They have good fatigue resistance and vibration dampening, which are required in applications such as aviation products.

Apple used ease of use as the vector of differentiation (see Chapter 7) for its Macintosh. Its operating system was developed specifically for this differentiation. The Macintosh hardware was designed for easy installation and was integrated with the operating system to make the system easier to use. Apple also invested in peripheral products and communications software and integrated them to make the complete system easier to use.

It should not be surprising that some of the most successful products come from platforms that are clearly differentiated:

- NEC designed its UltraLite Versa personal computer platform for versatility.

- Stratus and Tandem designed their computer platforms for fault tolerance.

- Digital Equipment designed its Alpha workstation platform for superior price performance.

- Hewlett-Packard designed its OmniBook computer platform for portability (the lowest weight and longest battery life).

- Microsoft designed its Office 4.0 product for integration of common functions.

When a new product platform is a success, a proprietary or defensible platform makes that success more sustainable, and in high-technology products, a sustainable advantage can be achieved only through technology. Thus, the most successful strategy for a new product platform is to achieve a competitive advantage based on proprietary or defensible technology. IBM's System/360 platform and Polaroid's instant photography platform are classic examples of this strategy. The strategic trade-off to a proprietary technology advantage in many markets is the need for open and compatible products. Proprietary products may be sustainable, but they may also be at a competitive disadvantage. The IBM PC and the Apple Macintosh demonstrate different strategies.

IBM's first personal computer, launched in August 1981, was a big success. The IBM PC immediately became the market leader and instigated a shakeout in the personal computer industry. To get to market faster, however, IBM broke from its tradition and used outside suppliers for key components. The defining technology of the IBM PC platform was not IBM's.

It was based on the Intel 8088/8086 microprocessor and the Microsoft-developed PC DOS operating system. While the IBM PC was a very successful product platform, it did not give IBM a sustainable advantage. PC-clone manufacturers were able to acquire the underlying technology and reproduce the platform. As a direct result, IBM was forced into price competition much earlier and lost market share trying to maintain prices. An alternative strategy for a company with IBM's resources could have been to acquire all rights to the defining technology, make the system open for software developers, and license the defining technology to a limited number of competitors.

Apple Computer pursued a very different strategy with its Macintosh by maintaining strict control of the defining technology, the Macintosh operating system. The Macintosh operating system permitted Apple to clearly differentiate its personal computer from all others. If Apple had lost proprietary control of its defining technology, then it probably would have had to share its market segment with many competitors.

The problem with Apple's sustainable advantage strategy was the exact opposite of IBM's; it held on too long, thinking that Microsoft would never catch up to the Mac's ease of use. It did not anticipate the continued dramatic increase in memory, which allowed Windows to be success-

Experience suggests that core competencies should never be outsourced.

ful. It also did not foresee the PC price wars that rapidly expanded the market, dwarfing Mac sales in the process. In desperation, Apple tried to sue for infringement by claiming that Windows copied the Mac's "look and feel," but it lost. If Apple had licensed the Mac operating system, it could have supplanted Microsoft as the dominant operating systems company. Even innovative platforms can be difficult to sustain as competitors quickly follow a company's early success. The result is rapid dispersion of new product platforms. Consumer electronics product platforms have been particularly vulnerable. Sony, for example, was successful with its 8mm compact camcorder based on a new platform that enabled hand-held video recording. However, the success was short-lived as competitors copied the platform.

In 1991, Sony upgraded the 8mm platform with the Video Hi8 system, which offered hi-fi stereo sound and improved picture quality. Several products with new features, such as a color viewfinder and an active prism to compensate for accidental movement, were released from this new platform, helping to stimulate sales for a short time. In this market, platform life cycles are very short, and sustainability of a platform advantage is almost impossible.

Robustness is a key element of any platform strategy. All opportunities such as proprietary technology, patents, or operational advantages should be considered as part of the strategy. All too often, high-technology companies make a fatal misjudgment regarding ownership of defining technologies and core competencies. Experience suggests that core competencies should never be out-sourced. When a sustainable advantage cannot be achieved in a platform, a shorter platform life cycle should be planned.

4. *No more than one product platform should serve a market.* We've found this statement to be controversial, but it has provoked strategic decisions in the right direction. Sometimes a company has multiple product platforms addressing the same market. Each may use different underlying technology, target different market segments, and be at a different point in its life cycle. Proponents of multiple platforms for a market argue that a single platform may leave market opportunities open to competitors by not effectively addressing the needs of certain segments. In most cases, however, offering different platforms in the same market has more disadvantages.

Multiple similar platforms can retard development and hinder competitiveness. For example, one data communications company maintained two network management systems: the first on a powerful workstation platform, the other on a PC-based platform. Two platforms required twice the effort to update with new communications devices, delaying by 6 to 12 months the release of new versions of each network management system, as well as new communications devices. It would have been cheaper for the company to sell the more powerful workstation platform at the lower price instead of investing in redundant development. Mistakes like this usually occur because a company can't decide which platform to develop; instead, it develops more than one platform without considering the strategic implications.

In addition to eroding economies of scale, too many overlapping platforms can confuse customers. IBM fell into this trap in midrange computer systems when it had five separate and incompatible platforms: the System/3 platform for small business, the System/38 and System/36 platform, the 8100 platform for distributed processing, the Series/1 platform for transaction processing, and the 4300 platform for running mainframe software on a minicomputer. Customers became confused and frustrated as IBM salespeople contradicted one another while maintaining that different IBM platforms were their best solution. It was difficult for customers to use multiple platforms, because the application software was not compatible among them. For IBM, the cost of maintaining and enhancing five different platforms became a competitive disadvantage.

By 1982, IBM realized that it needed to merge these into a single platform and launched the Fort Knox project—one new, midrange system platform that would be compatible with all five platforms. However, this was too difficult a problem to solve quickly. Even with 4,000 people working on it for four years, the new platform proved to be too ambitious and was canceled.[4]

In many cases, a company ends up with multiple product platforms through acquisitions. When this happens, it must continue supporting these platforms while developing a strategy to rationalize them in the market. One company ended up with four platforms serving the same general market for diagnostic testing. One was a low-cost manual test; two others were automated test systems, but one was based on a chemical process and the other on a biological process. The fourth platform, based on an emerging technology, was under development.

After struggling with the issue, the company decided to reposition the manual test to serve a different market, and discontinue the chemical system because the biological system was more accurate and provided a higher profit margin. At the same time, the company decided to phase out the biological system over the next five years, replacing it with the new platform based on emerging technology, as it was accepted in the market. This change in its platform strategy enabled the company to better focus its product development and leverage its R&D investment.

Benefits of Platform Strategy

Adopting the principles of platform management and developing a platform strategy have several important benefits that could, in fact, mean the difference between success and failure.

1. *A platform strategy focuses management on key decisions at the right time.* Developing product strategy at the platform level simplifies the product strategy process, enabling senior management to concentrate maximum attention on the most critical decisions. Strategic decisions are simplified, because there are fewer platforms than products, and major platform decisions are made every few years, not every few months. With this sharper focus, senior management spends 90 percent of its time on the few most critical decisions that determine 90 percent of the success of the products from that platform.

In most companies what's needed is a process to force executives to focus on these important decisions of platform and product strategy. This is one reason that a formal product strategy process, and within this the application of platform strategy, can be so useful. Platform strategy leads senior management to focus on important platform-level decisions, instead of diluting attention across numerous products. It separates platform strategy decisions from individual product decisions, raising the importance of the former. Some companies even distinguish the level of authority between these two levels of decision making. In this case, platform strategy is the responsibility of senior management, while the next level of management makes individual product decisions.

If they are sufficiently rigorous about platform management, most companies can generally anticipate when they will be approaching major platform management decisions. They can then schedule the necessary time. An executive in one very successful high-technology company allocates his time accordingly. Looking ahead to his calendar for the upcoming year, he is reminded that his company will be facing some critical decisions on a next-generation product platform in the spring. "I saw that we planned a new platform decision session at the end of May, so I blocked off half of my time in April and May for it. Right now I don't really know what I'll be doing, but I don't want to be distracted by other, less critical meetings and commitments. If I need less time, that's fine; this is just so important that I want to make sure I have the time that's needed."

2. *A platform strategy enables products to be deployed rapidly and consistently.* A platform strategy leverages the cost of developing individual products and can introduce a commonality that reduces manufacturing costs. Developing a platform approach to product strategy requires more discipline than simply developing the first product in a product line, without much thought to subsequent products. Conversely, setting product strategy at the individual product level dilutes focus, diffusing senior management's attention across all products. It also diminishes the leverage gained from using a common platform as a foundation and can create confusion about individual products. One company that set its product strategy at an individual product level developed 10 different products, many of whose capabilities overlapped. The differences among the products confused customers, as well as the company's own salespeople. Even more important, the company could not keep all these products competitive. The cost of repetitively making similar improvements for each of the products was simply prohibitive.

In spite of its importance, many companies tend to skip this foundation level of product strategy and go directly to product line strategy—or skip that, too, and go directly to the development of specific products. Eventually, they look back and realize they have developed a new platform for one of these products and say, "If only we'd thought of subsequent products before we completed the platform." For example, a computer company had difficulty separating platform strategy from product line strategy. Its new product attempted to address the collective requirements of many vertical market segments instead of being built as a platform from which various configurations could be developed to address the different vertical markets. As a result, there was just enough wrong with the product for each vertical market segment to reject it in favor of a competitive product that was better focused.

On the surface, skipping over platform strategy looks faster, easier, and less restrictive. The usual pattern is to develop a high-end product incorporating new technology and numerous features. Then the company decides it needs more than one product, typically a lower-priced version. It tries to reduce the cost of the original product as much as possible, but runs into constraints created by the original product design and, in some cases, may even need to make the products incompatible to achieve different goals. A product platform strategy would have prevented these problems. Multiple products could have been developed from the same platform, each implementing different features and functions to focus on specific market segments and distribution channels.

A consumer telephone products company used platform strategy and avoided these problems. Various models of cordless phones were developed from the same base platform, which consisted of a few circuit boards that contained the common radio technology and software. The physical styling and extra features varied for each model, according to the targeted market segment and distribution channel. Models developed for high-end channels, such as phone centers, contained many extra features and combinations of features, while models developed for low-end channels, such as Wal-Mart, were basic products with a minimal number of extra features. This approach leveraged a single platform rapidly into multiple products, to get the most from the R&D investment. An additional benefit, lower manufacturing costs by the use of common components, proved to be extraordinarily important when the market became more cost-competitive.

By initially developing a product platform and then leveraging this platform to create multiple products, a company gets a lot more from its R&D investment, spreading investment across multiple products. Although the extent of the benefit varies with the products, it can be significant in almost all cases when a company intends to develop multiple products.

One electronics company, over approximately four years, developed seven related products that individually addressed the unique needs of different market segments. Different teams developed each product, although there was some overlap from earlier product development teams to later ones. Because each of these was an independent effort, there was little reuse of technology, and the product architectures were different. Each product was developed from the ground up to be optimized for its target market segment, although many of the differences among the products were merely preferences of the team designing the product and not really unique requirements of the target market segment. But while a new product is developed, it's often difficult to distinguish unique requirements from preferences.

This individual product approach to development instead of a platform development approach came at a price. The electronics company later estimated that it could have saved as much as 50 percent of the development costs and released the last few products at least a year sooner if it had first designed a common platform.

3. *A platform approach encourages a longer-term view of product strategy.* When a medical products company was developing a new biosensor product, it had the choice of using two alternative base chemistries. One was low risk, but could be used only in a stand-alone product for the company's existing home-testing market. The alternative base chemistry was higher risk, but it could also serve as a platform to create devices for a series of other tests, thus opening the door for expansion into new markets. By taking a platform approach, the company created a longer-term opportunity that it would have neglected otherwise.

> *Platform life cycles drive the major competitive changes in high-technology industries by introducing new product generations, forcing companies into dramatic changes in product strategy.*

It takes a product platform much longer to progress through a life cycle than the individual products derived from that platform. Plat-form life cycles drive the major competitive changes in high-technology industries by introducing new product generations, forcing companies into dramatic changes in product strategy. If there is one common strategic error that has proved to be fatal to previously successful high-technology companies, it's this: They don't anticipate the threat to their primary product platform in time to react. We look at this in detail later in this chapter.

It is the *platform* life cycle that needs to be managed, not the individual *product* life cycle. Platform life cycle management begins with the strategic decision to develop a new product platform and continues with the strategic decision to replace that platform with a next-generation platform or retire it and go on to a new market.

4. *A platform strategy can leverage significant operational efficiencies.* In the previous example of an electronics equipment manufacturer, a lot of inefficiency arose from minimal reuse of components that were potentially common in the seven products. Only 25 percent of the components were common to more than four of the products, and only 10 percent to all products. Subsequent analysis indicated that as much as 60 percent of the components could have been common. Manufacturing cost savings could have been in the tens of millions of dollars. Additional savings

could have been achieved through leveraging support costs, particularly spare parts.

In another example, a company discovered three areas in which using product platforms had a significant impact on cost:

- *Engineering headcount.* Modeling headcount allocation against platform elements can be very revealing. If supporting elements do not provide differentiation at either the platform or the product level, the appropriate level of engineering support should be low relative to other elements. The company in question had 46 percent of its engineering staff allocated to supporting element engineering (chassis, etc.). With better use of product platforms, these engineers could have been allocated to revenue-generating activities.

- *Materials cost savings.* By using product platforms, the company was able to share defining and supporting elements. Usually, the architectural rules drive this building block, giving products based on a common platform a unique vector of differentiation (carried across all products), built on a common set of supporting elements that can perform (technically, visually, etc.) very differently by the creative application of segmenting elements. The commonality of key components can enable a 10 percent to 30 percent reduction in materials costs, depending on the platform. In high volume, the numbers add up. In this company's case, the cost saving was approximately $100 million a year.

- *Supply chain costs.* This is where product strategy drives operations strategy. With products based on a common product platform, a producer may choose to have platform-focused factories. This can optimize manufacturing costs and perhaps reduce materials costs further by leveraging local supply, reducing supply-side tariffs, and optimizing the supply line on the factory. Even geographically focused factories can take advantage of some leverage if they use the same tooling, processes, and equipment. In reality, companies usually take a combination approach because of regional product preferences that skew product mix and tariff incentives that create labor and supply cost dislocations. This company estimated $71 million in materials savings, $4 million to $8 million in labor savings, and $24 million in shipping and duties savings from aligning the operations strategy with the platform strategy.

5. *Product platform principles help management anticipate replacing a major product platform.* The biggest advantage of platform management and platform strategy is discussed in the previous section: being able to identify when a major product platform needs to be replaced in time to react. All product platforms have a life cycle; inevitably, revenue derived from products based on that platform begins to decline. When it does, a com-

pany must be ready with a new product platform to replace the one that is in decline, or it should be prepared to downsize its business. We discuss this in detail later in this chapter.

Product Platform Examples

The concept of product platforms is a powerful one, but its application differs widely from platform to platform. For this reason, there is no single description of a product platform that applies in all cases. One example is different from another, and each company must work at understanding the characteristics of its own product platforms. The platform examples that follow illustrate a wide range of platforms with different characteristics.

Apple Computer's 25-Year
Platform Strategy[5]

Like most companies in the last 25 years, Apple didn't manage its product strategy explicitly in terms of product platforms. It's fair to say that this description of Apple Computer's major product platforms and the product platform strategy it followed is a narrative of its actual strategy, not a case study of its intended strategy. Apple Computer has had a much publicized history of product development. Its major computer product platforms are outlined in Figure 3-2.

The Apple I was originally intended to be a hobbyist's build-your-own computer kit, but it was turned into an assembled microcomputer board. It was originally priced at $667, with a wholesale price of $500. The Apple II was derived from the Apple I.

In 1978, Apple began developing a powerful business computer that was a major departure from the Apple II platform architecture. The Apple III was its first major product platform failure. The Apple III platform was based on a Synertek 8-bit 6502A microprocessor running at 2 MHz, along with a built-in keyboard and a 143K internal disk drive. It used the Sophisticated Operating System, but it also ran in Apple II emulation mode, although not very well. The Apple III was announced in May 1980, but it was recalled for quality problems. In February 1981, Apple fixed the quality problems, dropped the price to $4,200, and then further reduced it to a base price of $3,500.

The Apple III Plus replaced the two original models of the Apple III in December 1983. Finally, with total sales of about only 120,000 units, Apple killed the product platform in April 1984 and wisely focused its resources on the Apple II and the Lisa and Macintosh product platforms. Four product platforms were too many to support.

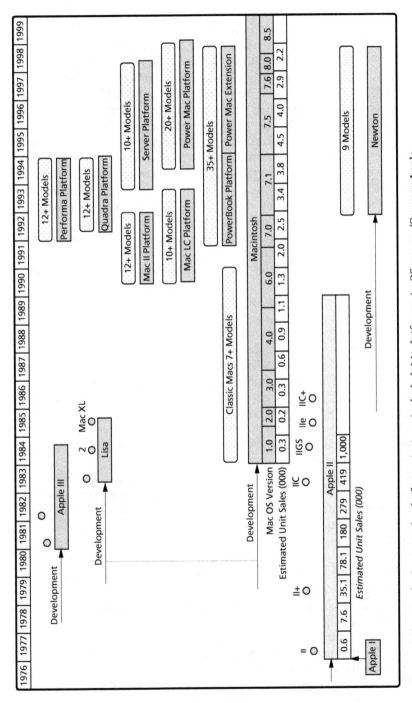

Figure 3-2 Apple Computer's platform strategy included 14 platforms in 25 years. (Source: Apple Computer; Owen W. Linzmayer, *Apple Confidential*, No Starch Press, 1999.)

When Steve Jobs and others from Apple visited the Xerox PARC laboratory in 1979, they were inspired to create the Lisa product platform. In exchange for the opportunity to invest in Apple, Xerox demonstrated some of its technology, including the graphical user interface, the mouse, and technology for networking computers and printers. Development of the Lisa took much longer than Apple anticipated, costing an estimated $50 million and taking 200 worker-years of resources (100 times more than the Apple II). Formally introduced in January 1983, the Lisa weighed 48 pounds and featured a Motorola 68000 microprocessor, two 860K floppy drives and a 5MB hard disk, a detachable keyboard, a one-button mouse, and a 12-inch, built-in monochrome display. Since the Lisa was incompatible with software on the market, seven applications programs were included to help justify the steep initial price of $10,000.

Even before the Lisa was shipped to the first customers, rumors began to circulate about a "baby Lisa," which was, of course, the Macintosh. The news diminished buyer interest in the high-priced Lisa. In September 1983, Apple reduced the price of the Lisa by 30 percent to $7,000 and introduced a high-end model, the Lisa 2. In January 1985, the Lisa 2 was renamed the Macintosh XL, and an emulation program was released to run Macintosh software in order to consolidate around a single brand. A short time later, in April, the Lisa was discontinued.

Apple began development of the Macintosh platform in 1979, and the first offering from the Macintosh platform was released in 1984; approximately 300,000 were sold in the first year. Seven different offerings were developed as part of what was later to become known as the Classic product family from the original platform, and more than 2 million units were sold.

In the 1990s, Apple created several derivative platforms from the original Macintosh platform. The Mac II and Mac LC platforms were launched in 1990. Eventually, each of these created more than 10 product offerings. In 1991–1992, Apple created the Performa and Quadra platforms, as well as the very successful PowerBook portable computer platform. The Power Mac PowerBook later extended the PowerBook platform. Collectively, the PowerBook and Power Mac extensions were responsible for more than 35 product offerings. Apple created the Power Mac and server platforms in 1993–1994. In 1998 and 1999, the iMac platform further extended the life cycle of the Macintosh platform.

In 1987, Apple began development of an entirely different product platform: the Newton, a personal digital assistant. The defining technology of the Newton was its ability to recognize handwriting as the primary user interface. Development of this new platform proved to be much more ambitious than Apple estimated. After approximately $500 million in development costs, the first Newton was shipped in 1993. Eight different models of the Newton were created over its five-year life cycle. Yet, while personal digital assistants became an important market, the Newton was a failure. Its defining technology, handwriting recognition, wasn't valued by the market.

Microsoft's Windows NT Platform History

Microsoft's Windows NT operating system is related to, but different from, its Windows 95/98 platform. NT is a more complex 32-bit platform primarily for use on servers as a networking operating system. Microsoft began development of NT in 1988 and released the first version of the platform, Windows NT 3.1, in 1993. The second version, Windows NT 3.5, released in 1994, was faster and more stable. In 1995, with Windows NT 3.51, Microsoft made NT compatible with its Windows 3.5 desktop applications. These were improved versions of the NT platform, rather than replacement platforms.

In 1996, Microsoft released Windows NT 4.0, which was more a platform replacement than an improvement. It was much larger (19 million lines of code compared with 10 million) and was able to run large, data processing tasks. A 1997 revision extended the platform to cluster computers together for large jobs. Microsoft started to replace Windows NT 4.0 with Windows 2000 in March 2000. The much larger platform had an estimated 30 million lines of code.[6]

AT&T's Service Platforms

Even a gigantic service business such as AT&T can be understood better by looking at its major service platforms in 1999.

- *Long-distance communications,* AT&T's primary service platform, supported a number of products. In 1999, the business long-distance product family was approximately $24 billion and the consumer long-distance product family was approximately $22 billion.

- *Wireless communications* was AT&T's fastest-growing platform, with a 40 percent growth rate and approximately $7.5 billion in revenue.

- AT&T expanded into a *cable television* service platform through acquisitions, making it potentially the largest cable television business in the United States. The wide range of product offerings from this platform included different service options and entertainment packages.

- AT&T's new *broadband* platform used its cable TV network to provide high-speed Internet access through Excite@Home, in which it had majority control.

- *Local phone service,* a new platform that used the cable TV network, was perhaps AT&T's most strategically important service platform.

Walt Disney's Families of Product Platforms

Although AT&T is a large business with several very large service platforms, it's a simple business compared with The Walt Disney Company, which has *families* of platforms. As illustrated in Figure 3-3, Walt Disney has five major business segments, each of which has multiple product and service platforms.

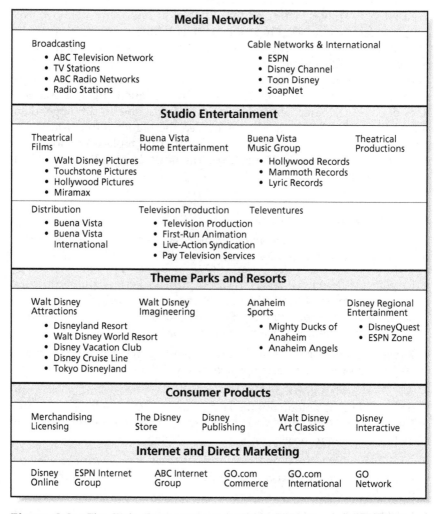

Figure 3-3   The Walt Disney Company has created five primary platform families.

Media Network Platforms. Of Disney's total revenue of $23 billion in 1999, $7.5 billion came from its media product platforms. In broadcasting, Disney had its ABC television network platform with a variety of programming product offerings, as well as the ABC radio network. In addition, it had a TV station platform with 10 stations and a radio station platform with 42 stations. In its cable network platform family, it had ESPN, Disney Channel, Toon Disney, and SoapNet channels, each a distinct platform with multiple program offerings. For several of these, Disney created platform variations, such as ESPN2, ESPN Classic, and ESPNews from ESPN. It also had minority ownership in several other cable platforms, including Lifetime, E!, A&E, and the History Channel.

Studio Entertainment. With approximately $6.5 billion in revenue in 1999, studio entertainment was Disney's second-largest family of product platforms. Within this family, there were four theatrical film platforms, each a studio with a different focus: Walt Disney Pictures, Touchstone Pictures, Hollywood Pictures, and Miramax. Each studio platform produced several product offerings (movies) a year. In 1999, Walt Disney Pictures produced *Inspector Gadget, Mighty Joe Young,* and *My Favorite Martian.* Touchstone/Hollywood Pictures produced *The Sixth Sense, Enemy of the State, The Waterboy,* and *Bicentennial Man.* Miramax produced *Shakespeare in Love, Life Is Beautiful, She's All That, The Talented Mr. Ripley,* and *The Cider House Rules.* Buena Vista Home Entertainment was Disney's platform for videotape and DVD versions of its pictures for home use. It released approximately 10 animated video products each year. Additional platforms in this group included movie distribution, the Buena Vista Music Group, theatrical productions, television production, and Televentures.

Theme Parks and Resorts. Theme parks also represented a large family of numerous product platforms, with more than $6 billion in revenue. Walt Disney Attractions is the largest in this family and includes five major attraction platforms: The Disneyland Resort, Walt Disney World Resort, Disney Vacation Club, Disney Cruise Line, and Tokyo Disneyland. We examine the product offerings from the Walt Disney World Resort as an example of product line strategy in Chapter 4. The Mighty Ducks professional hockey team and the Anaheim Angels professional baseball team were also entertainment platforms, as were the Disney Regional Entertainment platforms (DisneyQuest and ESPN Zone), and Walt Disney Imagineering platforms.

Consumer Products. The platforms in the consumer products family licensed the name "Walt Disney" as well as the company's characters to various manufacturers, retailers, and others. It included a merchandise licensing platform, Disney Publishing, Walt Disney Art Classics, and Disney Interactive. It addition, there was a strong retail platform with more than 700 stores.

Internet and Direct Marketing.   This diverse family of platforms represents the operations of Disney's online activities and the Disney Catalog. In 1999, it included a portal site platform (GO.com), a news platform (ABCNEWS.com), sports site platforms (ESPN.com, ABCSports.com, NFL.com, NBA.com, etc.), entertainment platforms (ABC.com, ABC Radio, etc.), kids and family platforms (Disney.com, Disney Club Blast, etc.), and e-commerce platforms (DisneyStore.com, Disney Travel Online, toysmart.com, etc.). As with most Internet platforms, costs of $300 million exceeded revenue of $200 million.

Amazon.com's Common Platform

In 1996 Amazon.com pioneered a revolutionary product platform for retail sales, enabling customers to order books over the Internet. Its early platform focused on providing information and processing customer orders for books over the Internet. In most cases, Amazon didn't even handle the stocking of these books, leaving that to publishers and wholesalers. Since then, Amazon has leveraged its platform into other product offerings, including music, video and DVD, electronics and software, toys and games, and home improvement. It has also expanded the capabilities of its platform to include more inventory stocking and distribution.

Amazon also created a platform variation when it entered the online auction business. The auction platform links buyers directly to sellers and provides the capability to auction a specific product to a high bidder, instead of selling the item to anyone who wants to purchase it at a set price.

Amazon's Internet-based platform was clearly different from traditional retail channels and offered many advantages that may very well prove to be superior for major segments of the market. Bricks-and-mortar competitors quickly (and in some cases not so quickly) moved to copy Amazon, since it clearly posed a threat to their retail store platform strategy.

However, there is another Internet-based alternative platform that may threaten a portion of Amazon's market. Companies using this platform also take orders over the Internet, but offer same-day direct delivery. Thus Peapod, Homeruns, and Webvan deliver groceries and can also deliver products like books and CDs. At the time of writing, Barnesandnoble.com was experimenting with a same-day delivery platform using the Barnes and Noble network of 350 retail stores to supply books by messenger and van. This example of an alternative platform shows the importance of understanding all aspects of a product platform, not just the obvious ones.

American Express's 100-Year Platform History

Even an old-line company like American Express has product platforms. The Travelers Cheque was its initial product platform in 1890, and since then there have been several variations of it. Its next product platform came in the 1950s, when it introduced the personal charge card. American Express developed multiple product offerings from this platform, including the green card, gold card, silver card, platinum card, and card variations in more than 30 national currencies. The American Express corporate card platform was released in 1970, and a platform derivative, the small business card, followed in the mid-1980s. The Optima platform, another credit card, was introduced in the mid-1980s, and in the 1990s, American Express began to issue cobranded cards.

Medtronic's Pacemaker Platform Evolution

Medtronic provides a fascinating example of how high-technology platforms evolve over time. Medtronic was originally formed as a service company in 1949, making 100 different custom products during the 1950s with no real platform strategy. Toward the end of the 1950s, Medtronic became closely involved in helping one of the pioneers of heart surgery, Dr. Walton Lillehei of the University of Minnesota, improve AC-operated pacemakers. It found that heart rates could be controlled when a pulse generator was combined with a wire electrode. This early pacemaker platform was then applied successfully to heart-block patients.

Building on this technology, Medtronic developed a new kind of pacemaker that was not much larger than a paperback book. The Bakken pacemaker platform was powered by mercury batteries and could be worn comfortably by young patients. The Hunter-Roth electrode had a plastic patch that was sutured to the heart, concentrating the electrical field where it was needed. The electrode was first implanted in 1958.

Medtronic developed the Chardack-Greatbatch implantable pulse generator platform in the early 1960s. By the mid-1960s, it introduced its first transvenous pacing system platform, in which leads could be maneuvered through a vein to the heart without opening the chest. In the 1970s, Medtronic introduced the Byrel platform, the first dual-chamber pacemaker. It synchronized the upper and lower heart chambers. In 1980, the Spectrax SX multiprogramming pacemaker platform was introduced. Its noninvasive programmability could adjust the pacemaker to the patient's needs without requiring another operation. All pacemakers now have noninvasive multiprogrammability.

By the mid-1980s, Medtronic introduced a rate-responsive, activity-sensing pacemaker platform, the Activitrax. Until that time, all single-chamber pacemakers functioned at a fixed rate, generally about 70 beats per minute, regardless of the patient's activity or blood-pumping requirements. Activitrax pacemakers used a sensor to detect blood pressure changes caused by a patient's muscle movement and then translated the pressure into electrical signals to trigger the appropriate response from the pacemaker. This technology was later incorporated into the dual-chamber pacemaker platform.

Medtronic went on to introduce the Thera (I-series) pacemaker platform. In 2000 it planned to introduce a next-generation pacemaker platform, the Medtronic Kappa pacing systems, which will offer therapeutic and diagnostic capabilities in addition to new capabilities that make it easier and faster to implant and track. This strategy of continuous improvement of its product platforms helped Medtronic achieve approximately 50 percent of the 1999 $2.4 billion worldwide market for pacemakers.[7]

Product Platform Management

For high-technology companies, the most important judgment for senior executives pondering their product development portfolio is, "What is the remaining life cycle of our primary product platforms?" When a primary product platform enters its decline, the entire business is threatened if the company doesn't react in time. Deciding when and how to react is a critical judgment that once-respected companies like Wang and Digital Equipment failed to make. More often than not, the delay proves fatal.

> *When a primary product platform enters its decline, the entire business is threatened if the company doesn't react in time.*

Platform management addresses this key strategic issue by focusing attention on major product platforms throughout their life cycle as part of a formal product strategy process. It enables senior management to address platform management issues, such as the following, at the appropriate time.

1. *Identify where a platform is in its life cycle.* When a major product platform enters the later portion of its life cycle and revenues begin to decline, a company must find some way to replace that revenue. Developing another product offering from the same platform is not the solution. While this may help for a short while, the real problem is the

underlying platform, so the most a new product offering can do is extend the life of the platform for a little while. Squeezing the tube can sometimes be misleading, though: The products at the end of a platform's life cycle can sometimes create enough revenue from that platform to create an illusion that it is invulnerable.

Figure 3-4 illustrates this key strategic question: Where is the platform in its life cycle? Although such a question is critical for every company, it is usually overlooked. In most companies, senior managers spend little or no time answering the question, even though their entire business strategy may rest on the answer. In these cases, the default assumption is: "The platform is still in the early portion of its life cycle, and we don't need to consider replacing it." When this default assumption is wrong, however, the result is usually disastrous.

2. *Synchronize the replacement of a major platform with a next-generation platform.*   Once a company recognizes that one of its major product platforms is approaching the declining stage of its life cycle, it needs to replace the platform. Data General Corporation faced this challenge in 1988 as its proprietary 32-bit ECLIPSE platform became less competitive. It had been a successful platform, providing computing cost advantages using Data General's proprietary architecture. Then the applications soft-

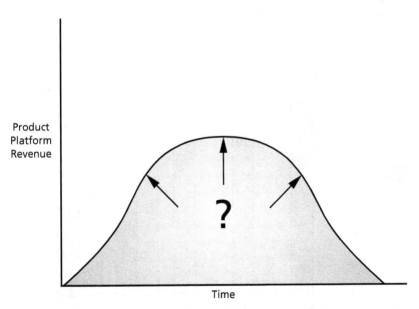

Figure 3-4   A company may not know where a product platform is in its life cycle.

ware business changed. Software developers moved toward open, non-proprietary platforms, and the ECLIPSE platform started its decline.

In 1989, under the direction of its new CEO, Ron Skates, Data General initiated a strategic shift to a new platform, the AViiON, based on the Motorola 88000 RISC (reduced instruction set computing) microprocessor and the UNIX operating system. This platform generated a wide range of workstation, server, and multiuser system product offerings. Data General's strategy was to release new products from the AViiON platform at a fast enough rate to offset the decline in the ECLIPSE platform.

AViiON revenue grew steadily, as can be seen in Figure 3-5. Despite this growth, total Data General revenue declined during the period, as the ECLIPSE platform moved to the end of its life cycle faster than AViiON grew. This is a classic case of a high-technology company racing to replace a dying platform with a new one. Data General eventually realized that it was not going to offset the decline in its ECLIPSE revenue fast enough, and in 1992 it launched another product platform aimed at a different market. The CLARiiON platform was an open data storage system based on disk-array technology. By 1996, the AViiON platform was generating $570 million in revenue; sales increased to more than $600 million in 1997, continuing at approximately the same rate through 1999. The CLARiiON platform was generating $355 million in revenue in 1996 and increased to $500 million in 1997, dropping to more than $400 million in 1999. In late 1999, Data General was acquired by EMC Corporation.

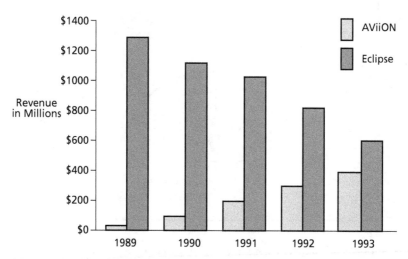

Figure 3-5   Revenue from Data General's Eclipse platform declined faster than revenue from AViiON grew between 1989 and 1993.

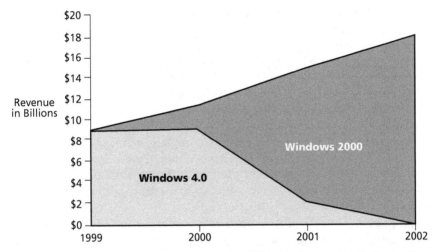

Figure 3-6 A next-generation platform should be synchronized with the decline of the platform it is replacing, as this example of Windows 2000 shows. (Source: *Computerworld*, December 6, 1999; Gartner Group, Stamford, CT.)

Microsoft's plan to replace Windows 4.0 with Windows 2000 shows how a next-generation platform should be synchronized with the decline of the platform it is replacing. As can be seen in Figure 3-6, Windows 2000 was expected to replace Windows 4.0 over a few years, while combined sales were expected to increase year to year.

To be fair, the difficulty of replacing a product platform with a next-generation platform varies considerably by the type of product. Software platforms are much easier to replace than hardware platforms, since the inventory and manufacturing issues are much simpler. The changeover also depends on a company's position in the marketplace and the superiority of its technology. Microsoft's leadership position in the operating system marketplace gave it more control over timing and synchronization than Data General had.

3. *Extend the life of a major platform.* Improving the underlying technology or redesigning some of the platform elements can extend the life of a major platform. While this is less expensive, the return on the investment is limited. At some point it becomes a matter of throwing good money after bad. Because of resource limitations, companies frequently need to make strategic choices among platforms. Should they continue to invest in extending an existing platform or invest in developing an entirely new one?

Pratt & Whitney faced this choice in its jet engine business. It planned to invest $2 billion in an all-new engine, the Advanced Ducted Prop, intended for the Airbus A340. At the same time, however, its PW4084 engine for the Boeing 777 was reaching range limitations. The engine was effective at a 5,000-mile range, but to be effective at a range of more than 8,000 miles, it required a major redesign, which would cost more than $500 million. Pratt & Whitney could not afford to do both and had to choose which platform to support.[8]

Frequently, the decision to extend or replace a product platform is driven by the company's core strategic vision. This was the case with Boeing and Airbus, described in Chapter 2. Boeing decided to invest $2 billion to extend its 747 platform, while Airbus decided to invest $12 billion in an entirely new platform, the A-3XX.

4. *Understand what causes a platform's life cycle to decline.* Identifying where a product platform is in its life cycle requires an understanding of what may cause it to decline. Typically, the continuation of a platform's life cycle is threatened by competitive products based on a superior platform, the development of a superior new technology, or, in some cases, market decline.

> ## A change in the desirability of a technology can be behind the decline of a product platform.

A change in the desirability of a technology can be behind the decline of a product platform. CFCs (chlorofluorocarbons) were hailed as a technological advance in the 1930s. They were safe (i.e., nontoxic and nonflammable), energy-efficient, and cheap. But scientists later discovered that CFCs were depleting the ozone layer. Governments and industry initiated actions to replace CFCs, and the $1.5 billion market for CFCs was on its way to elimination. By 1993, U.S. taxes on CFCs increased the cost to more than $5 a pound, providing an incentive to switch to alternatives such as 134a and HCFCs. As is the case whenever the market fades, the market leader—in this case, DuPont— had more to lose while new competitors had more opportunity.

Changing platforms is sometimes necessary because a platform depends on another platform. For example, when the DOS operating system became the standard for personal computers, a new market was created for DOS applications. Companies such as Microsoft, Borland International, Lotus Development, Software Publishing, WordPerfect, and others were successful with DOS-based application products. Then, with the advent of Windows 3.0 in 1990, the preferred operating system changed, and another totally new market was created: Windows-based applications.

This new market brought with it totally new criteria for success. It was not enough for products to simply run on Windows; they had to take advantage of its graphical environment. Once they did that, however, it was difficult to differentiate products according to user interface, or "look and feel," since these were now managed by the operating system. Less differentiation led to more price competition and to the increased importance of other differentiators, such as integration with other applications.

Many of the leading DOS-based software companies failed to anticipate the change correctly. They bet on IBM's OS/2 as the operating system to replace DOS, and went on to develop products based on OS/2 rather than Microsoft's Windows. As a result, WordPerfect, Lotus Development, Borland, and Symantec were late with Windows-based products. Microsoft, of course, placed the right strategic bet, as did Intuit, with its Quicken financial software product.

Alan Ashton, the founder of WordPerfect, thought the company's hold on word processing customers was so strong that it did not need to rush a Windows version of its word processing product to market. He later acknowledged that this was a mistake. Along with Windows, Microsoft introduced a new version of its word processing software that took advantage of these easier-to-use features. WordPerfect's sales declined as Microsoft Word took the market lead. By the time the WordPerfect product caught up in 1993, Microsoft changed its product platform again, this time by bundling separate applications into a single suite to create an integrated platform with a price slightly higher than the separate applications. WordPerfect had to lower its prices to compete and then had to eliminate free customer support and lay off 1,000 employees to reduce losses.[9]

Sometimes the market served by a product platform begins to decline. A market could be large and successful today, but gone tomorrow. Frequently, the cause of this phenomenon is a new alternative technology that provides advantages so significant that customers begin to use a different type of product. Disruptive technology is more likely to affect high-technology companies, so they need to be skeptical, perhaps even paranoid, regarding the long-term prospects for their markets. Ironically, it is the market leader that needs to worry the most. In his book *The Innovator's Dilemma,*[10] Clayton Christensen argues that companies, particularly industry leaders, sometimes listen too much to their customers, who put a low value on disruptive technologies that are not initially attractive to them.

The precipitous decline of IBM's large-scale systems business is perhaps one of the most dramatic examples of a collapsing market. IBM had dominated the market for large-scale computer systems since the 1960s. This dominance drove the company's growth through the 1980s. Starting in 1990, however, the market began to collapse, eroded by high-power workstations and networks of smaller computers. As shown in Figure 3-7, IBM's large-scale systems business dropped off a cliff, falling 50 percent, or almost $6 billion, from 1991 to 1993. The impact was even more severe on

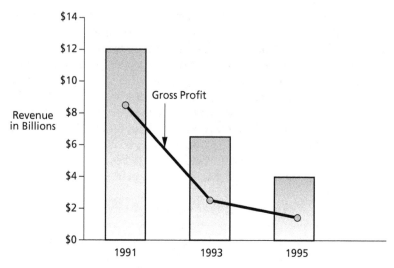

Figure 3-7   IBM's large-scale systems business fell 50 percent from 1991 to 1993. (Source: Ira Sager, "Lou Gerstner Unveils His Battle Plans," *Business Week*, April 4, 1994.)

gross profit margins, which declined from 70 percent to 40 percent at the same time that revenues were declining. The combined impact was an estimated drop in IBM's mainframe computer gross profit from $8.5 billion to $2.5 billion.

The loss of $6 billion in gross profit in two years can cause problems for any company, even an IBM. As a result, it needed to refocus its strategies and substantially cut overhead. The drop in mainframe revenue also shifted the thrust of its business. By 1993, IBM's personal computer revenue (almost $10 billion) exceeded its mainframe revenue, and by 1995 mainframe revenue was expected to become relatively small, compared with personal computer revenue. The PC business is very different from the mainframe business. It has different economics and a different competitive model, and it requires different product strategies to be successful.

In some cases, a market declines because it becomes saturated. When a new technology creates a market, there is rapidly growing demand for the resulting products. However, the market eventually becomes saturated as potential customers buy the product and have no need to buy another. The automobile radar detector market suffered this fate. Created by technology, it grew to more than $200 million (retail) during the 1980s. Eventually, the market became saturated and began to contract in the 1990s, as manufacturers ran out of ideas for improving their

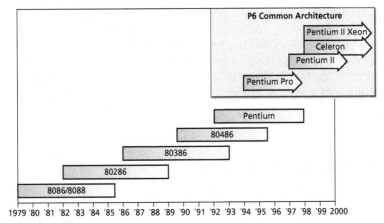

Figure 3-8 Intel's product strategy is based on introducing new product platforms in regular cycles.

products enough to get customers to replace the detectors they already owned.

5. *Regularly replace platforms with short life cycles.* Product platform life cycles for most high-technology products are notoriously short—and in some cases, are getting even shorter. The life cycle of microprocessors, for example, is approximately 3.5 years. Short cycles can be a competitive advantage for the company that establishes a cadence to replace its product platforms regularly. The need to replace a platform is never a surprise; it becomes a normal part of life.

Figure 3-8 illustrates product life cycles for microprocessors, using the Intel microprocessor product platforms as an example. Each of these is a distinctly different product platform; within each platform there are a number of product variations (devices with differing speeds or power consumption) and product line extensions. Sometimes short, but regular, platform life cycles are an advantage. For example, Intel can plan strategically to replace its microprocessor platforms with new ones approximately every 3.5 years.

Companies that successfully manage short platform life cycles can achieve a competitive advantage. IBM, for example, introduced the IBM PC in August 1981 and then replaced it with the XT in early 1983, only 18 months later. IBM began working on the XT even before it introduced the PC. It then replaced the XT with the AT in August 1984, again only 18 months later. By 1984, IBM's PC revenue was $4 billion, and it dominated the market for personal computers.

Short platform life cycles require a company to make product strategy decisions more frequently. If the decisions are right, then it wins—but only for a short time. If they are wrong, then the competition wins. IBM also provides this example. After the success of its AT, IBM made a strategic error on the next life cycle change, letting Compaq take advantage of the increased power of the Intel 80386 in 1986, while IBM delayed its next-generation platform trying to develop a "clone-killer" strategy. By the end of the decade, IBM lost its dominant position and 20 percent of its market share, equivalent to more than $5 billion per year in revenue.

Platform Strategy in Action

The three case studies that follow illustrate expert product platform strategy in action. The first case looks at how NCR deftly created a new product platform to capture the automated teller machine (ATM) market. The second shows how Xerox used platform strategy to make the life-or-death transition of its primary product platform—a transition that more often than not has destroyed high-technology companies. The third shows how Intel changed its product strategy over the course of 25 years and grew in its product platform management skills at the same time.

NCR's Dundee ATM Division: Creating a Competitive Advantage through Platform Strategy

NCR's ATM division in Dundee, Scotland, is a good example of product platform strategy. When Jim Adamson, the dynamic VP of the NCR Dundee ATM business, took over in 1980, he realized that the then-current 1780 product platform had severe quality problems. As he visited customers to resolve their complaints, Adamson also began to realize that NCR had an exciting opportunity.

His strategic vision was to make NCR the world leader in the ATM business by offering a wide range of superior-quality products that fit customers' key needs and by releasing those products ahead of the competition.[11] Jim Adamson's vision identified superior quality as the key differentiator. In the ATM business, this included reliability, simple maintenance, and low cost of total ownership. Banks wanted their ATMs to be available to customers as much as possible. Units that were down with malfunctions cost them business and created ill will. The banks wanted to be able to repair their ATMs infrequently and easily.

Achieving this vision would require a new platform, one that emphasized quality and reliability. However, NCR Dundee also faced some immediately pressing problems of satisfying angry customers. The Dundee division decided to develop an interim platform that would be a step on the way to a new platform, but that could be released sooner. It released the 5080 interim platform as a replacement for the 1780 platform in 1982, incorporating an improved printer and cash dispenser.

Adamson set a goal for the new platform: It needed to be twice as reliable as the next best competitive product. This would be the platform's vector of differentiation (see Chapter 7). When that goal became feasible, he changed it to three times as reliable. This required a significantly new platform in addition to the improvements incorporated into the 5080 platform. More reliable components were designed into the new platform, using replaceable modules that were easier to maintain. New computer software was written for the embedded computer.

The new platform achieved its reliability target. The first product from this platform was the 5070, a full-function interior ATM, released in November 1983 at ATM-5, an industry trade show. Seven months later, the 5081, a full-function through-the-wall ATM, was released from the same platform. It was followed by the 5084, a cash-dispensing-only version, in June 1985. In 1986, the 5080 interim platform product was replaced by the 5085, based on the new platform. Also in 1986, the new platform was used to release the 5088 (a drive-through-island version), 5571 (a machine for inquiry and document printing), and 5572 (an interactive video machine). In 1987, the 5070L, a low-priced model, was released.

The new platform gave NCR vital competitive advantages. Higher reliability was a vector of differentiation greatly valued by ATM customers. Competitors could not easily copy NCR Dundee's strategy, since they needed to develop entirely new platforms. Meanwhile, NCR continued to release many product offerings from its new platform. Competitors did not know whether to design new products from their old platforms that could compete on variety, or to develop a new platform that could compete on reliability.

Burroughs and Docutel withdrew from the ATM business, followed later by IBM and others. NCR captured the major share of the worldwide ATM market. By 1990, NCR was well on its way to developing its next-generation platform.

Xerox: Making a Life-or-Death Platform Transition

As we previously discussed, many once high-flying, technology-based companies came to an unfortunate end when the defining technology of their critical product platform became less competitive. Digital Equipment and Wang are two notable examples. Transition failure happens so frequently that some believe it is all but inevitable. Xerox is proving to be the exception to this rule.

Xerox's core strategic vision is based on being a document company, but it articulates its vision in such a way that it doesn't put strategic restrictions on what this means and how it gets there. With its leading position in a market where it had literally established the name of the market itself and with extensive patent protection, Xerox was the classic example of the dinosaur that would eventually be replaced by new technology. But it wasn't. Instead, Xerox became the leader, implementing new technology into new product platforms that displaced its previously successful product platforms.

Xerox copier platforms were based on light-lens (analog) technology. The advent of digital technology posed a serious threat. With effective peripheral vision, Xerox anticipated the potential impact of digital technology and moved quickly. In 1990, it first applied digital technology in its DocuTech Production Publisher, the first high-resolution digital publishing system. The DocuTech product platform created a new vector of differentiation for productivity. Prior to digital publishing, most business reports, forms, and brochures were printed on offset presses, using a labor-intensive prepress process to make printing plates.

Revenue from product offerings based on the DocuTech platform was $200 million in 1991. It more than doubled in 1992 to $500 million, and continued to increase to $750 million in 1993, $1 billion in 1994, and $1.4 billion in 1995. An interesting part of the strategy was that this first target market for a new product platform based on digital technology did not cannibalize Xerox as much as it could have in other markets.

Xerox continued to develop new product platforms based on digital technology, gradually replacing its light-lens product platforms. By 1996, it had introduced digital product platforms beyond the DocuTech for production publishing—color copying and printing, data center printing, multifunction products, and network printing. Figure 3-9 shows this transition. By 1998, more than half of Xerox's revenue was derived from digital product platforms. Most important, Xerox was able to make the transition relatively smoothly, so smoothly that many have underestimated the significance of this accomplishment.

There are several important lessons to be learned from the successful replacement of product platforms at Xerox. First, Xerox was able not only to see the impending technological threat but to react quickly. Its management process initiated the appropriate actions. Second, Xerox was able to introduce the new technology in a product platform targeted at a market that was not one of its primary markets, thereby creating incremental revenue and not confusing the market with multiple platforms. Once the technology was established in this new platform, Xerox implemented it in product platforms that served more mainstream markets. Finally, Xerox could afford to invest in creating new product platforms while still invest-

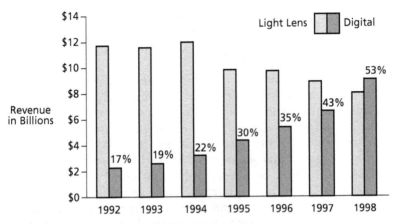

Figure 3-9 By 1998, more than half of Xerox's revenue was derived from digital platforms introduced since 1990.

ing in supporting the product platforms it continued to sell to its customers. It was able to do so because it dramatically increased the productivity of its product development process at the same time. With this increased productivity, Xerox was able to develop more than three times the number of platforms and product offerings with the same investment in R&D.

Intel: An Evolving Platform Strategy

Intel developed its first microprocessor product platform, the 4004, in 1971, followed by the 8008 six months later. The 8008 microprocessor was used in embedded products such as digital scales, traffic lights, and gasoline pumps. Intel developed an improved version, the 8080 microprocessor, in 1974.

Intel introduced the 8086 16-bit platform in 1978, and the 8088 8-bit platform in 1979. IBM selected the 8088 as the basis for its personal computer, and Intel's microprocessor business was born. The 8086/88 platforms performed from 5 to 10 MHz, much faster than previous platforms. Intel continued to introduce new product platforms every few years, as illustrated earlier in Figure 3-8.

Up until this time, Intel's platform strategy was limited. It developed only one product offering from each platform. Starting with the 80286 platform introduced in 1982, Intel began to release multiple products for each platform. The 286 was a 16-bit platform that offered products that ranged from 6 to 12 MHz. It incorporated on-chip memory management and was the first microprocessor that offered software compatibility.

The 80386 platform introduced in 1985 was based on a new 32-bit architecture that increased performance to 12 MHz. Intel designed a range of products from this platform, including the DX family and the SX family. The 80486 platform replaced it in 1989. The 80486 platform had a built-in math coprocessor and performance that ranged from 25 to 33 MHz. The product line strategy for this platform is described in Chapter 4.

In 1993, Intel introduced the Pentium platform, with five times the performance of the 80486. In 1995, it introduced the P6 architecture with the release of the Pentium Pro platform, which incorporated a second die with a high-speed memory cache to accelerate performance. Performance increased to 200 MHz.

At this point, Intel changed its platform strategy. The original strategy had been to design ever more powerful processors aimed at the top end of the computer market segment as previous-generation platforms migrated to the lower-end market segment. Intel's new strategy used one core technology as the foundation for developing several platforms tailored to meet the needs of multiple markets with multiple products. This strategy made sense for Intel, because there was sufficient volume in each market segment to begin to view each as a market and tailor a specific platform for each market. Intel was also able to develop and leverage a common architecture to reduce the investment in each platform.

Intel developed the MMX technology with a new set of instructions designed to enhance multimedia. This was incorporated into all platforms using the P6 architecture. The Pentium II platform was introduced in 1997. Intel optimized its design to deliver exceptional performance for business applications. A derivative platform was created for mobile applications. In 1998, Intel introduced two new platforms using the same architecture. The Intel Celeron platform was developed to meet core computing needs at an affordable price. The Pentium Xeon platform was developed for higher-end server and workstation computers and integrated large caches into the processor.

The Intel product platform strategy shows an interesting evolution over the last 25 years. It shifted from a single product per platform, to leveraging numerous product offerings from each platform, to customizing unique platforms for each market while using a common architecture. The transition illustrates not only the growth of its markets but also an evolution of Intel's platform management skills.

Notes

1. For additional definitions and examples of product platforms see Marc H. Meyer and Alvin P. Lehnerd, *The Power of Product Platforms* (The Free Press, 1997).

2. Alan Deutschman, "Steve Jobs's Next Big Gamble," *Fortune*, February 8, 1993.

3. When the first edition of this book was published, I wondered how Bill Gates would relate to this claim. Interestingly he later made the same statement in one of his books.

4. Roy A. Bauer, Emilio Collar, and Victor Tang, *The Silverlake Project* (Oxford University Press, 1992).

5. The information in this example is derived from a variety of sources, including Apple Computer, Apple Computer Annual Reports, and Owen W. Linzmayer, *Apple Confidential* (No Starch Press, 1999).

6. *Business Week*, February 22, 1999, p. 72.

7. Information provided by Medtronic.

8. Howard Banks, "Desperately Seeking Partners," *Business Week*, November 22, 1993.

9. G. Pascal Zachary, "Consolidation Sweeps the Software Industry," *The Wall Street Journal*, March 23, 1994.

10. Clayton M. Christensen, *The Innovator's Dilemma* (Harvard Business School Press, 1997).

11. John P. Kotter, *A Force for Change* (The Free Press, 1992).

4

Defining the Offerings: Product Line Strategy

A product line strategy is a time-phased conditional plan for the sequence of developing product offerings from a common platform, with each product offering targeting a specific market segment.

Product line strategy is where specific product offerings are defined. We use the term *product offering* to emphasize that the product sold by a company today is frequently more than what was traditionally considered to be the product. It includes the options for configuring and using the product, the way the customer purchases a product, the positioning of the product in the market, and the way the product is supported. In some cases the product offering includes product options, related products such as supplies for the basic product, and related services. A product offering can be a service as well as a tangible product.

Product line strategy is a time-phased conditional plan for the sequence of developing products from a common product platform. There are several important elements in this definition. A product line strategy determines the *sequence* in which products are developed and released. This sequence is *time-phased* throughout the life cycle of the platform and the product line. Finally, it is *conditional* in that it can change with evolving market conditions, competitive factors, or resource availability.

Without an effective product line strategy, the true potential of a platform strategy will not be realized.

In some ways, product line strategy can be considered less strategically critical than platform strategy. The defining technology has already been selected. The primary vector of differentiation has been decided. The general cost structure has been determined. A brilliant product line strategy is unlikely to save an inept platform strategy. Don't be deceived by this thinking, because without an effective product line strategy, the true potential of a platform strategy will not be realized.

Too many companies neglect to create any comprehensive product line strategy. They develop products in sequence, without really giving much thought to what comes next. Only when one product is complete will they start to think about which one to develop next. Products may not cover the appropriate segments of the market, or they may be released in a less effective sequence. By developing products in this manner, these companies lose the opportunity to implement a clear strategy to improve their position in the market.

A division of a major computer company developed a completely new product platform with some unique characteristics, but failed to think beyond the first product based on this platform. As soon as it completed this first product, the company began working on its next product. Because the engineering group was excited about applying the latest version of the technology, it began developing a more powerful version of the product. After almost a year of development, the company realized that the more powerful version would appeal to only a very small segment of the market. The largest segment wanted a less expensive, less powerful version. Because it got sidetracked, the company lost out to competition that beat it to this critical segment.

Ingredients of Product Line Strategy

A poorly implemented product line strategy can restrict the success of even a brilliant platform strategy. Without an effective product line strategy, companies fail to develop and release products in the proper sequence. They miss opportunities to target distinct product offerings in specific market segments, or confuse the market with a proliferation of products. In our experience, several ingredients are common to a successful product line strategy.

1. *The product line covers all primary targeted market segments.* Various product offerings within a product line are intended to appeal to different market segments; otherwise, there would be no reason to have more than one product. Collectively, the products within a product line should cover the major segments of the market; the primary objective of product line strategy is to achieve this coverage. Dell Computer faced such a problem in 1993 when it found itself under pricing pressure as IBM and Compaq came up with lower prices. Its strategic response borrowed a lesson in marketing from the auto companies, which targeted variations of the same basic chassis to different market segments. After conducting market research, including an analysis of its telephone-order database, Dell redesigned its product line. It organized its products around product families by configuring its computers differently. Each product family was aimed at a specific type of customer. Dell believed that it had four customer types, each of which it considered as a segment within the market[1,2]:

> ## Collectively, the products within a product line should cover the major segments of the market.

- The Dimension family was aimed at customers ("techno-to-go") who wanted a simple, affordable home computer that was ready to use out of the box. Maximum value and simplicity were the main focus. Prices ranged from $1,299 for the 486/25S to $1,799 for the 486/33.

- The Dimension XPS family included jazzed-up computers with fast graphics, enhanced video, built-in CD-ROM, and audio capabilities. It targeted sophisticated users ("techno-wizards") who buy "hot" components from computer magazines. This was a segment targeted successfully by Dell competitor Gateway 2000. Dell's family of products maximized video performance. Configurations were priced from $2,498 for the XPS 450V to $2,999 for the XPS 466V.

- The OptiPlex family was an advanced set of computers aimed at high-end corporate buyers ("techno-criticals") who were interested in advanced features and enhanced productivity. It stressed maximum performance and upgradability. In September 1993, prices ranged from the 433S/L at $1,878 to the 433/MX at $2,548.

- The NetPlex family with built-in networking was aimed at price-sensitive corporate buyers ("techno-teamers") who sought networking capabilities, name brands, and reliability.

By using the same platform, but targeting different segments with each product family, Dell avoided fruitless product proliferation while broadening its offerings.

Sometimes a company overlooks certain market segments in its product line strategy. Until Dell introduced the Dimension XPS product family, it missed the high-performance graphics segment of the market. The key to avoiding this mistake is an understanding of the market and how it is segmented. Market segments are groupings of customers with similar characteristics who choose a similar product or service. While there are many ways to segment a market, the key is to segment it in a manner that provides competitive advan-

> *While there are many ways to segment a market, the key is to segment it in a manner that provides competitive advantage.*

tage. For example, in the previous case, Gateway identified the segment of sophisticated users and targeted a product offering at it, while Dell initially missed that opportunity. Successful segmentation requires knowledge of how to match product capabilities to each segment of the market.

Without a product line strategy, individual products will be shaped by other criteria. For example, instead of designing a series of product offerings for clearly defined market segments, a company will design the initial product by including all the features it believes are possible. The next product will be slated to contain the additional features possible at that time. These product decisions are made without consideration of the market segments the product will address. The inevitable consequence is a range of products, none of which matches a defined market segment.

Market segmentation should not be analyzed statically . Segmentation can change rapidly, particularly in high-technology markets. As new segments emerge, product line strategy needs to be modified; new product offerings may be necessary to address these newly emerging market segments. Inflexibility

> *Segmentation can change rapidly, particularly in high-technology markets. New product offerings may be necessary to address these newly emerging market segments.*

leads to failure when conditions change. Either the company will continue to march down a path that is no longer viable or the entire plan will be discarded, and the company will hop from one product to the next in an effort to catch up.

This is what happened to a company that dominated its segment of the transaction terminal business. Unwilling to recognize that the market and technology were shifting, it stuck to its initial product line plan. The result: overpriced products leading to slippage to the number-three market position.

Variation of product offerings within a product line is limited by the constraints of the product platform. Differentiation of the product platform is usually the primary way that a product appeals to a market segment. For example, a high-performance, high-priced platform will appeal to the segment of the market willing to pay for that performance. Variations in performance and price can make a product more attractive to some market segments, but the appeal to other segments may be limited.

Fault-tolerant computer manufacturers Stratus and Tandem targeted companies willing to pay for this capability. Companies in this market segment are those with mission-critical transaction processing requirements, such as banks and airlines, as well as companies with process control requirements, such as utilities. Within this segment, Stratus and Tandem could offer products with a range of capacities and interface capabilities that subsegment the market.

2. *Each product offering is sufficiently focused to avoid product proliferation and market confusion.* In an effort to cover all market segments, a company may have a tendency to release too many products. Product proliferation is the result of a company's failure to focus on selected segments. The company tries to be all things to all people, and, in the process, it confuses customers. Apple Computer suffered from product proliferation in early 1993.[3] It was selling the Macintosh product line using a variety of overlapping product families: Centris, Performa, Quadra, Classic, LC, PowerBook, Duo, and Workgroup. The PowerBook was clearly different from the others, except for the Duo, which was a combination notebook and desktop.

At the low end of the Mac product line were the Classic products, followed by the LC. The Performa products were renamed versions of other products. The Performa 200 was a renamed Classic II; the Performa 400 was a renamed LCII. The Performa 600 was an LC III with a CD-

> ***Product proliferation is the result of a company's failure to focus on selected segments.***

ROM. The only difference in this product line was that it was sold through mass-market retailers with different software and support.

The Centris was the middle of the product line, replacing the IIci and the IIsi. The IIvx remained in the product line as part of the Centris family, but was not renamed. The Quadra family was the high end of the product line. There was little difference between the 800 and the 950. The Quadra 700 was the low end of the Quadra family and equivalent to some of the Centris products. The Workgroup 60, 80, and 95 models combined the Centris 610, Quadra 800, and Quadra 950 with networking software.

Sound confusing? It was. This proliferation of products confused and frustrated many customers. It also increased Apple's inventories. Apple finally learned the lesson of product proliferation and simplified its Macintosh product line—offering the Quadra for desktops, the PowerBook for notebook computers, and the Workgroup for servers.

Product proliferation can result from the company being overly customer-focused as well. A manufacturer of equipment for the cable TV industry focused too much on its customers. Since the cable TV business is dominated by large customers, this company began all its development projects at the request of specific customers. When it completed the product, the company found that it had to be modified for other customers. This led to product proliferation.

> ***Product proliferation can result from the company being overly customer-focused.***

The point of creating a product line strategy is to comprehend the market and competition and to make the difficult decisions about which products to develop. In the absence of a product line strategy, a company tends to become too reactive instead of proactive.

3. *The product line development schedule is time phased.* Another essential ingredient of product line strategy is the time-phased introduction of individual product offerings. Each potential product offering in the product line needs to be prioritized and then sequenced, since all versions cannot be released simultaneously. For example, Intel first released the 25 MHz DX product within its 486 product line, directly addressing the middle of the market for midrange performance, but also covering a little of the higher-range performance segment. The 33 MHz product was released next to cover the needs of the high-performance midrange segment better and begin to cover the server-multiuser segment. The 50 MHz product eventually gave better coverage to this segment. As part of its product line strategy, Intel covered the key market segment first with some applicability in other segments.

Predictability of the timing for individual product releases is also key. If the scheduled product releases cannot be predicted accurately, then the product line strategy may be questionable. One company with an overly optimistic product line strategy wanted its initial product to have a rich feature set; however, the allotted development time was too short to allow all the features to be developed. Instead of prioritizing the features and matching them with required development resources, the company based its initial product on whatever features were ready. Because there was no rationale for this feature grouping, the product did not address any specific market segments. The next product release was then rushed to market, and some of its planned features were not ready when the product was launched. These leftover features formed the next release.

As a result, the timing of release did not follow the original product line strategy, and the products did not match the needs of any market segments.

The product line plan is a critical element of the development plan. It should match the product release schedule with the resources required to meet it, enabling the company to validate this schedule with the rough estimate of required resources and the needed start dates for all projects.

4. *Similar product families and product lines are coordinated.*   Product line strategy needs to coordinate similar product lines, particularly when there are multiple product lines from the same or similar platforms. Trying to serve a large, broad market with a single platform can be a limiting product strategy. IBM, Apple, and Compaq tried this for a while in the PC market. Each offered a premium-priced platform, competing on advanced technology and new features. Together, these market leaders captured only 30 percent of the world market in 1992; the remainder of the market was divided among numerous companies selling PCs primarily on the basis of low price.

Market shares like this are not characteristic of a relatively mature market. It became clear that the market leaders were focusing on a single product line, leaving the bulk of the market to be divided among competitors with a lower-priced product line. IBM and Compaq saw the light in 1992, and each launched a new low-cost product line: IBM, the PS/ValuePoint product line, and Compaq, the ProLinear product line. Their early success was dramatic, and by the end of 1995 they were on the way to capturing market share in the low-price segment of the PC market. One can only wonder how the PC market would be different if IBM or Compaq had launched a low-cost product line three years earlier.

In some markets, it may be desirable to base more than one product line on the same or similar platforms. All are aimed at the same market, but each has characteristics that are meant to address a different segment. Typically, each product line is distributed through a different channel, sells in a different price range, and carries a different brand name or product designation. IBM implemented this strategy in its personal computer business, eventually offering four product lines in 1993. The IBM brand-name product line, selling the PS/2 and other products, was its traditional offering. The PS/2 carried a premium price and was positioned as a premium product. It had a three-year onsite warranty, faster disk drive, better graphics, and higher-quality components. In early 1993, there were 36 models in the PS/2 product line.

The PS/2 product line contained 21 models and targeted the consumer market segment, while the ValuePoint product line consisted of 21 models of low-cost computers sold through retail outlets and through IBM PC Direct. By early 1994, IBM concluded that there was little difference between the ValuePoint and PS/2 product lines, and the two were combined.

Ambra was IBM's other personal computer product line, which targeted the high-performance non-IBM market segment. Although based on a similar product platform with minor variations, it was promoted as a different product line, sold by a separate company. Ambra Computer Corp. was a small "virtual corporation" owned by IBM, which marketed a product line of low-cost personal computers to customers who bought PCs on the basis of price. The strategy of this product line was to attack competitors such as Dell, Zeos, and Gateway 2000 with non-IBM brand-name computers. The Ambra product line was aimed at more sophisticated customers who bought for price through telephone ordering and did not need technical support through retail stores.

Using the same platform for multiple product lines is risky, because the burden of differentiation between the product lines is placed more on feature differences and brand name than on the underlying platform. It can be done, but only if the discipline of separating features is rigorously applied. Unless differentiation creates a sufficient increase in volume, it simply dilutes resources. In the extreme case, one product just cannibalizes the other. Typically, the lower-priced product line cannibalizes the more expensive one.

One consumer electronics manufacturer fell into this strategic trap. The company had two product lines: one with a premium price and high margins sold through specialty dealers, and the other with lower prices and lower margins sold through high-volume outlets. Originally, each product line was based on a different platform, but the company slipped into using the same platform, differentiating the two product lines through features. Tempted by opportunities in the high-volume segment, it began to migrate features from the premium-priced product line. This left the brand name as the only differentiating factor between the premium and low-priced product lines, and eventually the entire market shifted to the low-priced products. Specialty dealers stopped selling the premium line. The resulting profit margins were too low to sustain its business, and the company was forced to downsize.

Product Line Strategy Examples

Product line strategy varies significantly with the nature of the product offerings, the market, and the competition. In the examples that follow, we try to demonstrate how product line strategy is applied in different situations.

Amazon.com Product Lines

Amazon.com is an interesting example of a successful product line strategy in the Internet age. Amazon's core strategic vision defines it as a company that has a single product platform, but a wide and almost unending range of product offerings from this platform:

> The company's objective is to become the best place to buy, find, and discover any product or service available online. Amazon.com will continue to enhance and broaden its brand, customer base, and electronic commerce expertise with the goal of creating customers' preferred online shopping destination, in the United States and around the world.

This core strategic vision contains all the vital elements: It states where the company wants to go, how it will get there, and why it will be successful. It also clearly guides Amazon's product strategy: a single platform that serves as the launching pad for an unending series of product offerings, clearly a very exciting strategy for an enormous emerging market.

Amazon's product platform consists of several important elements: software for browsing, searching, and reviewing content; availability checking; order processing, especially its one-click technology; secure credit card payment; and fulfillment. The company launched its product platform in July 1995 with its first product offering—online sale of books. Although Amazon was initially recognized as an online bookstore, its core strategic vision clearly extended beyond that initial product offering. Yet books were the right first choice. They showcased the power of the Internet in providing a lot of information, such as reviews and rankings, and also the ability to maintain a database of hundreds of thousands of items. Books were also easy to handle and ship, and required Amazon to maintain little inventory, since book publishers traditionally stock an inventory of all their books.

Amazon expanded beyond books in June 1998 when it started offering music products, and by the third quarter of 1998 it became the number-one online music seller. In November 1998, Amazon.com launched its video and holiday gift offerings from the same product platform. By the fourth quarter of 1998, it was the number-one online video seller.

The expansion of Amazon.com product offerings continued aggressively. In March 1998, it launched an online auction and later teamed up with Sotheby's and LiveBid.com to extend its auction product offerings even further. In April of that year it launched electronic greeting cards, and in June it offered the ability to download digital songs. In July 1999 Amazon.com released two additional product offerings: electronics, and toys and games. Realizing that it was easier to bundle the release of product offerings, in November 1999 Amazon launched four new offerings: home improvement, software, video games, and gifts.

At the same time, Amazon continued improving its product platform elements, which enhanced all its product offerings. It introduced purchase circles in August 1999, enabling groups to combine purchases. It launched Amazon.com Anywhere, providing access to shopping from wireless devices. On the international front, Amazon created two platform variations with Amazon.co.uk and Amazon.de. Eventually, these will support all product offerings in the United Kingdom and Germany, customized to their language and currency requirements. Amazon.com also continued to upgrade its software to improve the user experience and expand the capabilities of its distribution infrastructure. In addition, Amazon began to partner with other Internet sites for further expansion of its product offerings. These include drugstore.com, Gear.com (sporting goods), HomeGrocer.com, and Pets.com.

The Amazon.com example shows the power of a single platform that can be leveraged into numerous product offerings in an emerging marketplace. Spreading the investment in technology across multiple products provides significant competitive advantage, as does leveraging a common brand name in the Internet market,

> *The Amazon.com example shows the power of a single platform that can be leveraged into numerous product offerings in an emerging marketplace.*

where brand name is critical. What is most remarkable, however, is Amazon's ability to create and launch so many products in such a short period of time. This is an example of how something that would be impossible in the bricks-and-mortar world is possible in the world of the Internet.

HP Color Workgroup Printer Product Line

Hewlett-Packard was the leader in producing a variety of printers, and its color workgroup printers provide a good example of product line strategy. All used the HP ImageREt 2400 toner-blending technology for photorealistic images, the HP JetDirect 600N EIO internal print server, and the HP WebJet Admin printer management software. Within this platform, HP created two families of products, each aimed at a different price/performance market segment depending on print speed. To target the product offerings even more within each segment, HP developed three products with different features for each price/performance segment.

The 8500 Series. The 8500 family of products was targeted at the "standard" department color-printing market segment by fulfilling requirements for fast and versatile high-performance color printing as part of a network. The product printed 6 ppm (pages per minute) in color and 24 ppm in black and white, and it could handle media from 3.9" × 7.5" to 12" × 18.5". Within this product family, HP developed three products, each priced differently depending on features:

- $5,999—Color LaserJet 8500: 3 paper trays, 32 MB, not network ready
- $6,799—Color LaserJet 8500 N: 3 paper trays, 32 MB, network ready
- $8,699—Color LaserJet 8500 DN: 4 paper trays, 64 MB, network ready

The 4500 Series. The 4500 family of products was targeted at the lower price/performance segment of the same workgroup color-laser printing market with a price range some $3,000 less than the 8500. These products were slower—4 ppm in color and 16 ppm in black and white—and handled a somewhat more restrictive range of media—up to 8.5" × 14". Within this family of products there were also three products similar to the variations offered in the 8500 family:

- $2,499—Color LaserJet 4500: 2 paper trays, 32 MB, not network ready
- $2,949—Color LaserJet 4500 N: 2 paper trays, 64 MB, network ready
- $3,799—Color LaserJet 4500 DN: 3 paper trays, 64 MB, network ready

Dell Desktop Product Line

By 1999 personal computers had reached the point where they could be configured into almost infinite variations, depending on customer preferences. Yet even within this range, product line strategy was possible. Dell, for example, had three families of Dell Dimension desktops that it positioned toward different market segments, as follows:

- Dimension L, with prices starting at $899, included Intel Pentium III or Celeron processors up to 550 MHz and up to a 20 GB hard drive with up to 512 MB SDRAM. These were targeted for market segments interested in home finances, e-mail, word processing, productivity, and educational software.

- Dimension XPS T, with prices starting at $1,299, included Intel Pentium III processors up to 750 MHz and up to a 37.5 GB hard drive with up to 768 MB SDRAM. These were targeted for the market segment primarily interested in high-speed Internet use, demanding multimedia, games, and digital imaging.

- Dimension XPS B, with prices starting at $1,939 included Intel Pentium III processors up to 800 MHz and up to a 37.5 GB hard drive with 512 MB of RDRAM memory. These were targeted for the segment of the market interested in streaming video and audio, digital imaging, and intense gaming.

One-to-one marketing is the ultimate market segmentation and product line strategy.

The Dell product line raises issues related to individually customized products and what is emerging in some markets as "market segments of one" or what is sometimes referred to as one-to-one marketing. This is the ultimate market segmentation and product line strategy.

Tylenol Product Line

Tylenol is a product platform based on acetaminophen as the active chemical ingredient for all products in the platform. Acetaminophen has different characteristics from aspirin, the alternative, and all products from this platform share those characteristics. Many product offerings have been created from this basic ingredient, and the variety of offerings has enabled McNeil Consumer Healthcare, a division of McNeil-PPC, Inc., to sell 240 billion tablets in Tylenol's 38-year history. Let's look at how McNeil has achieved its success through product line strategy from this platform.

Adult Pain Relief Products. By varying two product elements—dosage and form—McNeil was able to create six adult pain relief products. Regular-strength products contain 325 mg of the critical platform element acetaminophen, while the extra-strength products contain 500 mg of acetaminophen. Each of these was targeted at a market segment for a different degree of pain or at least at a different segment based on the *perceived* degree of pain. Beyond this, the product was offered in different forms to address customer preferences within each segment. Regular Strength Tylenol is offered in caplets and tablets, while Extra Strength Tylenol is offered in tablets, caplets, gelcaps, and geltabs.

When the market segment for extended pain relief became apparent, McNeil created a product specifically targeted at that segment. Arthritis Extended Relief lasts for 12 hours instead of the 8-hour maximum for the previous pain relief products. McNeil designed this product by creating two layers—one for immediate release and the other for extended release. It contains 650 mg of acetaminophen.

Another product was targeted at the segment of the market for people with pain who have trouble sleeping. Tylenol PM contains 500 mg of acetaminophen, the same as Extra Strength Tylenol, combined with another ingredient (25 mg of diphenhydramine) to help cause sleep. It is offered in three forms: caplets, gelcaps, and geltabs. While we're at it, McNeil thought, why not offer a product that simply helps sleep? So the acetaminophen was removed to create a product called Simply Sleep. Technically, this is not from the same product platform, since it doesn't contain acetaminophen, but as a matter of convenience it can be managed in the same product line.

Cold and Flu Products. McNeil then targeted Tylenol at the related market for cold and flu. Tylenol Sore Throat is a liquid with 1,000 mg of acetaminophen offered in cherry or honey lemon flavors. Three product variations—Complete, Non-Drowsy, and Severe Congestion—contained additional active ingredients for cold symptoms along with 350 mg of acetaminophen. These are offered in caplets, tablets, and gelcaps. A line of flu products containing 500 mg of acetaminophen included Non-Drowsy and Nighttime in gelcaps. The nighttime liquid and powder product offerings contained 1,000 mg of acetaminophen. Variations of these products are targeted to the sinus and allergy market segments.

Children's Products. McNeil also targeted a number of its product offerings at the children's market segments. Its Infants product used concentrated drops of 160 mg of acetaminophen. Children's Tylenol liquid for 2- to 11-year-olds also had 160 mg per dose and came in three flavors: grape, cherry, and bubble gum. The Soft Chew product, also for 2- to 11-year-olds, contained 80 mg of acetaminophen per tablet and came in grape, fruitburst, and bubble gum. Junior Tylenol was aimed at the older-child segment, ages 6 to 12. It contained 160 mg of acetaminophen and came in chewables and caplets, each in grape and fruit.

There was also a line of children's products targeted for the related cold market. They included the same variations noted above—flu, sinus, cold, and allergy—but used a lower dosage of acetaminophen as well as a lower dosage of the other active ingredients.

Walt Disney World Product Line

A fun way to understand product line strategy is by looking at Walt Disney World as a product line. Walt Disney World can be viewed as a product/service platform, with multiple product offerings organized into product offering families. The objective of having multiple product offerings in this case is to attract more people to a single destination, get them to stay longer, and get them to spend more money.

The Walt Disney World product/service platform physically encompasses 43 square miles, approximately twice the size of Manhattan Island, and comprises several families of product offerings, including attractions, resorts, water parks, and shops. Even though it was built in 1971 with the Magic Kingdom as its original product offering, the Walt Disney World platform has grown well beyond that. Epcot, opened in October 1982, was its second major attraction product offering, combining Future World and World Showcase. Disney-MGM Studios opened in 1989, at a cost of more than $300 million. Also in 1989, Disney opened Pleasure Island, a one-admission, multi-nightclub entertainment complex. The latest product offering in the Walt Disney World attraction family was Disney's Animal Kingdom, opened in 1998.

The Walt Disney World product offerings include three water theme parks. Water Country was the original. When competitive water parks started to attract visitors from the older and more adventurous segment of the market, Walt Disney World responded by building Typhoon Lagoon in 1989. It later created a third, Blizzard Beach.

The Walt Disney World platform also includes numerous resort and hotel product offerings. The first three, opened in 1971, were the Contemporary, Polynesian, and Fort Wilderness. Over the last 30 years, 13 resorts have been added. By the beginning of 2000, Walt Disney World had a capacity of almost 20,000 hotel rooms, each catering to various preferences and price options.

Other of Walt Disney World's diverse product offerings are aimed at specific entertainment segments. Most notable is the 200-acre Walt Disney World of Sports, a state-of-the-art sports competition and training facility. It has a 7,500-seat ballpark, multiple baseball and softball fields, competition tennis courts, a track-and-field facility, volleyball courts, and more than 20 other sports facilities. It is also the spring training home of the Atlanta Braves. It attracts a unique market segment, and the numerous amateur and professional competitions encourage family and friends to spend money at the other Walt Disney World product offerings. Other specialty product offerings include the Disney Institute and Disney University, Disney BoardWalk, and Downtown Disney.

Product Line Management

Product line management is the process of defining and maintaining a product line strategy. This is an ongoing process, not just a one-time effort. In our experience, successful product line management includes the following activities.

1. *Defining product offerings from a common platform.* A product line is built on a product platform, and all product offerings within the product line incorporate the critical elements of that common platform. In particular, they all use the same defining technology, which is the essence of the product platform. More can be invested into the product platform elements, because they can be leveraged across all products in the product line.

For example, NCR's automated teller machine (ATM) product line, described in the previous chapter, used a common platform that was three times more reliable than competitive products. The product line included the 5070 full-function interior ATM, the 5081 full-function through-the-wall ATM (used outside of a bank on the exterior wall), the 5084 cash-dispensing-only ATM, the 5088 drive-through-island ATM, the 5571 inquiry and printing machine, and eventually the 5070L (a lower-priced version of the 5070). Each of these products varied in size, shape, and mix of functions, but all leveraged the reliability advantages of a common platform.

As elements of the product platform are improved, these improvements can be incorporated directly into all products from that platform. We saw this earlier in the Amazon.com example. Platform improvements such as Amazon.com Anywhere and the two national variations (Germany and the United Kingdom) were enhancements to all products.

For simplification purposes, we use the convention that a product line and its underlying product platform serve a market. This raises questions such as: What is the market? And when does a market segment become a market? There is no magic to these definitions. What is most critical is that they are clearly defined and understood. With the respect to printers, if color printers make up a sufficiently different platform from black-and-white printers, then color printers could be defined as a different market, especially when there is a reasonable expectation that customers will not routinely substitute a black-and-white printer if they need a color printer. If portable computers are a sufficiently different platform from desktops, they might be considered to be different markets, especially when customers are really looking for portability. Sometimes it's simply a matter of choice in defining the market scope.

2. *Targeting specific product offerings at specific market segments.* While the product platform targets the market in general, specific product offerings within the product line target individual segments of the market. Each product within a product line is modified to appeal to customers in a particular segment. High-priced, high-performance products, for example, appeal to the segment of the market that will pay more for increased performance.

Product line strategy starts by identifying and understanding each major segment in order to define the necessary product variations for each segment. As a result, each product offering varies from others in the product line by specific characteristics, such as the following:

- *Capacity.* Product offerings in a product line may differ by capacity. Examples of capacity differences include disk drives (data storage), airplanes (number of passengers), switchboards (number of lines), and voice-mail systems (number of messages).

- *Performance.* Performance differences may distinguish product offerings in a product line. Examples include microprocessors (processing speed), airplanes (speed and distance), data modems (data transmission speeds), printers (speed/pages per minute), and database software (response time).

- *Features.* Features frequently define product differences within a product line. Examples include cellular telephones (models with number recall, hands-free operation, etc.), personal computers (models with color monitors, different keyboards, etc.), and consumer electronics.

- *Quality.* Quality differentiation in the sense described here does not mean that some products are poorly made. It means premium-quality versions of the product, and, of course, higher-quality products are sold for a higher price. Examples include advanced materials (higher-quality materials with fewer impurities are necessary for certain applications), higher-grade semiconductors, and ruggedized computers (made to withstand field conditions for military use).

- *Packaging.* Packaging or configuration differences can also distinguish product offerings. Examples include ATMs (designed for different currencies), personal computers (predefined configurations and options), and videoconferencing systems (predefined communications and display configurations).

In some cases, the characteristics for differentiating product offerings in a product line are clear; in other cases, the issue is more complex. Deciding how to differentiate product offerings in a product line and how many to have are critical aspects of product line management.

Besides the primary products in a product line, add-on products, product upgrades, and custom products also may be part of a product line. Add-on products could simply be accessories, such as ribbons and toner for printers, but they could be even more important, as the following razor-blade example shows. For razor makers, the real profit comes in selling a continuing supply of blades, not the original razor. The principle applies in technology-based businesses as well. For example, medical diagnostic instruments require disposable reagents for each test. Usually, reagent revenue is where the company makes its profit. In this case, the product line strategy is to sell or lease the instrument at an attractive price, creating a guaranteed revenue stream because the reagent will work only with that instrument. In personal computers, add-on products include additional computer memory, modems, extra disk drives, and so on. These may be more profitable than the original product. In the prepress industry, the major image setter manufacturers such as Agfa, Crosfield, and DuPont relied on sales of film products to support lower-priced offerings on their electronic products.

Product upgrades are a form of add-on product important to many high-technology products, particularly computer software. Product upgrades provide additional revenue from the existing customer base, and can be critical to

> *Once a market approaches saturation, upgrades may become the primary source of continued revenue growth.*

extending the life cycle of many high-technology products. Once a market approaches saturation, upgrades may become the primary source of continued revenue growth. In the software market, some companies have implemented product line strategies entirely on the basis of future upgrade revenue. They offer the initial product at almost giveaway prices for the opportunity to sell upgrade versions in the future to a large installed base.

Some product line strategies revolve around providing customized products. Large, high-priced products, such as commercial aircraft, are built to customer configuration requirements. Personal computers can be ordered with customer-defined configurations for memory, software, and other options preinstalled. Custom products can be the primary basis of a product line strategy, or they can be an adjunct to it. Even in 1994, IBM's Ambra product line offered "custom-built" products. A customer could choose one of five system types (Slimline, Desktop, Minitower, EISA Desktop, or EISA tower), one of six microprocessors, numerous memory configurations, one of six hard disk alternatives, one of four monitors, a variety of preloaded software applications, and numerous other options.

3. *Phasing the sequence of development.* Each product in a product line requires some development in addition to the original platform development. In some cases, this may be significant (e.g., performance improvements in a microprocessor), while in other cases, it may be relatively simple (e.g., different configurations of personal computers). Since each product offering requires additional development, not all products can be released at the same time.

Product line mapping can help managers analyze and plan the priority, sequence, and timing of product releases within the product line.[4] In some cases, the initial market segment addressed should be the one served by the easiest or quickest product to develop. After all, there is an enthusiasm to bring the new platform to market and get real revenue. Amazon.com did this with its first product offering, addressing the book segment of the market. In other cases, competitive pressure creates the priority to address a particular market segment. If competition successfully captures a market segment, it may be more difficult to attack in the future. For example, some companies accelerated the priority of the online commerce segment in reaction to the success of such companies as eBay. In still other cases, the highest-priority segments are the largest ones, since they represent the highest potential revenue.

Market segments can also subsegment over time. When this happens, new product offerings can better address these subsegments. Tylenol, discussed earlier, is an excellent example of subsegmenting with product variations.

For high-technology products, the primary rollout of products in a product line is typically completed in the first half of the platform life cycle. Since life cycles tend to be short, it is rarely worthwhile to introduce a new product at the end of a platform life cycle, when a product may have only a one- or two-year life remaining. The exception is a product that is a "midlife kicker," extending the life of the product platform through increased performance.

The product line plan dictates product development by scheduling individual products backward from their planned release date. This is typically an iterative process, with the desired schedule matched to available development resources and then modified to meet constraints. Without a product line plan to schedule development, there is no trigger point to initiate the next product, and the company would start thinking about the next product only after finishing the current one.

When development teams understand product line strategy, the rollout of the entire product line is usually quicker and better. By understanding the targeted market segments for each of the products planned for the product line, these teams can design products to better fit those segments or implement designs that are flexible enough to make subsequent product variations easier to develop. For example, they can make the design more modular, anticipating changes to some modules for future product variations.

Product Line Strategy in Action

The two case studies that follow show how two companies followed different product line strategies over a period of years.

IBM's ThinkPad Product Line Strategy

IBM's entry into the portable computer market began in May of 1989 when it launched the Personal System/2 P70 portable computer, weighing 14 to 20 pounds. This product became noncompetitive five months later when Compaq introduced the Compaq Lte Notebook PC, weighing only 6 pounds, and the market began to shift toward smaller and lighter notebook computers. IBM tried to develop several other portable computers without much success. Products such as the L450SX and the CL57SX were bulky and heavy, weighing 8 to 11 pounds. Eventually, IBM realized this was going to be a strategic market, and it needed to leapfrog the competition, not just catch up. The strategy shift gave birth to the ThinkPad development effort.[5]

The ThinkPad platform was launched in October 1992. Key to the success of the ThinkPad platform was the first-generation 10.4-inch panel display. IBM had exclusive access to the worldwide supply of these displays, providing a sustainable vector of differentiation. It also introduced the TrackPoint to enable the functions of a mouse on a notebook keyboard.

As part of launching the new ThinkPad platform, IBM developed a general product line strategy. It decided on three families of products based on price and performance: The 700 series would be the high-end family, the 500 series would be the midrange family, and the 300 series would be the low-end family. Providing coverage of the market on the basis of price sensitivity such as this is typically the initial way to structure a new product line. Within each price/performance market segment, IBM would further segment the market with both black-and-white and color display offerings.

The ThinkPad 700 and 700C (color display) were the first two products released from this new platform. When IBM later replaced its proprietary Micro Channel with the AT bus, because the MC was too expensive and independent peripheral suppliers didn't like it, the 700/700C became somewhat obsolete. IBM continued to release additional high-end products with the 750/750C in September 1993 and the 755/755C in May 1994. In general, the new product offerings used faster microprocessors and more memory, so they tended to replace rather than supplement the previous ones. IBM's product line strategy within each family was not to further segment the market but to keep up with technology changes.

Although the low-end product family (also referred to as the Value Notebook family) was launched at the same time as the high-end one, the Think Pad 300 was not originally based on a common platform. It was designed and manufactured by Zenith under an alliance with IBM. Because of quality and production problems, the IBM 300 didn't work very well and was replaced in May 1993. Subsequent product offerings in the low-end family came from the same platform and were released in parallel with the high-end offerings in September 1993. The next addition to this product family wasn't made until May 1997, when the 380/380D was introduced. With a built-in CD-ROM, floppy disk drive, and hard disk, it was positioned for the general business user segment.

In March 1995, IBM introduced the "butterfly" expandable keyboard in the 701C, enabling a larger keyboard with the same form factor and thus creating a subnotebook computer. Initially, the keyboard was thought to be a great feature, destined to be part of the entire product platform. When the industry started moving to a larger screen size, however, the monitor dictated the size of the computer, and the "butterfly" was no longer useful.

IBM's product line strategy evolved as it gained experience in the market. The 700 series continued to focus on performance, and the 300 was focused on value, but there was no real need for pricing segmentation of anything in between. The 500 series, introduced in June 1993 as a subnotebook computer, focused on portability, with the 510Cs added in June 1994.

In September 1995, IBM introduced a number of product variations aimed at specialized market segments. The 755CD had a built-in CD-ROM. The 755CV had overhead projection capability. The 760CD had MPEG-2, and a traveling version offered fax modems and other features. The ThinkPad 760 series was extended to reach the broader midpriced market.

In May 1996 the ThinkPad 560 was introduced. The advantages of this smaller, lightweight product offering made it a more attractive product than those in the 700 series. The 560 weighed 4.1 pounds, while the 760 weighed 6.4 pounds. At this point, the 560 and 760 became the basis for a new product series. The 365X weighed about 5.9 pounds.

The ThinkPad 380 was launched in May 1997 and was aimed at the segment that wanted leading-edge technology at an affordable price. The ThinkPad 770 was launched in September 1997 with a 14.1-inch screen. In June 1998 IBM introduced the ThinkPad 600 upgrade to the 560 by incorporating a CD-ROM, and in April 1999 it introduced the 570 ultraportable. The 600 was one of the fastest-selling computers in IBM's history. The 240 ultralight was introduced in June 1999.

By the beginning of 2000, IBM's ThinkPad product line was structured as follows, with product families targeted at specific market segments, and specific products configured within each product family:

- *IBM Think Pad 240 Mini-Notebook Product Family.* The ThinkPad 240 mini-notebook was designed to be an easy-to-carry, easy-to-use, easy-to-connect superslim notebook targeted at the segment of professionals who value portability.

- *IBM ThinkPad 390X Notebooks.* The feature-packed IBM ThinkPad 390X was targeted at the market segment of businesses looking for an affordable, all-in-one business notebook.

- *IBM ThinkPad 600X Notebooks.* The ThinkPad 600X models incorporated Intel Mobile Pentium III processors up to 500 MHz, hard drives as large as 12 GB, and memory up to 576 MB. Its technical performance, optional upgrades, and IBM's service and support made the ThinkPad 600X appropriate for the market segment that balances performance and portability.

- *IBM ThinkPad I Series 1500 Small Business Notebooks.* The ThinkPad I Series notebooks were targeted at small businesses interested in productivity, reliability, impressive performance, and essential small business tools. Features such as the ThinkLight, Media Center with Instant Audio, and Easy Launch buttons were emphasized.

- *IBM ThinkPad I Series 1400 Notebooks.* The sleeker ThinkPad I Series 1400 notebooks were targeted at customers interested in productivity combined with style. Features include ThinkLight, Media Center, and Easy Launch buttons with emphasis on style; seven optional color covers enabled customers to personalize the outside.

- *IBM ThinkPad 390E Notebooks.* The IBM ThinkPad 390E was targeted at businesses looking for an easy-to-use notebook computer.

In addition, IBM continued to offer a few of its older ThinkPad products, including the 600E, 570l, and 770.

Intel's 486 Microprocessor Product Line Strategy

The Intel 486 microprocessor is an excellent example of product line strategy and a product line plan. Intel introduced the Intel 486 DX microprocessor in 1989 as the first in a new family of 486 products based on a new platform intended to replace the 386 product line. The 486 featured 1.2 million transistors on a computer chip and had twice the performance of the 386 product line. At the same time, the Intel 486 DX was 100 percent compatible with the previous generation of software developed for the 386.

Figure 4-1 illustrates the Intel 486 product line plan. It diagrams the introduction time frame and relative performance of each product. The table at the bottom of the figure shows how well the products cover various market segments. Fully shaded boxes indicate complete segment coverage, while partially shaded boxes indicate partial segment coverage.

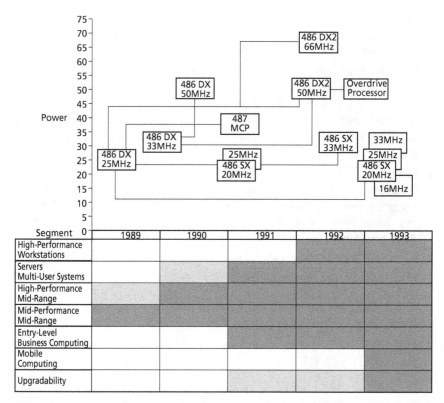

Figure 4-1 As Intel's 486 product line expanded, it progressively covered more market segments from 1989 to 1993.

The 486 was among the most powerful and complex microprocessors developed at that time. It integrated many system-level functions, including a 32-bit integer processor unit with an instruction set and a variety of addressing modes. The 486 DX was available in 25- and 33-MHz versions to serve the high-performance requirements of the midrange computing environment. The 50-MHz version of the 486 DX was introduced in June 1991 for the large server and high-end workstation segments.

Intel introduced the 486 SX product in April of 1991 for the entry-level business computing segment. The new microprocessor used the same architecture, but was less complex, less powerful, and less expensive than the DX products. Technically, the SX had a lower bus bandwidth (16 MB instead of 160 MB), had less memory addressability, and did not have an integrated math coprocessor. The 486 SX replaced the high-end processor in the 386 product line, the 386 DX. The 25-MHz 486 SX had twice the processing power of the 33-MHz 386 DX.

Intel's strategy was to overlap the two product lines (386 and 486) by providing more power at a higher price with the 486 DX versions. The overlap provided a continuing 386 market for almost two years. Then in 1991, Intel cannibalized the 386 market with the SX low-cost version of the 486 product line and ceded the 386 market to AMD and other competitors.

Intel also provided two 486 products that upgraded the performance of the SX processors, enabling customers to initially buy a lower-cost PC and then upgrade later on. The first was the 487 Math CoProcessor (MCP), which performed floating-point mathematics. The second was the OverDrive Processor, which doubled the 486 SX's internal speed using the DX2 speed-doubling technology.

The Intel 486 DX2 incorporated the speed-doubling feature, which let the microprocessor run at 50 MHz while interfacing with the system at 25 MHz. Computers using this processor could be designed for high performance without the complex issues of high-speed design.

The last set of products in the 486 product line was the Intel 486 SL, which specifically targeted the mobile computer segment. The features of this product were designed to reduce the power requirements and manage power at a system level.

The rollout of the 486 product line took four years. By the time the rollout was complete, it covered all major segments of the microprocessor market. Intel's sales of 486 microprocessors increased to 27 million units in 1993 and to an estimated 40 million units in 1994.

To accomplish this product line rollout, Intel developed a product line strategy detailing the products expected. Development of some of these products had to begin even before the initial 486 product was introduced. Fortunately for Intel, it understood the market from its 286 and 386 product line experience, and could base its 486 product line strategy on this experience.

The product line plan in Figure 4-1 is historical, but the same format could be used as a plan for a new product line. It combines three elements. First, it defines the anticipated time-phased plan for the introduction of products in the product line. Second, it matches this schedule to its coverage of the various market segments. Finally, it shows expected unit sales based on the time-phased plan. If additional products and coverage of market segments are important, then this plan becomes the best way to develop a sales forecast for a new product line.

Once a product line strategy is developed, the resulting product line plan links to the product development schedule. This schedule shows when development is anticipated to begin for each product in the product line plan. This is an iterative process. When the development plan for the product line is prepared, it may reveal that too many projects are scheduled at once, or that insufficient resources are available to complete the work required. The development schedule needs to be adjusted to meet these constraints, which may force a change to the product line plan. If this change is acceptable, it is made. If it is not acceptable, priorities need to be shifted in order to implement the strategy. Unfortunately, many companies do not link the product line plan to the development plan, and do not do the necessary reprioritization.

Figure 4-2 illustrates a hypothetical six-year product development schedule for the Intel 486 product line, starting in 1988.[6] It shows some interesting characteristics. The 486 DX was already under development at the beginning of 1988. Toward the end of its development, but before testing, two additional projects were scheduled. The first was the SX version of the 486. The second was the faster 33-MHz version of the DX.

The number of projects and resources increased during 1990–1991 as the first products began to generate revenue. In total, 14 product development projects were planned, with some taking much more time and resources than others. At the peak of the development effort, there were five projects in process at the same time. By the end of 1991, resource requirements began to decline, and 60 percent less were required by the end of 1993 than were necessary at the beginning of 1988. The freed-up resources were assigned to other product line developments, such as the Pentium.

Estimating the schedule of project start dates enables management to schedule the appropriate event for initiating a new project, such as a Phase 0 review in a phase review process. This review would typically trigger the formal decision to start, cancel, refocus, or delay the specific project.

> ### The time horizon of product line plans is typically two or three times the longest development cycle time.

When development capacity and load are balanced, this scheduling approach is similar to establishing a train schedule. A development project will start and end as scheduled. The estimated time between the start date and complete date is based on known development cycle times for new products of various levels of complexity. If a project is canceled at the Phase 0 review, another product opportunity can enter the process to take its slot in the product line plan.

The time horizon of product line plans is typically two to three times the longest development cycle time. This is long enough to provide visibility into the future and short enough to be realistic. Such a clearly articulated plan of future programs prevents one of the high-technology industry's cardinal sins: overcommitting scarce development resources.

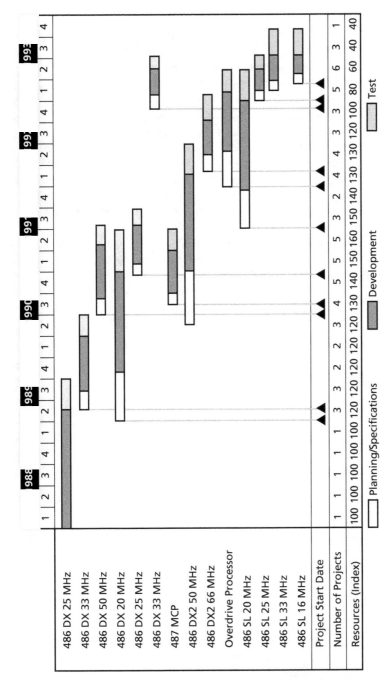

Figure 4-2 A hypothetical product development schedule for the Intel 486 product line shows how resources and timing can be synched for strategic balancing.

Notes

1. Scott McCartney, "Dell Programs New Products, Sales Strategy," *The Wall Street Journal,* August 2, 1993.

2. Pricing and other information provided by Dell in September 1993.

3. Phillip Robinson, "Centris, Performa, Quadra: All Apple Macs, Despite the Confusion," *The Boston Globe,* April 20, 1993.

4. For a discussion of product line mapping, see Steven C. Wheelwright and W. Earl Sasser, Jr., "The New Product Development Map," *Harvard Business Review,* May–June 1989. Also see an example of product line mapping in Figure 4-1 in this chapter.

5. Deborah A. Dell and J. Gerry Purdy, *ThinkPad: A Different Shade of Blue* (Sams., 1999). This is an excellent reference on the ThinkPad Story. Prior to developing the ThinkPad product platform, IBM had used the ThinkPad brand name on a series of tablet products that had little success.

6. The schedule and implied cycle times in this plan are illustrative only and are not based on actual Intel schedules. The estimates and the sequencing are considered realistic, based on experience.

5

Addressing Market Realities: The MPP Framework

Platform and product line strategies are powerful concepts
if applied effectively; a Market Platform Plan (MPP) framework
integrates knowledge about the market and knowledge about
the product and its defining technology.

Too often we've found that executives embrace management concepts such as those discussed in earlier chapters, but they are unable to put them into action. They understand the concept but need to get down to a more detailed level to understand what to do. To take these concepts down to the next level, we've developed several frameworks, which we describe and illustrate in this chapter. The first framework (Figure 5-1) simply summarizes the hierarchy of the primary levels of product strategy.

The second is the most critical; it's what we call the Market Platform Plan (MPP) framework (Figure 5-2). The plan itself can be prepared in a variety of formats, such as a presentation or a document. We represent the MPP framework as a cube to illustrate the relationship of its major components. One of the primary MPP components is the product platform, and we expand the detail of this using another framework, the Platform Technology Element Framework (Figure 5-3).

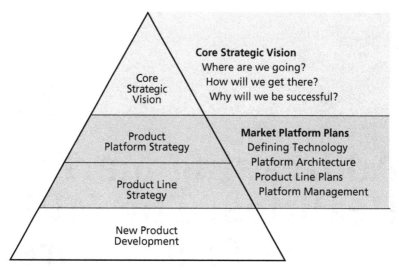

Figure within the pyramid:

Core Strategic Vision
Where are we going?
How will we get there?
Why will we be successful?

Core Strategic Vision

Product Platform Strategy

Market Platform Plans
Defining Technology
Platform Architecture
Product Line Plans
Platform Management

Product Line Strategy

New Product Development

Figure 5-1 Product strategy can be viewed as a structure consisting of six core elements.

Product Strategy Structure

The development of product strategy tends to flow from vision to platform strategy and then to product line strategy and finally to new product development. This might appear to be the opposite of what some entrepreneurs would envision as the way the process works, focused as many are on the individual product as "the big idea." History has shown repeatedly, however, that long-term success takes more than one good product idea. It requires a sustainable strategic vision successfully implemented with a product strategy.

> *Long-term success...requires a sustainable strategic vision successfully implemented with a product strategy.*

The *core strategic vision* (CSV) is at the top level of the pyramid shown in Figure 5-1. As we discussed earlier, this is where a company determines the answers to the critical strategic questions: Where are we going? How will we get there? Why will we be successful?

Product platform strategy, as we discuss in Chapter 3, is derived from the CSV. For example, a CSV focusing on success through price leadership would suggest a low-cost product platform. A CSV embracing

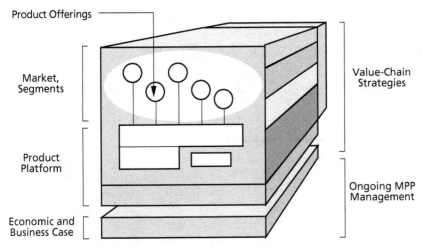

Figure 5-2   This MPP framework provides a structure for developing a market platform plan.

growth by expansion into new markets would suggest the development of new product platforms for new markets. *Product line strategy,* the third level and the subject of Chapter 4, defines the conditional time-phased product offerings from a particular product platform. Each product offering targets a specific market segment. The fourth and final level of the pyramid is *new product development.* Here, specific functionality for each new product offering, consistent with the overall product line plan, is defined.

The Market Platform Plan Framework, shown in Figure 5-2, focuses on the middle two levels of this pyramid.

The MPP Framework

A market platform plan enables companies to translate platform strategy into a practicable attack plan for a target market. It focuses their attention on the critical issues with the most leverage for understanding the interface between a market and the products developed to meet its needs and wants:

- Characterize and prioritize customer segments.
- Define the basis of customer value and differentiation that will be used to win high-priority customer segments.

- Define the offerings to the customers and outline the building blocks used to develop these offerings.

- Define a monitoring plan to sense external developments that could alter strategy.

- Establish economic metrics for measuring success in the market.

Markets and Market Segments

Before defining a market platform plan, let's revisit the basic notions of a market and a market segment. A *market* is a large group of potential customers, with common needs or problems, who purchase a common class of products and/or services for similar use or application. A *market segment* is a group of customers within a market with very similar concerns and requirements. They have behavior sets—patterns of why and how they use a product, how they purchase it, and how they perceive the risk of purchasing it—that are distinctly different from those of other segments. For example, the personal computer (PC) market has several different segments. In the corporate user segment, the issue is application integration using networked PCs. In the mobile segment, the focus is on portability, where weight, size, and battery life are important. The SOHO (small office/home office) segment wants price, ease of use, and sufficient capabilities. In the education segment, price becomes even more important, since the users are very price-sensitive. Customers within a market segment often act as buying references for each other.

Effective segmentation requires iterative analysis and validation. Frequently, segmentation can be done hierarchically, with the most easily perceived and easiest to implement characteristics considered first, followed by those that require increasingly more insight and creativity and greater skill to implement. Organizational demographics, such as industry, customer base size, and location are usually the easiest characteristics to identify. Others that are not so easily identified are likely applications of a product by a segment and the operating circumstances of its use. Some print and copy shops, for instance, specialize in printing product manuals, while others specialize in full color brochures. Some print and copy shops use stand-alone copiers, while others integrate all of their printing and copying equipment using local area networks.

The purchase decision-making process may be important in segmentation. For some computer products, for instance, the chief information officer may be the primary decision maker, while for others the role may fall to technically minded end users. Situational variables may come into play. For example, Federal Express initially targeted customers who required relatively small but urgent shipments. Other situational variables for something like customer orders could be large versus small, urgent versus planned, or routine versus customized. Finally, personal characteristics of customers could be the basis for segmentation. These include such factors as attitudes toward innovation and risk.

Developing a market platform plan involves selecting, deselecting, and prioritizing market segments—meeting the needs of a targeted market through a consistent winning vector of differentiation (see Chapter 7). A market platform plan may require more than one product platform to effectively address a given market space, but, as we discussed

Developing a market platform plan involves selecting, deselecting, and prioritizing market segments.

previously, this is to be avoided if at all possible. Having multiple platforms serving the same market is almost always too expensive and almost always confusing to the market. We've found, however, that organizational dynamics all too frequently encourage platform proliferation within a given market. Political fiefdoms often want to create platforms they can call their own. Frequently, such fiefdoms are created by those who prefer one technical approach to another. This is accentuated in cultures that value and reward clean-sheet engineering initiatives that spawn new product platforms instead of new products from a current platform.

The MPP helps companies avoid this problem by being focused as much on markets as on product platforms, effectively forcing reconciliation of multiple platforms for the same market. In reality, this reconciliation is far from easy and is often messy organizationally, but it forces the critical decision to choose among alternative platform strategies at the point where it should be made—when confronting market realities.

The exception, of course, is when a new product platform is introduced and gradually phases out an older one. The relative positioning of these two platforms is important, since companies usually need to continue selling products from an old platform as long as possible, while developing a more complete range of products from a new platform. Price differences are frequently used as a way of distinguishing the two platforms in the market.

Economic and Business Case

We refer to the thematic characteristic that consistently differentiates a market platform plan as the *vector of differentiation*. The vector of differentiation is consistent across all product offerings based on the product platform and therefore across all market segments. The vector of differentiation also provides the long-term competitive advantage not usually achieved by individual product features. It enables the MPP development team to focus its efforts on continuous improvement along a single high-priority vector so it can stay ahead of advancing competition and customers' increasing expectations.

A vector of differentiation can be derived from problems, purchasing behavior, economics, and requirements shared by customers across all targeted segments within a market. It determines the degree to which the product platform addresses or has the potential to address key customer requirements. The success of a vector of differentiation is usually relative to competitors' abilities to satisfy those requirements.

> *A vector of differentiation can be derived from problems, purchasing behavior, economics, and requirements shared by customers across all targeted segments within a market.*

If an MPP requires more than one product platform to effectively address its given market space, it is likely that each product platform may deliver a different vector of differentiation. In such cases, market communication and positioning must be carefully managed to minimize customer confusion.

Market and platform economics define the economic viability of an MPP based on the dynamics of the segment, revenue, and costs from the complete set of product offerings. A *value proposition* for a product offering is a brief statement of the customer benefits delivered by that product offering to its target market segment(s). A successful value proposition matches the customer's highest priority requirements in the target market segment(s).

Product Offerings and Product Lines

Whole product offerings are increasingly important. A specific *product offering* is more than the physical product. It includes the complete set of activities—support, professional services, and so on—that delivers value to the customer. Each product offering usually targets a market segment or a small subset of market segments within the total market. Typically, it makes sense to create a distinct product offering from a common platform for each distinct market segment, since the value profiles and customer needs vary by segment. The benefits of customizing product offerings to a segment, however, must be balanced against the associated design, manufacturing, delivery, and support costs.

As described in Chapter 4, the *product line* is the time-phased conditional plan for the sequence of developing products from the product platform. Each product in the product line targets a specific market segment. The product line plan in the MPP should cover the major segments of the market, but it doesn't require that all segments be covered. Some may be ignored, with the expectation that a portion of that segment will purchase one of the product offerings anyway, even if it is customized for another segment. In most cases, the vector of differentiation chosen for the product platform will effectively target certain market segments. For example, a vector of differentiation focused on high performance may effectively deselect those segments that prefer low cost to performance.

Market and technology readiness, resource availability, strategic objectives, and related factors determine the timing of the introduction of each product offering in the product line. This product line plan then influences the timing and initiation of development of platform technology elements.

Product Platforms

As described in Chapter 3, a *product platform* is primarily a planning construct. It is the set of architectural rules and technology elements that enable multiple product offerings and define the basic value proposition, competitive differentiation, capabilities, cost structure, and life cycle of these offerings. *Architectural rules* govern how the technology elements are integrated, along with other required technologies to form the specific product offerings in the market platform plan. These rules define the capabilities, partitioning, and interfaces of the technology elements. A product platform consists of a number of *platform technology elements,* such as components, subsystems, technologies, and processes. These characteristics vary by product platform. We focus here on the most critical elements, which are reused within the products that come from the platform. These are typically long lead-time items that require a high investment and significant management attention. The defining technology element is the most important. *Other technologies* are the remaining technologies required to develop the complete set of product offerings. These technologies are readily available and not critical to the platform.

Effective product platforms are not static, of course. They have the flexibility and speed to incorporate new technology and stay ahead of customer requirements. Instead of allowing the platform and product offerings to react to individual customer's needs, a well-developed product platform will show that customer needs from all relevant markets have been integrated and prioritized within the platform. Instead of bringing products to market with no consistent theme, a product platform continues to evolve along a desired vector of differentiation. This vector is based on the defining technology of that platform. Continuing improvement of the defining technology is emphasized in technology development.

While some companies may need to delay product development when key supporting platform elements are not available, those that manage their platforms effectively avoid this problem. They clearly define the underlying platform elements and construct a schedule for inserting new and improved elements from appropriate sources. They use product platform requirements to drive the development of technology platforms.

Effectively managing the product platform requires understanding the platform technology elements and their characteristics. We classify technology elements into three categories: defining, supporting, and segmenting. These are illustrated in Figure 5-3. The first two apply across all product offerings from the platform, while the third is the basis for the differentiation of product offerings.

Defining technology elements enable the vector of differentiation and establish the performance characteristics and limits of the product offerings from the platform. They also define the relative cost structure of the product platform. It's preferable that the defining technology reside within a company, if at all possible. It's also preferable that the company have some barriers to entry around the defining technology that will impede competitors from copying or possibly improving the defining technology. The active chemical ingredient acetaminophen is the defining technology

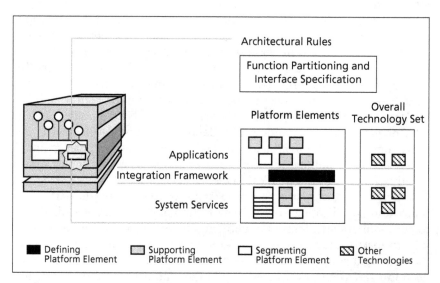

Figure 5-3 Effectively managing a product platform requires understanding the platform technology elements and their characteristics.

for the Tylenol platform, for example. All products from that platform share the performance characteristics of acetaminophen. Individual products vary the concentration of acetaminophen to alter the degree of expected performance.

Supporting technology elements support or enhance the defining technology element. While not critical to success, the selection of these supporting technology elements is still important, since they can affect overall performance or hinder the success of a product platform. These may be worth some increased attention if the technology is new to the company or it presents a time-to-market obstacle. The additional active ingredients in the Tylenol cold and flu products are supporting technology elements. They enhance the basic performance of Tylenol in alleviating cold symptoms.

Segmenting technology elements address the specific customer value propositions of high-priority segments of the market. They may add cost in order to address these specific segment needs. Usually, they require at least parity performance with competitors. Segmenting technology elements in the Tylenol example include the technologies for different forms, such as tablets, caplets, gelcaps, and geltabs. To some degree, they also include flavors for addressing the taste segments of the market.

Value-Chain Strategies and Ongoing MPP Management

The two remaining components of the MPP framework in Figure 5-2 address the value-chain strategies critical to support the market platform plan and the ongoing management of the MPP.

Today it takes more than just a good product to make that product successful. The product offering must be aligned with many other strategies. We refer to these collectively as value-chain strategies. *Supporting capabilities* include services, marketing, distribution and logistics, manufacturing, technology, and other resources.

> *The product offering must be aligned with many other strategies. We refer to these collectively as value-chain strategies.*

These must be coordinated with the platform and product line strategy to deliver and support the product offerings. *Standards* can also be a critical part of some MPPs, but their importance varies. In some MPPs they are critical, while in others they are not a consideration. Standards are the set of product requirements that all products must comply with to meet corporate business objectives and legal codes. Examples of standards are health and safety requirements, product appearance requirements, and enterprise coherence and interoperability requirements.

The final component of the MPP framework identifies the need for ongoing management of the market perspective. This includes the management processes already discussed in platform management and product line management, and platform technology management. Frequently, it also includes the monitoring of key assumptions, such as anticipated competitive products and technology evolution. Should any of these change in a way different from what was expected, it should trigger a redo of a market platform plan.

Managing the Technology Elements

The technology elements within a product platform also need individual management attention. They don't simply take care of themselves. Technology elements have unique characteristics, and, as such, they require some unique management practices.

1. *Technological change must be anticipated.* In many high-technology products, technology strategy serves as a long-range proxy for customer needs, as long as the evolution of technology is perceived in terms of customer needs. We refer to the measure of value of a technology as the *driving metric* when value is perceived by the customer. A driving metric chart can serve as a forecast of product requirements when technology development takes place in advance of a product line plan. While most product line plans cover two to three years, many technologies take longer to develop.

Driving metrics are defined by what is important to the market. For example, customers in the mobile disk drive market may value low power consumption, ruggedness, and the agility of a drive maker to fit given drive capacity into a compact space. Driving metrics change over the course of a platform's life cycle. They may change from performance and innovation-oriented metrics to cost metrics as a market matures.

A good technology strategy enables a company to properly model today's priorities as well as anticipate tomorrow's.

Some driving metrics are valued more than others. These need to be prioritized by market importance. While customers typically understand today's driving metric prioritization, they may not be able to anticipate tomorrow's. This is

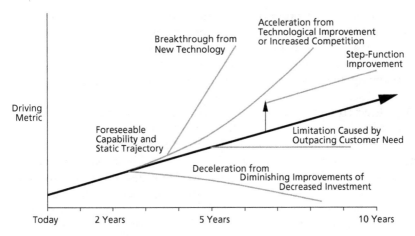

Figure 5-4 Technology trajectories can accelerate or decelerate and are dependent on many factors.

because they are typically influenced by their immediate problems and not in touch with long-range technology capabilities. A good technology strategy enables a company to properly model today's priorities as well as anticipate tomorrow's.

Figure 5-4 illustrates the range of trajectories for the evolution of technologies. Technologies can improve along a predictable curve. Sometimes these are referred to as sustaining technologies. Leaders in an industry can usually navigate the technological changes involved in a shift in sustaining technology, and continue to remain the leaders as the technology evolves.

In some cases, the trajectory will accelerate from technological improvements or possible increased competition, or it may decelerate from diminishing improvements or decreased investment. It's also possible to see a relatively quick step-function improvement. Another possibility is that improvement in the driving metric may be restricted, because it outpaces the customer's ability to absorb it.

Disruptive technologies or breakthrough technologies[1] redefine the driving metrics, causing a change in the basis of competition in an industry or market. Market leaders often falter when faced with a disruptive technology change. These disruptions may be due to architectural changes or changes in defining technology elements or supporting technologies, as when 5.25-inch disk drives replaced 8-inch drives.

2. *A technology platform is managed differently.* A technology platform is a set of initiatives organized around a macro-level functionality that

helps to manage and optimize technology investments across multiple product platforms—in fact, across the entire business, as well as across time. From a management perspective, a technology platform is best viewed as a collection of initiatives based on different groupings.

Supporting elements or technologies of current product platforms or current processes can be managed most easily, since it's only necessary to manage their cost and performance improvements. A traditional technology roadmap will usually be able to predict the improvements.

Sometimes, technology initiatives are not related to a particular element of a current platform, but come from a continuing commitment to a particular vector of differentiation, even if it leads to a new platform technology element. Vectors such as ease of use or highest performance may lead to technology development in totally new areas. Potential improvements can be so dramatic as to open entirely new markets or bases of competition. These are breakthrough technologies.

Technology platforms are managed differently from product platforms. Product platforms are a market-facing construct, and, although developed collaboratively with R&D, they are managed by a business unit. Technology platforms are, in a sense, a core competency for

> ***Technology platforms are in a sense a core competency for technology-based companies.***

technology-based companies. They don't lend themselves to the building block modules and interface structure of product platforms.

Whereas the key technical issues for a product platform revolve around the design of the element integration and the architecture, for technology platforms, they are more complex. They include roadmapping of relevant product platform elements and predictable, on-schedule technology delivery. But they also include identification of new areas for development that could lead to new product platforms.

The make/buy decisions are also different. For the product platform, these decisions are made at the element level. For the technology platform, make/buy and licensing decisions are made at the technology, patent, and portfolio levels.

3. *Technology roadmaps chart the planned application of technology.* Charting technology roadmaps is a useful technique to forecast how key technologies are expected to evolve or change over time. Of these, the roadmap for the defining technology is by far the most important. It indicates when the product platform may be made obsolete and need to be replaced.

Mapping key technologies against the product and platform elements that will incorporate these technologies enables a company to illustrate

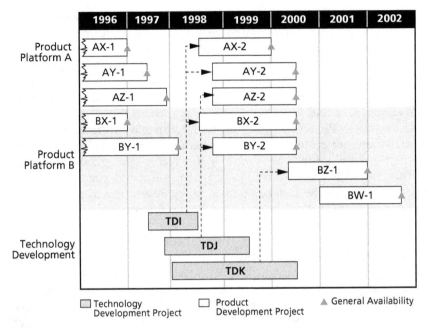

Figure 5-5   A common practice is to "insert" technologies into products as they evolve.

critical technical dependencies. Some companies view this as "inserting" technologies into products as they come along. Figure 5-5 illustrates the relationship. In this example, three technologies are being developed: TDI, TDJ, and TDK. Technology TDI will be applied to two products in product platform A (AX-2, AY-2) and one product in product platform B (BX-2). TDJ will be applied to two products, and TDK won't be applied until product BZ-1.

Market Platform Plan in Action

Let's look at a disguised case study to see how one company applied the MPP framework in a joint venture. An e-commerce software start-up had developed a unique service for creating and managing legally binding "electronic original" documents. The start-up approached one of the world's largest financial-services firms with a joint venture proposition that would allow the giant company to eliminate the paperwork—or at least the paper—from its lease transactions. It quickly became apparent that the two parties had very different agendas and very different levels of interest with regard to the proposed venture. The start-up was betting heavily that the joint venture's success would put it on the map, and it had a great deal at stake. The financial-services firm, on the other hand, merely saw the deal in terms of a productivity boost for its internal operations. The partnership would scarcely make a ripple in the giant company's annual revenues.

Using the MPP framework, the two companies were able to find enough common ground to make the joint venture work. It began with the parties coming up with a mutual and viable strategic vision of the partnership. This core strategic vision (CSV) provided a mechanism for representatives of the two companies to reconcile their disparate goals and perspectives and set the stage for the development of a market platform plan.

The CSV was developed by a cross-functional team of senior executives from both companies, known as the Decision Team, and then communicated to the Market Attack Team (MAT). The MAT, responsible for developing a market platform plan, helped ensure that the strategy would be consistent with this shared vision. The MPP provided the link between the core strategic vision and the joint venture's actual product and technology development. It also aligned the development of supporting value-chain capabilities, such as marketing, sales, and service, with the CSV. Instead of describing an individual product plan, along with its development and commercialization plans, the market platform plan described the market opportunity and corresponding development plans for a family of products, including the value-chain requirements for attacking a selected market.

The market attack team identified approximately 20 possible market segmentation criteria. The criteria that best segmented the industry into clusters of customers with unique requirements were selected from this set. The chosen segmentation axes were "annual number of transactions" and "average transaction size." The "annual number of transactions" axis was selected as a proxy for business process complexity. The greater the volume, the more likely that it would find decentralized business operations, functional specialization, and processes that required greater coordination. The "average transaction size" axis reflected the complexity of the transactions themselves. Larger transactions (e.g., commercial aircraft leases) are often individually unique, with a greater degree of negotiability and a larger number of documents per transaction. Smaller transactions (e.g., photocopier leases) typically use a handful of highly standard documents, with little scope for modification.

These two criteria were applied to an industry database of leasing companies in order to size the market opportunity for each of the market segments. Based on the relative size of the opportunity and the product fit for each segment, the MPP included a strategy for attacking the overall market. This attack plan was then applied to the joint venture's R&D efforts in order to link and align technology and product development initiatives with the intended strategy.

Considerable attention was also given in the MPP to a pricing model that incorporated the many possible points of value extraction (such as postsale service), yet had the flexibility to exploit the "willingness to pay" of customers in different segments. The result was a profit model that identified annuity, growth, and risk components of the revenue stream.

Alternatives and recommendations for market segmentation, pricing, and other key elements of the strategy were prepared by the MAT and reviewed with the Decision Team. Fundamental trade-offs in the strategy were decisively addressed at Decision Team meetings. The company, a financial-services firm, preferred a conservative market entry. It wanted the venture to go after a small number of customers and generate market pull through testimonials, initially. It wanted to manage the start-up investment more as a variable cost, with the lead customers sharing the investment in further development. From a service development perspective, the larger company's main focus was on optimizing the productivity enhancements that the service could provide for its own leasing operations.

The software start-up wanted a more aggressive approach, in terms of both customer engagement and service development. It envisioned the service evolving into a more sophisticated electronic marketplace for trading financial instruments. This strategy would require accelerated investments.

A decision team reviewed these alternatives and identified a strategy to which both partners could commit. At the final Market Platform Plan approval session, it reached agreement on the key elements of the strategy:

- Detailed lead product definition
- Long-term product roadmap and supporting value-chain plans
- Incremental funding requirements and contingencies for each partner
- Business case demonstrating positive earnings during the second year of sales

Notes

1. These definitions are a modified version of those presented by Bower and Christensen, "Disruptive Technologies: Catching the Wave," *Harvard Business Review* (January–February 1995), but the notion of continuous and discontinuous innovation has been discussed previously by others.

6

Successful Expansion Paths: The Leveraged Expansion Framework

Why does expansion into new markets sometimes succeed and sometimes fail? The answer is leverage. Companies that leverage their market knowledge and technology are most successful.

Create and launch a continuing series of products that open new markets and fuel rapid growth: This is the dream of most high-technology companies. Expansion into new markets was behind the growth of success stories such as Motorola, 3M, IBM, Hewlett-Packard, and Microsoft. While some other companies were more like one-shot wonders relying on a single, successful product line, these companies were able to continually expand in multiple directions.

For example, Motorola expanded its original AM (amplitude modulation) car radio business into FM (frequency modulation) radios in 1940. FM technology led Motorola from car radios into two-way radio businesses, such as Handie-Talky radios for the Army during World War II and police radios. The skills and experience developed with these products eventually led to cellular phones and pagers.

3M became a very large and diversified company by consistently building on its core competencies over several decades, with more than 50,000 products and $13 billion in revenue by 1992. It expanded from adhesive products into products as diverse as magnetic tape, medical supplies, medical devices, and medical instruments. Its skills with adhesives also led to the famous Post-it® Note business, as well as materials for safety products, such as traffic signs and license plates.

Lotus Development Corporation and Microsoft followed very different growth strategies in the late 1980s. A comparison of the two illustrates the difference between a strategy for expanding into related markets and one that primarily focuses on a single product platform.

Lotus rode the success of its 1-2-3 spreadsheet application software product to significant growth. From a $157 million company in 1984, it grew at a 25 percent annually compounded rate to $900 million by 1992. Most of this growth came from variations of its one successful product. Expansion into new markets was limited, and where Lotus tried to expand into unrelated fields, such as stock market data transmitted over radio waves, it was unsuccessful. Even though it was very successful with its primary product, Lotus did not follow a product strategy of growth through expansion.

With $125 million in revenue, Microsoft was a little smaller than Lotus. Yet it pursued a strategy of growth by expansion into related markets. The result was a compound annual growth rate of 45 percent and revenue of $3.7 billion for the year ended June 30, 1993. Microsoft grew to become more than three times as big as Lotus. This difference is illustrated in Figure 6-1.

In addition to being much larger than Lotus, Microsoft had pretax income of $1.4 billion, compared with $120 million at Lotus. Its market value was $23 billion, compared with Lotus's approximately $2 billion. Microsoft diversified more, developed more core competencies, and created more potential expansion paths that it could follow in the future.

This is not to take anything away from Lotus. It was a successful company. The comparison simply illustrates the benefit of a growth strategy by expansion into new markets. This difference was not lost on Lotus. It began to follow an expansion strategy of its own in the early 1990s with Lotus Notes. This very exciting expansion path fueled most of its growth in 1993 and accounted for an estimated 15 to 20 percent of its revenue.

Why is an expansion strategy so attractive? Some companies have been successful with a single product platform, but want to continue growing and need to expand into new markets to fuel this growth. Polaroid faced this challenge when the instant photography market

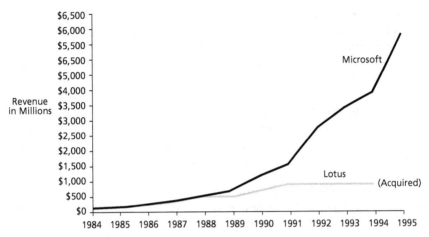

Figure 6-1 Microsoft became much bigger than Lotus by following a growth strategy of expansion into new markets.

began to turn sour. In 1982, Polaroid tried to expand by acquisition and development into unrelated areas, such as fiber optics, ink-jet printers, and medical diagnostics. All these expansion efforts failed—some, after significant investment.

In 1993, Polaroid continued its expansion into new markets, trying to build a $2 billion electronics business by the year 2000. Its CEO, I. MacAllister Booth, thought, "There are many more opportunities in the business world than just selling cameras and films."[1] However, the initial results of its lead product for this expansion, the Helios Laser Imaging System, were disappointing. Introduced in 1990, it was not readily accepted by hospitals or medical equipment manufacturers. The primary problem was that it made an 8" × 10" print instead of the 14" × 17" print preferred by doctors who read X rays and CAT scans.[2]

In spite of the risk of failure, expansion into new markets is sometimes necessary for survival. High-technology markets have a unique characteristic: They appear and disappear relatively quickly. When a market begins to disappear, companies relying on it need to expand into a new one, or face extinction themselves. Without expansion, a company could end up following the hundreds of other high-technology compa-

High-technology markets have a unique characteristic: They appear and disappear relatively quickly.

nies that went out of business when their primary market disappeared. For example, Wang replaced its calculators with word processing systems and then expanded successfully into minicomputers, but its next move was not as successful. Wang was not able to expand into another market in time to replace its disappearing word processing and minicomputer businesses.

Sometimes, companies fueled by their success in one market confidently expand into new ones, only to fail; all too frequently, this failure also drags down their existing products by diverting limited resources. Take WordStar, for example. Its pioneering word processing program made it one of the early software success stories, with revenue of $67 million in 1984, which was significant for a software company at that time. Then it tried to expand into new markets, such as database and spreadsheet products. While diverting resources to its expansion efforts, WordStar let its word processing products become less competitive. By 1993, it was roughly half the size it had been 10 years earlier, losing nearly $20 million in nine months.[3]

Why do some expansions into new markets succeed, while others fail? Experience, cases, and research studies show that the answer is *leverage*.

> ### *Leveraging a company's technical and marketing experience is one of the key determinants of new product success.*

Companies following expansion strategies that leverage their market knowledge and technology are much more successful than those following strategies with little leverage. In what was perhaps the best study on the success and failure of new, high-technology products, M. A. Maidique and B. J. Zirga determined that leveraging a company's technical and marketing experience was one of the key determinants of new product success.

This study, which was part of an innovation project at Stanford University, looked at 158 products, half successes and half failures.[4] To successfully expand into new markets, a company needs to leverage its strengths, particularly its core competencies. Leverage provides the basis for a framework to plan and evaluate expansion strategies.

Leveraged expansion builds upon what a company already does well. For example, a company may have underlying core technology or unique expertise in selling products in a particular distribution channel. By leveraging these capabilities—generally referred to as core competencies—a company has some advantages to build on in its expansion. When a company expands without any leverage at all, on the other hand, it is merely providing capital and has no more of an advantage than any other investor. In most cases, it may not be as good at being an investor as oth-

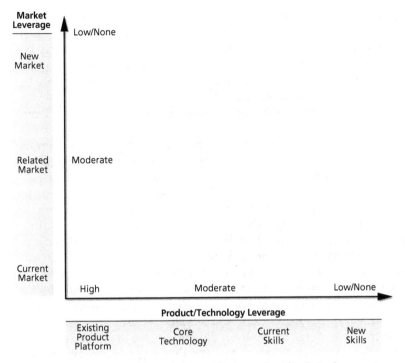

Figure 6-2   Companies can leverage their product/technical competencies or their market competencies.

ers, such as venture capitalists. What makes expansion into an unknown market so deceptively alluring is that a company really does not know what it is getting itself into.

Leverage follows two basic directions: a product/technology direction and a market direction.[5] Figure 6-2 illustrates these two directions, expanding from the starting point of existing products.

Leveraging Product or Technical Competencies

The horizontal lines in Figure 6-2 illustrate leveraging product and technical competencies. As one moves to the right, leverage is reduced.

The strongest, easiest, and fastest form of leverage is using an existing product platform to enter new markets. There are several ways of doing this. It can be done by creating a derivative platform, such as a portable computer platform from a desktop computer platform. The product platform can be modified for the unique requirements of a related market. Using an existing product platform as the starting point, a company can usually create a new product quickly, enabling faster expansion into the new market. Existing product platforms have other advantages. They are proven in both manufacturing and customer use, reducing many new product risks.

Unfortunately, opportunities for this type of leverage tend to be minimal, since most new markets—as opposed to new segments of the current market—require changes to the product platform.

When a product platform cannot be applied to a new market, the underlying technology can sometimes create a new product platform. In this second type of leverage, the source is core technology. The form of core technology varies by product. It could be critical subassemblies in an electronic systems product, or software modules in an application software product. It could be the type of composite material in a materials-based product, which in some cases can be used for additional applications. For example, fiber-based core technology used to reinforce aircraft bodies could also create golf clubs and bicycle wheels.

The *degree* of leverage depends on the importance of the existing technology to the new product platform. The defining technology provides the most leverage. Leveraging only ancillary or supporting technology provides little advantage.

Unique technical skills form the third type of technical leverage. Generally, these are the same skills used to create the core technology in product platforms, such as Microsoft's skills in writing software, and cable TV equipment company General Instrument's skill in analog design.

To be of significant value, the skills need to be reasonably distinctive. Existing or potential competitors should not have the same or better skills. Here again, skills related to the defining technology are most successful. The skills should already exist, as opposed to being a latent capability that can be acquired through new experience.

> **The degree of leverage depends on the ratio of existing skills to new skills.**

Leveraging unique skills differs from leveraging core technology. When leveraging skills, it's the skills that created the previous technology that are important to have. When entirely new skills are required, on the other hand, a company has little or no leverage. The degree of leverage depends on the ratio of existing skills to new skills.

Leveraging Market Competencies

Leverage can also be gained from market knowledge and distribution experience. A company uses its understanding of customers and markets to design a new product that leverages this understanding. It uses its presence in the channel of distribution to bring a product to the customer the same way it has other products.

Selling a new product to the existing customer base provides an opportunity to leverage both the market knowledge and the channel of distribution. The combined experience of knowing what these customers want and knowing how to sell to them can provide powerful leverage in expansion. The same customers may purchase other products through the same channel. For example, customers who purchase personal computers also purchase the application software for those computers. The degree of customer-base leverage depends on the breadth of the products purchased by that customer base. Some customers purchase a range of products, while others make more limited purchases.

There are some subtle, but critical, differences in access to customers that affect the strength of the customer base as an asset. For example, companies that manufacture and sell to resellers are not close enough to the final customer to have significant leverage. Some companies are in the envious position of having strong relationships with a large, fertile customer base. IBM, for example, has long-established relationships with corporate information technology (IT) departments.

Expansion into a related market is easier than expansion into an unrelated market, because a company has some understanding of the related market; it has some experience with related customer needs and desires through the products it already sells. It may be able to leverage its reputation. It may also be able to use its same distribution channel. Related markets are those adjacent to the current market. Notebook computers and laser printers, for example, are markets related to the desktop computer market.

The significance of leverage to related markets varies. A market could be related because the same customers purchase a different product. The directly related market offers significant leverage in either the direct knowledge of the market or the distribution channel—sometimes both. The market for

> *Leverage comes from understanding how to meet the needs of a different customer with a similar application.*

desktop computers is different from the market for mainframe computers and servers, yet for a company like IBM, the corporate market for desktop computers is a related market.

A market could also be related because the products in it are reasonably similar applications. Leverage comes from understanding how to meet the needs of a different customer with a similar application. For example, electronic scanners developed for package tracing are similar to retail scanners originally developed for supermarkets.

In a new market, there is little if any leverage. A company expanding into an entirely new market needs to realize that it may not know much about the customers and what they want in that market.

Leveraged Expansion Framework

The concept of leverage provides the basis for constructing a framework to analyze and, more importantly, develop strategies for expansion into new markets. Figure 6-3 illustrates this expansion framework. An existing product platform is positioned in the lower left-hand corner of the framework, at the intersection of the current market and the current product

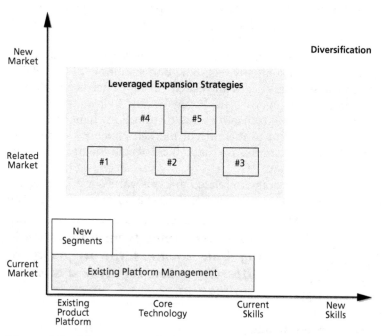

Figure 6-3   The expansion framework helps companies map the risks and opportunities of expansion.

platform. This expansion framework defines expansion strategies by their emphasis in each of the two directions.

Strategies along the horizontal axis emphasize changes from current platforms. The greater the distance to the right along that axis, the greater the change from the current platform and technology. Eventually, there is no leverage at all from existing product platforms, core technology, or unique skills. *Product diversification* occurs at this point.

Strategies along the vertical axis represent changes from the current market. Eventually, there is little or no leverage from experience and reputation in either the market or channel of distribution. *Market diversification* occurs at this point.

Diagonal strategy paths represent simultaneous changes in both dimensions. Expansion a short distance in this direction enables a company to leverage both technology and marketing. Eventually, expansion along this path loses all leverage, becoming what is essentially a completely new business venture.

While leverage diminishes along a path, opportunity generally increases. Going further along an expansion path provides more opportunities, since the scope of opportunities becomes broader. This implies that intermediate paths—those just far enough away to be interesting, but not so far as to be dangerous—are frequently the best opportunities.

Under this framework, expansion can be viewed as a series of alternative paths, each offering a different type of opportunity. By defin-

> *Along each strategic path, a company knows what it can leverage and what it needs to learn.*

ing these alternative strategic paths, a company can evaluate the opportunities and challenges associated with each. Along each strategic path, a company knows what it can leverage and what it needs to learn.

Expansion by introducing new products into the present customer base has a low risk. A company leverages its understanding both of the market and of how to sell the product, since it is already selling to the same customer base. When combined with leverage derived from using proven core technology, the result is likely to be a successful product—if the opportunity is large enough. The problem with this path is not the risk involved in expansion, but the lack of opportunities at the end of it.

Expansion like this into new market segments is addressed in Chapter 4, on product line strategy. By creating new product offerings, a company can generate more revenue by addressing new segments not sufficiently covered by current products. Tylenol, for example, created new product offerings from its acetaminophen platform to address new market segments.

Expansion by creating a new platform for the same market is addressed in Chapter 3 on product platform strategy. Since the new platform generally cannibalizes the existing one, incremental revenue comes only when the new platform achieves better market penetration.

Diversification brings a company into completely uncharted territory, where it knows little or nothing about the market. Unfortunately, just like explorers who don't know where they are going or what terrain lies ahead, a company may underestimate what it needs to be successful in this new market. For example, Texas Instruments tried to expand into an unfamiliar market in the 1970s to leverage its calculator technology and get away from the increasing price competition for basic calculators. Leveraging its calculator platform, TI sold a math instructional package with calculators to school systems. This was a terrible failure; TI found out that it did not know how to sell to school systems.

Following this experience, Texas Instruments decided to follow a more leveraged expansion strategy and developed the Little Professor. The Little Professor was a "calculator in reverse" sold to a related market—retail stores that also sold TI calculators. The Little Professor presented the math problem, and the child entered the answer. TI introduced the Little Professor in 1976, and it could not make enough of them for the Christmas season. It then leveraged this success into new expansion, with additional products like the Speak and Spell that helped children learn how to spell.

Diversifying in both directions is risky because a company has nothing unique to bring along on the journey. In this case, being more successful than others might require more luck than skill. One unlucky automotive electronics company decided that it would expand by diversifying into marine electronics. This was an entirely different market, with no commonality in customers or channels of distribution. The company had experience in designing consumer electronics, but little of its technology or unique skills applied to marine electronics. It lacked any experience in other required technologies, such as designing waterproof systems. The expansion effort was a failure that cost the company millions. Later, the company attributed its failure to the lack of leverage in its expansion efforts.

Leveraged Expansion Paths

The next set of expansion paths is the most exciting. The number of opportunities opens up significantly, since the combinations of related markets and alternative uses for the technologies are numerous. These also provide the advantages of leverage, to varying degrees. This is the area where most successful expansion occurs. We'll classify these into five different expansion paths, although in practice there may be degrees and variations of each.

1. *Build on the existing product platform to expand into a related market.* Directly related markets can sometimes offer opportunities for expansion by simply varying an existing product platform for unique needs. The defining technology of the platform generally remains unchanged, with changes or additions to the supporting platform elements creating a derivative platform.

Such was the case when Apple introduced its PowerBook notebook computer. The PowerBook used the operating system and microprocessor that were the defining technology of the Macintosh to develop a derivative platform. A different design, as well as the introduction of battery technology, made this derivative.

The market was related because the customer base was similar. Some of the customers were the same (those who wanted a PowerBook as an additional computer), but some were different (those whose priority was a notebook computer, not the Macintosh platform). With the PowerBook, Apple was able to expand along two paths: into a *derivative* platform for the same market and into a *related* market. This expansion path was very successful, providing Apple with $1 billion in additional sales in the first year.

In another example of this expansion strategy, AutoDesk scaled down its very successful AutoCAD computer-aided design software to run on personal computers at a lower price. AutoCAD LT targeted the related market: architects, designers, and engineers who needed a design tool that did not require the most advanced features or development tools. The goal of AutoCAD LT was to increase revenue by expansion into a related market.

America Online's expansion into AOL Anywhere is another interesting case. AOL Anywhere provides a gateway to the AOL platform from portable equipment, such as Palm devices and Motorola's smart wireless devices. For AOL, this is a market different from, but related to, its dial-up Internet access services. AOL has the potential of creating a new user base as well as reinforcing its value to customers who use both forms of access.

Unfortunately, opportunities along this path can be limited, since most product platforms are not versatile enough to provide new products in related markets. Component and material suppliers tend to have more opportunities in this category than companies building final products. For example, flat-panel displays were originally developed for portable computers. The flat-panel product platform has been successfully expanded into other markets that are related because of similar applications, such as video cameras and automobile navigation systems.

Advanced composite materials created new product platforms that found initial product applications in the space program (for the Space Shuttle and satellites). These materials offered greater stiffness at a lower weight than aluminum or steel. Later, these advanced composite materials platforms were applied to the related aircraft market. But, increasingly, they are also being applied in similar applications in unrelated markets, such as automobiles. The opportunity for growth by expanding the application of advanced composite materials into new markets is limited only by creativity.

In this expansion strategy the risks are low. The company will have some understanding of related markets, so it should be able to understand those customers' unique requirements. Development investments are also curbed, since a derivative platform generally requires only a small investment.

Companies should not pass up these expansion opportunities. Yet many do, simply because they never get around to looking for them. With a more disciplined expansion strategy, they would find them.

2. *Leverage core technology into a related market.* With this expansion path, core technology—not the existing platform—leverages expansion into a related market. Historically, this has been a prolific expansion path. Motorola, IBM, Hewlett-Packard, and 3M consistently used this strategy in their expansion. Adobe followed this strategy when it leveraged its core technology in printing to expand into a related market with its Acrobat software. Acrobat enables information prepared by almost any application to be displayed on a computer without the original application software. For example, using Acrobat, a newsletter can be produced by page-layout software, distributed throughout a network, and viewed just as it would have been printed.

Adobe built Acrobat on its Postscript core technology by creating data files in a portable document format (PDF). In doing this, Adobe essentially used its technology to do "pseudo printing." It sold Acrobat to a directly related, but different, market. Although the customers of Acrobat ran it on their PCs, just as other Adobe products, it had an entirely different use. Adobe's previous channel of distribution was OEMs (which built Postscript into their products) and resellers such as dealers. Acrobat was sold to dealers and system integrators who incorporated it in integrated systems.

AT&T, on the other hand, aggressively acquired cable networks, not in order to get into the cable TV market, but to get access to the core technology to build a new broadband platform and a new local phone service platform. The new broadband platform offers Internet access using the cable TV technology and infrastructure. This is a market related to, but different from, cable TV. Likewise, using this technology and infrastructure to provide local phone service is different from, but related to, AT&T's long-distance services.

Related markets enable leveraging of market experience, but not without risk. IBM found this out when it expanded into the home personal computer market with its PCjr. The PCjr's awkward keyboard, lack of appropriate software, slow processing speed, and high price caused one of the highest-profile failures in IBM's history.

The distinction between a derivative platform and a new platform based on the same defining core technology is actually a matter of degree, as is the distinction between a related and a new market. Microsoft's Windows CE operating system could be classified as a platform derivative of Windows, but we believe that it is different enough to be better classified as a new platform using the same defining technology. Similarly, the market for device operating systems could be classified as related to PC operating systems, or it could be called a new market.

Most of the risk in this expansion strategy is in creating a new platform. It also requires a larger investment and longer development cycle. When Boeing began developing the 717 short-haul plane, it found that the development costs were substantial, compared with the opportunity in this related market.

3. *Use unique skills to expand into a related market.* Expansion opportunities in directly related markets are sometimes found by combining existing skills with some new ones. This expansion path builds more on knowledge of related markets than on technology, although skills for developing the key technology are necessary.

Similar to the previous strategy, this path leverages presence in a market to define new products for existing customers or customers with similar applications. These new products use some of the same unique skill competencies, but they do not rely on an existing core technology.

Banyan Systems used a component of its networking software to create a new Internet product for a related market in 1996. Switchboard provides online white pages that contain addresses and phone numbers for millions of individuals. Compaq Computer's 1992 expansion into laser printers provides an interesting example of this strategy. By using its unique skills in designing and manufacturing high-quality, low-cost electronic systems, Compaq developed a line of printers that appealed to its customer base. It leveraged sales by selling these printers to its own customers, with whom it had already built a reputation. "We wanted to have a Compaq printer for anybody who wanted to have a Compaq PC," said David Black, general manager of Compaq's peripheral division. Even leveraging an existing customer base does not ensure success, however. After a fast start, capturing 10 to 15 percent of this market segment, Compaq's sales stalled.[6]

Here we see one of the less obvious risks of this expansion strategy. In the printer market, Compaq was a distant second to Hewlett-Packard, which already had an established reputation. Compaq realized that it needed to continue to make substantial investments to keep its printer platform competitive as technologies continued to advance. To justify this investment, it needed to increase its market share to have sufficient economies of scale, but it couldn't expand market share without expanding its market outside its customer base. That moved it from a related market (current customers) to a new market (noncustomers and different channels of distribution). Compaq realized that this wasn't feasible. David Black was replaced, and a number of new printer projects were canceled in order to reduce losses. By December 1993, Compaq abandoned the laser printer business, even though it sold $120 million in 1993 and had a 15 percent market share.

Eastman Kodak used its skills in digital graphics to create a market related to its strong customer base: 35-mm photography. In 1992, it introduced the photo CD player, which stored 100 photos on a CD, prepared by local photo finishers. In addition to the consumer market, the photo CD could be a tool for businesses such as real estate firms and retailers, thus creating the opportunity for Kodak to expand into a directly related market at the same time.

Similarly, IBM, Digital Equipment, and Hewlett-Packard expanded into the market for RAID (redundant arrays of independent disks) drives. These drives use multiple lower-capacity disks that perform the data storage function of a high-capacity drive. These companies sold these products primarily to their own customer bases, optimizing the drives to work with their own computer systems.

Sometimes expansion along these lines can completely regenerate a business. EMC Corporation was moderately successful building add-on memory boards for large computers. In 1988, it used its unique skills to expand into data storage systems. This was a directly related market that required a totally new platform. EMC's storage system platform was designed using many small disk drives strung together to create a large, efficient data storage capacity. This new platform was tremendously successful, and EMC expanded to become one of the fastest-growing companies in the United States, achieving $780 million in revenue in 1993 and $6.7 billion in 1999. Net income for the 1999 fiscal year was $1.2 billion. Not a bad expansion strategy.

4. *Leverage core technology into a new market.* The path of leveraging core technology into a new market provides many opportunities for expansion, since there are obviously more new opportunities than related ones, though it can also be much riskier. It can be particularly successful for companies that have a robust core technology with many potential applications.

For Dow Chemical Co., Methocel (sometimes referred to as "slime") provided a core technology with numerous potential new markets. When Methocel is heated, its molecules bond together to form a gel. When it cools, they thin out again into an oozing slime. Dow aggressively sought new market applications for this core technology. Now it's used in food products such as Twinkies, Burger King onion rings, salad dressings, and soups. It can make cheese cheesier, gravy creamier, and fillings richer. Pharmaceutical companies use it for time-release medicines and coated capsules. Museums use it as a mud mask to clean paintings. By 1999 it was used in more than 200 different products in a variety of markets.[7]

In the late 1990s, some companies found a variation of this expansion path to be very lucrative: selling technology or incorporating technology developed for a company's own products to competitors or potential competitors. IBM, for example, formed the IBM Technology Group to license and sell core technology to other OEMs. In 1999, this group signed deals for more than $30 billion:

- $16 billion with Dell computer to supply storage, microelectronics, networking, and display components

- $3 billion with EMC to provide disk drives to be incorporated into EMC's Symmetrix Enterprise Storage system

- $1 billion with Nintendo to design and manufacture a 400-MHz processor

- $8 billion with Acer to provide hard disks, microelectronics, and networking

- $2 billion with Cisco for microelectronics and IBM for switching and routing intellectual property

To some extent, this expansion strategy may be changing the paradigm for technology-based companies. The ability to leverage R&D beyond incorporation into the company's own products provides a much higher return on its R&D investment. This is also the primary expansion path followed by defense contractors looking for ways to expand into commercial markets. Take microwave technology as an example. The U.S. Department of Defense funded the development of gallium-arsenide–based core technology for monolithic microwave integrated circuits through development funding and purchases of devices for communications and smart bombs. With the market for these devices greatly curtailed, manufacturers expanded into new markets for products that could use this core technology for wireless communications.[8]

Raytheon used its microwave-circuit core technology to develop devices for satellite television broadcast receivers and microwave systems for satellite-based communication networks. M/A-COM expanded into components for wireless phones and collision-avoidance systems. Alpha Industries expanded into components for wireless phones and automotive systems.

Following this path for expansion into new markets with similar applications presents the risk of misunderstanding what those markets want, and particularly trying to force core technology on new markets. Most companies are biased toward their own core technology. For example, Polaroid assumed that its wet-chemistry core technology was just what the market for instant movies wanted and invested a lot in the development of Polavision, only to discover that the market preferred videotape technology.

5. *Use unique skills to expand into a new market.*   This expansion path combines a little leverage in each direction. It is clearly the weakest of the leveraged expansion paths, since it does not leverage very much. However, it can be successful in certain cases and is still less risky than diversification.

Cirrus Logic, Inc. provides an excellent example of how this type of expansion strategy works. The company's CEO, Mike Hackworth, positioned the company to grow by developing a wide range of semiconductors for controlling peripheral functions. The expansion strategy was based on leveraging unique skills: the company's storage/logic array (S/LA) VLSI design software.

Cirrus Logic's initial products were disk-drive controller chips for disk-drive manufacturers, such as Seagate and Conner. Next, it expanded into video graphics array (VGA) controllers for PC manufacturers. Continued expansion followed, with controllers for flat-panel, liquid-crystal displays (LCDs), data-fax modems, and graphical user interface (GUI) accelerators.[9]

The RAID drive example shows another application of this strategy. Data General used a different expansion strategy from that used by IBM, Digital Equipment, and Hewlett-Packard. Its CLARiiON product line targeted not only its own customer base, but other UNIX systems as well. This gave Data General a much broader market opportunity, although it had less leverage. It took advantage of the opportunity and achieved considerable success with this strategy.

Similarly, Texas Instruments (TI) used its component technology skills to expand into radio-wave-based antitheft devices for automobiles. These devices are built into the car key and send a radio signal to a receiver in the steering column. The car's ignition system will work only if the correct signal is sent. Ford Europe was TI's first customer for this product.[10]

This expansion path also incurs the risk of misunderstanding the preferences of a new market with a similar application. DuPont discovered this with Corfam, a synthetic leather it hoped would be as successful for shoes as nylon was for stockings. The lesson DuPont learned—at a cost of more than $80 million—was that it was not. Similarly, RCA's Videodisc failed because it could not record television programs, which customers wanted to do.[11]

One version of this strategy is to use technical skills to provide services for other companies. This expansion strategy is popular among companies that find they have excess technical staff when their major market deteriorates. Banyan Systems did this when it formed an alliance with its former rival, Microsoft, to support Microsoft products. Digital Equipment followed by redeploying its technical staff to support Microsoft products also.

Microsoft's Growth Strategy in Action

Microsoft Corporation is an exciting example of applying expansion strategy for growth into new markets. Expansion strategy has been the driving force behind Microsoft's rapid growth. Starting from its early skills, Microsoft expanded from $2.5 million in 1979 to $2.7 billion in 1992.[12] Its expansion paths went in four directions: languages, applications software, operating systems, and consumer products. Each expansion path established a new position for future expansion.

In 1979, Microsoft began its growth from a small ($2.5 million) base by building on its core technologies in microcomputer languages and knowledge of microprocessors. This included the early experience of founders Bill Gates and Paul Allen in trying to build a traffic-counting computer in their Traf-O-Data venture. Microsoft developed a Convergent Technologies version of its existing BASIC compiler platform and a new assembler language using its skills in developing language software. Both of these expansion paths were closely related to its existing business.

> *Microsoft's new core competency in operating systems led to the most significant expansion path in its history—perhaps one of the most significant expansion moves in business history.*

In 1980, Microsoft expanded into a similar, but not directly related, market with Softcard, a hardware emulation board enabling an Apple II to run the CP/M operating system. It sold more than 100,000 Softcards. More important, while this expansion strategy used some of its unique skills, it also required Microsoft's programmers to learn more about operating systems. With these new skills, it launched development of XENIX, a version of UNIX for microcomputers.

This new core competency in operating systems led to the most significant expansion path in Microsoft's history—perhaps one of the most significant expansion moves in business history. In 1981, Microsoft developed its first major operating system, PC-DOS for IBM (MS-DOS for the Microsoft version). Microsoft actually did not have sufficient experience or time to develop this product on its own. So it licensed 86-DOS from Seattle Computer to form the core for PC-DOS. IBM originally approached Microsoft only to develop languages such as BASIC, FORTRAN, and COBOL for the new IBM computer. However, Bill Gates saw a big opportunity for expansion when he realized that IBM did not have the operating system it needed. Microsoft made a deal with IBM to develop four languages and PC-DOS, retaining the right to resell DOS to other companies as MS-DOS.

The following year, Microsoft completed development of COBOL and FORTRAN for DOS. It also followed a new expansion path in operating systems by licensing MS-DOS to 50 other computer manufacturers. And, somehow, Bill Gates and Microsoft found the time to embark on a totally new expansion strategy: applications software. The first application product was Multiplan.

Expansion along these diverse paths shows that massive resources are not always necessary for expansion. Microsoft was a small company with limited resources, but it intuitively had a clear strategic direction. Microsoft's strategy of growth by expansion into new markets accelerated in 1983 as it pursued expansion paths in many exciting directions. It developed the mouse for personal computers, reflecting its skills in operating system interfaces and its knowledge of user needs, as well as new skills in hardware development. It launched Microsoft Word, one of its most successful application software products. The remaining languages—Pascal, C, and BASIC—were completed for MS-DOS during 1983, and it completed XENIX 3.0 as well. Finally, Microsoft also followed an unleveraged expansion strategy, Microsoft Press, to publish guidebooks for personal computer users. It was generally an unprofitable venture for Microsoft, showing again that unleveraged expansion has more risks than benefits.

Microsoft's expansion did not slow down in 1984, as it turned its attention to the new Macintosh computer. Multiplan and Word were converted to the Macintosh platform, as was the BASIC language. Microsoft continued its expansion into new applications with Microsoft Project, Microsoft Chart, and Microsoft File. It also pursued the path of a derivative platform with DOS for the IBM PCjr. (Even Microsoft does not always pick successful paths.)

Microsoft began to pursue fewer expansion paths in 1985. The two that it did pursue, however, were major successes. In September 1985, it released Excel for the Macintosh, eventually beating out Lotus Jazz as the most successful spreadsheet application on the Macintosh. It sold Excel into an existing customer base (Macintosh spreadsheet users who were already being sold Multiplan). Excel was a completely different platform from Multiplan, but used Microsoft's unique skills.

Windows was a totally new user interface for the DOS operating system. Development of Windows began in 1981 as the Interface Manager project, and it was first announced by Microsoft in 1983. After many delays, Microsoft finally released it in November 1985. Windows was built on a highly leveraged expansion strategy, and Microsoft sold it to a directly related market—DOS users. It leveraged Microsoft's unique skills both in operating systems and in applications software development.

1986 was a relatively slow year for Microsoft's expansion, as it tried to digest some of its major expansion strategies of the previous two years. However, it did launch its first expansion into multimedia with the establishment of a CD-ROM division and the development of Bookshelf, a CD-ROM product.

In 1987, Microsoft returned to exploring new strategies for expansion. It acquired Forethought's PowerPoint presentation software. It released the IBM PC Windows version of Excel, leveraging Excel's core technology into a directly related market. Microsoft Works for the Macintosh, an integrated application aimed at beginning users, was released in September 1987. Works leveraged several existing platforms into a directly related market. Finally, in 1987, Microsoft released the OS/2 operating system developed jointly with IBM.

Microsoft's pursuit of expansion strategies began to slow in 1988. Building on the success of Works, Microsoft released the PC version. It also released two OS/2 related products: LAN Manager with 3Com and Presentation Manager. In 1989, Microsoft pursued relatively minor expansion paths with Quick Pascal, SQL Server, Excel for Presentation Manager, and the acquisition of printer driver software. In 1990, the company also engaged in another kind of unleveraged expansion: It formed a consulting division. In 1991 Microsoft returned to expansion, using some of its traditional technology. It developed a new mouse, the Ballpoint mouse for laptop computers, and it developed Visual BASIC.

In 1992, Microsoft launched Windows 3.1, which was the version that launched the success of the Windows platform. It also released other derivative Windows platforms. Windows for Workgroups integrated networking directly into the operating system and Windows NT aimed at the server market. Microsoft also continued expanding into new applications markets with the release of Access Database.

Microsoft entered the multimedia market in 1993 with the release of Encarta, the first multimedia encyclopedia designed for a computer, in

March. It quickly added to this product line with five other multimedia titles. In addition, it released improved versions of many of its products. In 1994, Microsoft continued to add more products, albeit mostly smaller ones.

In 1995, Microsoft introduced a new operating system, called Bob, that was targeted for the home computing market. Unfortunately it was not successful. Windows 95, a next-generation version of the Windows operating system, was released in August and sold more than 1 million copies in the first four days. Microsoft expanded into a new Internet market with MSN, The Microsoft Network, and Internet Explorer. Of much less importance, it released SideWinder, a digital optical joystick.

Through its acquisition of Vermeer Technologies in 1996, Microsoft expanded into the market for software to create Web pages. In March, it introduced ActiveX, a set of development tools for the creation of active content on Internet and PCs. It continued expansion into new markets with a joint venture with NBC called MSNBC, as well as the introduction of *Slate,* an online magazine.

In 1997, Microsoft continued its expansion by acquiring WebTV to expand into the market for Internet access via television. It also created a new product line of online city guides, called Sidewalk.

By 1999, Microsoft had created a $21.9 billion business by leveraging its capabilities to expand into many new markets. Operating systems platforms were a $9.0 billion business, up from $1 billion in 1992. Developer platforms, including languages, were a $2.3 billion business, up from $150 million in 1992. Business applications were $7.8 billion, up from $1.3 billion in 1992. Consumer products were $2.5 billion, up from less than $300 million in 1992.

Notes

1. Gary McWilliams, "A Radical Shift in Focus for Polaroid," *Business Week,* July 26, 1993, p. 66.

2. McWilliams, p. 67.

3. *The Boston Globe,* August 18, 1993.

4. Robert A. Burgleman and Modesto A. Maidique, *Strategic Management of Technology and Innovation* (Irwin, 1988), p. 321.

5. H. Igor Ansoff also used a similar matrix with the added dimension of geography to describe strategic portfolio strategy and mission. See H. Igor Ansoff, *Corporate Strategy* (McGraw-Hill, 1965; rev. ed. 1987).

6. Kyle Pope, "Compaq Is Revamping Its Printer Line," *The Wall Street Journal,* August 13, 1993.

7. Susan Warren, "Why Dow Finds Slime Sublime," *The Wall Street Journal,* November 15, 1999.

8. Aaron Zitner, "Cutting the Cords," *The Boston Globe*, August 24, 1993.

9. Bill Arnold, "Cirrus Takes PC Market by Storm," *Upside*, August 1993.

10. Kyle Pope, "Ford Taps Texas Instruments to Supply Security Device for Cars Sold in Europe," *The Wall Street Journal*, August 25, 1993.

11. "Flops," *Business Week*, August 16, 1993.

12. Sources: Microsoft company literature; Daniel Ichbiah, *The Making of Microsoft* (Prima Publishing, 1993); Stephen Manes and Paul Andrews, *Gates* (Doubleday, 1993).

PART 2

Competitive Strategy

Beneath every successful product strategy is an interlocked set of competitive calculations. First and foremost, what will separate your technology-based product or service from those of your rivals? Why should anyone buy your offerings instead of someone else's? Differentiation can be achieved through obvious means, such as offering the cheapest or most reliable product. But other "vectors of differentiation" are available as well, and may be more successful, especially if they can occupy unclaimed avenues of differentiation. Such alternative "VODs" run the gamut from ease of use, to the psychological assurance that goes along with a trusted brand name, to positioning a product or family of products as a "total solution" to an entire set or class of business problems—comprehensive product development planning software, for instance.

Part 2 begins by reviewing the gamut of differentiation strategies, including pricing strategies, both offensive and defensive. It goes on to offer a balanced analysis of time to market as a competitive strategy, noting both the power of "first mover" status and the technology- and product-development risks inherent in strategies based on timing. This section of the book also assesses the lure of the so-called world products—technology-based products that can be sold around the world with minimal modification—and the risks of a "world product" competitive strategy. Part 2 concludes with a discussion of cannibalization—perhaps the most misunderstood or overlooked product strategy in the technology sector. A company doesn't want to kill its profits from current products by introducing replacement products prematurely, but neither does it want a competitor to beat it to the dinner table by introducing such replacement products first. That's the cannibal's dilemma, and it's dissected in Part 2.

7

Achieving Sustained Differentiation Using Vectors of Differentiation

A vector of differentiation enables sustained competitive product differentiation by continuous improvement along a specific path with a distinct benefit or value proposition. This is by far the most successful competitive strategy for high-technology companies.

Products achieve competitive advantage through competitive strategy, and there are two primary types of competitive strategy: product differentiation strategy and price-based strategy.[1] Of these two, product differentiation strategy provides the primary source of competitive advantage for most high-technology products.

What do we mean by differentiation strategy? Differentiation is a way of distinguishing a product's value from that of competing products, but it means more than being different. The Edsel automobile was different, but customers did not value its combination of features, and the car was one of the biggest failures in the history of the auto market. Differentiation is a strategic approach to positioning products advantageously as customers decide which product to choose.

Differentiation is a *relative* comparison. A product is differentiated only because it offers something superior to what is available in competitive products. Absent any competition—as is the case when a company creates a new market—differentiation can be considered only against imaginary competition. This is where second or subsequent companies to market may have an advantage. They can better position their products through differentiation against competitive products already in the market.

Effects of Differentiation

Successfully applying a differentiation strategy requires an understanding of the four basic concepts of differentiation.

1. *Differentiation positions a product in the market.* Product differentiation combined with price define the relative positioning of competitors in a marketplace. Figure 7-1 illustrates this as a market with five competitors. Products A and B are the market leaders, but they are pursuing very different strategies. Product A is highly differentiated and sold at a premium price. It is much more successful than products C, D, and E because it offers much more for about the same price.

Product B is the price leader in the market. It is less differentiated than products C, D, and E, but is successful because it is sold at a much lower

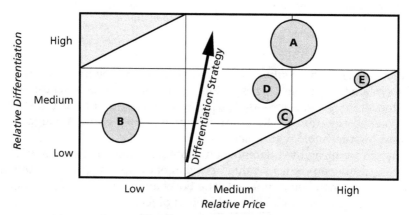

Figure 7-1   Product differentiation and pricing define the relative positioning of competitors in a market.

price. Competition between products A and B is determined by customer preference. Some customers are willing to spend more for the advantages that product A offers; others are not and will choose product B.

Products C, D, and E are in less competitive positions in the market. Their success is based on a unique appeal to certain segments or on imperfections in the market, and they need to reduce their price or increase differentiation to be more competitive.

An analysis like this provides a two-dimensional snapshot of a market, showing the relative positioning of competitors. Each product is more or less differentiated than others and can command a relative price reflecting the value of this differentiation. If the market does not value the differentiation of a product, then the price is usually reduced, or the product will die. The goal of a product differentiation strategy is to move a product toward the upper right of this chart (Figure 7-1), while still capturing the largest market share. A company not continuously moving in this direction will drift toward lower product differentiation, and ultimately a lower price. With most companies preferring to compete on this basis, average product requirements increase over time, and a company not continuously moving will drift to the bottom.

This snapshot analysis can also show whether the market is relatively differentiated or undifferentiated. In markets that are relatively undifferentiated, products are generally clustered together. Undifferentiated markets are commodity markets, where price becomes the primary basis of competition. Progressive snapshots of a market over time would show its evolution.

2. *Differentiation segments the market.* The success of differentiation varies by market segment as each segment values a particular vector of differentiation based on its unique preferences. In this sense, market segmentation has two related, but different, meanings. A population or group can be segmented by various customer characteristics. Examples are companies with earnings under $1 million,

> *The success of differentiation varies by market segment as each segment values a particular vector of differentiation based on its own unique preferences.*

college-educated workers, businesses by industry type, people by age group, and so on. This is the traditional definition of market segmentation, but it only provides demographic information about the market. It usually doesn't establish the basis for competitive advantage.

The other meaning of market segmentation is based on the differentiation of competitive products. Various vectors of differentiation segment the market as customers choose products differentiated by that vector. In

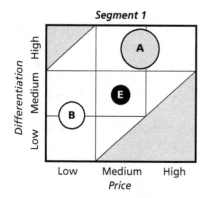 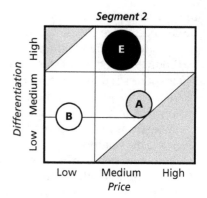

Figure 7-2 The relative value of differentiation can change in different market segments, even though pricing remains the same.

this view, the market is segmented not according to characteristics of the customers, but according to the vectors of differentiation selected by competitors.

In Figure 7-2, two different market segments are compared. Note that the price positioning of each product does not change, since the products are priced the same regardless of market segment, but the relative value of differentiation does change. The differentiation of product A is more valued in Segment 1, while the differentiation of E is more valued in Segment 2. Product B competes on price and does not have any significant differentiation.

Handheld computers exemplify how differentiation applies to market segments, as illustrated in Figure 7-3. Although handheld computers are generally similar, the market can be divided into four segments based on customer requirements. One group of customers uses its handheld computer primarily for personal information management (PIM), such as calendars or address books. Within this group we've defined two segments: customers who primarily use their handheld computer as a convenient extension of the desktop (remote devices) and those who use it on a standalone basis. Two other segments are customers who integrate their handheld computers with other applications on their desktop, such as word processing, and those who use them as a primary computer ("little computer").

We then evaluated four products against these segments. Since they used a compatible version of the Windows desktop operating system, Windows CE devices were strong in application integration and for use as a little computer. The Apple MessagePad was strong only in the little computer segment, and it eventually failed since this segment evolved to

Handheld Computers

	PIM Remote Device	PIM Stand-Alone	Application Integration	"Little Computer"
Windows CE Devices	Some	Some	Strong	Strong
Apple MessagePad	Some	Some	Strong	Strong
PalmPilot	Strong	Strong	Some	
Psion	Some	Strong		

Figure 7-3   Differentiation varies by market segment in the handheld computer market.

be relatively small. The Psion, which was the pioneer of this market, was strongest in the stand-alone market. The Palm Pilot appealed to those who wanted a handheld computer for PIM in both the remote device and stand-alone segments. These turned out to be the largest and second-largest segments as the market emerged, making the Palm Pilot the most successful of these handheld computers.

Relating the two types of segmentation enables a company to effectively target prospective customers. This is crucial, since without this relationship a company cannot focus its marketing and sales efforts.

Sometimes differentiation can be so significant that it creates new markets. That was the case with fault-tolerant computers. What began as a vector of differentiation grew to be an entirely new market with its own group of competitors. The opposite can also happen. Differentiation diminishes to the point where a market based on differentiation no longer stands out from a broader market. Again, fault-tolerant computers provide an example. Eventually general-purpose computers became so reliable as well as less expensive that fault-tolerance was no longer supportable as a unique market.

> *Sometimes differentiation can be so significant that it creates new markets.*

3. *Differentiation evolves throughout a market's life cycle.* As a market evolves, so does the relative differentiation in that market. Understanding and predicting these evolutionary stages of differentiation are essential to competitive strategy.

- *Market development.* In the nascent stage of a market, customers and competitors don't know which characteristics of a product are important differentiators. Initially, a wide variety of attributes may be perceived as important by the companies entering the market, but customer acceptance of these qualities varies. As customers begin to express their preferences for differentiation, they determine winners and losers. Products that win in this initial stage can begin to solidify their differentiation vectors, while others copy the attributes preferred by the market. In the early days of the personal computer market, for example, nobody really understood what customers would value or establish as a standard. There were numerous operating systems, different microprocessors, various types of printers, bundled applications software, multiple configurations, and a variety of expansion capabilities. The market was confused.

  The market for the next-generation product to replace audiocassettes was also confused. Philips was pushing the digital compact cassette technology, which featured CD-quality sound and the ability to play standard audiocassettes. Sony was offering the minidisk technology, which was the first recordable 2.5-inch optical disk for consumers. Each had varying support from record producers, and neither had emerged as the new standard by 1993. By the middle of 1993, Philips had sold fewer than 20,000 units in the United States, and Sony had sold only 40,000 units.[2] The market was confused by the differentiation and had not yet decided which version it preferred.

  Early-stage markets are usually confused. Nobody is sure what is really important. Markets generally do not begin to grow until this confusion starts to diminish.

- *Market growth.* As a market grows, products become more clearly differentiated. Their qualities become known. Customers classify products into various categories, and market share starts to correlate to the relative importance of the vectors of differentiation. When a particular vector of differentiation is less attractive to customers, the product is typically discounted or discontinued. Usually, a market shakeout begins in this stage. In some markets, a competitor can begin to take a commanding lead with a vector of differentiation that is not easily copied by others. In other markets, a successful vector of differentiation is more easily copied, and everyone incorporates the product attributes that customers prefer. As a result, minimum product requirements increase.

■ *Market maturity.* As a market matures, it becomes relatively undifferentiated. Product characteristics preferred overwhelmingly by customers become requirements that every product must have. As a result, most products tend to be similar, and "soft differentiators," such as service and price, become more important bases for competition. Anticipating the evolution into this stage is critical to product strategy. In some cases, product strategy can even forestall maturity or initiate redifferentiation of the market.

Personal computers became a mature market by the turn of the century. It was virtually impossible to differentiate them, since all competitors used the same microprocessors, the same operating systems, and the same components. There was little variation in design or configuration. At this point price, service, and the like were the only remaining bases for differentiation. Some customers preferred one brand name, such as IBM or Compaq, and were willing to pay a little more for this preference. Others were attracted to the convenience of ordering online from companies such as Dell and Gateway. Still others didn't care about differentiation and opted for the lowest-price products from companies with aggressive price promotions or "no-name" companies.

■ *Redifferentiated market.* Sometimes a market can be redifferentiated after it reaches maturity by establishing new differentiation vectors that are important to customers. This shifts the basis of competition away from price and back to differentiation. Even a very mature market can be redifferentiated by applying new technology. Take the $7 billion market for sports shoes and sneakers as an example. Several competitors were able to differentiate their products through investments in new technology: Reebok introduced the Pump, Nike introduced Air, ASIC introduced gel, and LA Gear introduced fiber-optic materials.

These companies redifferentiated a mature market through new technologies, and in the process they were able to raise the price of their

> **A vector provides a path for continuous differentiation in a specific direction.**

sneakers from $15 a pair to more than $100. They succeeded in growing the market (in revenue, if not units) and capturing more market share, while the share of market for companies without any unique differentiation declined significantly.

■ *Market decline.* As a market begins to decline, differentiation is much less important as a competitive strategy. By that time, competitors have already positioned themselves in the market. Competition continues to be based on price, service, brand name, or simply convenience in purchasing the products.

4. *Differentiation should be managed as vectors, not points.*   Differentiation along a vector is much better than individual points of differentiation. A vector provides a path for continuous differentiation in a specific direction. It says, "This is the direction that we are taking in differentiating our products, and we are going to stay ahead of competitors by doing it better and better." A vector of differentiation is not stagnant; it is a direction for continuous improvement. An individual point, on the other hand, implies that it alone is sufficient differentiation and that competitors will not catch up.

> ***Products differentiated by a single point have nowhere to go next, and products differentiated by multiple points in many directions generally do not get as far as those that go in a well-determined direction.***

There is either no need or no opportunity to go further with the same type of differentiation. The next step in differentiating a product can be entirely unrelated.

Products can be differentiated in alternative directions, and vectors establish the directions for differentiation. Products differentiated by a single point have nowhere to go next, and products differentiated by multiple points in many directions generally do not get as far as those that go in a well-determined direction.

When competitive products in a market are differentiated along alternative vectors, customers select the vector they value most. Some products may "own" a particular vector of differentiation. They continue to be improved along the vector, and no one can catch up. For example, the computer workstation market became very competitive, but one company was able to maintain consistently higher margins by "owning" a key differentiation vector. Silicon Graphics was the clear leader in workstations customized for graphics manipulation. This was a rapidly growing market segment, with uses ranging from three-dimensional scientific modeling to the lifelike animation in Hollywood motion pictures. Silicon Graphics tailored its workstations' hardware and software to serve this market segment and, as a result, could not be matched by the producers of general-purpose workstations.

Benefits of Vectors of Differentiation

It's easy to see that the most successful products achieve a vector of differentiation (VOD). These products deliver a specific benefit to customers and are continuously differentiated along this specific benefit or value proposition.

1. *Vectors separate the strategic from the tactical.*   It's important, especially for senior management, to focus on the most important strategic decision and not get mired down by the details. Vectors of differentiation enable a clear focus on the unique *way* a product will be successful, instead of on individual details. Strategically, a VOD answers the following questions:

- What is the primary value to customers of alternative VODs?
- How will various market segments value this VOD?
- Will a particular VOD enable us to win against expected competitive products with alternative VODs?
- Do we have sufficient advantages to prevent competitors from more successfully incorporating this VOD?
- Will we be at a disadvantage relative to other VODs?

Continuous improvement of the product or service, or new releases of product offerings, on the other hand, are more tactical. They don't *define* the vector of differentiation; they *implement* it.

Some companies back into a vector of differentiation. They determine the characteristics or feature set for a new product or new product platform without any particular vector in mind. This is characteristic of determining a strategy on the basis of tactics. The success of the strategy is then left up to chance.

2. *A VOD focuses product improvements.*   Once a company has determined its vector of differentiation, then this becomes the focus for all product development. The common goal of all products is to be the best at achieving this particular VOD. The company is willing to sacrifice performance in other product features to be the best in one focused benefit. Over time it can increasingly distance itself from competitors.

SAP shows how a VOD can increasingly differentiate a product over time. As illustrated in Figure 7-4, it continuously differentiated its enterprise resource planning (ERP) application software from 1972 well into the 1990s. SAP's original product release, R, integrated manufacturing and accounting information in a single common application. In its next generation, R2, SAP continued the integration with releases that added more integrated functions, such as order processing, purchasing, and shipping, as well as additional materials management and integrated accounting. Competitors followed SAP, but they could never catch up as SAP continued to add more integrated capabilities. In the 1990s SAP released R3 and added integrated capabilities for human resources, sales force automation, taxes, and the like. It continued to add capabilities along this vector for large multinational corporations, including currency management, multiple plant integration, and multiple languages.

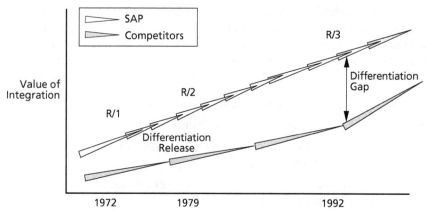

Figure 7-4   SAP continuously improved its vector of differentiation and conse-
quently increased the gap between it and its competitors between 1972 and 1992.

Competitors that tried to compete on the same basis were unable to keep
up with SAP's continued movement along this vector. Others competed
with SAP by offering single products with the integration capabilities of
SAP. Referred to as "best of breed," these applications were frequently better at doing specific tasks, but lacked the integration. Some were successful,
but none was to the degree of SAP. SAP's original vector of differentiation
enabled it to grow to 367 million DM in 1989. Its ability to stay ahead of its
competitors along this vector enabled SAP to grow to 8.5 billion DM.

3. *The length and slope of a VOD provide strategic insights.*   In addition to
the relative distance from competitive products, a VOD provides strategic
insights for two other important geometric properties: length and slope
(Figure 7-5). A company needs to understand these for each of its major
vectors of differentiation. The potential *length* of a VOD determines how
long a product can be continuously improved along one vector.
Strategically, it provides a sense of the time before competitors can catch
up. In the example just discussed, SAP had a long vector of differentiation.
Before competition could catch up to where it was, SAP progressed further
along the vector. For its competition, SAP was a moving target that was
able to maintain competitive advantage. Assuming the product continues
to improve along a vector, it can generally stay ahead of competition until
it gets to the end. At this point, a product differentiation strategy may not
be viable. Generally, this happens when the market matures.

The *slope* of the VOD shows how fast a product can improve. A VOD
with a rapid (steep) slope can increase the relative competitive advantage
over time. A VOD with a relatively gradual slope cannot increase its rela-

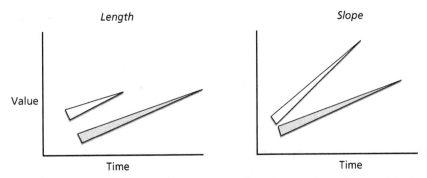

Figure 7-5   The effectiveness of a vector of differentiation depends on its length and slope.

tive competitive advantage very quickly. Strategically, it's important to understand which slope applies.

4. *The relative value of a VOD changes over the market life cycle.*   Earlier, we discussed how differentiation evolves throughout a market life cycle. A VOD demonstrates this over time as the market and competition evolve. As the VOD evolves, the difference between it and that of competitive products will begin to diminish. The rate at which a VOD diminishes depends on its length and slope, as discussed earlier.

Figure 7-6 offers the Apple Macintosh as an illustration. Initially, the Macintosh was highly differentiated on ease of use through its graphical operating system, mouse, bundled application software, and easy-to-con-

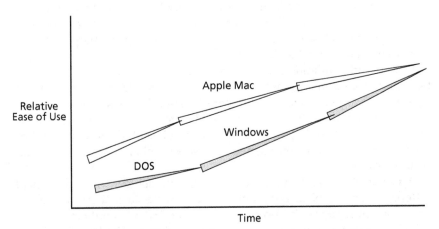

Figure 7-6   Over time, other PCs caught up with Macintosh's vector of differentiation—ease of use.

nect peripherals. Apple continued to extend the differentiation with every new Macintosh product offering and system upgrade, but eventually its basis of differentiation began to diminish. Other peripherals became more standardized, and connections were easier. Other PCs incorporated the mouse. Finally, Microsoft replaced the DOS operating system with Windows. Apple's advantage began to diminish.

Differentiation Strategies

High-technology products can be differentiated along many types of vectors, each of which represents a strategy for differentiating products. The experiences of high-technology companies lead to generic differentiation strategies that can serve as models.

Differentiation Using Unique Features

Many high-technology companies are drawn to differentiation by product features, since advances in technology provide many opportunities for new and interesting features. This is generally the easiest differentiation to select, but one of the most difficult to define as a continuing vector, especially if the features are unrelated.

Differentiation can sometimes be achieved on the strength of a single feature. Sharp, for example, was able to differentiate itself in the very competitive camcorder market by replacing the conventional viewfinder on its ViewCam with a 4-inch color LCD panel. Users could watch what they were filming in color, as if it were on a small TV. The competitive advantage of this feature was so successful that in Japan, Sharp increased its market share from 3 to 20 percent.[3]

Feature differentiation is most successful if several unique features can be grouped around a common theme or vector. NEC's UltraLite Versa personal computer grouped a number of related features on the vector of versatility. The monochrome screen could be replaced with a color screen. The screen could be flipped around to show presentations, or it could be used as a pen-based tablet. There were also a number of options, all related to versatility.

A vector of related features could be used to achieve various types of differentiation. In 1972, for example, Hewlett-Packard (HP) introduced one of its most successful products ever—the HP-35 handheld scientific calculator—using new features as its differentiation. The HP-35 had several unique, but related, features: 17 arithmetic, trigonometric, and logarithmic functions; the capability for data storage; and 10-digit accuracy.

These features significantly differentiated it from other calculators, enabling HP to target engineers as a very specific market segment. At the start of development, HP projected sales of 10,000 units in the first year. It sold over 100,000.[4] However, competition eventually caught up with HP's vector of differentiation. Today, there are many calculators with these features, all at 10 percent of the original price of the HP-35.

Microsoft Word for Windows 6.0 provides another example of a vector of differentiation relying on related features. In this case, features were grouped around the vector of improving the process of writing. They included automatically correcting misspelled words as they are typed, automatically reformatting documents to make them look better, listing most commonly used fonts at the top of the font menu, enabling a user to drag text from one document to another, and permitting a user to undo the past 100 changes.

Feature differentiation can also be used to address a specific segment of the market. In February 1993, Lotus Development released a new product called Improv that targeted the so-called power users of spreadsheet software. Improv was differentiated from the Lotus 1-2-3 product by its flexibility and use of plain English commands instead of variables in formulas. For example, a cell could be defined as "Sales-1993" instead of "C12." As part of its product line strategy, Lotus chose to introduce Improv as a totally new product rather than as an upgrade or new version of 1-2-3. The strategy was aimed at increasing revenue by targeting a different segment of the market.

Although attractive, differentiation based on features can be a limited strategy. As in the case of the HP-35 and the Sharp ViewCam, the competition can copy features, neutralizing any competitive advantage. Without any consistent theme for the features, the product doesn't create any long-term brand recognition. Eventually, the impact of a product having more and more features diminishes. Japanese consumer electronics companies saw this with VCRs as they struggled to find new features with enough value to maintain prices. When the feature war ends, the baseline product incorporates all important features, and there is little basis for any differentiation.

Differentiation by Measurable Customer Benefits

All differentiation should benefit the customer in some way; however, when a product is differentiated with directly measurable benefits, customers will prefer it even at a significantly higher price. The challenge of differentiation based on measurable benefits goes beyond achieving the benefits. It requires clearly quantifying and communicating them. For

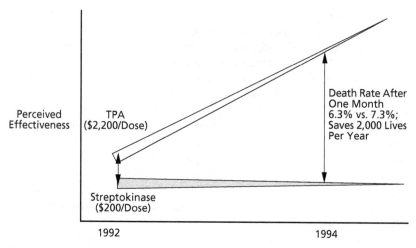

Figure 7-7 When a product is differentiated with direct and dramatic measurable results (as with the pharmaceutical TPA), customers will prefer it, even at a higher price.

example, in the medical device and pharmaceutical industries, health care reform sharply focused buying behavior on "measurable patient outcomes," rather than simply cost reduction. In these industries, the story related below and illustrated in Figure 7-7 is becoming commonplace.

In 1992, Genentech, Inc., one of the world's first biotechnology companies, tried to differentiate its blood-clot buster, TPA (sold as Activase), which was priced at $2,200 per dose, from a competitive product, streptokinase, priced at $200 per dose. Of the 900,000 people who suffer heart attacks in the United States each year, only about 20 percent received thrombolytic drugs like these, and TPA was used in only half of those cases. Genentech had a significant opportunity to increase both its share of the market and overall use, but only if it could clearly differentiate the benefits of TPA.

In order to statistically prove the performance difference, Genentech funded a $55 million, 41,000-patient study by the Cleveland Clinic. Genentech's objective in this study was to show that heart attack victims' survival rates were higher with TPA, which would induce cardiologists to administer TPA despite its higher price.[5] The study results showed that TPA, compared with streptokinase, saved one additional life in every 100—a death rate of 6.3 percent one month after heart attack, compared to 7.3 percent. Genentech's differentiation was clearly stated by G. Kirk Raab, its president: "If everyone used TPA, we could save six lives a day in the U.S., or 2,000 people per year. It used to be that doctors had to find a reason to use TPA; now they're going to have to find a reason not to use TPA."[6]

The competitive response claimed that other studies did not show any significant difference. Genentech obviously anticipated the claim, which is why it invested $55 million and studied 41,000 patients.

Cost benefit is a critical metric in promoting measurable benefit differentiation. In this case, the benefit is one life per 100, and the cost is an additional $2,000 per treatment. Put another way, an additional $200,000 saves one life.

Genentech could have chosen a strategy of lowering the price of TPA to achieve proximity to the price of streptokinase. In 1992, Genentech sold approximately $180 million of TPA. Cutting the price in half would have cost it $90 million at the same volume. It would need to sell at least twice as much to offset this price cut, while still having a significantly higher price of $1,100 compared with $200 per dose for competitive products. If it met the $200 per-dose price, it would need to sell at least 10 times as many doses of TPA to break even—more than the total size of the market.

Even though lowering the price to meet competition is a normal tactical response, Genentech considered alternative strategies before acting. With

> *Ease of use has become a very popular vector of differentiation in today's increasingly complex high-technology products.*

the strategy it chose, even a slight increase in TPA market share would more than pay for the $55 million invested in proving this differentiation, and a significant increase was possible given the market characteristics. This strategy was sound for Genentech. The major risk was that, despite its investment, the study could have showed no significant performance difference. That could have been the end of TPA, at least $2,200 per-dose TPA. The market share of TPA increased from 50 percent to 66 percent within three months, while the share for streptokinase dropped from 50 percent to 33 percent.

Differentiation through Ease of Use

Ease of use has become a very popular vector of differentiation in today's increasingly complex high-technology products. Ease of use definitely appeals to a large segment in most markets, especially consumer markets. Except for a period of time in the 1990s, Apple consistently focused on ease of use as a vector of differentiation. For example, the Macintosh user-friendly interface enabled people to learn how to use the computer more quickly, leading to less frustration. This difference translated into more productivity, which is usually why the customer purchases a computer in the first place. Although user-friendly advantages are difficult to quantify, they do provide a difference that is easy to communicate. Apple promoted this advantage in its commercials, which compared frustrated businesspeople trying to use a competitive product (the IBM PC with the DOS operating system) with someone easily using a Macintosh.

Apple continued emphasizing the ease-of-use vector with the iMac, introduced in 1998. It made the iMac easy to buy (It comes complete with everything you need). It's easier to set up ("There's no step 3") and easier to use (One click and "hello, Internet"). Apple emphasized connection to the Internet. The iMac came with everything needed to send and receive e-mail and surf the World Wide Web. A friendly Setup Assistant asked a few simple questions and then walked customers through the steps of getting online.

Intuit's Quicken for computerized checking and Quickbooks for accounting also emphasize ease of use and simplicity. They are designed to be used by the customer who is willing to sacrifice features for simplicity. Intuit also illustrates another principle of differentiation. It's always better to carry a constant vector of differentiation through all products, creating a single message and common brand recognition.

Differentiation by Improved Productivity

Increased productivity is frequently claimed as a benefit of differentiation. The customer can get more done with this product than with competitive products.

Increased productivity was the benefit of Lotus 1-2-3 Release 4's workgroup capability vector of differentiation. It allowed multiple users to work on common spreadsheets, significantly increasing productivity. A workgroup could distribute and manage 1-2-3 data using Lotus Notes. This was a powerful vector for Lotus, because it offered continued differentiation of similar features along the vector, and it used Lotus' proprietary Notes technology.

Increased productivity is frequently touted as a primary benefit for many high-technology products, such as application software. The primary value proposition is that the product saves the user money by reducing the labor required to complete specific tasks; however, since this is the basis of all competitive products, it's difficult for it to work as a vector of differentiation. Usually it's how the product improves productivity that defines the vector of differentiation.

Differentiation by Protecting the Customer's Investment

Since advances in technology create change, a product can claim a competitive advantage by differentiating itself to protect a customer's existing investment, thus avoiding or reducing the loss incurred by upgrading to an improved product.

This was the primary differentiation advantage of the extremely successful IBM System/360 product line in the 1970s. It provided a compatible family of computers, enabling customers to upgrade to more powerful computer hardware without losing their investment in software or peripherals.

Digital Equipment's "one company, one architecture" strategy in the 1980s successfully differentiated the VAX computer family from competitors by providing a range of compatible products. Companies that wanted a common set of products using the same operating system chose Digital VAX computers over IBM and others. To these companies, the savings in software, development, and operating costs outweighed any other factor.

Differentiation through Lower Cost of Product Failure

The cost of a product's failure can be a very significant vector of differentiation to some users. The direct cost of repair or maintenance is obvious. It drove the differentiation advantage for Japanese cars in the 1980s. With some products, there is also a significant indirect cost of product failure when the product is not available because of repair or maintenance. Computer systems are the obvious example.

When Bill Foster founded Stratus Computer in the early 1980s, he intended to build a computer company based entirely on a strategy of product differentiation. This differentiation, or as Foster liked to call it, the "Stratus Difference," is continuous availability. He believed that the company would "retain the Stratus Difference by concentrating on hardware and software designs that achieve continuous availability." This differentiation enabled Stratus to grow to almost $500 million in 1992 and, more important, because of this difference, Stratus continued to increase profitability during 1990–1992 while most other computer companies were losing money.

The value of this differentiation to customers is measured by the cost of system downtime. In 1992 Stratus promoted its systems by estimating the cost of downtime as follows:[7]

- The average direct revenue loss is $78,000 per hour.

- The loss per incident, including revenue and productivity, is $330,000.
- Some companies lose $500,000 per hour of downtime.

Because of these savings, Stratus computers could be priced at a premium compared with computers that were not fault-tolerant.

Differentiation with Higher-Performance Products

Performance advantages are a popular vector for differentiating high-technology products, since advances in technology usually improve performance. Differentiation can be achieved in many dimensions: speed, power, and capacity, among others.

Digital Equipment used performance as the vector of differentiation in its Alpha AXP Workstations (DEC 3000 product line), which incorporated its Alpha microprocessor. Digital positioned its DEC 3000 workstations as the best in price/performance (using a computational performance measure called Spec92), comparing performance to competitive products. Digital claimed price/performance advantage for the DEC 3000 at all major price points, proving the differentiation of the AXP platform, not just a single model in the product line. Digital's comparison showed how competitors Sun, HP, and IBM all clustered together at a lower price/performance level.

Hewlett-Packard used battery life and size to effectively differentiate its OmniBook computer. The OmniBook was a DOS/Windows-compatible notebook computer weighing less than three pounds. Most important, it could run for up to six hours on four ordinary AA alkaline batteries—far longer on much less power than other notebook computers. This clearly differentiated the OmniBook in an increasingly crowded market. New technology was the key to the differentiation. The OmniBook used "flash cards" (PCMCIA cards) instead of disk drives. These are semiconductor chips sealed in a card to store data, saving space and power over normal disk drives with spinning magnetic platters and moving read/write heads.

By using this design approach, HP was able to differentiate the OmniBook without sacrificing other features, such as the size of its keyboard and screen. By using new technology to differentiate the OmniBook, HP achieved an advantage over competitors that did not have a core competency in that technology.

Performance can also be used to place a product into a new segment in the market. This is what Convex Computer did in 1984 when it positioned its products between Cray and Digital Computer based on performance. It created the "minisupercomputer" market by offering a product with a price/performance ratio in between Cray's $5 million to $15 million supercomputers and Digital's $300,000 to $750,000 minicomputers.[8]

Differentiation by Unique Fundamental Capabilities

Differentiation based on unique fundamental capabilities can be one of the most successful vectors of differentiation, one that usually can be continuously improved, and sometimes sustained for a very long time.

Polaroid cameras are clearly differentiated on a unique fundamental capability: They instantly develop pictures within the camera itself. This is a unique capability that no other camera can match, and has been protected by patents vigorously defended by Polaroid.

While other camera manufacturers were fighting fiercely for survival, Polaroid was able to stand on the sidelines and watch the battle, protected by its unique differentiation. However, in high-technology markets even a unique capability can be attacked. The spread of one-hour film developing diminished the value of Polaroid's instant cameras and forced it to lower prices. Video cameras then provided new competition.

Differentiation through Design

Even high-technology products can be differentiated to some extent using product design, especially where the design differentiation promotes ease of use for new users.

Apple has always tried to differentiate its computers through design, if not as the primary vector then as a secondary vector. The first Macintosh portable was a failure. It weighed 17 pounds and underperformed most other portables on the market. While different, the basis of differentiation was not advantageous, and even the Macintosh user interface could not save it. Potential customers either stayed with Macintosh desktops or went with IBM-compatible portables.

Determined to learn from its mistakes, Apple wanted its next try, the PowerBook, to have advantageous differentiation as a notebook computer, not only as a smaller Macintosh. The entire PowerBook development team studied how potential customers used notebook computers. They discovered that people did not really want small computers *per se*; they wanted mobile computers, size being just one aspect of mobility.[9]

The PowerBook was designed with two unique advantages: the TrackBall pointer and the palm rest in the front of the keyboard. These made the PowerBook more comfortable to use and therefore more user-friendly, supporting the overall ease-of-use differentiation vector for the Macintosh family of computers. In the first year, Apple sold more than $1 billion of PowerBooks (440,000 units).

By the second year, however, competition began to catch up to Apple on this vector of differentiation. Sales growth began to slow to an estimated 580,000 PowerBooks in 1993.[10] Apple did not continue introducing improvements, although improved battery life and smaller devices in PCMCIA cards could have been natural extensions along this vector.

The Apple iMac, introduced in 1998, renewed the emphasis on design as a basis for differentiation.

The Apple iMac, introduced in 1998, renewed the emphasis on design as a basis for differentiation. To some extent it changed the idea of what a consumer computer was expected to look like. The new look included sleeker, more rounded lines, and a move away from the traditional beige box. The iMac's shell is made of translucent plastic in five dazzling colors: strawberry, blueberry, grape, tangerine, and lime. Some believe that its differentiation through design was a large part of the iMac's success in selling 2 million computers in its first year.

Rarely is design the primary basis for differentiation, particularly in high-technology products. But in some cases it can be a supporting or secondary vector of differentiation.

Differentiation Based on Standards

It's easy to overlook standards as the basis for differentiation, but in some markets this has been critical. In the early days of the personal computer market, the early 1980s, there was a variety of operating systems such as CPM, MPM, DOS, Apple Macintosh, and Apple II operating systems. Eventually the market began to settle on Microsoft Windows as the standard. Computer manufacturers that "differentiated" their products by conforming to the Windows standard prospered. The same was true with software that ran on Windows.

Differentiation based on standards is difficult to rely on. A company can't control establishing a standard, although many would like to. It really means recognizing this as a secondary basis for differentiation and knowing when to incorporate this change into products. It's also difficult to stand out with a standard as a vector of differentiation, since almost by definition most other competitors will convert to the same standard. In some ways it's more a matter of avoiding a negative—nonstandard—vector of differentiation.

Differentiation by Total Solutions

Total solutions offer customers savings in the costs of using products. Total-solution differentiation is achieved in electronic systems by bundling software and hardware or by offering a range of compatible products.

IBM's AS/400 generated an estimated $14 billion revenue in 1991. If it had been an independent company, the AS/400 division would have been the world's second-largest computer company at that time. While the AS/400 offered price-performance advantages, its chief vector of differentiation was that it gave customers a total solution, eliminating the need for systems integration. The AS/400 included virtually everything needed: hardware, operating system, database software, and support. This made it not only cheaper for customers to use, but also easier for independent software vendors to develop application products for it.

Open systems can also provide total systems differentiation, but in a very different way. Sun Microsystems built its success on the differentiation provided by open systems. As a result, Sun grew from start-up to more than $3.5 billion in 11 years. Ironically, the company stumbled into a successful product differentiation strategy based on other factors—lack of sufficient financial resources was much more of a factor than strategy in its decision to publish the specifications for its SPARC microprocessor architecture in 1986.[11]

Integration is a frequent theme of a total solution vector of differentiation. Microsoft used integration to deliver a total solution when it launched Microsoft Office 4.0, a bundled and integrated set of application software products (spreadsheet, word processor, presentation maker, and database). This also illustrates how a vector of differentiation evolves. Microsoft's first step toward a total integrated solution was offering related applications that had the same type of interface (touch and feel), reducing user learning time. The next step was bundling these together at a lower price. Substantial integration came next. Microsoft Office 4.0 provided a common integration framework called Object Linking and Embedding (OLE). This gave Microsoft a significant lead over competitors that were still cobbling together applications with different software frameworks. Microsoft's framework enabled users to take a document-centric view of their work, erasing boundaries among applications. Microsoft used this fresh vector to maintain its lead over competition by continued enhancements. It continued along this vector for many more years, adding integration of Internet capabilities in subsequent products, especially Office 2000.

Differentiation by Total Cost of Ownership

The selling price of the product is only one aspect of the total cost to the customer. Over the ownership life cycle, costs such as routine maintenance, service and repair, lost revenue due to downtime, cost of consumables, and residual value can amount to substantially more than the initial purchase price, especially for high-value, relatively long-lived products.

NCR, with its range of highly reliable and easily serviceable automated teller machines (ATMs), prepared tables showing its cost of ownership compared with that of competitive machines. The tables took into account all cost factors and demonstrated the savings that would result over the life of the product, enabling NCR to charge a premium price.

Differentiation in the cost of ownership for many high-technology products often comes from different architectures. Compare Microsoft Windows 2000 with the Sun Solaris UNIX operating systems. Both targeted the Internet server market, but each had very different architectures. Sun's architecture enabled it to scale *up* by supporting server hardware that incorporated multiple microprocessors. Windows 2000, on the other hand, was designed to scale *out* to manage many smaller and cheaper PC-based servers. Microsoft claimed that its approach produced the lower total cost of ownership for two reasons: A customer could use a rack of standard PCs linked together and besides enabling lower-cost modular expansion, standard PCs were much less expensive than Sun's higher priced servers. Microsoft also claimed a lower cost for hardware maintenance, since one computer in the rack could be replaced while the others kept working.

This vector of differentiation strategy relies on relatively sophisticated customers who are not easily seduced by a lower list price. It is particularly effective in the high-value capital purchase markets, where products are expected to have a long life.

Differentiation through Brand Name

Brand name is not generally a primary vector of differentiation, especially in high-technology products. However, brand name reputation can effectively suggest an underlying vector of differentiation. It can trigger a customer's feeling of value from the underlying vector, and the underlying vector can establish and maintain the value of a brand name.

> *Brand name is not generally a primary vector of differentiation, especially in high-technology products.*

It's imperative that the underlying vector is understood; otherwise, a company can delude itself into believing that differentiation based on its brand name is sufficient. We sometimes see this as a convenient differentiation of last resort. The following case illustrates how companies come to rely on this type of differentiation.

Senior management asked the product development team leader how the product he proposed would differentiate itself in the market. The product was a next-generation data communications switch with features different from those of the company's existing products. Compared with other products recently introduced, it was competitive, but not unique.

The team leader compared the new product against others on the market and showed that it was competitive, having all the same capabilities as those products.

"But how is this product different?" he was asked again.

After thinking for a moment he responded, "Our reputation for service and support is highly respected by our customers."

"Some of the new competitors in the market are highly respected multi-billion-dollar companies," one of the executives pointed out.

"But they are new to the market," the team leader responded.

Senior management bought this argument as sufficient differentiation, and the company invested $20 million to develop the product. It was unsuccessful in the market.

Differentiation Based on Convenience

Like brand name, convenience is not usually a primary vector of differentiation for high-technology products. In the PC market, Dell and Gateway enabled customers to order computers directly to their desired configuration and loaded selected application software on the computers before shipping them to customers. This made the purchase and setup more convenient for customers and provided a competitive advantage to some extent. Similarly, Amazon.com can be more convenient than going to a bookstore to purchase a book, especially for corporate purchases in quantity.

> *Like brand name, convenience is not usually a primary vector of differentiation for high-technology products; as a vector of differentiation, frequently it can be copied by competitors.*

Convenience has a higher value in markets where little else distinguishes products. The PC market is a good example. However, as a vector of differentiation, frequently convenience can be copied by competitors.

Risks of Differentiation

Like other strategies, differentiation strategies have risks. Companies frequently encounter these risks by chance, even though they are able to anticipate them.

1. *Differentiation can't be sustained.* To be successful, differentiation must be sustained long enough. What frequently happens with a new technology is that one company innovates a really different new product or service; however, it then finds that other companies copy its approach because it didn't have adequate barriers to entry. So while the company initially had significant differentiation from the original competitors, it now has little or no differentiation from the new set of competitors.

Hundreds of Internet-based companies, particularly those doing e-commerce, fell into this trap during the 1998–2000 time period. Internet-based commerce provided exciting new opportunities for selling products online instead of through traditional brick-and-mortar retail stores. There were opportunities in almost any product category, including pet supplies, pharmaceuticals, food, books, computer equipment, travel, etc. These services were very different from retail stores. With an ample supply of venture capital and the hype of initial public offerings, many new companies were launched in each category, and the number of companies offering the same products rapidly proliferated. The problem was, there was nothing to differentiate one from another, and the market became crowded.

With no other opportunity for differentiation, Internet-based commerce became the ultimate commodity market: multiple companies selling exactly the same products in the exact same location—your computer. There weren't even the traditional differences in location that might discourage some from driving a little farther for a better price. In desperation these "e-tailers" tried to establish a brand name though massive advertising, including mil-

Few e-commerce companies will ever have profitable product offerings in this ultimate commodity marketplace [the Internet].

lion-dollar advertisements during the Super Bowl. Some spent more than $100 million trying to establish a brand name. Others desperately cut prices, frequently below cost, trying to establish customer loyalty—as if price-based customers are loyal.

All in all, by the beginning of 2000, this looks like a multi-billion-dollar lesson in product strategy for many young companies and their financial backers. This is not to say that Internet-based e-commerce won't be successful. On the contrary, it's likely to become the dominant form of retail commerce in the future, and many, if not most, brick-and-mortar stores will be replaced. The point is that few e-commerce companies will ever have profitable product offerings in this ultimate commodity marketplace.

2. *There is insufficient proximity to price.* A differentiated product must maintain price proximity to products without that differentiation. This means that a customer faced with two alternatives will pay X dollars more for the product with the differentiation advantage. At much more than X dollars, the customer would decide to purchase the lower-priced product and forgo the advantages offered by the differentiation. The value of X varies among customers, but these values tend to be distributed so as to make rough approximations possible.

In the first few years after it released its personal computer, IBM was able to differentiate its computer against IBM compatibles by the extent of compatibility with application software and peripherals. Only IBM's PCs were truly compatible; others were mostly compatible. However, this difference was important to customers who found that a particular software package or printer would not work with the IBM compatible. In 1984, IBM dominated the PC market with a 70 percent market share and was able to charge a premium of $1,000. Customers were willing to pay more for the assurance that the computer they bought would work with all IBM PC software and peripherals, so IBM could charge this premium for its PCs and still maintain sufficient proximity to IBM compatibles.

As the IBM compatibles became truly compatible, the value of this differentiation changed, and IBM lost price proximity (Figure 7-8). By 1990, the value of differentiation based on compatibility was down to $50.

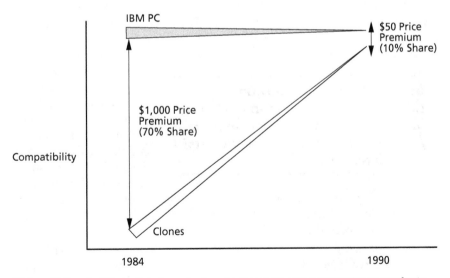

Figure 7-8 A differentiated product must maintain price proximity to products without that differentiation, as IBM learned with its PCs from 1984 to 1990.

That's all customers were willing to pay for the assurance of compatibility, since it was no longer much of a problem. IBM misinterpreted its initial success in the market. It thought that its differentiation advantage was based on reputation and service. Over time, the IBM name alone was not a significant differentiator, and service became less of a differentiator. One PC customer put it this way, "I can buy three compatible PCs for the price of two IBM PCs, so service is not important."

IBM was slow to lower its price and rapidly lost market share. To some extent, IBM was slow because its PC revenue was still increasing, just not as fast as the market, so the loss in market share wasn't as painful as it might have been. By 1990, IBM's market share was down to 10 percent. This drop cost IBM approximately $50 billion in revenue, and it lost the opportunity to be the leader in a very important market.

Industry standardization and common components eliminated most vectors of differentiation, turning the PC market abruptly into a commodity business, with price being the primary competitive factor. In a highly differentiated market, price proximity can be maintained, even with a significant price difference. When the value of differentiation is virtually eliminated, it becomes a commodity market.

The market places a value on any new vector of differentiation. Price proximity is equal to that value. If the price difference is higher, the product will not attract as many customers. In 1989, Sega of America introduced the Sega Genesis 16-bit video game player to compete with Nintendo, which had almost 90 percent of the market. Genesis was more advanced than Nintendo's 8-bit game player, but at twice the price ($199 versus $100), it was not very successful. The price differential was greater than the value placed on it by the market. It did not have price proximity.

In 1990, Sega reduced the price of Genesis by 25 percent to $149 and bundled in it one of its most popular games. This change brought its price within proximity, and its vector of differentiation was a success. Sega's market share skyrocketed from 7 percent in 1990 to almost 50 percent in 1993, while Nintendo's dropped from almost 90 percent to 50 percent. Sega's U.S. sales increased from $80 million to more than $1 billion.[12]

> *Successful differentiation requires advantages that customers value. Misjudge what the customer values, and the resulting product will most likely fail.*

3. *Customer preferences are misunderstood.* Successful differentiation requires advantages that customers value. Misjudge what the customer values, and the resulting product will most likely fail.

For example, the IBM PCjr was very different from the IBM PC and other personal computers. It had scaled-down characteristics that IBM thought were important to the targeted home computer market. These features included a smaller keyboard, an infrared connection of the keyboard to the computer, and a limited operating system.

IBM found out the hard way that this differentiation was not of much value to targeted customers. The product was a monumental failure, despite tens of millions of dollars spent on advertising and promotion. The features may have been different, they may even have been features that some customers liked, but they were not features that most customers preferred.

4. *The cost of differentiation is too high.* Differentiation can be costly. Each additional capability or feature can add to the cost of the product. Differentiation can go beyond the point of diminishing returns, and eventually the cost of differentiation exceeds its value.

The Apple Lisa computer suffered this fate. It introduced some new and valuable features—namely, the user-friendly interface that has since become so successful in the Macintosh products. However, at a list price of $10,000 (down from the $13,500 initially considered), it was priced beyond its value. The Lisa example also provides a lesson in the cost of differentiation for high-technology products. As a technology evolves, its cost decreases. Technology that was too expensive in the Lisa was cost-effective in the Macintosh. In between, there was a decline in the cost of other technology—memory chips, processors, and disk drives—needed to implement that vector of differentiation.

A company making electronic instruments also fell into this trap. It developed a new product based on customer input that incorporated every feature its customers said they would like to have. The company thought it had developed the perfect product; its new instrument did everything that any competitive product did all at once, and more. The company totaled the cost for making the instrument, added a 50 percent gross margin, and set the selling price. In the end, however, few customers were willing to pay that much for this perfect product. Customers preferred to buy instruments that had the feature set they sought and did not want to spend more for additional features that were of little importance to them.

Not all differentiation is costly. Inexpensive differentiation can provide exciting opportunities. For example, Whistler Electronics increased differentiation of its product at almost no cost. The company made radar detectors for automobiles, entering a market that at the time was very competitive. In order to differentiate itself from competitors, it developed "pulse protection" that immediately signaled the driver that police radar ahead was using pulse detection (radar that is shot from hand gun pulses instead of operating continuously). It implemented this feature entirely in the software of the product, requiring no additional cost, except for a label put on the box promoting "pulse protection." Whistler was able to price these products at a premium and take away significant market share from competitors.

The cost of differentiation varies by company. Economies of scale, shared costs, and technology can all be different. The same vector of differentiation can be more expensive for one competitor than another, making a vector of differentiation successful for one competitor but not the other.

5. *There is too much unfocused differentiation.* Some companies incorrectly think that a differentiation strategy means adding more and more features. A typical example is the "checklist syndrome," in which product designers believe they need to add every feature included on competitive products or every feature request-

> **Some companies incorrectly think that a differentiation strategy means adding more and more features.**

ed by customers. They visualize customers as using a checklist to tick off features, making purchase decisions by adding up the number of features included. So they design the product to include everything.

In reality, most customers do not make decisions this way (although product reviewers use this approach to rate competitive products). Customers base their decisions on the features that are most important to them. The results of too much differentiation are a price that is too high (as was seen in the electronic instrument example), confused customers, and lack of distinction in the market. For example, advances in electronics and software made VCRs a formidable challenge to the average person. At this point, simplification became a differentiator. Some manufacturers brought out de-featured machines that had remote control pads with only eight or so buttons. These machines could tune themselves to the local TV stations, thus eliminating the daunting setup requirement. This is an example of technology going beyond the point of value to the customer, leaving the market open to resegmentation.

6. *A new vector subsegments the market.* In some cases, differentiation can create a market segment that is large enough to become a significant market. A new vector of differentiation can then subsegment this market. Let's look at examples from the computer industry to illustrate this point. Tandem and Stratus differentiated their products along the vector of fault tolerance, creating a large, successful market segment. However, as standard operating systems, such as UNIX, became an important vector of differentiation in the general computer industry, they also became more important in that market segment. New competitors began to subdiffer-

entiate the fault-tolerant market segment by introducing UNIX-based network servers. These were differentiated from Hewlett-Packard, SUN, IBM, and DEC servers by fault tolerance and permanent availability.

The problem of subdifferentiation also affected Raytheon's Patriot defense missile. The original intent of the Patriot missile, when it was developed in the late 1960s, was to work on a range of threats, including aircraft, ballistic missiles such as Iraqi Scuds, and low-flying cruise missiles. The Patriot used a fragmentation warhead to explode near the incoming threats, crippling them with fast-moving fragments.

While still effective against these threats, to many military officials the Patriot was not as effective against a specific new subsegment of this antimissile market: modern ballistic missiles carrying high-penalty warheads, such as chemical or biological agents. In these cases, the hit-to-kill approach of the Erint missile made by Loral was considered superior. The Erint missile carried no warhead, but destroyed enemy missiles by hitting them at high speeds. This approach vaporized any chemical agents, whereas the Patriot missile permitted a higher percentage of those agents to reach the ground. Raytheon's vector of differentiation proved to be less important in this new subsegment of the market.[13]

7. *Emerging technology can change a vector of differentiation.* New technology, or sometimes continuing advances of the same technology, can reduce or eliminate a vector of differentiation as rapidly as it was created. In some cases, it can eliminate an entire market segment in the process. For example, desktop publishing systems became feasible when printshop-quality printers such as the Apple Laser Writer and publishing software such as Aldus PageMaker created a system under $10,000. This differentiation took a segment of the market away from large electronic publishing systems, since desktop publishing software enabled text and graphics to be combined.

Technology eventually enabled this capability to be included in many word processors as well as operating systems such as Windows, in turn reducing the differentiation in products such as PageMaker.

8. *A company fails to build the perception of differentiation.* Differentiated products position themselves uniquely in the minds of potential customers. Differentiating a product in fact but not in perception does not help customers see the advantages of the differentiation.

There are several causes for failure to build perception. It can happen when a company does not recognize how its customers are valuing its product. For example, when Cullinet first introduced its report writer software, it differentiated the product on flexibility. After a while, Cullinet noticed that most of its customers were using the software for auditing EDP systems. So Cullinet renamed the product EDP Auditor and charged more. Its sales took off. Cullinet succeeded in building the perception to match its differentiation. Similarly, Reebok, Nike, and others clearly built the perception of their differentiation in sport shoes, possibly even more than the actual differentiation itself.

Failure to build the perception of differentiation can also be a failure of marketing. One software company developed spreadsheet software in the early 1980s that was clearly differentiated on its virtual capacity, a major advantage to many users who were frustrated by the limited capacity of spreadsheet applications at that time. Unfortunately, the company was unable to reach the segment of the market for whom this differentiation was important, and the product was unsuccessful.

Sustainable Differentiation

Sustainability is a major consideration in selecting the vector of differentiation. If the vector is successful, a company would like to stay on that vector as long as possible and distance itself from competitors. When a vector is not sustainable, a company needs to anticipate what it will do when competition catches up.

> *Sustainability is a major consideration in selecting the vector of differentiation.*

Apple Computer ran into this problem when it was unable to sustain the differentiation of its Macintosh computers. For many years, the Macintosh was able to justify a higher price for the superior user interface that made its computers easier to operate. Apple's difference was primarily in its software, not its hardware. The Macintosh was clearly worth more than an IBM PC with a DOS operating system. Price proximity was maintained at a higher price of $500 to $750.

When Microsoft introduced Windows 3.0 for the IBM PC in May 1990, this differentiation began to diminish. Gradually, Windows became more stable and ran more application software packages that used its features. The Macintosh differentiation shrank, and maintaining price proximity meant closing the pricing gap. By June 1992, Apple's price difference was down to $200 and declining.

Obviously, Apple would have preferred to continue moving along its vector of differentiation to justify its premium price, but it could not. It had to compete more on price. Apple also found that it was spending more on R&D and not getting a competitive return for its investment. As Figure 7-9 shows, Apple was spending approximately $70 million of R&D for each percentage of market share in 1991, and Compaq was spending $60 million. However, Dell was spending only $20 million. Compaq

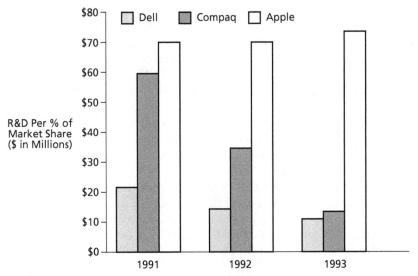

Figure 7-9 In the early 1990s, Apple had a higher development investment than its competitors, without the differentiation to justify it.

changed its strategy to compete more on price and reduced R&D spending to approximately $15 million per market share percentage. Apple was left with a much higher development investment without the differentiation to justify it.

Sustainability comes from establishing barriers to entry.

Sustainability comes from establishing barriers to entry. These delay the time it takes for competitors to catch up and erode the basis of differentiation. Barriers can be established in several ways.

Maintaining Technological Advantage

When a company can base a vector of differentiation on its technical core competencies, it can establish a competitive advantage. To copy the basis of differentiation, competitors need to catch up technically by improving their core competencies. In some cases, they pay a penalty, because they do not own the technology themselves. In other cases, they need to invest heavily to acquire the technology.

Motorola capitalized on its semiconductor technology when it differentiated its MicroTac portable telephone on size and weight. It continually pursued this vector of size and weight differentiation, introducing even better models as competitors were able to match earlier versions.

Sharp's introduction of the color LCD in its ViewCam was based on its underlying technological strength in LCDs. Many of its competitors did not have this technology, so it took some of them a little while to catch up.

Possessing or cultivating technical core competencies is important only insofar as they are applied to achieve a vector of differentiation in actual products. This is overlooked by companies that invest in technical competencies, then let them go to waste by not applying them to differentiate their products. Xerox's Palo Alto Research Center (PARC) was infamous for developing groundbreaking technology that was not capitalized on by Xerox. One notorious example was PARC's invention of the graphical user interface for computers that Steve Jobs later applied to create the Macintosh.

Using Patent Protection

When available, patent protection is the ideal sustaining vector of differentiation, because it locks out the competition. The challenge is to select the appropriate patent strategy for breadth and completeness. Patents should be as broad as possible to erect the widest barrier against competition. Many companies initiate the patent application process too late in product development, or apply for patents on detailed design elements that often do not provide sufficient protection. But patents that are too broad can also fail in court, as evidenced by Apple's unsuccessful attempt to defend the Macintosh's "look and feel" against emulation by Microsoft and HP. An outstanding example of appropriate breadth is Polaroid's patents on instant photography, which allowed it to own this significant differentiation vector.

> *When available, patent protection is the ideal sustaining vector of differentiation, because it locks out the competition.*

Completeness is also critical to full patent protection. An animal health biotechnology firm developed a new, general-purpose antibiotic for livestock. The patent specified mammalian treatment at a low dosage. Unfortunately, coverage did not extend to high-dosage applications and excluded the largest animal health market segment—poultry! Not covered by the patent, this application was in the public domain and available to any other drug company.

Rapidly Advancing the Vector

A final way to sustain a competitive advantage is to move along the vector of differentiation so fast that competitors cannot catch up. This is the implied strategy when a company does not think about how it will sustain its differentiation. For years, Sony managed to maintain high margins in the cutthroat Walkman business by staying a step ahead of copycat Japanese competitors. From the basic Walkman platform, Sony stayed ahead by continued miniaturization and by subsegmenting the market with products such as the waterproof Sports Walkman.

Earlier we used the example of SAP and its vector of differentiation based on an integrated system. The rapid slope and length of the vector gave SAP the opportunity to sustain competitive advantage by moving rapidly along it. SAP seized that opportunity and the competition couldn't catch up for more than a decade.

Notes

1. Michael F. Porter introduced this classification in his three generic competitive strategies. The application of differentiation, particularly the concept of differentiation vectors, expands on this. See Porter, *Competitive Strategy: Techniques for Analyzing Industries and Competitors* (The Free Press, 1980), and Porter, *Competitive Advantage: Creating and Sustaining Superior Performance* (The Free Press, 1985).

2. Patrick M. Reilly, "Sony's Digital Audio Format Pulls Ahead of Philip's, But Both Still Have Far to Go," *The Wall Street Journal*, August 6, 1993.

3. Gale Eisenstadt, "Unidentical Twins," *Forbes*, July 5, 1993.

4. Charles L. Leath, "40 Years of Chronicling Technical Achievement," *Hewlett-Packard Journal*, October 1989.

5. Marilyn Chase, *The Wall Street Journal*, April 29, 1993, p. 1.

6. Marilyn Chase, *The Wall Street Journal*, May 3, 1993, p. B1.

7. Stratus Computer, Inc., 1992 Annual Report.

8. Regis McKenna, "Marketing Is Everything," *Harvard Business Review*, January–February 1991.

9. "Annual Design Awards," *Business Week*, June 7, 1993.

10. James Daly, "Can PowerBook Regain Its Cutting Edge?" *Computerworld*, November 15, 1993.

11. Mark Stahlman, "The Failure of IBM," *Upside*, March 1993.

12. Nikhil Hutheesing, "Games Companies Play," *Forbes*, October 25, 1993.

13. Aaron Zitner, "Rival Haunts Patriot Missile," *The Boston Globe*, March 25, 1994.

8

Product Pricing Strategy

Too often companies ignore pricing strategy, and it shows.

Price is a competitive factor in all high-technology markets, and it is an element of strategy—whether explicit or implicit—for all high-technology products. Eventually, the success or failure of many products may depend on their pricing strategy. Yet, despite its importance, pricing strategy is often neglected in many high-technology companies. It becomes a financial computation instead of a strategic consideration. We find that marketing managers and product developers will sometimes spend only a few days— sometimes only a few hours—working on the pricing strategy for a new product. They do not estimate how customers will value the product, project how price will evolve in the market, understand how competitors will price products, or consider alternative strategies. In short, they fail to think about price strategically.

The underlying cost structure of high-technology products is also unique. Profit margins are generally high, because development costs are large, and some technology-based cost elements decrease rapidly during the product life cycle.

Appropriate price strategy varies by product, competitive pricing, and stage in the life cycle of a market. Products with distinctive vectors of differentiation can sustain a higher price. Market share leaders can introduce a lower price, because they have scale advantages, particularly in products that have high fixed-cost requirements, such as R&D or capital. Aggressive pricing by competitors such as market share leaders can force lower-than-desired pricing. Pricing strategy also changes during the life cycle of a market, typically getting more aggressive in later stages.[1]

High-technology products are more susceptible to price wars. Businesses with high fixed costs and high margins are ripe for price wars, particularly when there is excess capacity in their industry. A company needs to anticipate how competitors will react to a price reduction in order to outmaneuver them. Successful pricing strategy for high-technology products requires an understanding of customer perceptions and an anticipation of competitor strategies.

The sources for cost advantage provide the foundation to support price strategy. Without a cost advantage, a company competing on price is really just cutting its profit.

Competitors in a market have different cost structures, and eventually these differences provide a source of competitive advantage, whether price is used as an offensive or a defensive strategy. The sources for cost advantage provide the foundation to support pricing strategy. Without a cost advantage, a company competing on price is really just cutting its profit.

Since we introduced these concepts in the first edition, pricing strategy is being influenced by a new phenomenon: the Internet. Internet companies have introduced radical new pricing strategies, not only for their products and services, but also for the non–high-tech products they sell. We expect that some of these companies create entirely new pricing strategies and others may prove to be unsustainable fads. We cover the implications of these new strategies later in this chapter.

Effects of Pricing Strategy

Setting effective strategy based on price in high-technology products starts with understanding three basic underlying concepts.

1. *Price positions a product in the market.* Relative price combined with relative differentiation positions a product in the market. In Figure 8-1, product B is the price leader in the market. It also has a lower relative differentiation than the others. Products C, D, and E compete in the middle of the market; they are not competitive on price or differentiation. Product A competes on its higher differentiation and is priced the highest. The objective of offensive price-based strategies is to move a product

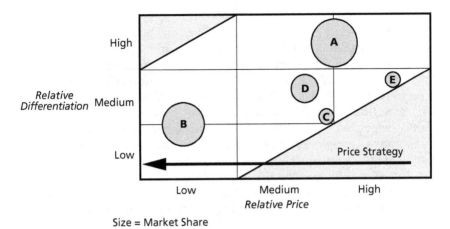

Figure 8-1 Products are positioned relative to each other on the basis of price and differentiation.

to the left of this chart, while preserving sufficient profit and increasing market share.

In today's markets, it's not that simple. The relative positioning of products actually varies by segment within the market. Each segment places its own value on the differentiation among products. For example, if product E were a multimedia PC, it would be positioned much higher on the differentiation axis for the multimedia segment of the market. And beyond segment differences, there are variations caused by differing perceptions on price and imperfect knowledge of alternatives.

2. *Prices decline throughout a market's evolution.* As the life cycle of a high-technology market evolves, competitive characteristics of the market change. As we discuss in Chapter 7, differentiation changes throughout the life cycle. Price also changes. Unit price can decline significantly during the evolution of a market, and, generally, this decline can be anticipated. Perhaps the exact timing or amount of decrease cannot be accurately projected, but the general trend can be estimated.

- *Development.* In its nascent stage, a market is still developing. Costs are initially high, and products are generally at their highest price. Differentiation is not established, and a pricing framework may not yet be set. Since the products are new, they can be value-priced according to the benefit they provide the customer. Competition has not yet set in. Everyone—customers as well as competitors—is groping to understand the price framework within this new market.

- *Growth.* In the growth stage, a new market begins to define itself. Customers select their preferences. They are better able to evaluate alternatives than in the development stage and place a higher value on some vectors of differentiation than on others. High-technology product prices generally decline during the growth stage. Competitors also begin to define how they intend to compete. Vectors of differentiation become firmly established, and price reductions are used to compensate for products with differentiation that is not valued sufficiently by customers. Competitors with weak differentiation continue to use price reductions to compensate.

    This stage provides the first signs of how pricing will be structured in the market. Competitors that expect to compete aggressively on price begin to make those strategies apparent, introducing lower-priced products to establish their position, although it may be difficult to distinguish their efforts from those of companies compensating for noncompetitive products.

    In 1993, the personal computer industry was in its growth stage, and prices had been declining rapidly for two years. The price of a Macintosh IIvx, for example, dropped almost 50 percent, from $2,595 in October 1992 to $1,369 in June 1993. During that period, the price of a Compaq DeskPro 4/25 fell almost 25 percent, from $1,742 to $1,355, and a Zenith Z-station 425Sh plunged more than 50 percent, from $3,083 to $1,419.[2]

    Price-based competitors captured almost two-thirds of the market until the more established companies reduced their prices to be more competitive. Then competitive advantage shifted. In one year, from 1992 to 1993, the top five PC vendors increased their share of the U.S. market from 36.9 percent to 48.8 percent.[3] The decline in PC prices also accelerated the growth of the U.S. market from 11.8 million PCs in 1992 to 13.8 million in 1993, with all this growth going to the top five companies.

    The decline in price continued through the 1990s and beyond. Interestingly, though, except for the low-price segment, price levels remained relatively constant while capabilities increased.

- *Maturity.* Price competition accelerates as a market moves from the growth to the maturity stage. Competitors are able to imitate the successful vectors of differentiation, and with products less differentiated, price becomes a more important competitive strategy.

    Loss of market share in the mature market stage has different implications than it does in the growth stage. In the mature stage, losing market share causes a decline in sales, not just slower growth. Competitors that have already made investments in capacity and inventory are hit with losses as sales decline. They react aggressively, usually by cutting prices. Costs are also lower in the mature stage. Initial investments in developing the product platform have been recovered. The costs of developing the market are lower. The defining technology underlying the product platform generally has matured, and the manufacturing costs have been lowered through experience and volume.

- *Decline.* Market declines are usually messy. Some competitors exit the market, but they do not go gracefully. They typically dump their excess inventory at fire-sale prices. Those companies that remain in the market usually have reduced margins. At this point, there is little to differentiate competitive products. As a result, there is little justification for a high-margin, high-price strategy.

3. *Lower prices increase market penetration.* High-technology markets tend to be very elastic; lower prices drive higher volumes. This was true for calculators, VCRs, televisions, telephones, personal computers, computer networks, application software, portable telephones, and pharmaceuticals. As prices decline, products become affordable to more customers willing to try them for the first time.

Figure 8-2 dramatically illustrates this relationship in the calculator market during the 1970s. At a price of ¥180,000 (approximately $750) in 1967, the calculator market was very small—only 63,000 units were sold. They were used in critical applications or shared among work groups. By 1976, their price declined to ¥4,800 (approximately $21), and production volume increased to more than 40 million.

However, price reductions increase volume only up to a point. When the price becomes so low that it no longer matters or when the market becomes saturated, price reductions have little or no impact on volume.

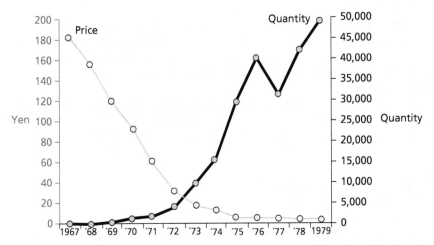

Figure 8-2   Lower price increases market penetration, as shown by the sales of calculators from 1967 to 1979.

This happened in the calculator market, where the product eventually cost less than $10 and was offered free with magazine subscriptions.

Offensive Pricing Strategies

Pricing strategies can be classified as primarily offensive or primarily defensive. The following offensive strategies are used when a company intends to use price as the principal competitive weapon.

Establish Price Leadership as the Basis for Competing

Price leadership[4] is the primary competitive strategy based on price. Customers buy the product because it is the least expensive. This strategy is particularly effective in a mature market, when the price leader can narrow the differentiation between its products and those of higher-priced competitors.

For example, in the microprocessor market, Intel competes on performance using its market standard architecture. A nonstandard (not Intel-compatible) microprocessor cannot be successful at any price, since it will not run standard software. This is the "negative differentiation" discussed in the previous chapter. A compatible microprocessor can compete very successfully, however, as a lower-priced alternative. Companies such as Advanced Micro Devices (AMD) and Cyrix Corporation grabbed 80 percent of the 386-microprocessor market in 1993 by using a price leadership strategy for a compatible product.[5]

Intel's strategy was to avoid price competition, staying ahead of its competitors by introducing more advanced products. It abandoned the 386 market in favor of the faster 486-microprocessor market. The objective of AMD and Cyrix was to take sales away from Intel, not to increase the size of the market.

One critical aspect of this strategy is that only one company can successfully execute it, since there can be only one price leader. We'll discuss price-based strategy more when we talk about risks at the end of this chapter.

Use Penetration Pricing to Increase the Market

As was seen earlier in the calculator example in Figure 8-2, lowering the price increases the size of the market. This is another price-based offensive strategy: Rapidly decrease the price to increase the size of the market. It is both a growth strategy and a competitive strategy.

In a penetration pricing strategy, price is set far below the economic value of the product to encourage more customers to purchase the product. This accelerates the natural evolution of a market. It may also take much of the profit margin out of the market, so lower profit can be a side effect of accelerating a market's evolution.

Penetration pricing is a variation of the price leadership strategy. It is similar in that it is a strategy to compete on price, but it is different in that its primary intent is not to take today's customers away from competitors. Its objective is to increase market share while growing the market. Competitors' sales may not decline. The IBM-clone manufacturers competed on price using a penetration strategy. They increased the size of the market by making personal computers more affordable to many people. Meanwhile, personal computer sales at Apple and IBM continued to increase.

In the first edition of this book, we wrote that the extreme penetration pricing strategy is to give the product away, and used the example of Computer Associates and its Simply Money and Simply Tax accounting products. Computer Associates offered the product free to customers willing to pay the $6.95 for postage and handling. The objective of its strategy was to penetrate the market to create a strong position and then use this position to generate upgrade revenue. We saw this as a unique strategy for software products when the cost of each new product was relatively low.

Since then, the trend seems to have gone even further. Some companies are giving away personal computers in return for monthly Internet access fees, although the strategy hasn't proved to be successful. One Internet company, iWon, actually pays people to use its product, an Internet portal. It gives out prizes, $10,000 each day, $1 million each month, and $10 million once a year, to get people to go to its Web site. This is an extreme example of what happens when there is no differentiation.

Eventually, a penetration strategy runs out of gas. The market becomes penetrated to the point where growth inevitably slows. A penetration strategy then shifts to a price leadership strategy, and competitors become more aggressive. Losing market share in a growing market is one thing; it's not really painful. Losing sales in a flat market is another. That's painful. It usually precipitates a price war.

Use Experience-Curve Pricing to Discourage Competition

Experience-curve pricing is a preemptive strategy. Some may even call it predatory. It's an aggressive strategy that prices products below cost in hopes of forcing those already in the market to exit, while keeping others out of the market. The key to success with this strategy is that cost benefits are achieved at a *predictable* rate. For example, unit costs can decline at 20 percent to 30 percent each time accumulated experience doubles.[6]

What do we mean by the experience curve? Almost any task increases in efficiency when performed repeatedly. People who begin jogging after not running for many years, for instance, find that their elapsed time the second time they run is faster than the first. The fourth is faster than the second, and the eighth is faster than the fourth. In fact, the percentage improvement may be the same at each of these intervals. This is the experience-curve theory.

Each time the number of repetitions doubles, the process improves by a specific percentage.

> *Experience-curve pricing is a pre-emptive strategy. Some may even call it predatory.*

The experience curve is especially important to high-technology products because of the rapid cost drop at early volume levels. Remember that improvement comes when the cumulative experience doubles, and cumulative experience comes rapidly in the early stages of a new market. The cumulative volume for personal computers doubled frequently during the first five years of the market. In comparison, for a product like light bulbs it may take 40 to 50 years before the cumulative production volume and experience doubles again.

This strategy has been successfully employed in industries such as digital watches, calculators, specialty chemicals, and semiconductors. Experience-curve pricing was a particularly popular strategy in the 1970s. For example, in 1976, when Gillette entered the market for digital watches, most observers expected that it would not be long before the big marketer would take a significant market share. But in early 1977, Gillette announced it was pulling out of the market because of "the continual erosion of the retail price structure and because the watches failed to produce the profit levels it was seeking."[7]

Several companies had preceded Gillette in dropping out of the market, and more followed. Experience-curve pricing was the reason for this shakeout. Gillette was selling its digital watches in the $40-to-$75 price range; Texas Instruments (TI) priced its watches in the $40-to-$50 range; and Litronix was the price leader with a low price of $39.95. However, TI surprised everyone by introducing a $20 watch, cutting the retail price by more than half in a dramatic bid to force others out of the market and block new entries.[8]

TI implemented an experience-curve pricing strategy. The strategy worked. Many competitors, including Gillette and Litronix, were forced out of the market. TI was beginning to achieve a cost advantage through its experience curve and projected even more reductions in the future, based on increased volume. It set its prices to make money in the future on the basis of these anticipated reductions.

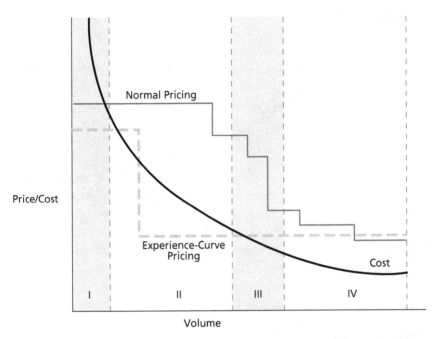

Figure 8-3   The cost curve is the same, but the pricing steps occur at different stages of a product's life cycle in the normal and experience-curve pricing models.

Figure 8-3 illustrates an experience-curve pricing strategy at work. Under the normal pricing pattern, introductory prices are held throughout most of the first two stages of the product's life cycle. This permits margins (the difference between price and cost) to increase in stage II. During stage III, a shakeout occurs, and prices decline repeatedly. By stage IV, prices become more stable, with declines less frequent.

The experience-curve pricing strategy is entirely different. The expected eventual price is implemented early in stage II, creating a loss through most of that stage. This price can then be maintained, because most competitors have been forced out of the market, which brings on the shakeout much earlier, in stage II instead of III. It may also compress stage II because of increased penetration.

Figure 8-4 illustrates the experience-curve cost advantage in the digital watch example discussed earlier. TI achieved a significant cost advantage over Gillette through experience-curve advantages. At its cumulative volume of 3 million units, TI's cost was 50 percent lower than Gillette's at 250,000 units.

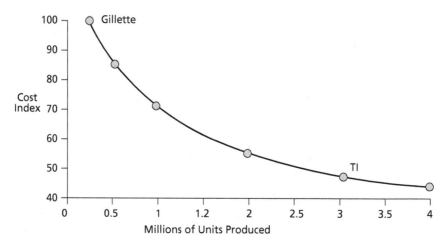

Figure 8-4   TI's position on the experience curve for digital watches gave it a cost advantage.

Compete on the Basis of Price/Performance

Price-based competitive positioning does not mean just lowest price. In high-technology products, a competitive strategy based on price/performance combines the performance vector of a differentiation strategy with a price-based strategy. The goal is to offer the lowest price for unit of performance.

Too many companies confuse three competitive strategies that are really very different. Competing on price leadership, as discussed previously, means offering the lowest price without an emphasis on performance difference, as in the low-end PC market. Performance does not matter, as long as it is sufficient. Competing on performance emphasizes performance without much regard to price. For instance, customers paid more for Cray supercomputers if they needed that level of computing performance. At that time, a customer couldn't buy several lower-priced computers to do the same job. Competing on the basis of price/performance combines elements of performance differentiation and price-based competition into a single strategy: to be the leader in price/performance. Digital Equipment used this strategy in its Alpha-based workstations. In 1993, it claimed an edge in price/performance over IBM, Hewlett-Packard, and Sun Microsystems, and it used independently audited comparisons to back up its claims. Compared with IBM's $70,000 high-end workstation, for example, Digital's system had equal performance at $36,000.[9]

This strategy usually requires some inherent cost advantage, usually in the design of the product and preferably in the defining technology. In Digital's case, it used the advanced Alpha microprocessor, which performed the same functions in a single chip that required an eight-chip set in IBM's workstations.

Use Promotional Discounting to Accelerate Purchases

Discount-based promotions are becoming more popular with high-technology products, especially higher-volume products and those sold to mass markets. The objective behind promotional discounting is to lower a product's price without diminishing its perceived value. This approach encourages people to buy now rather than defer their purchases (since the value is higher and the discount is only temporary).

Companies selling application software products use promotional discounting strategies to create incentives to accelerate initial product sales. There is another advantage also. Once customers purchase a software product, they are likely customers for regular upgrades, creating an ongoing revenue stream. Upgrades frequently have lower selling expenses and can be more profitable.

The economics of computer software make this type of pricing strategy particularly attractive. The unit cost of application software products is very low—only the material costs of disks and documentation, as well as some support costs. The original development costs are the greatest. These are amortized over the volume sold, so the higher the volume, the lower the unit cost. After-sales support is another variable cost, but, increasingly, this service is priced separately.

Following are a few examples of promotional discounting pricing strategies.

- *Competitive upgrades.* The competitive upgrade promotion is aimed at prompting customers to switch from a competitive product. For example, in 1993 Microsoft Word for Windows 6.0 sold for $320, but the price was reduced to $135 as an upgrade from either an earlier version of Word or a competitive product (WordPerfect or AmiPro). A customer needed to turn in the master disk or title page of the user manual of the older product in order to get the 58 percent discount.

  In order to gain enough market share to become competitive, Borland introduced Quattro Pro 5.0 with a competitive discount that reduced the price from $99 to $35. The workgroup version was introduced at a competitive upgrade discount, reducing the price from $495 to $99. Borland believed that strong sales from this promotion would offset lower margins and put it into second place in the market. It expected to sell 500,000 units during the five-month promotion period.

Even if competitive upgrades are discounted so deeply that there is little or no profit, the potential value of future upgrade revenue is high.

- *Bundles and packages.* Related products can also be grouped together and sold at a discounted price. The objective is to attract the customer to buy more for a slightly higher price, similar to the "buy one and get a second for $1" retail pricing strategy. It is a particularly effective strategy when the cost of the bundle or package is very low. Again, application software (combined with other software products or computer equipment) is particularly successful with this strategy because of its low unit cost.

Microsoft Office for Windows 4.0 was sold in 1993 as a bundle for $505 ($305 as a competitive upgrade). It contained four applications: Word, Excel, PowerPoint, and Mail. Purchased separately, they would have cost three times as much. Lotus SmartSuite bundled five applications for $484.

Defensive Pricing Strategies

Some pricing strategies are more appropriately categorized as defensive. They are secondary to a differentiation-based strategy, often supporting the implementation of that strategy.

Adapt Prices to Maintain Highest Competitive Price

With an adaptive pricing strategy, a company wants to maintain as high a price as possible. It is reluctant to lower its price and reduce its profit margin. Only when competitors lower their prices to the point where the company loses market share will it adapt by lowering its price. Adaptive pricing is one of the most popular defensive price strategies for high-technology products. In most cases, however, it is the default of *no* price strategy.

> *Adaptive pricing is one of the most popular defensive price strategies for high-technology products. In most cases, however, it is the default of no price strategy.*

When a company does not have any price strategy for a product and simply reacts to competitive changes in price, it follows adaptive pricing strategy.

A company following this strategy implicitly believes that more aggressive pricing is not to its advantage. Offensive pricing strategies have been discarded. IBM and Apple followed this strategy for their personal computers. They maintained higher prices—justified initially by significant vectors of differentiation—until low-price competitors captured the major share of the market. Then they adapted by lowering prices and margins.

Imagine what would have happened if IBM had pursued a penetration pricing strategy instead. It might have had a market share two to three times greater in 1992, increasing revenue by more than $10 billion. Or, even better, what if Apple had followed a penetration pricing strategy instead of a maintain-the-margin adaptive pricing strategy? The Macintosh could be the standard for personal computers, and Apple could be several times larger! Examples like these suggest that companies should pay more attention to pricing strategy. Adaptive pricing is appropriate in many cases, but it should not always be used by default.

Use Price to Segment the Market

Pricing strategy can be used to segment the market. One way is to sell a highly differentiated product at a premium price. When the differentiation is highly valued by specific segments of the market, the product will be most successful in these segments.

Computers with fault-tolerant capabilities, for example, were priced much higher than comparable computers without this capability. The higher price helped segment the market. If there were no significant price difference, then most customers would prefer fault-tolerant computers. At the higher price, fault-tolerant computers were attractive to companies with mission-critical applications, where downtime is very expensive. Airline reservation systems, bank ATM networks, and utility control systems are some of the mission-critical applications in that segment of the market.

Pricing can also be used to position products competitively in different channels of distribution. For example, drug companies charge more for prescription drugs sold through pharmacies than through health maintenance organizations (HMOs).

Use Skim Pricing to Maximize Profit

Skim pricing is intended to skim the cream off the top of the market by offering a premium-priced product that only a small portion of the customer base will pay for. It is a high-price, low-volume strategy, frequently employed by companies that can supply only a small volume of a highly differentiated product. While this is an effective strategy for prestige products, like designer clothes and fancy cars, it does not always work with high-technology products.

Apple attempted this strategy with the Lisa computer by pricing it at $10,000, twice as much as other desktop computers. The goal was to skim the market, selling as many units as Apple could produce at higher margins. The high price was justified on the basis of the Lisa's high development costs and unique differentiation.

What happened instead was that the pricing strategy segmented the market. Those who wanted a computer to prepare graphics and do presentations found the value of the Lisa worth the higher price. Others did not. Even executives who could afford the higher price for the additional ease of use didn't buy the Lisa—because it lacked compatibility with the other computers in their company—and the average user found the premium-priced Lisa too expensive.

Use Value-Based Pricing to Maximize Profit

A value-based pricing strategy is intended to maximize profit margins by setting prices at higher levels than justified by product cost alone. High-technology products typically have a high value, since they use advanced technology to solve critical problems or displace other costs.

CAT scanners, for example, provide extremely high value and were value-priced when they were introduced. Value pricing is usually possible only when there are no competitors or when a product is significantly differentiated on value. Polaroid could value-price its instant camera because there was no competition. Patents protected it. Genentech was able to value-price TPA at $2,200 per dose against $200 for streptokinase because its value was higher—it saved one more life per hundred.

Pharmaceutical companies use value pricing for prescription drugs protected by patents in order to recover the extraordinary development costs of $300 million to $400 million necessitated by the extensive and costly clinical trials. When the drug comes off patent, the value-pricing strategy changes to an

> *A value-based pricing strategy is most effective in the early stages of a market.*

adaptation strategy. This practice is frequently criticized because it's difficult for some to see the relationship between R&D costs and price. Companies tend to focus only on the relationship of manufacturing cost to price. However, without the use of value-pricing strategies in pharmaceuticals, new drug development would slow to a crawl.

A value-based pricing strategy is most effective in the early stages of a market. Once competition begins to set in, it becomes less tenable.

Redirect Product Line Sales by Bait-and-Switch Pricing

Bait-and-switch strategies are typical in sales of appliances, automobiles, and clothing, but they are not confined to these products. The approach is also used by high-technology companies, although it has not yet taken on the negative aura there that it has in other industries.

Companies that compete in markets with increasing price competition generally need to offer a low-priced product in their product line. The bait-and-switch strategy draws attention to the product line with the low price, but then tempts customers to purchase a higher-priced product with more features or capacity.

The laser printer market illustrates the bait-and-switch strategy. Increasing price competition and advancing technology drove prices from $4,000 to less than $1,000 in only a few years. To be competitive, companies needed a cheap product, but hoped to sell more fully featured products, which carried higher profit margins. Hewlett-Packard offered the LaserJet 4L, a low-cost version of its popular LaserJet 4, for $849 in 1993. The L-version printed 300 dots per inch (dpi) compared with 600, and offered no upgrade options. The $1,279 4ML model, however, offered upgradability, more memory, the ability to network, PostScript capability, and Macintosh/PC compatibility.[10]

Competitors followed a similar strategy. Texas Instrument's microWriter was priced at $729, but the $999 model included additional features. For $1,299 there was a model that had more fonts and the capabilities needed by most users. Similarly, Epson's ActionLaser 1000 was priced at $799 and had options for upgrading to higher-priced models.

Internet Pricing Strategies

The advent of the Internet era has introduced many changes, and pricing strategy is no exception. Internet-based products and services are still in the development stage, and it's too early to tell which ones will be sustainable pricing models and which may prove to be unsustainable fads.

1. *The Internet provides cost advantages for more aggressive pricing.* The Internet is a much lower-cost distribution channel than other alternatives. The cost of providing product information is lower. Centralized inventory management is generally cheaper than inventory maintained at multi-

ple retail locations. The cost of identifying availability of merchandise can be lower in some cases, and the cost of taking a customer order is less. These savings are offset to some degree by higher costs of shipping products to customers.

These cost advantages provide the basis for more aggressive lower pricing by Internet companies. The question still to be answered is: How much lower? The economic model for Internet transactions is still evolving. It's more sensitive to volume, and the predominant strategy is to focus on building volume, but it's not yet clear by how much.

2. *Many Internet companies price products and services below cost.* Most Internet companies sell products at a discount. The rationale is that they have cost advantages and can compete using a price leadership strategy. These companies also believe that volume is critical to long-term success because operating cost is volume-sensitive and because volume establishes the company's brand name.

Many companies are still trying to understand their economic model. Amazon.com's economic model looked something like this at the beginning of 2000:[11]

Revenue per customer	$160.01
Merchandise cost	$139.22
Gross margin per customer	$ 20.79
Marketing cost per customer	$ 42.68
Operating cost per customer	$ 19.83
Net loss per customer	$ 41.72

Is this a ridiculous pricing strategy? Maybe not. At a net loss per customer, Amazon obviously needs to change its economic model before it can be profitable, but here's how the process could evolve. The marketing cost per customer will decline when Amazon stops building its customer base and begins to rely on customer loyalty for repeat purchases. As we point out in earlier chapters, Amazon's strategy is to build customer loyalty by (1) making it the most convenient location to shop on the Internet, (2) selling a wide range of products to add to convenience, and (3) understanding and staying in contact with its customers. Also, by building its brand name, Amazon could become the initial location of choice for new Internet shoppers, and it won't need to spend much to acquire new customers. Much of its operating cost is volume-sensitive and will decline as volume increases. Finally, once it's

> *Generally, only one company can be successful as the price leader, and this truism is expected to carry over to e-commerce.*

comfortably established as the leader, Amazon may not need to offer such deep discounts, and it will be able to raise its prices.

Collectively, these changes lead to a profitable economic model, so Amazon may not be following such a poor pricing strategy. But remember that generally only one company can be successful as the price leader, and this truism is expected to carry over to e-commerce. Only the leader will be able to have the cost advantages to support the economics of a price leadership strategy.

3. *Some e-commerce companies have introduced creative pricing models.* The Internet has enabled several creative pricing strategies that were previously not scalable to broader markets. For example, Priceline.com introduced a "name your price" pricing model to sell cheap airfares. Airlines with excess capacity could negotiate online with subscribers. Other Internet sites enable customers to bid collectively, with all customers getting the benefit of volume discounts.

Internet companies such as eBay have popularized auction pricing. This has proved to be very popular with consumers and with some businesses, because they can become engaged in the process and, in some cases, get good deals. However, auction pricing over the Internet has done much more than provide a new competitive pricing strategy. It has created a bigger market for used products. It provides a way for the average person to resell used items to a much larger group of potential buyers than was ever possible before. It's very possible that used products could become a much larger market in the future, adding new meaning to recycling and eroding the sales of new products.

4. *Pricing strategy can become more important as the Internet automates price comparisons.* A number of Internet services provide product comparisons, including price comparisons, enabling customers to go to the Internet site selling that product at the lowest price. Now a customer can price-shop at a virtually unlimited number of locations in order to get the lowest price, without leaving his or her computer. In some cases, Internet shopping services are actually "shopping" electronically and compiling all the information for the customer.

Services like this on the Internet create an unprecedented ability for customers to price-shop and will put even more emphasis on pricing strategy and the need to manage cost.

5. *Free access to services and information is accepted on the Internet.* When it comes to service product offerings, the Internet has aggressively promoted the free access model, and it's not clear when, if ever, companies will actually make money. Early attempts to charge anything for access have generally been unsuccessful, supporting the belief that everything on the Internet should be free. Instead of revenue as a measure of success, the emphasis has been on clicks or eyeballs surveying a Web site. Some

Internet companies, like iWon, go beyond "free" and give cash prizes to customers to use their service.

Eventually, it's anticipated that these companies will be able to generate revenue through advertising or subscription fees. Certainly, television, radio, and publishing provide models, although it's not certain that the Internet will work the same way.

Risks of Offensive Pricing Strategies

Just as there are inherent risks in differentiation strategies, there are also risks in using price as the primary offensive strategy. Three major risks are described below.

1. *Price leadership may not be sustainable.* As stated previously, a market generally has room for only one price leader. Customers who are primarily influenced by price will buy from the competitor with the lowest price—and only one company can have the lowest price.

When a company embarks on price leadership as its primary competitive strategy, it's committing to maintaining the lowest price to be successful. If a competitor follows with a lower price, the company must respond by undercutting the competitor's price. Otherwise, it will not attract the segment of the market that buys because of price, and it has little else to offer (or it would compete on some other basis).

This risk is different from the risk of differentiation, since there are varied vectors of differentiation, but there is only one vector of price leadership. Competing on a vector of differentiation that is not as strong as others can still achieve limited success with customers in segments that prefer that particular vector. However, competing primarily on being the second lowest priced can be successful only if customers do not know the competitor's price or if the competitor is out of stock.

2. *Aggressive pricing could precipitate a price war.* Aggressive pricing, like price leadership, penetration pricing, experience-curve pricing, or promotional discounting, could precipitate a price war. Some companies may not be passive as others attempt to steal market share through price reductions. They may retaliate with even lower prices. When this happens, a price war erupts. Generally, all competitors lose in a price war—some just lose less than others.

Price wars were precipitated in the hard disk drive industry in 1993. The transition from the growth to the maturity stage happened quickly in this $24 billion industry. Coming off their most profitable year in the previous five, disk drive companies began slashing prices by over 30 percent (more than triple the usual rate of price decline) during the first six months of 1993.[12]

The disk drive industry at that time had many characteristics that made it ripe for a price war. Competitors rapidly expanded production to meet their individual sales growth expectations, which, in aggregate, exceeded industry demand. A slight reduction in the rate of growth triggered an exaggerated reaction, and market share shifts, common at this stage, caused a particularly acute problem for some of the Asian disk drive manufacturers. As a result, they began to sell their excess drives at bargain prices to distributors.

At the same time, technology shifts moved customer interest to higher-capacity drives. As a result, inventories of lower-capacity drives increased, precipitating fire-sale prices to move them before their value dropped even further. This scenario is reasonably typical of high-technology products during the maturity stage. Frequently, it drives industry consolidation.

> **A price leadership strategy is really a cost leadership strategy.**

3. *Aggressive pricing may not be supported by a sufficient cost advantage.* A price leadership strategy is really a cost leadership strategy.[13] A company that tries to achieve price leadership without a competitive cost advantage will make less money than its competitors. While this may be acceptable for a time—particularly if there is a price umbrella in the industry, with other competitors making "excess" profit—it's not sustainable over the long term.

For a while, this was the case in the personal computer industry. Market leaders such as IBM, Compaq, and Apple created a price umbrella for their competitors to compete on price, even though the cost structure of these competitors was higher than that of the market leaders. These low-priced competitors accepted making a lower profit. This made sense, since making a low profit was better than not being in the business at all.

Eventually, the market leaders realized that their profit margins were too large for the emerging high-volume market. When they lowered their prices to more competitive levels, they forced the low-priced competitors to accept an even lower profit; in fact, these competitors began to lose money.

Any aggressive pricing strategy, then, needs to be supported by an equally aggressive cost strategy. The company must understand its cost position relative to competitors and exploit all sources of cost advantage. Even when a cost advantage is achieved, it's not always possible to maintain it. Competitors can improve their cost advantages by copying improvements or by exploiting other sources of cost advantage. Changes in technology can also shift the sources of cost advantage. For example, the shift to standard microprocessors in the computer industry eliminated the cost advantage for companies that had their own semiconductor man-ufacturing facilities.

Sources of Cost Advantage

A price strategy, particularly an offensive strategy, must be implemented through cost management; otherwise, declining prices will simply result in declining profits. Companies pursuing an offensive price strategy must exploit all sources of cost advantage in order to be successful. Companies with a defensive price strategy need to keep costs under control. The sources of cost advantage vary by product and company, but the following are usually most important.

1. *Low-cost design can provide a competitive cost advantage.* The cost structure of a product is determined when a product specification is com-pleted. For many high-technology products, by the time the specification is completed, 80 percent to 90 percent of the product's life cycle costs are locked in, leaving only 10 percent to 20 percent of the cost to be man-aged after the product is released.

> *Traditional design approaches don't sufficiently integrate cost objectives into the design of a product.*

Traditional design approaches don't suffi-ciently integrate cost objectives into the design of a product. Traditional approaches to product design emphasize designing to a product specifi-cation that describes the product's functionality, performance characteris-tics, operating parameters, tolerances, and so on. Cost estimates are then based on the completed design, and gross margin is computed by sub-tracting this cost from the estimated price that the product can support. If the resulting margin is less than anticipated, the company must go back and redesign the product or proceed with lower margins, hoping to reduce costs in the future. Periodic future cost reductions are not planned in the initial design, and therefore are uncoupled from the process. With this approach, product cost is a consequence of product design, not a requirement.

When product cost is of strategic importance, it is better to use a design-to-cost approach, in which low cost is established as a product requirement of equal importance to other critical requirements. In the product specification step, the low-cost requirement is evaluated against other requirements. This is an iterative process. Each requirement or fea-ture has a different cost that needs to be compared against its value. The target price and cost are linked by the required gross margin, while the price that can be charged depends on the product specification. The product's design is a result of this process—unlike the traditional approach, in which product cost is a result of the design process. Also, unlike the traditional approach, future cost reductions are planned from the beginning.

A new test tube for medical applications made this trade-off in its design. The test tubes were very price-sensitive, because of budget constraints in research laboratories, but the company wanted to introduce an improved tube using advanced plastics to replace glass. The product would then be differentiated on safety, but the additional cost would result in a price that was too high. A solution was eventually found in the design by replacing the costly stopper at the end of the tube with a cheaper one. The new test tube could be sold at the same price, but it appealed to those research labs where safety was more important than the quality of the stopper.

Establishing target cost as a requirement also encourages creativity early in the design process. When Hewlett-Packard (HP) designed its DeskJet printer, 2,240 symbols representing 18 different character sets were necessary to meet the needs of international markets. Implementing the design would have required 9-bit characters and one megabyte of ROM (read-only memory), but this would have been too expensive for the market. To solve the dilemma, HP mapped the commonality among all the characters required. Next, it broke this character map into 256 elements. Finally, it developed software to reconstruct individual characters from these elements. The resulting ROM requirement was reduced to 30 K bytes.[14]

Price and the resulting cost target become primary design requirements for a product that competes on price. They can also be a helpful approach for products that use a defensive price strategy to make them less vulnerable to cost-based competitors.

2. *Superior manufacturing and economies of scale build cost advantages.* The usual source of cost advantages is, of course, manufacturing. Manufacturing cost advantages can be derived in several ways. Economies of scale are achieved through volume, particularly when there is a high fixed-cost content in the total product cost. When volume is higher, fixed costs are leveraged over many more units, reducing the cost per unit. Economies of scale are why most companies competing on the basis of price need high volumes. They cannot afford to concede this cost advantage to others with higher prices.

Highly automated manufacturing, as opposed to labor-intensive processes, is typical when there is a relatively high fixed-cost content. The manufacturing process offers other sources of cost advantage. This was demonstrated clearly by Japanese manufacturers in the 1970s and early 1980s, when they introduced JIT (just in time) and TQM (total quality management) manufacturing techniques. These techniques greatly reduced manufacturing cost while increasing quality. As a result, these manufacturers were able to compete with a strategy of lower price combined with higher quality differentiation. This proved to be a winning strategic combination, even though the assumed incompatibility of the two confused customers for a while.

This product strategy, enabled by manufacturing process advantages, became the dominant strategy. It changed the competitive balance of many industries, including automotive, consumer electronics, machine tools, and portions of the semiconductor industry.

Vertical integration can sometimes provide a manufacturing cost advantage. If a company manufactures most of its basic materials, semiconductors, or components, it gets these at a lower cost. However, vertical integration also reduces flexibility as technology changes. Internal suppliers must be competitive with external suppliers. If not, then what was a cost advantage can become a disadvantage.

Manufacturing process advantages can also come from creative changes. One of the most unusual examples of how to reduce manufacturing costs comes from Genzyme Transgenics, which is moving its manufacturing from sterile labs to livestock farms in order to reduce production costs of drugs like tissue plasma activator (t-PA). The cost savings could be substantial. Using cell cultures in a lab, scientists can get 2 to 20 milligrams of t-PA protein per liter of cell culture at a cost of $20 to $50 per liter. By contrast, goats can produce 10 to 40 grams of the proteins in a liter of milk at a cost of $.50 per liter.[15]

3. *A more efficient supply chain is a source of cost advantage.* Increasingly, high-technology companies need to look beyond manufacturing to achieve cost advantages. Other cost elements in the supply chain can frequently become a source of cost advantage. The supply chain includes the cost of materials acquisition, manufacturing, inventory, order management, distribution, invoicing, and warranty.

Gateway 2000 based its initial strategy for PCs on a low-cost structure throughout its supply chain, beginning with its location at the intersection of Iowa, Nebraska, and South Dakota, and extending to its mail-order distribution. Gateway's product strategy was clear: low-cost, no-frills computers sold through mail order. Its cost structure was one of the lowest in the industry. These combined to enable Gateway to grow to $1.1 billion in 1992 and maintain a 10 percent profit while being a low-cost provider.[16]

Dell followed Gateway and then became the leader in using the Internet to sell computers directly to customers, achieving an even lower cost structure than mail order. Dell went on to enable customers to customize their computer purchases over the Internet, building computers to their specifications in 24 hours. Dell achieved several important supply chain cost advantages. By selling computers directly, it eliminated the margin that would otherwise have to be paid to dealers. By taking orders over the Internet, it reduced order-processing costs and also used fewer mail-order catalogs. By building computers to customer order and then shipping them immediately, Dell reduced its inventory and related costs dramatically. Overall, by having the most efficient supply chain, Dell was able to become the lowest-cost competitor and therefore could compete aggressively on price.

Leading communications companies such as Cisco and Wellfleet Communications have kept pace with an explosive market by managing, but not owning, their complete supply chain. As a result, they can insulate themselves from viciously rapid technology advances and simultaneously gain a substantial cost advantage over their competition. This innovative approach of not physically touching the product at any time in its sourcing, building, or distribution enabled Wellfleet to claim the distinction of being the fastest-growing company in America for both 1992 and 1993.

4. *Superior technology can provide product cost advantages.* Technology can also be a source of cost advantage. In the case of a critical technology, it's an advantage not easily met by competitors. Motorola's PowerPC microprocessor, for example, used RISC (reduced instruction set computing) technology, giving it an advantage over the competitive Pentium microprocessor from Intel. RISC technology enabled Motorola to pack more processing power into fewer transistors, resulting in a computer chip half the size (120 square millimeters versus 262). Motorola could manufacture twice as many microprocessors in the same time and space as Intel, giving it a major cost advantage with a microprocessor of equal processing power. Motorola could initially sell the PowerPC 601 at $450, compared with the Intel Pentium at $965.

Cost advantages through technology are typically used as a defensive price strategy. Technology leaders usually are not low-cost competitors, since they invest heavily in technology and product development to position their product via a differentiation strategy. They make it very expensive for a competitor to copy their differentiation.

Price/performance advantages (which are a hybrid of price and differentiation strategies) are almost always achieved through technology. Digital Equipment's strategy of price/performance leadership with its Alpha workstations was based on the unique technology of its Alpha microprocessor.

Technology can also be a source of cost

> *Price/performance advantages... are almost always achieved through technology.*

advantage within a particular market segment. For example, Motorola used its microelectronics technology to introduce lightweight portable cellular telephones, thus creating a new market segment. Because competitors didn't have the same technology, Motorola enjoyed the advantage of having the lowest cost in the lightweight telephone segment for some time. Its lead was so significant that permission was delayed for Motorola to sell into the Japanese market in order to give Japanese competition time to catch up.

5. *A superior development process can provide product cost advantages.* Development can be one of the biggest cost elements in high-technology products. In some products, such as computer software and pharmaceuticals, the allocated development cost per unit exceeds the cost of goods sold. In many other products, the allocated cost per unit may exceed other controllable costs, such as labor and overhead.

Many companies have discovered that product development productivity can be considerably improved, and the resulting cost differences can be impressive. In working with more than 350 companies to improve product development, PRTM has found a 30 percent average improvement in development productivity (with an associated 40 percent to 60 percent reduction in development time). This improvement came from several sources. Improving time to market reduced new product development cost, since most development costs are based on run rate. Developing a product in one year instead of two required fewer worker-years of development resources. Another source of improvement was a reduction in wasted development. In 1992, electronic systems companies wasted an average 18 percent of their development on products that never came to market. Individual performance, however, ranged from 3.5 percent for the best-in-class companies to 40 percent or more for others.[17]

The amount of R&D investment can also provide a source of cost advantage. Gateway 2000, for example, supports its low-cost, low-price strategy by investing almost nothing in R&D. Compare this with Apple Computer, which at the same time invested 8.5 percent of sales in R&D. As long as Apple was able to sustain a significant vector of differentiation, the additional cost was worthwhile; however, when the Macintosh lost its differentiation, high R&D spending became a cost disadvantage. If Apple's investments had paid off by creating new products, it would not have been a problem.

6. *Cost advantages can come from global scale.* In the 1990s, large multinational companies achieved a new form of scale advantage as they integrated far-flung operations into a tightly integrated and flexible process. By doing so, they were able to increase this leverage due to their size, while simultaneously improving their flexibility.

This new scale advantage comes from increased integration both across and within all functions. When companies globalize their product development process, they are able to offer a single product to all world markets at the same time, while designing the flexibility to manufacture it wherever the cost is the lowest. They attain a significant cost advantage by leveraging development and lowering manufacturing cost.

The globally integrated company may supply its component plants with raw materials from a single source; standardize its manufacturing process in British, Taiwanese, and American final assembly plants; and enter customer orders into a worldwide order fulfillment system. Products can be assembled in and distributed from the most convenient sites. The globally integrated company can link all product developers, demand analysts, and production planners from all facilities through a worldwide network to coordinate and balance all activities.

Those large companies that successfully link their global resources are evolving into stronger, more responsive operations, better able to cut costs and serve a worldwide customer base. This new manufacturing scale advantage will provide a source of cost advantage that cannot be achieved by smaller, single-country competitors.[18]

Pricing Strategy in Action:
Compaq Computer

As discussed in the previous chapter, to be successful, a product differentiation strategy has to maintain prices in reasonable proximity to the prices of competitors' products, primarily with an offensive pricing strategy. Reasonable proximity equals the value of the differentiation. When this reasonable proximity is reduced—as is often the case in maturing markets—even companies with previously differentiated products need to shift their product

> *To be successful, a product differentiation strategy has to maintain prices in reasonable proximity to the prices of competitors' products.*

strategy toward more competitive pricing. Compaq Computer's 1992 shift in product strategy is a case in point.

Compaq Computer was founded in 1981 to develop and market a portable personal computer. The portable IBM-compatible computer was successfully differentiated by its smaller size, which enabled it to be carried from place to place. Compaq's revenues reached $100 million in its first year.

Later, Compaq offered desktop systems as well. Its product strategy shifted to differentiation on higher performance, using its ability to quickly develop products with leading-edge technology. In September 1986, Compaq got a jump on competitors by releasing the industry's first 80386 personal computer, beating IBM to market by several months. Compaq also developed some unique components and worked closely with key suppliers, such as Conner Peripherals, to introduce smaller form-factor disk drives. As a result of this strategy, revenue increased in 1988 by 69 percent to $2 billion, followed by a 40 percent increase in 1989.

In 1989, Compaq was a $2.9 billion company that competed on high performance and leading-edge technology and followed a skimming price strategy. Michael Swavely, president of North American operations, said, "We never positioned ourselves based on price. We sell a better product, not a cheaper product."[19] All this began to change in 1990. Penetration price strategy by clone competitors such as AST, Dell, and Northgate drove personal computer prices lower and lower as the market grew rapidly. The price difference between Compaq's PCs and low-priced clones exceeded 30 percent at a time when these lower-priced products were catching up in technology and performance. Revenue and profits were rising at these price leaders, but Compaq was beginning to have problems. It lost proximity with its differentiation. The differentiation that Compaq offered was not worth a 30 percent higher price to many PC customers. By mid-1991, Compaq lost market share, and its revenue began to drop. It had its first-ever loss and laid off 1,700 employees.

To some extent, Compaq's faulty product strategy was based on IBM's. It positioned its products primarily against IBM's, ignoring other competitors. Compaq's PCs were more innovative than IBM's and were sold at the same price. Together, they created a price umbrella in which lower-priced PCs flourished.

In October 1991, the Compaq board of directors decided that a low-price product strategy was required, despite recommendations by CEO and cofounder Rod Canion to continue a differentiation-based strategy. They ousted Canion and made Eckhard Pfeiffer the new CEO. The next day, Pfeiffer launched new efforts to develop lower-priced PCs. He believed a *new* PC design was needed, not just incremental improvement. He said it was needed because it was "far more difficult for a design engineer to achieve a 10% cost reduction than a 40% or 50% reduction, because no matter how hard you look at a problem, doing things the way they have always been done blocks your view of doing something fundamentally different."[20] Compaq's new product strategy was to close the price gap in order to compete directly with lower-priced competitors. Pfeiffer supported this strategy with initiatives to shorten product development cycle times and reduce manufacturing, materials, and overhead costs.

In the summer of 1992, Compaq launched its ProLinea line of cut-rate PCs, and in less than a year these new lower-priced PCs closed the gap in price to less than 15 percent—within a reasonable proximity. Sales in the third quarter of 1992 jumped 50 percent to more than $1 billion. Compaq's share of the U.S. PC market increased from 3.5 percent to 5.1 percent.

A lower-priced product strategy requires a lower cost structure. This means lower development costs, lower materials costs, lower manufacturing costs, and a lower profit margin. Compaq's low-priced ProLinea PCs and Contura notebooks had fewer features. Compaq reduced component and material costs by forcing suppliers to compete more aggressively. Manufacturing was streamlined, and capacity utilization was increased. Higher volumes offset lower profit margins.

Pfeiffer believed that winning at a price leadership strategy would depend on manufacturing efficiencies and economies of scale: "Only the most efficient manufacturers will be able to continue ongoing price reduction while achieving acceptable profitability. As we move into volume production, cost for every process comes down significantly." In 1993, as volume doubled from 1.5 million to 3 million computers, total manufacturing costs fell by almost $10 million.[21]

In implementing its new price-based strategy, Compaq changed the way it considered pricing in the design of its products. It identified price as a key to customer satisfaction. Compaq cut its prices dramatically in 1991 and 1992. As in many companies, the product price had previously been determined by computing cost after the product was designed and then multiplying that to achieve the appropriate profit margin. With the new emphasis on price in its product strategy, Compaq used price as the starting point instead of the ending point. Product development engineers started with the target selling price and then computed the cost budget they had to work with.

Compaq's new product strategy was to challenge competitors on price and then up the ante with more features, a broader product line, and better services, such as a three-year warranty. In March 1993, Compaq initiated another price cut, forcing IBM and Dell to follow. Compaq had reduced its cost structure below that of IBM and even Dell, so it had more profit margin to play with. At the same time, Compaq initiated direct-response selling for the first time, getting into a new, low-cost channel of distribution.

Compaq's shift to a price-based offensive strategy was very appropriate for that stage of the PC market. With this strategy, in 1993 Compaq went from being a company in trouble to the most successful PC company. Revenues grew to more than $6.5 billion, and it captured 10 percent of the market.

Unfortunately, Compaq fell prey to one of the risks of a price-based strategy. It was unable to sustain its cost advantage. One of its primary competitors, Dell, was able to achieve comparable cost savings in all areas, but then continued to achieve the dramatic cost advantages in its supply chain that we describe earlier.

Compaq was unable to react. Dealers were critical about its distribution, and it couldn't shift channels abruptly without massive losses in revenue. Dell beat out Compaq as the market share leader. Compaq's growth faltered and it replaced its CEO again. Frequently, lessons in product strategy can be very expensive to learn.

Notes

1. For a comprehensive review of pricing see Thomas T. Nagle, *The Strategy and Tactics of Pricing* (Prentice-Hall, 1987).

2. William J. Cook, "Computer Chaos," *U.S. News & World Report*, July 26, 1993.

3. Jim Carlton, "Popularity of Some Computers Means Buyers Must Wait," *The Wall Street Journal*, October 21, 1993.

4. "Price leadership" is sometimes used to describe the product in a market that establishes the price structure. While frequently this is also the lowest-priced product, it is not necessarily so. Here, "price leadership" means the lowest-priced complete product.

5. Catherine Arnst and Peter Burows, "Showdown in Silicon Valley," *Business Week*, November 1, 1993.

6. Bruce D. Henderson, *Henderson on Corporate Strategy* (Abt Books, 1979), p. 106.

7. "Why Gillette Stopped Its Digital Watches," *Business Week*, January 31, 1977, pp. 37–38.

8. "Litronix Cuts Out of Consumer Products," *Business Week*, February 28, 1977, pp. 32–33.

9. *The Wall Street Journal*, October 12, 1993.

10. Phillip Robinson, "Falling Laser-Printer Prices Can Put Them in Schools and Home Offices," *The Boston Globe*, July 27, 1993.

11. Eric Schonfeld, "How Much Are Your Eyeballs Worth?" *Fortune*, February 21, 2000.

12. Robert D. Hof, "Blood on the Tracks," *Business Week*, July 12, 1993.

13. In fact, Michael E. Porter refers to this strategy as a cost leadership strategy. See *Competitive Strategy: Techniques for Analyzing Industries and Competitors* (The Free Press, 1990). "Price strategy" is used here to emphasize that there can be a difference, but that there is a risk in not linking price and cost.

14. Donna J. May et al., "Data to Dots in the HP DeskJet Printer," *Hewlett-Packard Journal*, October 1988.

15. Ronald Rosenberg, "Down on the Farm," *The Boston Globe*, July 20, 1993.

16. Jim Impoco, "Milking the Market," *U.S. News & World Report*, July 26, 1993.

17. Pittiglio Rabin Todd & McGrath, *Product Development Benchmarking*, 1993.

18. For more information, see Michael E. McGrath and Richard W. Hoole, "Manufacturing's New Economies of Scale," *Harvard Business Review*, May–June 1992.

19. Rick Whiting, *Electronic Business*, October 30, 1989.

20. Eckhard Pfeiffer, "The Compaq Turnaround," *Audacity*, Spring 1993.

21. Stephanie Losee, "How Compaq Keeps the Magic Going," *Fortune*, February 21, 1994.

9

Taking Advantage of First-to-Market and Fast-Follower Strategies

Being the first to market can form the basis for competitive strategy, as can being a fast follower. Overall, being fast has tremendous competitive advantages.

Time is becoming an increasingly important competitive factor in product strategy, particularly in high-technology fields where the underlying technology advances rapidly and the markets change quickly. Companies using speed to get a jump on their competitors can also achieve advantages to help them stay ahead. Being first, however, does not guarantee success. Companies that move prematurely can stumble and fall, enabling competitors to walk over them on the way to success.

A timing advantage has to be paired with a primary competitive strategy of differentiation or price leadership, enabling a company to be the first to market with the chosen differentiation or price advantage. Without a primary strategy, a company is merely first with something that others will soon copy.

Two different types of time-based advantages are frequently confused. One is derived from being first to create a *new* market; the other comes from being the *fastest* to market. Being first is the usual focus of time-based competitive strategy. It is a glamorous strategy. Many of the legendary successes, such as Xerox, Polaroid, Kodak, DuPont, and Corning, were first to create a market. The first company to introduce a new technology that creates a new market is hailed as the innovator.

> ***Slow- or late-reacting companies are less competitive. They are followers not by intention, but because they don't have the core competencies to be leaders.***

Of course, not everyone will be the leader. But it's important to distinguish between intentionally being a follower and simply being late or slow. Slow- or late-reacting companies are less competitive. They are followers not by intention, but because they don't have the core competencies to be leaders. The term *fast follower* is used in this chapter to emphasize the difference between the slow company and the company that waits, poised to jump into a market when the timing is right.

If a company is slow, no competitive strategy can overcome this disadvantage, short of a dramatic innovation that is protected by patents. Any early successes usually will be matched and then improved on by a faster competitor. A company with a time-based disadvantage can be successful only if its competitors don't use a time-based strategy against it.

The primary concepts of time-based strategy come from understanding the two competitive advantages it provides. Though related, they are very different, and the difference is frequently overlooked in a company's haste to move quickly. In some cases, this leads a company to select the wrong strategy.

Advantages of Being First to Market

Surprisingly, a company can be first to market even though it is slower than competitors. It just needs to start sooner. Even if its development process takes longer, it can achieve the first-to-market advantage by identifying opportunities before its competitors. Beating the competition by being first to market has several advantages.

1. *The first-to-market company can capture a market share advantage.* Whether introducing a new product platform, a more advanced product, or a new feature, the first company to market can capture additional mar-

ket share simply by being first. Customers cannot buy a similar product from anyone else, so there is no competition. The first company to market has a temporary monopoly.

In addition to a stronger initial position in the market, there are other advantages. A company's reputation can be enhanced by being seen as more innovative. With enough of an advantage, a company can preempt competitors or establish barriers to entry. Competitors may see a follower strategy as less attractive, since someone has already established an advantage in the market.

In 1977, Larry Ellison cofounded Oracle Systems to develop relational database software. His inspiration came from reading an IBM research paper that described the concept of a relational database. Ironically, Oracle beat IBM to market by three years. It then modified its product to run on computers from a number of other manufacturers. By 1993, Oracle's revenue rose to more than $1.5 billion, and it had 34 percent of the market, compared with IBM's 26 percent.[1]

When Sega introduced its Genesis 16-bit video game player in 1993, ahead of market leader Nintendo, Sega was able to increase its market share from 7 percent to 50 percent after a slow reception because the game player was overpriced. Nintendo eventually came out with a 16-bit player, but because Sega was first with the new technology, it displaced Nintendo. Nintendo said that its goal was "to be best, not first." Bing Gordon of Electronic Arts believed this strategy was a mistake for Nintendo. "In technology the trick is to get in there first. Don't get killed, don't overinvest, learn quickly, and come out with a new generation of technology."[2]

First-to-market advantages can be particularly successful when a company targets niche markets. Raychem Corporation, for example, makes sophisticated materials, such as irradiated plastics and specialty connectors. Its chairman, Paul Cook, estimated that the company introduced 200,000 products in its first 25 years. Raychem's idea of a great product was one with a 90 percent operating margin and a 100 percent market share in a $10 million niche.[3]

2. *The first-to-market company gets earlier experience.* Being first enables a company to get earlier experience with customers, technology, suppliers, and channels of distribution. The company can then use this experience to refine the product to stay ahead of competition.

There is nothing like having an actual product in customers' hands to help a company understand what its customers really want. Being first to market provides the opportunity to get this experience before competitors. Competitors can get much of the information by interviewing customers, working with the same suppliers, or doing research. The information they get is usually not as accurate or detailed, but it is a lot cheaper. But surprisingly, some companies fail to follow up a first-to-market strategy with a process to capture this information. Their competitors study it more thoroughly and actually learn more.

The company that first develops a product based on new technology has a head start in refining the technology and its application to the product. Xerox (Haloid at the time) introduced its first commercial xerographic copier in 1949. At first the product was not very successful, and most customers returned it because it was too complicated and took several minutes to make a copy. The copier's only successful application was in making paper masters for offset printing.

Competitors such as 3M, American Photocopy, and Kodak followed Xerox into the market over the next three years. They were unsuccessful also. But Xerox kept refining and improving its product, and finally released the Xerox 914 in 1959. The 914 proved to be the successful product that launched Xerox. It was easy to use and made excellent copies for $.05 each. Xerox used its early experience to understand the market better and refine the technology. Competitors such as 3M and Kodak were not able to catch up.

The same advantage of early experience can be gained with channels of distribution, manufacturing processes, and suppliers. The key in all of these advantages is *applying* the early experience. The experience itself does not constitute the advantage.

3. *The first-to-market company can influence the definition of standards.* The first to market has a better opportunity to influence product standards. Informally, customers may make the first product to market the de facto standard. For example, in 1956 IBM introduced FORTRAN, one of the first high-level computer languages for machine-independent programming using mathematical notation. This language became widely accepted as the standard for early mathematical and scientific programming.

In fact, standards groups may use the first product to shape the approved standard. Being first does not necessarily confer control of standards, but it does give an advantage. Being first has a downside, however; it can reduce flexibility when it is time to change, since the first to market has already committed to a particular approach.[4]

Using its Betamax format, Sony had first-to-market advantages with an 18-month head start in the home VCR market. Competitors JVC and Matsushita followed, but they introduced a different and incompatible format: VHS. Betamax offered superior picture and audio quality, while VHS was less expensive and had a longer recording time. The longer recording time turned out to be the vector of differentiation preferred, and Sony lost the battle even though it was first to market.

The VHS-based competitors had more time to understand the market before they finalized their designs. When VCR technology was introduced, nobody was sure whether customers would use it for viewing prerecorded tapes, recording TV programs, or watching home movies. As customers showed a preference for recording TV programs, playing time became a more important vector of differentiation than quality.

Advantages of Being the Fastest

A company that is faster than its competition can be first to market even if it starts later. A last-to-start, first-to-finish strategy can be very effective. In most cases, the advantages of being the fastest are greater than those of being the first.

1. *The fast product developer is nearer in time to the eventual market.* There is an often overlooked advantage of faster time to market: The ability to predict what will be important in a market diminishes with the length of the prediction period. That is, the further ahead of time product development starts, the more difficult the prediction, since the evolution of

> *In most cases, the advantages of being the fastest are greater than those of being the first.*

technology affects product differentiation, and customer expectations change. New competitive products change relative advantage, and competitive prices also change over time.

When a company starts developing a new product, it must predict what the market conditions will be at the time the product will be released. It forecasts market size and price levels. It anticipates competitive products that will be on the market. It estimates the vectors of differentiation that will be preferred by customers. It predicts the impact of technology—its own and that of competitors.

These predictions are easier for a company with a faster product development process, since it doesn't need to forecast as far into the future. In Figure 9-1, the curve shows how accuracy declines over time. As with most predictions, such as the weather, accuracy drops at a faster rate as the length of the prediction period increases.

Two companies, A and B, are both bringing new products to market at the same time, but A's time to market (TTM) is only 18 months, while B's

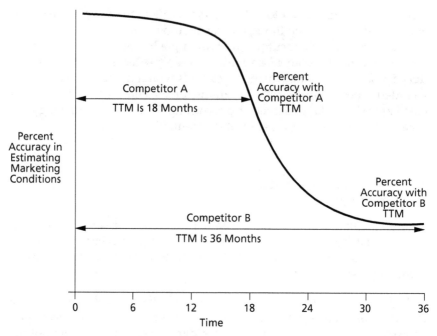

Figure 9-1   The accuracy of predicting the eventual market for a product declines over time.

is 36 months. When B started development, it needed to predict market conditions 36 months into the future. Company A started development 18 months later and had to predict only 18 months into the future. Company A will probably be more accurate.

2. *The fast product developer can get ahead and stay ahead.* By continuously staying ahead of its competitors, a company can eventually drive them out of the market. The source of this advantage is the speed of the product development process.

In Figure 9-2, assume that competitor A has a 33 percent advantage in TTM because of its superior product development process, and assume both companies start development of a first-generation product at the same time. Company A's TTM advantage enables it to bring its product to market a year ahead of competitor B. Then it starts developing the second generation.

Competitor A releases its second-generation product while Competitor B's product is still early in the life cycle of its first generation. Competitor B is forced to bring out its second-generation product prematurely. Competitor A introduces its third-generation product at the same time. In

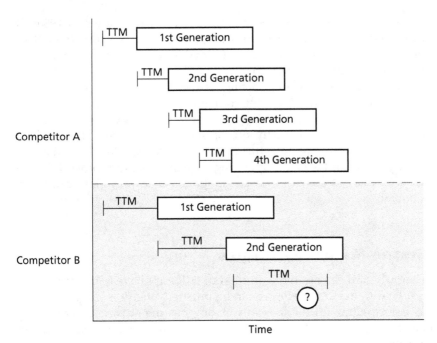

Figure 9-2   Faster product development can allow a company not only to get ahead, but to stay ahead.

order to be competitive, B starts development of its own third-generation product. Even before it is finished, competitor A introduces its fourth-generation product. End of competition. B withdraws from the market.

3. *The fast product developer can use newer technology.*   When a company has a shorter development cycle, it can incorporate more advanced technology into its products. Assume that competitor A has an 18-month time to market and competitor B has a 36-month time to market. If both companies introduced competitive products in 2001, then competitor A could use technology available in mid-1999 to design its products, while competitor B would still be using 1998 technology.

The advantages of incorporating new technology can vary from none to critical, depending on the differences in the technology used in the two products. In practice, if there is a major technology advantage, the slower competitor would cancel its product before completion and go back to redesign a more advanced version. However, it might not know if its disadvantage was the result of starting later than its competitor or having a longer time to market. If the company started later, it might be able to catch up, but if it had a longer time to market, it would have no chance.

Sun Microsystems achieved this time advantage in the mid-1980s. It introduced new product platforms every two or three years, more than doubling performance each time. Its major competitor, Apollo, introduced new platforms every four or five years. Eventually, Apollo was unable to keep up with Sun's technology advantage. The two companies followed different development strategies that enabled the differences in development cycles. Sun designed its products, including its UNIX operating system, with many off-the-shelf components. This strategy made its design and manufacturing very flexible. Apollo followed a proprietary strategy. Its Aegis operating system was more powerful than that of UNIX, but this also caused Apollo to be slower to introduce new technology.

First-to-Market Strategies

"The early bird catches the worm"—but it doesn't have to be the swiftest bird. First-to-market strategies can be pursued even if a company is not the fastest, although the fastest company has the advantage of waiting longer before it acts. There are four specific variations of first-to-market strategies.

Be the First to Upgrade Products with New Technology

First to upgrade is almost always a winning strategy when the market is well understood and the new technology is desired by many customers. The product incorporating the new technology will have a clear differentiation advantage over competing products.

Compaq executed this strategy in September 1986 when it got a jump on IBM by using the faster Intel 386 microprocessor. Compaq's market share increased dramatically as it took sales away from IBM and other competitors that were still using 286 technology. The strategy was clear in this case. There was no confusion about new standards or unproven features. It was a matter of offering

The first to market with the new technology wins, but how much it wins depends on how long it takes everyone else to catch up.

better performance for a higher price in a market that not only expected but eagerly anticipated continued performance improvements.

The first to market with the new technology wins, but how much it wins depends on how long it takes everyone else to catch up. Eli Lilly was first to market with a new technology applied to antidepressant drugs in January 1988. Prozac captured a significant share of the market, and revenues grew to $1.2 billion by 1993. Prozac, which enhances the action of serotonin, a chemical transmitter of messages between nerve cells and the brain, had the market to itself for nearly four years. Pfizer introduced Zoloft in 1992 and SmithKline Beecham introduced Paxil at the beginning of 1993. For these four years, Prozac competed only with older drugs that sold for pennies compared with the $1.75 per pill that Prozac was able to command. In addition, its early presence in the market gave it a significant lead over the other two drugs. In 1993, Prozac's sales were almost twice those of Zoloft and Paxil combined.[5]

First to upgrade can also be a risky strategy if the market is not well understood, and the new technology is not clearly anticipated by customers. For example, Philips was the first to market with a new multimedia technology called CD-i, which provided an interactive compact disk for use in entertainment, education, publishing, and training. Philips invested an estimated $1 billion in developing the technology platform, along with the related products and software.[6] To be successful with this new technology, Philips needed to establish it as a standard, either by achieving a significant market penetration on its own or by licensing it to others. This was a high-potential, high-risk strategy for Philips. In the first two years, it sold approximately 300,000 units using the new technology, too few to declare it a success at that time.

Respond Rapidly to Market Changes

When there is an important change in the market, the competitor that responds first can gain a major advantage. The change could be a shift in customer preference to a specific vector of differentiation; it could be mandated by law, such as the phase-out of CFCs; or it could be a result of the natural evolution of the market. In any case, those companies that respond rapidly can capture the advantage. Those that respond slowly may be left behind.

For example, when Microsoft introduced Windows 3.0 to the applications software market in 1990, it became the operating system preferred by most PC users. Some software companies moved quickly and converted their applications to the Windows operating system. Obviously, Microsoft was one of them, but so was Intuit with its Quicken financial software. The companies that responded quickly achieved competitive advantage as Windows-based applications became greatly preferred over DOS-based applications. Others, such as Lotus and WordPerfect, suffered by being slow to respond.

Introduce Continual Product Innovation

With a stream of small improvements, a company tries to get ahead of its competitors along a vector of differentiation, and then jump out ahead again as soon as they react. It places competitors in the position of continually reacting and playing catch-up, and eventually it can accumulate a decisive advantage.

Mitsubishi followed this strategy in residential air conditioners, a market that had been led by an American company.[7] In 1980, Mitsubishi introduced a product using integrated circuits to control the heat-pump cycle, increasing energy efficiency. The following year it modified the product with two improvements that enabled simpler installation, thereby bypassing HVAC dealers in the distribution channel. These modifications were quick-connect freon lines and use of a microprocessor to simplify wiring. In 1982, Mitsubishi introduced a new version with a high-efficiency rotary compressor and modified electronics that further increased energy efficiency. Electronic cycle control was improved in 1983 by adding sensors, and energy efficiency was increased still more.

The next step in increasing energy efficiency was to include an inverter in 1984 to manage the electric motor speed over a wide range of variability. In 1985, Mitsubishi introduced shape-memory alloys to automatically adjust to the most efficient circulation pattern. It upgraded its air conditioners with optic sensors to adjust for day and night conditions, and introduced a remote control. Learning circuitry was added in 1988, adapting each product to local environmental conditions and initiating defrosting. In 1989, electronic air purifiers were added as an option.

A slower American competitor only began to introduce electronics in 1986. It didn't have a chance. It was years behind Mitsubishi, and could not possibly catch up. It conceded defeat and started to source its advanced air conditioners, heat pumps, and components from Mitsubishi and other Japanese companies.

Mitsubishi's strategy incorporated frequent small improvements, instead of putting them all together into a single release of a new product. This can be a successful strategy, but it must be clearly established as the product strategy at the outset.

Be the First to Create a New Market

The innovative company that creates a new market can achieve significant first-to-market advantages. Alexander Graham Bell invented the telephone in 1875, and his company grew until it constituted a regulated monopoly. Xerox created the market for plain-paper copying with its application of xerography and, as a result, built a very successful business. Sony created the Walkman market and used first-to-market advantages to continue to lead this new market. Intel created the market for the microprocessor and continued to stay ahead of competitors.

Creating a new market often involves pioneering technology. Pioneering technology is usually buggy at the beginning of

> *Creating a new market often involves pioneering technology.*

the technology life cycle and improves greatly during its early stages. The first company to focus on a new technology also has the lead in improving that technology.

If a company creates a market, then by definition, it is the first to market; however, to be successful it needs to consistently build upon its first-to-market advantages. Corning, for example, made fiber optics feasible with its technology breakthrough in 1970. Corning scientists Robert Maurer, Donald Keck, and Peter Schultz developed an optical fiber that retained more than 1 percent of the light transmitted per kilometer. Optical fiber was first installed commercially in 1976, and since then, Corning has continued to improve this technology. It made an early long-term commitment to invest in the manufacturing processes necessary to mass-produce high-quality fiber. Corning continued to improve fiber-optic technology, reducing the transmission loss by nearly 100 times. After more than 20 years of consistently improving this technology, Corning was poised to take advantage of it as the basis for the communication highways of the future.[8]

A company has the opportunity to create a new market when it has new technology or sees a new market evolving. It can either choose to wait by putting the technology on the shelf for future rapid deployment or introduce the technology immediately. A market leader will decide to delay for one of two reasons. First, the company may not want to cannibalize its existing products until the last possible moment, waiting until competitive moves force it to deploy the new technology. Second, it may want to let other companies enter the unknown market first, observe their shortcomings, then introduce a better product. To be successful with this method, the company must have an excellent sense of the market and its competitors, so it can pounce as soon as market conditions are appropriate.

For example, IBM actually developed reduced instruction set computing (RISC) but did not want to immediately cannibalize its existing complex instruction set computing (CISC) product lines, so it delayed bringing out competitive workstation products and using RISC. It also delayed introducing RISC technology in microprocessors until the PowerPC in 1994.

Fast-Follower Strategies

Selecting the strategy of creating a new market is possible only if a company has the opportunity. It can then decide to act on the opportunity and be first to market, or wait until others act first and then implement a fast-follower strategy.

Being a fast follower is not the same as being slow. Fast-follower strategies can be very successful, particularly for companies with TTM advantages. The objective is to wait until the market is sufficiently clear before entering. There are two primary fast-follower strategies.

Wait Until a New Market Is Clarified

New markets are exciting. They have few competitors and offer the possibility of rapid growth. It's not clear how they will be structured, how customers will use the new products, or what competitive factors will be most important.

Fast-follower strategies can be particularly successful in new markets created by advances in technology, since nobody really knows how customers will eventually use the product or what they will prefer. The first company to market may fail because it guesses wrong about what the market wants. Others standing on the sidelines can watch and then move into the market when it is clearer.

For example, when microwave ovens were introduced, early manufacturers such as Litton saw them as a replacement for the conventional kitchen stove. The idea did not sell well. When microwaves were repositioned as a secondary method of cooking and their size was reduced, however, the success was enormous. Unfortunately, it was the later entrants, Japanese and Korean companies, that benefited from Litton's experience.[9]

New markets, particularly high-technology markets, must be educated. This is an expensive process, and its costs are usually borne by the first company to market. Competitors who cannot or do not want to educate initial customers will let someone else do it first.

Competitors who cannot or do not want to educate initial customers will let someone else do it first.

For instance, in the market for online home data services, competitors let Prodigy Services (a joint venture of IBM and Sears) educate the market. Prodigy aggressively went after the home market in 1984, and by 1993 it had 2 million users, but it also had cumulative losses of about $1 billion and was still not making money.[10] Prodigy needed to educate early customers in this mass market about why they needed the service and how to use it, a task requiring substantial investment for advertising and support. Many early customers didn't even know why they needed a modem to connect their computer to the telephone line. Competitors let Prodigy make this early investment in developing the market, and then entered the market when customers were better educated.

Market segmentation, pricing, and the vectors of differentiation valued by customers are also unknown in a new market. To return to the Prodigy example, competitors CompuServe and America Online positioned themselves in more profitable segments of the market and fine-tuned their pricing. CompuServe focused on business users and charged a premium for must-have data. America Online focused on home users. Both were profitable in 1993, while Prodigy continued to lose money.

Sometimes a fast follower can actually develop a product and put it on the shelf until the timing is right. One communications company did this by developing an ISDN (integrated services digital network) product in the late 1980s, but did not release it until the company saw what the competition was doing. At the appropriate time, it announced the product with better price/performance than the competition. By that time, it had also developed the capability to deliver multiple releases of new ISDN products every six months.

Reverse-Engineer Successful Competitive Products

Reverse engineering is the process of designing a product by copying the function of a successful competitive product. It is different from directly copying the product itself, since the emphasis is on copying function, not the specific design. Reverse engineering reduces development costs and eases market entry, since there is already a comparable product that is successful in the market.

For example, PC-clone manufacturers reverse-engineered the IBM PC to create a product that was functionally similar. They avoided large investments in technology and reduced market risk because they copied a product that was already accepted by customers. Amdahl used a similar process, which it called "better engineering," when it consolidated IBM's logic design to achieve higher performance at lower cost.

Cyrix reverse-engineered Intel's 486 microprocessor by looking at how the 486 processed software and then developing its own architecture. Its microprocessors were compatible with Intel's, since it followed identical software interface protocols. Cyrix also claimed that its CX 486 microprocessors were faster and more efficient than Intel's.

Risks of Timing Strategies

While a timing strategy can provide competitive advantage, it is also risky. Too many companies blindly proceed with these strategies, assuming there is no downside. They believe first is always better. Then they discover the cost of failure. The primary risks of a timing-based strategy fall into three categories: premature market entry, compressed product life cycles, and an inferior product development process.

Entering the Market Prematurely

"Pioneers get arrows in their backs." This old saying applies to product strategy as well. The company that pioneers the application of a new technology or creates a new market is not necessarily the one that will be most successful. The failure of Sony's Betamax standard is an example.

Another of the more famous exemplars of this principle is the CAT (computer assisted tomographic) scanner, which was invented by Britain's EMI Ltd. EMI was originally a record company that became successful marketing Beatles records. It used some of its profits to diversify into electronics. As part of this diversification, one of its engineers, Godfrey Housefield, invented the CAT scanner, inspired by a neighborhood surgeon who complained about not being able to "see" brain tumors.

EMI became an instant sensation, outdoing traditional suppliers of X-ray equipment, such as General Electric, Siemens, and Philips. But even though the CAT scanner was easy to improve—since it was early in its technology cycle—EMI didn't have the technical resources to keep up with competitors or the marketing and support resources to be competitive. While Housefield received a Nobel prize and knighthood, EMI exited the business in 1979.[11]

Japanese electronics companies have successfully used first-to-market strategies to secure dominant positions in most major consumer electronics markets: home VCRs, video cameras, the Sony Walkman, compact disk players, digital tape players, and so on. In many of these efforts, they skillfully used government support and consortia to strengthen development and initial entry. This was also the strategy they used in creating the market for HDTV (high-definition television), but their first efforts failed. The Japanese consumer electronic companies, its Ministry of Post and Telecommunication, and its public broadcasting network (NHK) formed a triad for nearly 30 years to develop Hi-Vision. NHK invested ¥19 billion ($100 million). The product platform used analog technology, but the United States and Europe waited until more advanced digital technology was feasible. Even in Japan, only 15,000 Hi-Vision televisions were sold per year.[12]

Companies need to ask themselves this question: Is it better to be first in the market or to let others do the initial pioneering, watch their experience closely, and then respond quickly? A conscious strategic choice must be made between a first-to-market and a fast-follower strategy.

Compressing Product Life Cycles

Product strategies based on speed can shorten product life cycles as major competitors battle aggressively to be the first to introduce the latest incremental improvement in technology and the newest features. For example, in consumer electronics products during the late 1980s, the life cycle of new products was reduced to as little as several months. The result was lower profit margins because of price reductions on the inventory of products that were replaced, inadequate returns on the investments in new product development from products having only a six- to nine-month life, and customer confusion about the proliferation of new products with negligible differences.

A company basing its strategy on a speed advantage should identify the potential outcomes of its actions, including expected competitor responses, such as escalations that may lead to deterioration of the entire market through factors like compressed product life cycles.

Relying on an Inferior Product Development Process

Companies that use a strategy dependent on timing but do not have a superior product development process are setting themselves up for failure. Any strategy based on timing—whether first-to-market or fast-follower—requires a competitive advantage in product development. A company with a product development process superior to that of its competitors can successfully execute a time-based strategy. The minimum performance characteristics of a superior product development process are:

- Time to market must be at least as fast as that of competitors.

- The company must be capable of quickly reacting to new technology and changes in the market.

- The company must integrate the product development process with the product strategy process.

What makes a timing-based strategy most interesting is that there are significant time-to-market differences among companies, and these differences can be used to achieve competitive advantage. Our experience shows that the best companies (those in the top 20 percent of performance) have an advantage of more than 50 percent in time to market. These companies have the opportunity to implement first-to-market or fast-follower strategies better than their competitors. The results of a TTM difference of this magnitude can be dramatic. Many companies recognize the strategic implications of time to market and have begun implementing major improvements in their strategies.[13]

Notes

1. Alan Deutchman, "The Next Big Info Tech Battle," *Fortune,* November 29, 1993.

2. Nikhil Hutheesing, "Games People Play," *Forbes,* October 25, 1993.

3. Thomas Peters, "The Mythology of Innovation, or a Skunkworks Tale, Part II," *Readings in the Management of Innovation,* edited by Michael L. Tushman and William L. Moore (Ballinger Publishing, 1988), p. 143.

4. For a comprehensive discussion of standards, see H. Landis Gabel, *Competitive Strategies for Product Standards* (McGraw-Hill, 1991).

5. Milt Freudenheim, "The Drug Makers Are Listening to Prozac," *The New York Times,* January 9, 1994.

6. Merrill Lynch estimate, November 10, 1993.

7. George Stalk, Jr., and Thomas M. Hout, *Competing Against Time* (The Free Press, 1990), pp. 112–114.

8. Information provided by Corning.

9. Thomas S. Robertson, "How to Reduce Market Penetration Cycle Times," *Sloan Management Review,* Fall 1993.

10. Nikhil Hutheesing, "The First Shall Be Last," *Forbes,* October 25, 1993.

11. Richard Foster, *Innovation—The Attacker's Advantage* (Summit Books, 1986), pp. 193–194.

12. Takeshi Matsuzaka, "HDTV Shift Stuns Industry," *The Nikkei Weekly,* February 28, 1994.

13. For additional insights into improving the product development process, see Michael E. McGrath, Michael T. Anthony, and Amram Shapiro, *Product Development Success Through Product and Cycle-Time Excellence* (Butterworth-Heinemann, 1992).

10

Thinking Globally about Product Strategy

Recognizing that global high-technology products have some significant advantages over national competitors, it's important to understand the unique requirements of global markets.

Selling products globally became an important source of growth for high-technology companies in the 1970s. With limited modifications, they were able to export products successfully to selected global markets. Competing was not the primary goal; incremental revenue was a sufficient achievement. In some cases, global markets even gave companies the opportunity to sell older products that were no longer competitive in their home markets.

During the 1980s, global competition intensified, and, by the 1990s, high-technology companies had to compete globally to be successful. Any one national market, even the American or Japanese market, became too small a portion of the total worldwide market. A company concentrating on one market was vulnerable to global competitors. The cost of developing a high-technology product could be so large that spreading this cost across many worldwide markets provided an economic advantage.

Products vary among countries for many reasons. Languages, preferences, and uses vary. Technical standards and certification requirements differ. From country to country, market segmentation can be different, and protectionism and nationalism can influence product preferences. Yet customers throughout the world are expecting products, particularly high-technology products, that meet global standards. They are increasingly reluctant to pay more for local products that are less advanced.

> **Customers throughout the world are expecting products that meet global standards. They are increasingly reluctant to pay more for local products that are less advanced.**

Theodore Levitt used this trend to distinguish between multinational and global corporations:

> The multinational corporation knows a lot about a great many countries, and continually adapts itself to their supposed differences. The global corporation knows one great thing about all countries, and lures them to its custom by capitalizing on the one great thing they all have in common. The global corporation looks to the nations of the world not for how they are different, but for how they are alike. While it recognizes the presumed need to be globally competitive as well as nationally responsive, it constantly seeks in every way to standardize everything into a common global mode.[1]

As worldwide product requirements become more common and the advantages of commonality are preferred to local alternatives, the opportunity for global product strategy increases. While a global strategy can offer great advantages, it needs to be implemented with an understanding of the reasons behind the international product differences. In addition, global product strategy is part of a broader global strategy, and its interdependence must be understood before a successful product strategy can be formulated.

The economic advantages of global products can be so great that such products will eventually dominate most offerings from national competitors. With sales in multiple worldwide markets, global products attain a much higher level of revenue, which can be used to fund even more advanced product development, and provide the global competitor with a much higher return on product development investments. A hypothetical example is electronic instrumentation for medical diagnostics that is sold in four countries: the United States, Japan, the United Kingdom, and Italy. Figure 10-1 shows the market size in each of the four markets. The market in each country has an indigenous (domestic) competitor (A-1, J-1, U-1, I-1) with approximately 40 percent share of the market. This is a typ-

Country Market ($M)	United States $800	Japan $500	U.K. $300	Italy $100	Total $1,700
A-1					
Market Share	30%				14%
Revenue ($M)	$240				$240
R&D ($M)	$10				$10
ROI	140%				140%
J-1					
Market Share		40%			12%
Revenue ($M)		$200			$200
R&D ($M)		$10			$10
ROI		100%			100%
U-1					
Market Share			40%		7%
Revenue ($M)			$120		$120
R&D ($M)			$10		$10
ROI			20%		20%
I-1					
Market Share				40%	2%
Revenue ($M)				$40	$40
R&D ($M)				$10	$10
ROI				-60%	-60%
G-1					
Market Share	30%	20%	20%	20%	25%
Revenue ($M)	$240	$100	$60	$20	$420
R&D ($M)	$10	$1	$1	$1	$13
ROI	140%	900%	500%	100%	223%

Figure 10-1   Global products have significant economic advantages, as this example in the diagnostic instruments market proves.

ical market share for the leading national competitor. In the American market, both the national competitor (A-1) and the global competitor (G-1), which is also an American company, have 30 percent.

Assume that the market for the new product in all four countries totals $1.7 billion over its entire life cycle. Also assume that the $10 million development costs are the same for each competitor. The global competitor (G-1) incurs an additional $1 million for customizing and qualifying the product in each additional market. In order to isolate the effect of global R&D leverage, it is assumed that each company makes 10 percent profit on sales. In reality, manufacturing and distribution economies of scale would favor the global competitor even more.

Figure 10-1 shows the differences in the competitive economics. The American competitor (A-1) and the Japanese competitor (J-1) achieve a good return (simple ROI with no consideration of the cost of capital) on their investment in developing this product—140 percent and 100 percent, respectively. The competitor from the United Kingdom (U-1) receives some investment return (20 percent), but not enough to justify the risk. The Italian competitor (I-1) loses money. The global competitor (G-1), on the other hand, does extremely well, achieving a 223 percent return on investment and capturing 25 percent of the global market.

This analysis leads to some interesting conclusions about a global product strategy:

- Global competitors have a significant economic advantage.

- Competitors that focus exclusively on smaller national markets cannot afford to develop many high-technology products because the return on investment is insufficient.

- Global competitors need to have a significant share of major markets, particularly their own. This is an advantage for competitors from large markets.

These conclusions led to the formation of the European Economic Community (EEC). Indigenous competitors in individual European countries could not compete against larger global competitors, and they could not themselves become global competitors without having a larger domestic market.

A telecommunications switching system, for example, could cost approximately $1 billion to develop. In Europe, five different companies had developed switches for the unique standards in their own countries. Each investment was spread over a much smaller base than the equivalent investment in a telephone switch for the American or Japanese market. Even in a large market, R&D costs are a high percentage of the cost of a telephone switch. In 1993, AT&T estimated that R&D could run 8 to 15 percent of the price of a switch.[2] The same is true in pharmaceuticals. With development costs estimated at $300 million to $400 million for a new drug, it's likely that global competitors will be the only ones that can afford the R&D investment.

A competitive advantage is achieved by developing a product for most major worldwide markets, but the problem is that product requirements do differ from country to country.

International Differences in Products

There are many reasons for international differences in products. Some of them are unavoidable, yet in the right circumstances they can be managed.

Certification Requirements

Government agencies require numerous certifications for high-technology products. For example, telecommunications products must be approved by the various national telephone systems. The process of adapting and certifying foreign designs to meet these telecommunications standards, called *homologation*, can be quite extensive and varies among countries. Medical, pharmaceutical, and biotechnology products require approval from regulatory agencies in individual national governments. Some of these requirements are being standardized in Europe with EEC unification practices. In turn, different approval requirements affect product design, and must be incorporated into the initial design or modified later to meet each country's requirements. Extensive approval processes can also delay the release of new products in some countries. For example, the United States has one of the longer approval cycles for new drugs, which are sometimes introduced in other countries before becoming available in the United States.

Standards

Differing standards are a major problem in high-technology markets. Standards vary by country or groups of countries, and products that work in one country may not work at all in another.

Televisions and VCRs made for the United States will not work in Europe or Japan. Three standards were originally developed for color television broadcasting: NTSC (National Television Standards Committee) in the United States and Japan, based on the original RCA technology with 525 scanning lines per screen; SECAM (segmented color memory) in France, with 825 lines per screen; and PAL (phased alternate line) in Germany, with 635 lines per screen. The three standards continue to be used throughout the world, but they remain incompatible.

In 1988, there were 18 cellular networks in Europe, which served more than 1 million subscribers with six different and incompatible standards. The Scandinavian PTTs developed NMT (Nordic Mobile Telephone) in the late 1970s. Variations (NMT-450 and NMT-900) were implemented differently in several countries. TACS (total access communications systems) was a refinement of the American 800-MHz AMPS system and used in the United Kingdom and Ireland. Radiocom 2000 was developed by Matra and used in France. C-450 was developed by Siemens in 1985 and used in Germany. RTMS was the Italian standard, and COMVIK was a unique network used in Sweden.[3]

Variations in standards, such as these in the European cellular industry in 1988, made it very difficult for a company to design and market a global product. The products were technically very different—by intention. Each country wanted its "national champion" (the company based on its own soil) to be the one that dominated its national market.

The EEC recognized that this practice also handicapped national companies in developing the economic leverage to become global competitors. As a result, it formed the GSM (Groupe Spécial Mobile) to develop standards and specifications for a pan-European digital cellular system. A common denominator was feasible, since new standards were needed for the next cellular platform that would be based on digital rather than analog technology. The systems and equipment for the digital technology were developed by joint ventures of European suppliers. However, the common standard created for Europe was different from the digital cellular standards in other countries.

Many standards will come together over time, particularly as changes in technology require new ones. Some standards that are deeply entrenched, such as electric power specifications and left- versus right-drive cars, may never change.

Language Differences

In high-technology products, language differences are important in user instructions, training materials, control panels, and user interfaces in computer systems. English can serve as a universal language in some products, particularly the more technical ones, such as complex technical support manuals used by a limited number of customers. In most products, however, the benefit of translating user instructions and manuals into the most common foreign languages is worth the added cost.

It's more difficult to solve the problem of local language friendliness for computer software products than for other high-tech products. It is difficult to translate all the words and messages that must appear on the computer screen. Today, some application software products are customized automatically for language differences.

Differences in Use

Products are varied to accommodate the different ways that people throughout the world prefer to do things. For example, in some countries, supermarket checkout clerks stand as they work, while clerks in other countries sit. Automatic supermarket scanners need to be designed accordingly.

Differences in use can also come from a difference in infrastructure. For example, newer technology can have very different applicability in less developed countries. In some cases, new technology that overcomes the lack of existing infrastructure may find an even broader market, as evidenced by the explosion of cellular phones in Latin America and China, where the existing phone systems are primitive. In other cases, new technology may not be successful, as is seen in low sales of disposable syringes (more expensive than reusable syringes) in less developed countries.

Eventually, many of the ways people throughout the world do things may be standardized by technology. To some extent, cultural difference is an excuse used by country managers within multinational companies to get specific product models designed for each country. Whirlpool challenged these differences with good results. People in every European country wanted a different type of washing machine: the French preferred top-loading machines, for example, while the Germans preferred front-loaders. However, Whirlpool found that customers would give up these cultural preferences for machines that had superior performance, were easier to use, and were more economical. By devising a uniform product line, Whirlpool eliminated half of its European warehouses, simplified distribution, and increased profits by 27 percent.[4]

Demographic Differences

Demographics such as population distribution, income levels, and income distribution differ by country. For example, 1993 income per capita was $23,000 in the United States, but only $3,000 in Latin America. The richest 10 percent of the population in Brazil had more than 50 percent of the national income, while the same proportion in the United States had only 25 percent of the national income.

Differences in demographics can create dissimilar market segmentation from one country to another. In the pharmaceutical industry, for example, the size and composition of the population, as well as the standard of living, affect the market. Age distribution changes the market size for particular products. For example, an older population shifts the emphasis to geriatric drugs.

The size of the pharmaceutical market in a country is directly related to its standard of living. As a result, the U.S. market is many times larger than the Chinese market. In fact, most of the worldwide pharmaceutical market is in the United States, Japan, and Western Europe, particularly France, Germany, and the United Kingdom.

There are also differences in business market segmentation among countries, as in computer-buying patterns in Europe. Italy, with numerous midsize companies, has a larger midsize computer segment, and computers such as IBM's AS/400 have been very popular there. The United Kingdom progressed faster than other European countries in the application of desktop computers. Some European countries, particularly Germany, maintained the old centralized approach to management. As a result, they continued to prefer large, centralized mainframe computers.

National Preferences and Protectionism

Customers in most countries prefer to buy products that were made in that country. They see the local company as being more committed to their country by providing jobs. This preference will become even more important as global unemployment increases.

National preference is particularly important when the primary customer is a national government or government-owned company, which is the case with many high-technology products. In addition to the obvious defense products, most telecommunications products are purchased by government agencies. In countries with national health care, the government is the primary customer for medical and pharmaceutical products.

National governments also influence buying practices to entice foreign companies to locate facilities (and jobs) in their country. Several major computer companies, for example, have received computer purchase inducements to locate facilities in a particular country. After building a new plant, they received large orders from government agencies and educational institutions.

Nations also use trade barriers, such as tariffs and quotas, to protect their local industries. The motivation behind these barriers is simple: preserve jobs. All countries want to support companies that provide jobs to their citizens.

Subtle protectionism is often behind other stated reasons that a product cannot be sold in a foreign country. For example, one telecommunications company was the leader in its own country, but could not get the required approval in a foreign country for its communications switch. Finally, it met with the minister of trade in that country to resolve the issue. The company was told that the real reason was that it did not invest enough in the country. When it acquired a local company that was going bankrupt, and thereby preserved 1,500 jobs, its communications switch was approved.

Sometimes, protectionism is not so subtle. In the early days of the computer industry, Japan placed a high tariff on imported computers and refused to let IBM build a manufacturing facility there until it agreed to Japanese restrictions. Likewise, Texas Instruments was prohibited from producing semiconductors in Japan until it licensed its technology to Japanese companies and agreed to limit its penetration of the Japanese market.[5]

National Laws

Products can also be restricted by legal regulations that differ from country to country. Microsoft confronted the problem when it released Windows 2000 in China. Chinese regulation prohibits products that contain foreign-designed encryption software. Windows 2000 uses encryption to encode transmission over the Internet so that electronic eavesdroppers—such as governments—can't intercept or monitor e-mail or financial transactions.

Labeling requirements and restrictions placed by the EEC and some European countries on genetically engineered foods have constrained the import of American foods and genetically engineered seeds.

Global Product Strategy Integration with Other Global Strategies

Global product strategy is so closely linked with other global strategies that it is difficult to succeed at one without integrating the others. This close integration has led to confusion and frustration as some companies try to make progress on improving one element of global strategy without addressing the others. Deconstructing the different elements of global strategy helps clarify the role of each (see Figure 10-2).

Global market strategy defines the national and regional markets in which a company will compete. *Global manufacturing strategy* determines where a company locates manufacturing facilities and how its global supply chain functions. The *global product development process* provides the framework for how products are developed for worldwide markets with worldwide resources. *Global product strategy* defines which products are developed for which markets and how the characteristics of these products address global requirements.

While global product strategy is the focus in this chapter, other global strategies with which it interacts must be explained.

Figure 10-2   A global product strategy requires the close integration of other strategies.

Global Market Strategy

Global market strategy determines where a company will sell its products. It is primarily a sales strategy, although it affects product strategy because of its implications for product variability and product priorities. While there are numerous country markets throughout the world, high-technology products are marketable primarily to developed countries, considerably limiting the number of country markets.

> *Global market strategy is primarily a sales strategy.*

In addition, the smaller markets may not be economically attractive. The advantages of selling products into multiple markets are offset by the costs of entering each market.

Most high-technology companies concentrate on North America, Western Europe, and Japan—a triad that constitutes the largest portion of the global market for most high-technology products. Usually, a company is based in one of these regions and then expands into the others. Expansion into Europe, which was previously done country by country, became a pan-European endeavor in the 1990s.

Some companies go beyond the triad of major markets into smaller developed and larger undeveloped country markets. Companies relentlessly pursuing this expansion strategy enter one or more new country markets each year. There are advantages to this strategy. Smaller markets tend to be less competitive, and, in some, there is no competition at all. Moreover, once a company dominates a small market, it discourages competitors from entering. Eventually, a sufficient number of smaller markets can increase the overall global volume needed to achieve economic advantage.

Emerging country markets have long-term potential; some of them can eventually grow to be larger than the big market triad. For example, the pharmaceutical market in China is today estimated at only a few billion dollars; however, it could be a $50 billion market by 2010, and possibly the largest pharmaceutical market in the world by 2050.

> *From a product strategy viewpoint, the sequence of expansion should be based on the size of the country market, the strength of competitors, and the suitability of current and planned products.*

From a product strategy viewpoint, the sequence of expansion should be based on the size of the country market, the strength of competitors, and the suitability of current and planned products. From a sales strategy viewpoint, it is typically based on the feasibility or ease of expansion into targeted country markets.

Global Manufacturing Strategy

A global product strategy is tightly linked to a global manufacturing strategy in two ways. First, a company needs to have an international manufacturing capability as it adopts a more global product strategy. International manufacturing is helpful in implementing a global product strategy, although a universal global strategy does not require international manufacturing unless there are major trade barriers.

The second link comes from the leverage provided by manufacturing products in foreign markets. Companies with foreign manufacturing are much more successful in achieving foreign sales than those that do not manufacture in their target markets. In the late 1980s, we conducted an extensive study of international manufacturing that clearly pointed out the importance of global manufacturing in leveraging international sales. To be successful internationally, a company needed to operate manufacturing facilities in the major foreign countries where it sold its products. There were several reasons for this leverage. In many countries, customers prefer a product manufactured locally to an imported product. In some countries, protectionism in the form of tariffs or informal barriers provides advantages to locally manufactured products. Local manufacturing facilitates the understanding of local requirements and a faster response to changes in customer preferences. Finally, local manufacturing provides a focal point for customer visits, allowing a company to demonstrate the care and quality that go into production.

Global Product Development Process

Developing products globally requires a process that leverages resources scattered throughout the world.

Developing products globally requires a process that leverages resources scattered throughout the world. Many companies find such leveraging difficult to accomplish, as illustrated in the following scene, typical in many high-technology companies:

> The project team in an American high-technology company was proposing a new product, primarily for the American market. While the company was international and had a stated goal of becoming more global, the product requirements and sales forecasts for the product were based solely on the American market.

> "Will this product be successful in Europe?" the CEO asked the team leader.
> The team leader responded, "We believe it will be, but we don't have much information on the European market."
> "What does the European marketing manager think about the product?" the CEO asked.
> "He said he had other priorities and that he would look at it when it was close to completion."

> "I think we need to understand the worldwide requirements for this product," the VP of engineering said. "We don't have the resources to reengineer it for the European market."
> "What about the requirements for the product in Japan and Brazil?" another executive asked.
> "We don't know anything about those markets," the marketing member of the project team responded.

At this point, the VP of North American sales jumped into the conversation. "We can't delay development to find out what other countries want. We need this product yesterday. If they can't define what they need, that's their problem. The cost benefit is sufficient, and I think we should just go ahead and develop it. Then we can modify it to fit their needs later."

After more discussion, the CEO said, "We keep saying we are trying to become more global. Eventually, we need to begin making decisions on a global, not a national basis. I think we need to start now."

The other executives agreed, and they declined to approve the project until it integrated worldwide requirements. The CEO said that he would contact the marketing organizations in the other countries and get their participation.

To be successful, a global product development process must, at a minimum, accomplish the following:

- Priorities for assigning resources to new product opportunities must be determined at a global level. This is a subtle, but difficult change for most companies that are used to decentralized decision making. These companies need to place product approval authority at a worldwide executive level.

- Product marketing tasks such as product specification, competitive positioning, and sales forecasting need to be done through global collaboration. This requires coordination among multiple marketing and sales managers throughout the world, which is not an easy task for most companies.

- Worldwide sales organizations need to make commitments to support the product launch, sell the product, and achieve sales forecasts. This requires early involvement and coordination of all sales organizations throughout the world.

In addition, a company may develop products globally with design, engineering, and testing being done in multiple countries. With global development, resources are balanced throughout the world, and critical skills can be leveraged without restriction on where they are located.

Global Product Strategies

In general, a company should try to leverage its product development by selling products throughout the world, but, at the same time, it must sell competitive product offerings in each country market. This leverage ranges from selling exactly the same product in all countries to simply coordinating some research. In between, a company could leverage product platforms, modules, or technology.

Global product strategies are applied on an individual product platform basis, and a company with multiple platforms can follow multiple global product strate-

> *Global product strategies are applied on an individual product platform basis, and a company with multiple platforms can follow multiple global product strategies simultaneously.*

gies simultaneously. Competitive advantage can be achieved by applying a better global strategy than competitors; the catch is the degree of variation that restricts these strategies. When a low level of R&D investment is required, a global product strategy has less impact, and any global strategy can be equally effective.

Products change over time as they progress through their life cycle, and these changes can shift the competitive advantages of one strategy over another. For example, in the early days of the personal computer industry, R&D costs were relatively high, but over time these costs declined, as companies moved to standardized components, and sales volume increased. As a result, a more global strategy became less advantageous.

There are four alternative strategies for globalizing products.

Design and Develop Products
Uniquely for Country Markets

Products designed for customers in a single country or a few directly related countries follow a regional or country-specific product strategy. When the product is developed only for a single country, this is referred to as a local or domestic strategy. Most high-technology products are at least regionally focused and developed for the North American or European markets.

An international variation of this strategy is used to develop multiple products, each designed separately for an individual region, usually by a company's business unit in the region. This is referred to as a multiregional product strategy. Since there is little difference between a local, regional, or multiregional strategy from a product strategy perspective, we refer to them collectively as a regional strategy.

Within a regional strategy, product development priorities are established to achieve regional objectives. Product requirements and specifications are based on what is necessary to be successful in the targeted region. There is little or no sharing of product requirements from one region to another, and no reason to consolidate requirements. Each product is essentially developed in a vacuum, although there may be some sharing of common experience.

This is an appropriate strategy for some products, such as transformers. Asea Brown Boveri (ABB), with $1 billion in revenue, was the leader in designing these products, which are used in the transmission of electricity over long distances. ABB didn't see its operation as a global business, but as a collection of local businesses with intense global coordination. ABB transformer factories concentrated on maximizing design and production flexibility and focused closely on the needs of domestic customers.[6] Product strategy was regionally focused, but there was indirect leverage from global coordination in other activities. Global coordination included consolidation of material requirements to gain advantages from suppliers and shared learning on common processes and problems. ABB became excellent at attaining this leverage.

Developing multiple regional products can be an inefficient strategy, since it doesn't leverage development resources. This was the mistake one company made in designing and manufacturing computer-based industrial control systems. The company was the leader in the United States, and it acquired

> *Developing multiple regional products can be an inefficient strategy, since it doesn't leverage development resources.*

the leading company in the United Kingdom. It wanted to implement a customized global product strategy, but it was unable to do so because each country had what appeared to be different requirements. American customers preferred a computer terminal interface with keyboard entry and output displayed on the computer screen. The British preferred system controls with individual knobs, buttons, and switches.

Because of these perceived differences, the company used a multi-regional product strategy. In the end, it shelled out more than $20 million without gaining an economic advantage over local competitors. Ironically, the difference turned out to be a design trade-off, not a significant cultural difference. A local competitor in the United Kingdom was successful with a computer terminal interface.

Leverage a Country-Specific Product through Reengineering

This strategy follows the previous one. After a company develops a product for a specific region (typically domestic), it then decides to reengineer the product and sell it to another region (typically foreign). This is also the traditional export strategy. Companies develop a product for their home market and simply export it to foreign markets. Engineers in those foreign countries make the changes necessary, and then sales agents resell the product.

Generally, this is not a good strategy, since the reengineered product is usually not as successful as the original and is always more expensive. Unfortunately, it is one of the more popular strategies because of the organizational structure and product development process limitations of most companies. Product development decisions are frequently made on a regional basis, and marketing involvement is restricted to regional responsibility.

The experience of a medical diagnostic equipment company illustrates the inefficiency of this strategy. The company had facilities in multiple countries, each developing products for regional markets. When it began selling an American-designed product in Europe, it needed to reengineer the product design and remanufacture each product to fit local needs. The factory in the United States shipped completely tested diagnostic equipment to the factory in England.

When received there, the product was torn apart and rebuilt to meet British and European requirements. The necessary changes included additional shielding, substitution of approved materials to meet local government standards, and replacement of the power supply and related components. The equipment was then retested and put into inventory. Because this was a medical product, testing was a major cost. When shipped to yet another European country, the equipment was again modified for local needs and then retested.

This process of remanufacturing and retesting more than doubled the cost of the equipment. Eventually, the company found that it was able to design and test one product for global requirements. It was easier to put some of the additional requirements into all products than to remanufacture them individually for each country.

Such a strategy may be appropriate when there is a significant difference in the maturity or critical characteristics of regional markets. In this case, the timing of market entry may be so different that common requirements cannot be considered without causing a costly delay in entering the primary market. The Japanese PC market is an interesting example.

The Japanese PC was quite different from others until the middle of 1993. PCs could not handle *kanji*, the Japanese character set, so Japanese computer manufacturers "Japanized" standard PC hardware and operating systems. Since they had their own variations, the result was incompatibility among computers and software. Using a keyboard was also unusual in Japan, since *kanji* required thousands of pictograms instead of phonetic characters. Handwriting was used instead of typing. Computers made typing possible, but the market evolved as stand-alone word processors (*wahpuro*), instead of multipurpose computers. In 1993, PCs were used in Japan less often than in the United States—by only 9.9 per 100 Japanese workers, compared with 41.7 per 100 American workers.[7]

In 1993, Microsoft introduced a new Japanese-language version of Windows, Windows 3.1J. This version was fully bilingual and could run on almost any manufacturer's hardware. It also provided the easy-to-use capabilities that made Windows so successful throughout the rest of the world. Japanese companies could no longer compete using locally developed operating systems. Microsoft's economic advantages were just too big. Microsoft implemented this strategy by changing the Japanese market to some degree. (Alternatively, it could have followed a multiregional product strategy and designed a unique product for the Japanese market.)

There were also strategic implications for computer hardware and software companies. Windows 3.1J made a customized global product strategy possible for them, because the Japanese market became similar enough to the American and European markets. They could sell their existing products after modifying them for language differences.

The ability to use a customized global strategy provides significant advantages to global competitors such as IBM, Dell, and Compaq, which collectively had only 15 percent of the $6 billion Japanese market.[8] Local competitors like NEC, Fujitsu, and Toshiba were put on the defensive by the feasibility of a customized global product strategy instead of a regional strategy.

Customize a Global Product Platform to Meet the Needs of Different Regions

The customized global product strategy is perhaps the most successful. It involves designing a base product platform that is then customized for local requirements with minimal effort. The cost advantages and R&D leverage can be considerable. The key to this strategy is balancing

> *The customized global product strategy is perhaps the most successful.*

global changes to fit local market requirements and changes in the local market to fit global product requirements.

The customized global product strategy begins with a design that considers the requirements of all relevant national markets. Common requirements are designed into the base product platform, and variations are added as part of the final configuration.

A manufacturer of cable TV boxes executed this strategy brilliantly. It designed a common product platform for worldwide requirements that enabled high-volume, low-cost production of the electronics and box. Variations for different markets (the United States, Mexico, Brazil, Hong Kong, and Europe) were implemented before shipment by inserting the appropriate software code, enabling the common electronics to interface with the different protocols and transmission formats.

Xerox implemented a customized global strategy when it developed the Xerox 5100 copier in 1990. The design incorporated the requirements for U.S., European, and Japanese markets with input solicited from customers in each of these markets. In the past, Xerox had developed unique products for each market because the requirements for a successful product differ in each region, particularly in Japan. Copiers in Japan need to accommodate a lighter-weight paper, *kanji* characters are much more difficult to copy, and the use of blue lead pencil is common. The Xerox 5100 copier was introduced in Japan in November 1990 and in the United States in February 1991. It was the fastest global rollout for any new product at Xerox, and it saved Xerox $10 million in development costs.[9]

Key to the design of a customized global product is maintaining commonality for as long as possible. Country-specific variations are then added at the latest possible stage in the manufacturing process, preferably after the product is tested. Some companies use "country kits" for software, accessories, plugs, and so on to accommodate unique, country-specific differences.

One computer printer manufacturer had a creative approach. The only differences remaining in its manufactured product were the power converter and electrical plug used in different countries. The manufacturer left a small hole in the shipping box and put in the appropriate converter plug as the product was shipped to the customer.[10]

Biotechnology and pharmaceutical companies generally follow a customized global strategy. The basic drug is the same, but the dosage format and packaging may be different for each country. The approval process is also unique to each country, so a key aspect of a customized global strategy is the up-front planning of coordinated approval in multiple countries.

Develop a Universal Global Product

Developing a common product for all worldwide markets provides the highest leverage, both in development and in manufacturing. It enables a company to design a product once, eliminating costly redesigns each time the company enters a new market. Unfortunately, developing a universal global product is not always possible.

Raw material and component products are suited to this strategy. Many electronic components, such as semiconductors and disk drives, do not change with the requirements of national markets. Advanced materials and specialty chemical products are generally global.

Some products need only small modifications to be developed as universal global products. Mainframes and supercomputers, for example, require minor modifications for power and environmental factors in each country, but this adjustment is so negligible compared with their cost that they are virtually global products.

Still another class of product must have global interoperability. Data communication hubs and routers need to accommodate most international communications standards, so they are universal global products by requirement.

Risks of Global Strategies

The primary risk of product strategies that are less global, such as regional or leveraged regional strategies, is that competitors will gain an economic advantage with a more global strategy, such as customized global or universal global. However, there are also risks involved in strategies that are more global.

1. *It's difficult to execute a global strategy.* Many companies forget how difficult it is to execute a global strategy of any kind and formulate their global product strategy independently of their overall global capabilities. Then they fail to execute because they lack the necessary capability.

As was previously discussed, global product strategy is closely linked with other global strategies. If a company does not have the right global manufacturing or supply chain capability, it can-

> *Global product strategy is closely linked with other global strategies.*

not efficiently build or deliver a global product. If it doesn't have a global product development process, it can't develop a product that will be successful in multiple country markets. And if it doesn't have a global distribution capability, it can't sell the product in country markets, even if it has designed a global product.

Execution of a global product strategy isn't easy, even for the best companies. Microsoft attempted to penetrate the Chinese software market when it introduced a Chinese version of its Windows software, called P-Win, but by early 1994, it faced many obstacles. The powerful Ministry of Electronics Industry (MEI) promoted another operating system called Chinese Star, developed by SunTendy, a Chinese company.

(Interestingly, Chinese Star required both Microsoft DOS and Windows.) The MEI wanted Microsoft to drop P-Win and endorse Chinese Star so that Microsoft could not dominate the Chinese software market. It was reluctant to give licenses allowing software companies to write software for P-Win.

Microsoft had other problems with P-Win as well. Instead of developing P-Win in China, it decided to develop it in Taiwan, which was viewed as a renegade province by the Chinese. Also, the Taiwanese use a different set of Chinese characters and a different way of typing them into a computer. P-Win lacked the most popular Chinese input methods and did not support many application software products. On top of all this, software piracy was a major problem in China. Shenzhen University was involved in making unauthorized copies of Microsoft products. Microsoft estimated that 650,000 copies were made, costing it $30 million. The university was fined $260.[11]

> *Not all high-technology products can be successful as universal global products.*

2. *Global products may have insufficient proximity to national requirements.* Not all high-technology products can be successful as universal global products. Choosing this strategy and designing a product for all worldwide markets can backfire. For example, customers in major global markets may not be willing to trade advantages in price or capabilities for less customization to their individual needs. Or a product developed to meet the requirements of so many country markets becomes overly complex, compared with products developed for a single country market. An application software company fell into this trap when it developed one accounting software product to meet the needs of more than a dozen national markets.

For high-technology products, the size of investment in product development is an indicator of the likelihood of their success as universal global products. This correlation is an extension of the economic advantages discussed earlier. Supercomputers, for example, are successful universal global products because of their high level of R&D investment per unit. This is not always the case. Japanese consumer electronic companies developed analog-based, high-definition television, expecting their investment to give them a competitive advantage in the U.S. and European markets, but these markets decided to use a digital-based standard, and the Japanese products would not work.

The universal global product needs to maintain sufficient proximity to national products. The advantages of lower price or better capabilities need to offset the advantages of a product designed to specific national requirements.

Notes

1. Theodore Levitt, *The Marketing Imagination* (The Free Press, 1986), p. 28.

2. John J. Keller, "AT&T's Network Equipment Unit Is Bouncing Back," *The Wall Street Journal*, December 2, 1993.

3. John A. Quelch, Robert D. Buzzell, and Eric R. Salama, *The Marketing Challenge of 1992* (Addison-Wesley, 1992).

4. William Echikson, "Inventing Eurocleaning," *Fortune*, Autumn–Winter 1993.

5. Clyde V. Prestowitz Jr., *Trading Places* (Basic Books, 1988), pp. 34–35.

6. William Taylor, "The Logic of Global Business: An Interview with ABB's Percy Barnevik," *Harvard Business Review*, March–April 1991.

7. Andrew Pollack, "Now It's Japan's Turn to Play Catch-up," *The New York Times*, November 21, 1993.

8. Brenton R. Schlender, "U.S. PCs Invade Japan," *Fortune*, July 12, 1993.

9. For more information, see Michael E. McGrath and Richard W. Hoole, "Manufacturing's New Economies of Scale," *Harvard Business Review*, May–June 1992.

10. European consumers are used to assembling the plugs on appliances.

11. Jeffrey Parker, "Can Microsoft Bust China's Protectionist Strategy?" *Reuters World Report*, March 17, 1994.

11

Understanding the Opportunities and Risks of Cannibalization

You don't want replacement products to kill the profit of existing products prematurely. Yet you don't want someone else to do it either.

Cannibalization is perhaps the most misunderstood or most overlooked product strategy in high-technology companies, although it is a recurring issue. Emerging technology drives companies to continuously upgrade and replace existing products; cannibalization occurs when a new product replaces an existing product. There's good cannibalization and bad cannibalization, however. The latter takes place when companies inadvertently consume their own profits. We have found that very few companies understand the basic concepts of cannibalization. This was the case in the following company.

Members of the project team were proud of what they had accomplished; after all, they had been working on the new product for almost 18 months. They expected it would be completed and ready for release in another six months. It would be a very competitive product, with 80 percent of the capabilities of the company's existing product at less than 50 percent of the price, and these were the capabilities that were most important to customers.

The afternoon status presentation to the executive committee went very well. The engineering VP was pleased with some of the innovative design features, and the sales VP thought that the product would sell well. Only the chief financial officer seemed to be concerned. He kept asking project leaders about the impact on the company's existing product. It was as though he were in another meeting, they thought. The existing product was not their responsibility.

The team members were obviously shocked, to say the least, when they were told two days later that the project had been canceled. The prevailing opinion seemed to be that senior management was either crazy or incompetent. The reason for cancellation, they were told, was to avoid cannibalization of the existing product.

"This is stupid," they responded. "Our new product is a much better value for the customer. If we don't keep up with what the customer wants, the competition will."

They knew the CFO was behind all this and asked for a meeting to try to change his decision. He started by explaining his analysis to the team. He referred to their forecast that 5,000 units would be sold over the next three years, and then explained that 80 percent of these sales would come at the expense of the existing product.

"No kidding," the lead design engineer told himself sarcastically. "We have almost 70 percent of the market; where else is it going to come from?"

"As you know," the CFO went on, "the profit on the new product is a lot less than that of the existing product. When you compare the results of launching this new product with keeping the existing one, we would lose almost $50 million in profit. If you include the cost of excess and obsolete inventory on the existing product and incremental manufacturing overhead, this loss could go up to $65 million."

"What about expanding the market with the lower price?" someone asked.

"No, the market for our products is pretty well fixed in size," the marketing team member responded. "There is little or no price elasticity."

"What about the threat of competition?" another engineer asked.

"This is unlikely for the time being," the marketing team member responded. "Our existing product is only 18 months old, and the competition isn't expected to have a product in this range for at least two years."

"All of this work was wasted then," one project team member said in frustration.

"We were asked to see what elements of the design could be used to reduce costs on the existing product," the team leader said. "Maybe some of it can be used there."

As they got up dejectedly and began to walk out of the room, one of the engineers asked the CFO, "Couldn't this analysis have been done sooner?"

"Yes," he responded. "It could have been done at the very beginning, but it wasn't. Everyone was too excited about getting started and didn't think through the impact of cannibalization."

Unlike this situation, in a normal case of cannibalization, an improved version of a product or a new product platform replaces the one currently being sold. As illustrated in Figure 11-1, when the original product approaches the end of its life cycle, frequently sustaining sales by reduced price over the last couple of years, the replacement product is introduced, typically at a higher price. The company then implements an orderly transition, using the price difference between the old and the new products to manage the sales mix between them. Manufacturing can then phase out production and reduce inventory of the older product while ramping up production of the new product.

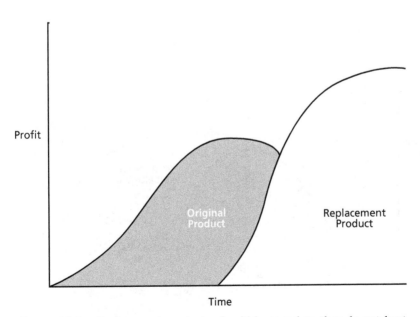

Figure 11-1　Replacement products should be timed so they do not hurt overall sales.

True cannibalization really occurs only when there is not an orderly or profitable transition. The replacement product kills the original product before its time. Companies make their strategic mistakes in not understanding when cannibalization should be avoided and when it is appropriate.

> *True cannibalization really occurs only when there is not an orderly or profitable transition. The replacement product kills the original product before its time.*

Figure 11-2 illustrates how cannibalization can reduce profits. The original product is still successful when the replacement product is released, but sales and profits begin to decline as sales are transferred to the replacement product. However, in this example, profit from the replacement product is lower than what the company would have made by continuing to sell the original product. Lower prices or higher costs of the replacement product can cause this difference. The remaining section of the curve represents lost profit.

Cannibalization is particularly important for the market leader. Introducing a new product at the expense of the most successful product in the market usually has little upside potential. Yet failing to introduce a new product or technology allows a competitor to attack the market.

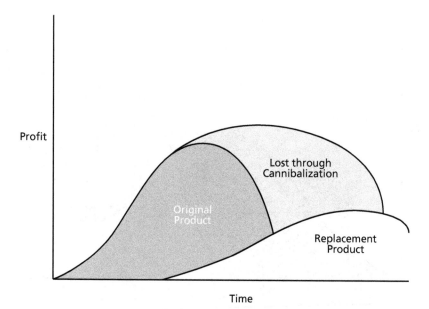

Profit

Lost through Cannibalization

Original Product

Replacement Product

Time

Figure 11-2   When replacement products are introduced too early, they can hurt overall sales and cannibalize profits.

Market cannibalization typically benefits the attacker rather than the defender, since the attacker has little to lose. We'll review the attacker's strategic alternatives and then look at the defender's strategies, but first we'll examine the causes of unfavorable cannibalization.

Causes of Unfavorable Cannibalization

Cannibalization should be approached cautiously when it may have an unfavorable economic impact. Lower profit contribution, unfavorable economics, substantial retooling, and higher technical risk are the typical cannibalization problems that arise.

1. *The new product will contribute less to profits.*   As our earlier example shows, a new product could generate a lower profit contribution than the product it cannibalizes. This happens when the new product is sold at a lower price, with a resulting lower profit per unit, *and* the lower price does not sufficiently increase market share or market size. Unit sales above those of the existing product can be achieved by gaining market share and/or by increasing the size of the market, as we discuss in Chapter 8.

2. *The economics of the new product might be unfavorable.*   Technology changes can sometimes force a product to be cannibalized by a completely different type of product. An example is business forms, a $6 billion market that is likely to be cannibalized by personal computers. It is much easier to enter information on a PC and print out the completed form than it is to type up a preprinted business form. The information can be entered automatically, edited, and integrated into other computer systems without retyping. Many business forms, particularly multipart forms, are thrown away without being used. Computer-generated forms eliminate this waste as well as a lot of time and labor.

One company that was a leader in multipart forms for financial services faced this issue of cannibalization. A team of computer-savvy forms designers proposed a new software product that would automate one of the company's most popular forms, permitting the company to expand into application software. Customers showed high interest in the software product.

The product was completed and released to the market 18 months later and proved to be a success. In the first two years, sales of the new product achieved $15 million, returning 10 times the development costs. Unfortunately, the company's sales of the form that it cannibalized were reduced by $30 million in the second year. When the company examined the economics of this cannibalization, it looked something like the following (in millions of dollars):

Year	Software revenue	Software profit	Lost forms revenue	Lost forms profit	Change in profit
1	$6.0	$3.0	$5.0	$1.5	$1.5
2	$9.0	$4.5	$30.0	$9.0	($4.5)
3	$10.0	$5.0	$50.0	$15.0	($10.0)
4	$6.0	$3.0	$60.0	$18.0	($15.0)
5	$5.0	$2.5	$80.0	$24.0	($21.5)

The analysis showed that the new software product was a one-time sale, but it was cannibalizing an ongoing revenue stream. By the time the company realized the economic impact, it was too late. The cost was almost $20 million per year. Although this type of cannibalization may eventually be necessary, since someone will be selling forms software, the dilemma illustrates what makes cannibalization such an important strategic issue.

3. *The new product will require significant retooling.* When the new product requires a different manufacturing process, profit is lower because of the investment in that process and because of the write-offs associated with closing or retooling current manufacturing plants. One company that faced such a problem was the market leader with a medical device that had 85 percent of market share. The company manufactured the product in high volume at three plants. Researchers saw the opportunity to redesign the device using a new material that would provide additional safety advantages to its customers.

While devices made from this new material were better, customers were not willing to pay very much more for them. Medical reimbursement schemes prevented customers from passing along higher prices. So the company had an opportunity for improving its product, but could not increase prices. Also, it had invested more than $50 million over 10 years to automate its manufacturing and thus reduce product costs as much as possible. The new material used in the proposed device would make these manufacturing facilities obsolete, and the company would probably need to close them completely and relocate production. The new product would require an investment in new manufacturing plants of more than $40 million over the next three years.

After developers produced a prototype of the new device, the company delayed its decision to complete development because of cannibalization. Management was split on this issue. Some believed that the company had to introduce the new product regardless of the financial consequences. If it did not, a competitor would, and the company would lose its position in the market. Others believed that cannibalization would only cause disruption and a significant reduction of profit for the next three years. To them, it was a big mistake.

After many months of discussion, the company finally decided on a compromise strategy. It completed development using the new material but only in a limited format—one aimed at a very small market segment in which the company did not have significant penetration. That way, it could test customer reception of the device with the new material, and develop production gradually.

4. *The new product has greater technical risks.* The new product may be profitable, but it may introduce much higher risk. In this case, a company can cannibalize its position in the market with a failed product. Again, the market leader has the most to lose.

A manufacturer of test equipment suffered this risk. It developed a new, fully automated test system that would handle 50 tests simultaneously, compared with the one-test-at-a-time capacity of its semiautomated equipment. It would be first to market with a fully automated system and would increase profits, even though it would cannibalize its semiautomated equipment. The advanced technology and high performance would enable the company to charge a premium and reap higher margins.

The company failed to recognize that this advanced technology had higher risks. After the company successfully introduced the new sys-

> *Cannibalization is not always bad. Deliberate cannibalization can be a key element of product strategy.*

tem and had more than 100 customers, it discovered a fatal software problem. When a power interruption occurred, the new automated system got confused and mixed up the data. One patient would get the reported results of another. Customers stopped buying the new automated system *and* the previous semiautomated instrument. Instead, they purchased a new, highly reliable semiautomated instrument from a Japanese competitor. A year after introducing the new automated system, the company had gone from a 75 percent market share to less than 30 percent.

Offensive Cannibalization Strategies

Cannibalization is not always bad. Deliberate cannibalization can be a key element of product strategy. For the attacker, the fear of cannibalization may be the defender's Achilles, heel. Since cannibalization hurts the market leader, it can provide attackers with an advantage. The attacker, either a new market entrant or a competitor with a much smaller market share, has less to lose than the market leader. It has several strategic alternatives.

Cannibalize the Market to Attack the Market Leader

Cannibalizing an existing market is a successful strategy for attacking an entrenched market leader. By upsetting the market, the attacker erodes the position of the dominant company, although the attacker cannibalizes its own products in the process. The attacker hopes to compensate for its cannibalization loss with increased market share in the redefined market.

Sega Enterprises' attack on Nintendo's dominance of the $3.5 billion American video game market included a strategy to cannibalize its own video game software with a new form of software distribution. In 1993 Sega formed a joint venture with Time Warner Entertainment and Telecommunications, Inc., to offer Sega's video games through cable television networks. The joint venture's Sega Channel provided Sega's 100 or more video games for a monthly fee of $20.[1]

This strategy could have significantly cannibalized Sega's own game software revenue, since Sega would receive a much lower license fee for software distributed through cable. However, as the market attacker instead of the leader, Sega sought to increase its overall market share in both game players and software by redefining the market. To be successful, it would need higher volume to offset lower profit per unit. This strategy also positioned Sega for future technology improvements, when interactive cable would enable groups of cable subscribers to play video games together.

In this product strategy, the attacker is willing to make the sacrifice of cannibalization, since it has less to lose and more to gain. Cannibalization favors the attacker rather than the market defender. High-technology companies that have a small market share, but desire to increase it, should consider alternative cannibalization strategies rather than simply trying to compete directly with the market leader. High-technology markets are unique in this regard. Constantly changing technology offers the opportunity to redefine products in a way that cannibalizes the market and delivers a competitive blow to the market leader, which is forced to sacrifice more.

Introduce New Technology First

The market leader has a vested interest in maintaining the current technology as long as possible at the most stable and profitable point in the product platform life cycle. When the market leader considers introducing replacement technology, cannibalization usually makes the financial return and risk unattractive. So the leader waits.

This delay provides an opportunity for an attacker to move first in introducing the new technology. The attacker can use this strategy, which is a variation of the first-to-market strategy, to leapfrog the market leader. Sega used it in introducing its 16-bit Genesis video game player ahead of Nintendo, which was content to continue with its 8-bit player as long as possible. Nintendo's share of the U.S. market dropped from 90 percent to 50 percent, while Sega's increased from 7 percent to almost 50 percent. Ironically, because Sega was successful, it had more to lose in the implementation of its previous cannibalization strategy.

This strategy of attacking a market leader with new technology while the leader is trying to hold onto the old technology is common in high-technology industries. The minicomputer companies used it against mainframe computer companies. PC companies used it against the minicomputer companies.

Defensive Cannibalization Strategies

For the reluctant defender, controlled cannibalization may be a necessary strategy to repel attackers. Cannibalization can also be a defensive strategy for the market leader. In these strategies, the market leader uses cannibalization as a defense, just as burning sections of a forest creates fire breaks to stop a forest fire. The leader has four defensive cannibalization strategies.

Cannibalize Yourself Before Competitors Do It

Self-cannibalization may be necessary as a defensive strategy to keep an attacking competitor from being successful. With this strategy, a company chooses to cannibalize its own products rather than let a competitor do so.

The drug industry illustrates cannibalization as a defensive strategy. Drug companies maintain high prices on patented drugs to cover research costs. They could reduce the price, but this would subsequently starve their research and development efforts. Once a drug comes off patent, however, ferocious price competition starts. At this time, the drug company usually phases out of the market for the drug and supports its business through other patented drugs.

In 1993, Merck began to implement a strategy of intentional cannibalization of some of its products as they came off patent. In a joint venture with Johnson & Johnson, it introduced an over-the-counter version of its popular ulcer drug, Pepcid. Merck also entered the generic drug market with diflunisal, made from the same compound as its branded arthritis drug, Dolobid. Both products were made in the same plant in West Point,

Pennsylvania.[2] Rhone-Poulenc Rorer, Marion Merrell Dow, Glaxo, and Warner-Lambert initiated similar strategies to selectively cannibalize their off-patent prescription drugs.

Timing is the key to cannibalization as a defensive strategy. Do it too soon, and cannibalization will result in unnecessary lost profits. Do it too late, and attackers will seize the market.

Sometimes a company can create a strategy to fend off competition without significantly cannibalizing itself, as when Eastman Kodak creatively defended its film and film processing market. Under the threat of digital photography and camcorders, Kodak developed the photo CD. Other companies in Kodak's position would have reacted by introducing a digital camera and cannibalizing their film and film development businesses, but Kodak found a way to integrate this business into its solution. It designed the photo CD player to use CDs prepared by the Kodak photofinisher from normal 35-mm film. A photographer takes pictures with existing camera equipment and film and then requests a copy on CD, at an extra charge. The CD can be viewed on normal television, using the photo CD player.

Introduce Cannibalization to Continue as the Technology Leader

The technology leader in a market regularly cannibalizes its existing successful products just as its competitors begin to catch up. Intel, for example, cannibalized its 2½-year-old 8088 microprocessor with its 80286 processor in February 1982. It replaced the 80286 with the 386 in October 1985, the 386 with the 486 in April 1989, and the 486 with the Pentium in May 1993.

> *Regular cannibalization by the technology leader is successful when the underlying technology continuously advances. When it does, the technology leader can pace the market.*

Regular cannibalization by the technology leader is successful when the underlying technology continuously advances. When it does, the technology leader can pace the market by establishing regular product life cycles. In the Intel example, it was able to establish half-life[3] cycles of three to four years.

In an interesting strategic adjustment, Intel lengthened the life cycle of the 486 by several months when it delayed the introduction of the Pentium because competition had not yet caught up. With this delay, Intel reduced cannibalization of the 486 and increased profits. One analyst estimated that for every new Pentium chip, Intel could churn out up to a dozen more 486 microprocessors, and the delay increased profits by more than $112 million in 1993.[4]

Manage the Rate of Cannibalization through Pricing

Pricing is used most often as the mechanism to control the rate of cannibalization. Where cannibalization is an issue, the price for the new product is set at a level that encourages a particular sales mix of the existing and new products. If the price of the new product is relatively higher, the rate of cannibalization will be lower. Reducing the price of the new product will usually increase the rate of cannibalization.

Intel uses this strategy to control the mix between old and new generations of microprocessors. It introduces new microprocessors at a high price, reflecting their higher performance. It then reduces the price of its older microprocessors to an attractive enough level so they continue to be purchased by some segments of the market. This makes for an orderly instead of an abrupt transition from the cannibalized product.

Restrict Cannibalization to Specific Market Segments

The medical device company discussed previously applied the strategy of minimizing cannibalization by restricting introduction of its new product to smaller market segments. Some market segments are less vulnerable to cannibalization, because there is either more to gain or less to lose in them. By tailoring the new product to a particular segment, a company can get the benefits without the loss, as well as the opportunity to gain experience with the new product.

Sometimes, however, a product drifts into another segment. In 1990, Boeing was uncomfortably aware of the threat that the Airbus A340 long-haul aircraft posed to its product line, and began development of the Boeing 777. Early sales for the 777 were encouraging, showing comparable performance against the Airbus product. Yet orders for the larger 747 "jumbo" plummeted to just two in 1993. There were many factors involved, such as deregulation of the airline industry, which resulted in many more direct city-to-city flights with lower capacity requirements (so-called long, thin routes). The high-capacity jumbos were in more demand when regulation permitted only the hub-spoke arrangement, in which all passengers flew into one international airport and took connecting flights to their destinations. Upgrade plans for the 777 indicated a passenger capacity of 550 compared with a 747 jumbo limit of 566, and the 777 started to become more of a competitor than a complement.[5]

Risks of Cannibalization Strategies

The risks of cannibalization strategies are quite clear: cannibalizing when it is *not* necessary and not cannibalizing when it *is* necessary. The strategic challenge of cannibalization strategy is knowing when to do it and when to defer it.

Premature cannibalization is the primary cannibalization risk. In some cases, the costs of cannibalization are higher than the costs to develop the new product.

Why do companies do this to themselves? Usually, it's not because they thought about it but made the wrong choice. Surprisingly, it's because they did not think about it before doing it. Some companies—particularly the conservative market leaders—err in the other direction. They avoid cannibalization too long and let competitors get an advantage. Instead of introducing new technology first, they let competitors bring it to market.

> *The strategic challenge of cannibalization strategy is knowing when to do it and when to defer it.*

IBM made some severe mistakes by avoiding cannibalization because it was the market leader, letting competitors succeed where it had developed new technology. It developed RISC technology, but delayed introduction, in part because RISC would cannibalize current products. It also intentionally restricted the capabilities of the PCjr so that the product would not take sales away from the PC. These restricted capabilities contributed to the failure of the PCjr. Lou Gerstner, the new CEO of IBM, recognized the problems created by IBM's avoidance of cannibalization when he said, "We've got to eradicate out of anybody's mentality in IBM that we don't cannibalize our product."[6]

Analytical Framework for Cannibalization

Companies frequently stumble in trying to evaluate the impact of cannibalization, and in doing so they end up making the wrong strategic decision. They may think they have a great opportunity when it really is not so great, because of the impact of cannibalization. They may decide against introducing a new product because of cannibalization and then lose market share that was not factored into their analysis.

Figure 11-3 shows alternative ways to analyze the impact of cannibalization. Many companies use one of the first two alternatives (usually they progress from the first to the second), but the third is the correct way to analyze cannibalization. The financial analysis is somewhat simplified to illustrate the main point.

The first approach (Alternative One) is a straightforward financial analysis of the new product opportunity. In 2000, 50,000 units will be sold, 400,000 the next year, and so on. Assuming a net income of 15 percent (to simplify the analysis), the new product will make a profit of $375,000 in 2000, increasing to $12 million in 2003 and 2004. Assuming an initial investment of $10 million to develop the product, the company will fully recover that investment in 2001 and make a net profit of more than $24 million. It appears to be a great opportunity!

However, the second analytical approach (Alternative Two) considers the impact of cannibalization. In 2001, 300,000 of the 400,000 units sold are expected to come from sales of the company's existing product. This is inevitable, since the company is the leader in the market. In the analysis, net income from the previous analysis ($375, $2,700, etc.) is the starting point, and the effect of cannibalization is an adjustment. The selling price ($40) for the current product is multiplied by the estimate of unit cannibalization to compute the revenue loss from cannibalization. This revenue loss is then used to estimate the net income cannibalized and the estimated income *net* of cannibalization. Cannibalization reduces estimated net income in 2001 from $2.7 million to $900,000, and it continues every year. For simplicity's sake, the analysis assumes the same profit margin, even though this is usually not the case. Considering cannibalization, the investment of $10 million is never fully recovered, leaving a loss of more than $1 million at the end of the year 2004.

What about the sales that would be lost if the company does nothing? The situation is considered in Alternative Three. This alternative includes an estimate of sales that would be lost to competition if the company did nothing. Sales would begin to erode in 2002, with an estimated 500,000 units expected to be lost. The figure will increase to 1 million in 2003.

Alternative One

Alternative One	2000	2001	2002	2003	2004
Revenue					
Units ($000)	50	400	1,200	2,000	2,000
Selling Price	$50	$45	$42	$40	$40
Total Revenue ($000)	$2,500	$18,000	$50,400	$80,000	$80,000
Net Income Percent	15%	15%	15%	15%	15%
Net Income ($000)	$375	$2,700	$7,560	$12,000	$12,000
Net Investment ($000)	($9,625)	($6,925)	$635	$12,635	$24,635

Alternative Two

Alternative Two	2000	2001	2002	2003	2004
New Product Income ($000)	$375	$2,700	$7,560	$12,000	$12,000
Cannibalization					
Units (000)	0	(300)	(1,000)	(1,500)	(1,500)
Selling Price	$40	$40	$40	$40	$40
Revenue Cannibalized ($000)	$0	($12,000)	($40,000)	($60,000)	($60,000)
Net Income Percent	15%	15%	15%	15%	15%
Income Cannibalized ($000)	$0	($1,800)	($6,000)	($9,000)	($9,000)
Income Net of Cannibalization	$375	$900	$1,560	$3,000	$3,000
Net Investment ($000)	($9,625)	($8,725)	($7,165)	($4,165)	($1,165)

Alternative Three

Alternative Three	2000	2001	2002	2003	2004
Income Net of Cannibalization ($000)	$375	$900	$1,560	$3,000	$3,000
Expected Lost Sales					
Units (000)	0	0	500	1,000	1,000
Selling Price	$40	$40	$40	$40	$40
Lost Revenue Expected ($000)	$0	$0	$20,000	$40,000	$40,000
Net Income Percent	15%	15%	15%	15%	15%
Lost Income Expected ($000)	$0	$0	$3,000	$6,000	$6,000
Income Net of Cannibalization with Adjustment for Lost Sales	$375	$900	$4,560	$9,000	$9,000
Net Investment ($000)	($9,625)	($8,725)	($4,165)	$4,835	$13,835

Figure 11-3 The impact of cannibalization on sales is significant, as this hypothetical example shows.

This analysis begins with the income net of cannibalization from Alternative Two and makes the adjustments necessary to consider the impact of sales that would be lost by doing nothing. The estimated units of lost sales are multiplied by the selling price and percentage of net income to compute the expected lost income. Netting the sales that are expected to be lost against cannibalization yields a net income of $9 million in 2003. Overall, the new product may again be attractive, returning the $10 million investment by 2003 and generating a positive net investment of more than $13 million by 2004. However, this return must be considered against other potential investments. It would also be a much more attractive investment if it were delayed two years to extend the life cycle of the current product.

By using this analytical framework, a company can do a sensitivity analysis to determine critical breakeven points, such as the level of cannibalization where a new product becomes uneconomical, or the level of erosion where cannibalization makes sense.

Notes

1. *The Nikkei Weekly,* April 19, 1993, p. 8.
2. Shawn Tully, *Fortune,* May 3, 1993, p. 66.
3. "Half-life" is used here to mean the period from when the product is introduced to when cannibalization starts. That is when the life cycle decline begins.
4. Richard Brandt, *Business Week,* February 22, 1993, p. 40.
5. *The London Sunday Times,* January 9, 1994.
6. Judith H. Dubrzynski, "An Exclusive Account of Lou Gerstner's First Six Months," *Business Week,* October 4, 1993.

PART 3

Growth Strategies

Edward Abbey, author of Desert Solitaire, *wrote that "growth for the sake of growth is the ideology of a cancer cell." At properly managed technology organizations, growth is a controlled outcome of a carefully designed strategy to achieve growth of a certain type or types. This is not to say that growth strategies should not aim for accelerated growth; they should. But the test of a growth strategy is whether it achieves the kind— as well as the amount—of growth the organization seeks.*

Part 3 begins by surveying the prominent pathways to growth, and their attendant risks. Selecting a mix of growth pathways is recommended over betting everything on a single pathway. Growth through innovation, for example, is a storied path to growth, but investment in innovation is risky and the returns can be notoriously slow to accrue. The increasingly popular acquisition route to growth is examined at some length, and advice is offered on applying the rudiments of product strategy to new ventures. (A new venture can be viewed as a product strategy aimed at creating a product platform that will culminate in a complete business.) Part 3 concludes by describing the different drivers of growth through innovation, enumerating the principal varieties of innovation strategies, and explaining why innovation cannot be planned or scheduled.

12

Highways to Rapid Growth

*Rapid-growth companies make a commitment to grow by following
a deliberate, proactive process. They identify the growth
highways and head down them.*

Rapid growth is an attitude, one that starts with an ambitious vision for growth that is transformed into a growth *strategy*. Some companies have the growth attitude firmly embedded. Microsoft is the best example. From 1990 to 1999 it grew from $1.2 billion to $19.8 billion by deliberately expanding into new markets.

A rapid-growth strategy is proactive, not reactive. Rapid-growth companies make a commitment to grow and have a deliberate proactive process to make sure they do it. Conversely, many other companies focus exclusively on profitability. They look at return on investment as the criterion for select-ing product develop-ment projects and fre-quently bypass oppor-tunities for growth.

> **The core strategic vision (CSV) is the starting point for accelerated growth.**

The core strategic vision (CSV) is the starting point for accelerated growth. Companies set their expectations for growth by describing where they want to go. While simply defining a vision of rapid growth doesn't ensure that a company will grow faster, a moderate-growth vision is unlikely to achieve rapid growth. When done properly, a rapid-growth CSV will not only guide growth; it will energize the entire company and give it a growth attitude. We can see this commitment in how Microsoft describes part of its core strategic vision, encouraging growth and expansion in many directions.

> Microsoft's vision is to empower people through great software—any time, any place, and on any device. That means helping companies build friction-free knowledge-management systems, so information flows effortlessly through their businesses, and to implement flawless e-commerce operations. It means helping developers create great Web-enabled products for a wide range of devices. It means making PCs simpler and more reliable. It means helping consumers transform the Internet into their own "personal Internet"—a resource that learns from them over time and empowers them with all of the information they need, while protecting their privacy.[1]

We also see the commitment to rapid growth in Nortel's CSV: "Nortel Networks is and must remain a growth company."

As part of the CSV alignment process, a company makes sure it has the product strategy to achieve that vision. This is where rapid-growth companies identify their highways to growth and explore them. They deliberately set out to identify and evaluate the possibilities.

For example, as part of its CSV exercise, one company identified a gap between its core strategic vision and its current product strategy. The current strategy simply wouldn't get it to where it wanted to go. To close this gap, the company assigned three product strategy teams to explore the three growth highways that offered the most promise. It didn't reject the other potential growth highways; it just didn't give them the same priority. Each team worked methodically to identify and assess the opportunities along each highway. At the end, each team selected one or two growth opportunities and evaluated the potential of each. The teams completed their work by presenting their recommendations to an executive strategy team, which picked one to fund and then launched a development effort.

Growth opportunities are unlimited. A company can go in any of several different directions—"growth highways"—to find opportunities to increase revenue. The opportunities along each highway are different; so are the risks and levels of investment. Rapid-growth companies regularly scan these highways, then choose one or more to travel.

The following is a roadmap to eight potential highways for growth. The first three focus on growth opportunities in markets in which a company might currently compete. The next three growth highways offer the greatest opportunity (these are the three that Microsoft prefers). The last two are the boldest and can create significant opportunity, but they are the riskiest and require a longer journey.

Generating Revenue from Additional Product Offerings

Recall from Chapter 4 that the purpose of product line strategy is to develop a continuing series of product offerings from a common product platform. Each product offering targets a specific market segment or group of segments. The objective of following this highway to growth is to create additional revenue by adding new product offerings to better penetrate specific market segments. In some cases, the new product offering will take market share from competitors, and in others it might actually expand the market by attracting new customers.

As discussed in Chapter 4, Amazon.com took this highway to growth. Although books were its first product offering, Amazon expanded in June 1998, when it started offering music products, and then added videos and holiday gifts. Amazon continued expanding in 1999 with online auctions, digital greeting cards, downloaded digital songs, electronic products, toys and games, home improvement products, software, video games, and gifts. By continually offering new products, Amazon built its revenue to $1.64 billion, an increase of 169 percent over revenue of $610 million in 1998.

Revenue created by adding new product offerings is generally added profit, but the question for growth is how much is really added revenue, since some of the new revenue may come from other product offerings in the same family. With Amazon, revenue from the new product offerings contributed almost entirely to growth, but didn't reduce revenue from other Amazon product offerings. Instead, they took sales away from competitors—in this case, the brick-and-mortar companies.

New product offerings are not always highways to growth, however. Frequently, much of the revenue will be taken from other products that the company already has in the market.

> *The real level of growth is the difference between the revenue from the new offering and the lost revenue from the others.*

The real level of growth is therefore the difference between the revenue from the new offering and the lost revenue from the others. In the Tylenol example discussed in Chapter 4, most of the revenue from additional adult pain-relief products, such as Extra Strength gelcaps, was taken from the company's other product forms, such as tablets and caplets. A very limited amount of *new* revenue comes from competitive pain-relief products, because the customer really wants the product in gelcap form. In cases like this, adding a new product offering is more of a competitive strategy than a highway to growth.

At some point in the life of a new product platform, often halfway through, the revenue increase from adding new product offerings diminishes. During the first half of a life cycle, new revenue from new product offerings can be a significant highway to growth as the product platform is realizing its potential. However, during the second half of the life cycle, revenue from new product offerings begins to diminish, and it's no longer a highway to growth.

Ironically, this is when opportunities for new product offerings seem to be the most attractive. Customers' desires push new product offerings tailored to specific segments. New offerings from a mature platform are easier to develop and less risky. Although the return on investment from new products appears to be very attractive, sometimes the degree of cannibalization is underestimated, and the net return can be disappointing, as discussed in Chapter 11. In general, new product offerings during the second half of the platform life cycle may increase profits, but are not a significant highway to growth.

Because new product offerings tend to be customer-driven, a company that is more reactive than proactive will be confronted with more of these opportunities at the beginning of its product development pipeline. Before anyone knows what's happening, the pipeline is full of these proposals, and the company unconsciously forgoes better opportunities in order to invest its development in alluring possibilities for growth.

Generating Revenue from Next-Generation Platforms

We explain the importance of product platform life cycles in Chapter 3. As a product platform approaches the end of its life cycle, it needs to be replaced with a new one before its revenue stream begins to decline. A new or next-generation platform may be a highway to growth, but it may not. The strategic and financial justification for a new product platform is usually compelling. When compared with the expected decline in revenue from the current maturing platform, the *difference* in revenue can be significant. Failure to act in time will invite certain revenue decline. Chapter 3 discusses several companies that failed to act in time to replace their maturing product platforms.

Developing a next-generation platform as a highway to growth can be deceptive. While the total revenue opportunity is large, revenue growth may be much lower, since much of it might be replacement revenue. We saw that happen at Data General, where increased revenue from its AviiON platform was offset by declining revenue of its aging ECLIPSE platform. This highway simply takes you back to where you started.

However, there are five next-generation platform strategies that *can* be highways to growth.

1. The next-generation plat- form can drive growth by taking market share away from competitors. Companies with aggres- sive growth strategies plan to boldly seize mar- ket share from competi- tors by introducing a new platform of prod-

   Companies with aggressive growth strategies plan to boldly seize market share from com- petitors by introducing a new platform of products. They don't aim just to replace their maturing product platform with one that is more competitive.

   ucts. They don't aim just to replace their maturing product platform with one that is more competitive; they set their sights on leaping over competitors. This was the case with NCR and its next-generation ATM, which helped it grow from a minor competitor to the market leader.

2. A next-generation platform can serve a broader market by being more successful in some segments. When Microsoft spent hundreds of mil- lions of dollars to replace Windows NT with Windows 2000, it was not only trying to replace an aging platform with a next-generation plat- form, but also expecting Windows 2000 to contribute to its growth, because the new platform would be more effective in the rapidly growing market segment for Web servers. Microsoft's share of the Web server market was estimated at only 25 percent at that time, and if Windows 2000 could increase its share of this estimated $56 billion market segment, it would contribute to Microsoft's growth.[2]

3. A next-generation platform can also contribute to growth when it is more expensive than the platform it is replacing. Even if market share doesn't increase or the market doesn't broaden, the average purchase per customer is higher. In this case, it's necessary for the new platform to provide increased benefit to customers to justify the higher price.

4. In some markets, a next-generation platform can induce customers to upgrade from the previous generation of products. If a large percent- age of customers upgrade to the new platform, this can mean sub- stantial growth. Windows 2000 also provided this growth opportunity for Microsoft. In general, markets that present replacement opportuni- ties provide an exciting highway to growth and also accelerate inno- vation.

5. A next-generation platform can expand a market—usually by making the product more affordable to a broader market. Here, the highway to growth is the increase in market size. This has been the case in many

exciting electronics markets, such as personal computers, portable phones, and calculators.

The next-generation platform as a highway to growth is tricky. High-growth companies look beyond high ROI and ask: How will this help us grow?

Growing by Strengthening Competitive Position

A stronger competitive position can sometimes be a highway to growth, but frequently the result is an increase in revenue. Adding improvements that make products better than those of competitors is always a good defensive strategy, and may be necessary to keep competitors from taking away market share. However, it's important to look at the added revenue that will come from a stronger product. This happens in several ways.

A stronger product may capture increased market share, and revenue could grow substantially. It's important to clearly distinguish whether a product improvement is intended as a growth strategy or not; the increase in market share will determine the direction. This highway to growth is open only to those with lower market share.

> *It's important to clearly distinguish whether a product improvement is intended as a growth strategy or not; the increase in market share will determine the direction.*

A company that has a dominant share of its market may need to continually improve its product offerings, but this will not be a highway to growth.

In a new, rapidly growing market, a winning and sustainable vector of differentiation will provide a highway to growth. We saw that in the SAP example in Chapter 7. By continually focusing on improving its products along its vector of differentiation, an integrated customer solution, SAP grew rapidly from 367 million DM in 1989 to 8.5 billion DM in 1998. The key to such growth is the ability to sustain the competitive advantage of a successful vector of differentiation. Once this advantage is lost, then it ceases to be a growth highway even in a growing market, as we saw in the IBM PC example.

In certain market conditions or at certain stages of the evolution of a market, a price-based strategy can sometimes be an effective highway to growth. By becoming the price leader, a company can increase its market share and create additional revenue, as long as the relative

281

increase in units sold is substantially higher than the relative decrease in price, of course. In some cases, aggressive pricing may also increase the size of the market by making the products more affordable to more customers.

Overall, a price-based strategy should be used cautiously. Competitive response is likely, and when this happens, revenue growth is unlikely.

Expanding into a Related Market by Leveraging Platforms, Technologies, or Skills

Leveraged expansion into related markets as well as leveraged expansion into new markets (discussed next) have proved to be superhighways to growth for many high-growth companies. By building on existing platform or technical capabilities, a company leverages the development of new product platforms and reduces the risks of development. By expanding into a related market, a company leverages some understanding of the market and what customers want. But by expanding into a new market at the same time, it creates a significant opportunity for new revenue growth.

In Chapter 1, we saw how Compaq shifted its focus in 1992 to develop a new low-cost PC platform to get it into the rapidly growing market for low-priced PCs. This market was related to the market for higher-performance PCs, but was different enough so that Compaq's product platform didn't serve customers in that market. Compaq's new platform became the driver of its growth, taking revenue from $4.1 billion to $18.2 billion in four short years.

Microsoft has used this highway to growth regularly. In 1992 it released Microsoft Access, a relational database software product, which expanded into a market closely related to its other desktop applications. In 1996, Microsoft introduced ActiveX Technologies, a set of tools to enable the creation of active content for the Internet and the PC. In 1997, it introduced the Sidewalk City guides on Microsoft Network.

Expansion into related markets is a proactive highway to growth. You need to keep looking for these opportunities in order to find them.

Expansion into related markets is often overlooked. *Reactive* companies are too focused on responding to the requests of their salespeople and customers and hence fail to see opportunities in related markets. Expansion into related markets is a *proactive* highway to growth. You need to keep looking for these opportunities in order to find them. Start by identifying markets that are related or potentially related, then evaluate and rank them for opportunity, with one or two selected for expansion. Some companies do this intuitively; others do it more formally by integrating identification and evaluation into their annual strategic process.

Expanding into New Markets Not Closely Related to Existing Markets

Expanding into new markets offers even more growth opportunities than expanding into related markets. The further a company travels from its current markets, the greater the number of opportunities. But it's also true that the further a company travels from what it knows, the greater its risk.

The difference between a related and an unrelated new market can be a matter of perspective. For Microsoft, the development and sale of a video game player meant a new market. It wasn't selling game players; in fact, it hadn't developed and built a computer hardware product of any significance. It had developed and marketed entertainment software for PCs, but not for stand-alone game players. The video game market represented a major growth opportunity for Microsoft, leveraging its exceptional systems engineering and software skills to enter a new market. Rapidly growing companies must periodically enter unrelated markets to find sufficient growth opportunities, because, eventually, they run out of growth opportunities in their current and related markets.

Microsoft's expansion into the business-to-business market is another example of how it uses its technical capabilities to create new products for a new market. In 1999, Microsoft began to release a new platform around Windows DNA and related products to provide a full range of software for building and deploying Web-based applications for business. The business-to-business market gave Microsoft a lot of opportunity to grow.

In March 1993, Microsoft introduced Encarta, the first multimedia encyclopedia designed for a computer. This was a very different market for Microsoft, but it did leverage some of its multimedia and software capabilities. In 1995, Microsoft created Microsoft Network (MSN) and enrolled over 500,000 members in the first three months. The Internet service provider market was a new one, but Microsoft leveraged its technical capabilities. Subsequently, as it learned more about this market, Microsoft significantly modified MSN, and then used this platform to expand into other markets by going into a joint venture with NBC to form MSNBC.

Expansion into an unrelated market is a riskier growth highway to follow. There is more opportunity at the end, but there are also many more obstacles to overcome along the way—much to learn about the new market, many new skills and technologies to develop, and many difficult decisions to make. With the X-Box, Microsoft faced two early decisions that could determine its eventual success. It decided, at least preliminarily, to include a disk drive to increase performance at a higher cost, and also to delay release until 2001, when it could have a really high-performance product.

Microsoft's TaxSaver tax preparation software is another example of the risks of expanding into a new market. Even though Microsoft has terrific application software capabilities, its expansion into the tax preparation software market failed, and it withdrew from the market in March 2000. Microsoft eventually realized that this market required a greater development effort than it originally expected. In addition to federal tax software, it needed to develop software for every state. Continual tax changes increased the investment even further. Since Microsoft was a late follower in the market, without any new vector of differentiation, it could not achieve the market share needed to have the volume to support this development.

Although this growth highway offers great opportunities, there are many potential new markets, and risk and ultimate potential vary. A company must take the time to evaluate an opportunity in a market about which it may know little.

Instead of taking the first highway that comes along, successful companies screen a range of opportunities. Those that pass the initial screening are then evaluated more thoroughly before one is chosen. Since the failure rate along this growth highway is much higher, a company must be willing to fail and have a process to determine when to exit.

Using an Acquisition to Expand into a Related or a New Market

Many rapidly growing companies, like Cisco Systems, have followed the acquisition highway to growth. It's a variation of the previous two highways to growth in that the acquisition itself is actually the trigger to pursue the opportunity. The acquisition is necessary for the expansion to be successful.

This type of acquisition is very different from acquisitions that simply add revenue by consolidating revenue from the acquired company. Those types of acquisitions are like adding 5 + 1 to get 6. It's really not growth at all; it's simply consolidation of the revenue from two companies. When an acquisition is used to grow revenue for both companies by expanding into a new or related market, it's more like adding $5 + 1$ to get 10! Cisco Systems and Nortel Networks are excellent examples of two companies that followed this highway to growth. Cisco has made numerous acquisitions, 65 in 1999 alone. From 1997 to 1999, Cisco grew from $6.5 billion to $12.2 billion. Nortel grew from $17.6 billion in 1998 to $22.2 billion in 1999.

The acquisition highway is bought with cheap currency, the company's highly priced stock. Only companies with the highest-valued stocks can play this high-stakes game.

We discuss the use of acquisitions to enable product strategy in the next chapter. As a growth strategy, driving the acquisition highway can be powerful, but it must be a deliberate, integrated strategy, not just opportunistic. It requires an absolute commitment to this strategic direction. The acquisition highway is bought with cheap currency, the company's highly priced stock. Only companies with the highest-valued stocks can play this high-stakes game, and once they start playing, they must commit to accelerated growth or get out.

Considering Diversification as a Way to Grow

The difference between acquisition and diversification may appear to be relatively small, but it's not. On the acquisition highway, there is little leverage from market experience, but there is still a reasonable amount of leverage from technology and technical capabilities. On the diversification highway, there is little leverage from either, and therefore we emphasize the term *diversification.*

Intel's historical growth became more and more difficult to sustain when it captured a dominant share of the microprocessor market and rapid growth in the market began to slow, so it began to look at growth highways outside its primary market. It pursued several growth highways, including the diversification highway. One of these was its entry into the Web-hosting business. In January 1999, Intel launched Intel Online Services. Its first data center in Santa Clara had a capacity for 10,000 servers, but nine months later only a dozen companies were using this service. Many questioned Intel's expansion, saying that the company lacked any experience in the online business. Intel's CEO, Craig Barrett, responded by claiming that Intel had experience running its own Web site, Intel.com.[3]

In 1993 Raytheon attempted to diversify into what it expected would be a significant new market opportunity: personal, rapid-transit systems. Seven years and almost $45 million later, Raytheon decided to cancel this diversification effort.[4] The twin risks of learning a new market and learning a new technology proved to be too much. The market for personal transit systems didn't materialize as anticipated, and the initial test cars were too heavy.

Traveling along this diversification highway to growth is risky, but it may become necessary when a company's prospects are not good, and it needs to reinvent itself. EMC is a great example of a company following this highway to growth. Its original business of building cables and sub-assemblies offered little opportunity for growth, so it decided to diversify into RAID disk drives. This diversification enabled it to build a $6.7 billion business by 1999.

When Digital Equipment stopped growing, it should have considered the diversification growth highway more thoroughly. It developed some interesting communications products that could have formed the basis for diversification, but didn't pursue them far enough. Because diversification as a means to growth is such a big change of direction, it requires changing the company's core strategic vision. This is what Digital failed to do.

In general, diversification is so drastic that it should be considered only when necessary.

Creating Opportunities to Grow through Innovation

Innovation is the most beloved highway to growth. It's the way many dramatic success stories, such as 3M, Xerox, IBM, Intel, and Polaroid, got started. Innovative technology is used to create opportunities for products that never before existed and establishes entirely new markets. Alexander Graham Bell's innovations created the

> *Innovation is the most beloved highway to growth.*

telephone and an entire industry. The microprocessor innovation provided Intel with one of the fastest growth superhighways ever. 3M's relatively simple innovation—the Post-it® Notes—fueled a major new product line. Growth rates from successful innovations can be spectacular.

Despite its attractiveness, innovation is difficult. Innovation can't be scheduled or planned like the other highways to growth. Not only does it take time; it happens only when a number of things come together.

Innovation is also risky. A company may invest in innovation and not achieve results for a very long time. In the meantime, it must seek other opportunities for growth. For these reasons, innovation frequently works best as a secondary highway to growth. That is, the company makes some continuing investments, but does not rely on them for supporting growth objectives until something shows promise.

Conclusion

A rapid-growth strategy requires an increased investment in R&D. A rapid-growth company is more aggressive, but it doesn't travel just one highway. Instead, it invests in a broad portfolio of product development projects. It invests in some of the highways for growth identified in the proactive process, but it also continues to

> *A rapid-growth company doesn't travel just one highway.*

invest in maintaining the competitive position of its current product offerings. The increased investment in R&D pays off once the company begins growing rapidly. And what is the rationale for growing rapidly? We can see three reasons. First, accelerating revenue growth is more important than increasing profit margins. (The assumption is that, eventually, a larger company will generate more profit than a smaller one.) Second, a rapidly growing company will be able to take advantage of more opportunities in the new economy, making it stronger and better positioned for the future. Finally, rapid growth is more exciting. This excitement attracts more ambitious management and investors willing to pay a premium.

Notes

1. Bill Gates, 1999 Microsoft Annual Report.
2. *Business Week,* January 24, 2000, p. 154.
3. Andy Reinhardt, "The New Intel," *Business Week,* March 13, 2000.
4. Ross Kerber, *The Boston Globe,* March 29, 2000.

13

Growth through Acquisitions

Acquisitions can be an integral part of product strategy. There are five types of acquisitions, and each enables product strategy differently.

The acceleration of new technologies over the last decade has increased business opportunities, while at the same time making it increasingly difficult for individual companies to take advantage of these opportunities on their own. Correctly handled, acquisitions and other business relationships such as mergers, joint ventures, partnerships, and strategic investments can provide the missing ingredients to make the most of these burgeoning opportunities.

Developing the needed capabilities internally can take a long time, often so long that a company can miss new market opportunities altogether. Through an acquisition, however, it can immediately access the technology or market experience it needs to expand into a new market. Acquisitions can also be used to strengthen a competitive position in the marketplace.

Although the primary focus of acquisitions in high-technology industries has been to support product strategy, that is not the only reason for making them. Some acquisitions are made to improve operational efficiency through increased economies of scale and consolidation of activities. Numerous mergers and acquisitions in the banking industry are made for this purpose. By combining banking operations, a number of branch banks can be closed, for instance, and internal support operations can be consolidated to reduce overall operating costs. Many telecommunications service companies, Internet service providers, and cable companies also have consolidated for the primary purpose of operational improvements.

This chapter focuses on acquisitions that enable product strategy. We build upon the frameworks and strategies presented in previous chapters and show how acquisitions and other business relationships fit into them. We treat mergers and acquisitions as the same, for they are similar when engaged in to enable product strategy. Although there are some important legal and even psychological distinctions between a merger and an acquisition, there is less of a distinction for product strategy purposes. To help explain the different strategic implications of acquisitions, we've grouped them into five types, describing how each contributes to product strategy. We then look at issues of acquisition valuation. How much of a premium should a company be willing to pay?

> ## How much of a premium should a company be willing to pay?

The expansion framework we introduce in Chapter 6 provides an effective way to explain how an acquisition enables product strategy. It assumes that there are three primary reasons for an acquisition: to improve a company's position in the current market, to leverage entry into a related market, or to enter an entirely new market. Using this framework, we've classified each of the strategic reasons into five distinct acquisition types. The first three acquisition types are engaged in to achieve the leverage necessary to expand into a new market. The fourth is undertaken for competitive reasons. The final type is undertaken to add a new platform for a new market, even though it doesn't leverage much of what the acquiring company already has.

Types of Acquisitions

Most acquisitions are not purely a single type, since it is hoped that there are many secondary benefits; however, most can be classified as one primary type (or reason). Without a primary reason for making an acquisition, a company may as well say, "Let's make an acquisition and see if anything happens." This is often the case with complex multipurpose mergers.

Type I: Acquire a Product Platform to Expand into a New Market

In a Type I acquisition, a company wants to expand into a related market, but can't do so with its own product platform and technology. It has two options: develop the platform itself or acquire it. Acquiring a product platform is usually more expensive than developing the platform internally, unless it's paid for with highly valued stock. But in either case, acquisition is faster; speed may be critical if the related market is strategically important.

The Type I acquisition strategy is illustrated using the expansion framework in Figure 13-1. An expansion platform is created for a related market through two ingredients: (1) the acquiring company leverages its understanding of the market, customer relationships, and distribution channel, and (2) the acquired company provides a new product platform for this market. Sometimes, the company's current platform and the acquired platform may be complementary, offering customers a solution that integrates both platforms. That's why the illustration shows some overlap. The increased importance of total solutions is driving this trend in many industries.

Type I acquisitions have proved to be especially effective when a large, mature company with a strong distribution capability acquires a start-up company that is just beginning to sell a new product. This is the favorite acquisition strategy of John Chambers, CEO of Cisco: "Our ideal acquisition is a small start-up that has a great technology product on the draw-

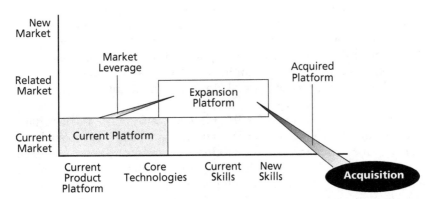

Figure 13-1   Type I acquisition: Acquire a product platform to expand into a new market.

ing board that is going to come out in 6 to 12 months. We buy the engineers and the next-generation product. Then we blow it through our distribution channels and leverage our manufacturing and financial strengths."[1]

As we discuss in Chapter 2, acquisitions of this type, as well as Type II, are an integral part of Cisco's core strategic vision. Its strategy for technical excellence is to blend internal product development with acquisitions. In 1999 alone, Cisco released 65 major new products and claimed to have the leading market share in 16 of the 20 markets in which it competed.

Examples of Type I strategy include Cisco's August 1999 acquisitions of Cerent Corporation and Monterey Networks, Inc., for a combined $7.4 billion in stock. With these acquisitions, Cisco entered a new related market, the optical transport market, which it expected to be a $10 billion market in 2002. Cerent was a leading developer of next-generation optical transport products. Monterey was an innovator of infrastructure-class, optical cross-connect technology used to increase network capacity at the core of an optical network.

Another Type I example is Cisco's acquisition of Summa Four, Inc., in July 1998. Summa Four's open-standards-based programmable switches enabled Cisco to offer value-added telephony applications to new and existing service providers, extending these services to a voice-over IP (Internet protocol) infrastructure. These switches are used by service providers for basic call switching as well as for delivering services such as voice mail, calling cards, and voice-activated dialing. This acquisition supported Cisco's core strategic vision to provide an open services environment, enabling applications for circuit- and packet-switched networks.

Microsoft sometimes uses Type I acquisitions to get into new related markets. For example, in April 1997, it acquired WebTV to get the platform needed to expand into the market for Internet access using television sets. In September 1999, Microsoft acquired Visio Corporation, the leading supplier of business diagramming and technical drawing software—for $1.3 billion—in order to get a platform to expand into a related market for business productivity.

A shared vision, at least for the market/platform, is an important ingredient of a Type I acquisition. If, after the acquisition is completed, the two companies can't agree on the product strategy for this new platform, then it's likely to fail. To avoid this risk, both companies need to discuss their core strategic visions prior to the acquisition and develop a market platform plan immediately. This helps align strategies and address differences in a rational manner.

Type II: Acquire Technology and Technical Skills to Develop a New Product Platform

A Type II acquisition strategy, depicted in Figure 13-2, is a variation on Type I. The objective is still to create a new platform to enter a related market, but in Type II the acquiring company is trying primarily to add technology and technical skills, instead of a complete product platform. The acquiring company intends to combine this new technology with some of its own to build a new product platform for a new market. The reason for acquiring the technology and skills is to develop the platform much faster or better than the acquiring company could do on its own. As in a Type I acquisition, the acquiring company usually provides the market and channel capability.

In other words, whereas in a Type I acquisition a platform is acquired to be sold to a related market with minimal or no change, in a Type II acquisition the primary intent is to acquire a new technology to build a new platform for expanding into a related market. The acquisition may include an existing platform, but if this is an incidental rather than a primary objective, it is considered to be a Type II acquisition.

Identifying the type of acquisition is important in knowing what to do *after* the acquisition. In some cases, it may also be important to distinguish between an acquisition of *technology* and an acquisition of *technical skills*. Although, frequently, this is a more granular distinction than necessary, refer to the first as Type IIA and to the second as Type IIB. In theory a company should be willing to pay more for a Type I acquisition than a

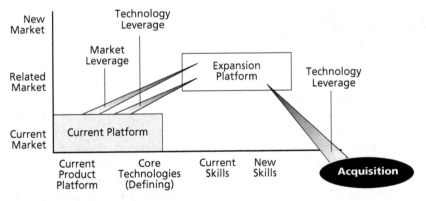

Figure 13-2 Type II acquisition: Acquire technology and technical skills to develop a new product platform.

Type II, because a Type I also includes the underlying technology and skills. Likewise it should be willing to pay more for a Type IIA than a Type IIB, because a Type IIA includes the underlying skills in addition to the technology.

In early 2000, Nortel Networks made several Type II acquisitions in order to get the critical technology to build a new platform for the high-speed optical Internet switching and transmission systems market. In March 2000 it acquired CoreTek for $1.4 billion. CoreTek had technology for tunable lasers that eliminated the need for different lasers for each optical wavelength on each line. By incorporating this technology into its new platform, Nortel could reduce costs by using a generic laser to generate multiple wavelengths and convert data transmission directly from one wavelength to another.

A couple of months earlier, Nortel had acquired Qtera Corp. and Xros, Inc., each for $3.2 billion, to provide other technologies for this same platform and related offerings. Qtera provided technology that increased the distance that optical signals could be sent without regeneration. Xros's silicon-based micromirror switch provided very high capacity for open optical networks. Xros was another key building block in Nortel Networks' strategy to develop an all-optical Internet platform.

Even more so than with Type I, it's critical to integrate a Type II acquisition immediately into product strategy. In a Type I acquisition, there is an existing platform ready to be launched into the related market, even if the company expects to develop a next-generation platform in the future. In a Type II acquisition, this new platform needs to be developed before *any* benefits accrue from the acquisition, so time is more critical.

Type III: Acquire Market Experience and Channel Capabilities to Enter a New Market

A Type III acquisition is the complement of the first two. In this case, the acquiring company has a product platform, but does not have the capability to offer it to a new market, so it acquires a company with a strong distribution capability to enable it to bring its platform or a derivative of it to the new market. This acquisition strategy is depicted in Figure 13-3.

One Type III acquisition was BASF's purchase of American Cyanamid (American Home Products Corporation's farm chemical business) for $3.8 billion in March 2000. BASF had a growing pipeline of new crop-protection products, but it had weak distribution in the United States. Cyanamid had strong U.S. marketing and distribution capabilities. The acquisition gave BASF leverage to expand the market for its new products.

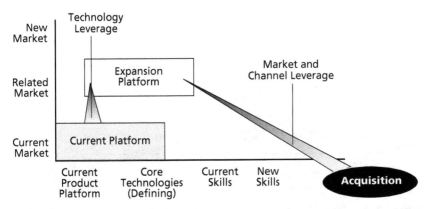

Figure 13-3   Type III acquisition: Acquire market experience and channel capabilities to enter a new market.

The ingredients for success in a Type III acquisition are the same as in a Type I. The only difference is the importance of leveraging the new market capabilities as quickly as possible. Overall, this is not a very popular acquisition strategy, since the acquiring company usually has the market and distribution capability.

Type IV: Acquire a Competitor to Strengthen a Current Market Position

In a Type IV acquisition, a company acquires a competitor with a product offering in the same market. The objective of such an acquisition strategy is to consolidate market share by combining the two companies. As illustrated in Figure 13-4, after the acquisition the combined company now has two product platforms in the same market, which in theory corrals more customers with different preferences.

The strategic value of a Type IV acquisition lies primarily in increasing competitive advantage. The dominant company in each market usually has significant advantages, but some of these advantages are diminished if the company is now selling two different product platforms to the same market. The downside is that it's difficult for the sales force to sell two competing products to the same customer base, and it's expensive to continue to support two different product platforms. Type IV acquisitions are how companies usually get into the problem of multiple platforms serving the same market, as we discuss in Chapter 3. Eventually, a Type IV acquisition results in consolidation of the two platforms into a single,

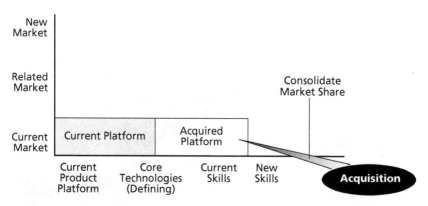

Figure 13-4   Type IV acquisition: Acquire a competitor to strengthen current market position.

new, next-generation platform so the company can achieve critical scale advantages.

Sometimes, a Type IV acquisition enables a company to reduce competitive threats enough to raise prices and profits, but in at least one case this strategy backfired. A company with 40 percent market share acquired its major competitor with 30 percent of the market, thinking that, combined, they would have a 70 percent share and could reduce competitive pricing pressure. Customers in this market routinely solicited proposals from two companies, however, and after the acquisition, the third-largest competitor got a lot more opportunities to bid. Its market share increased, and the combined company realized a market share of only a little more than 50 percent.

Frequently, a Type IV acquisition is made to strengthen a company's position in a market segment by providing a new platform focused on that segment. Such was the case in EMC Corporation's $1.1 billion acquisition of Data General. This acquisition enabled EMC to address customer requirements in the midrange storage market, an approximately $10 billion market segment in 1998. Data General's CLARiiON storage products were recognized as among the most advanced midrange storage systems. When combined with EMC's advanced software, distribution, and services capabilities, they enabled EMC to fully address all its customers' online storage needs in both new and existing market segments.

Too often, though, Type IV acquisitions are made with the vague objective of strengthening competitive position, with no clear idea of what that actually means. Managers may become confused after the acquisition, making objectives more elusive. The key to a Type IV acquisition is to start with a clear idea of what is intended, and then move quickly to get the desired benefits.

Type V: Acquire a Company with the Capability to Diversify into a Related Market

A Type V acquisition, depicted in Figure 13-5, is more of a stand-alone strategy. What do we mean by this? The acquired company is reasonably self-sufficient, since it provides both market capability and the product platform. The acquisition enables the acquirer to diversify into a related market without providing much assistance. Generally, there are additional strategic reasons for a Type V acquisition; otherwise, it's not worth paying a premium over the market price for the company, as is done in most acquisitions.

For example, AT&T's acquisitions of two major cable companies enabled it to protect its customer base and expand into new, related markets. In 1999 AT&T had approximately 60 million long-distance customers, but without controlling the point of origin of their calls, its hold on these customers was at risk. The local phone companies had more leverage to provide long-distance service to their customers, and more perceived proximity to the increasing opportunity for Internet access services. In order to protect its long-distance business, therefore, AT&T acquired cable companies TCI and MediaOne for $110 billion. AT&T intended to upgrade these cable networks to provide interactive TV, high-speed Internet access, and, most important, phone service. While these two cable companies could have upgraded their networks themselves, they were reluctant to make investments of the magnitude required. With the ability to offer local phone service, AT&T could retain many of its long-distance customers.

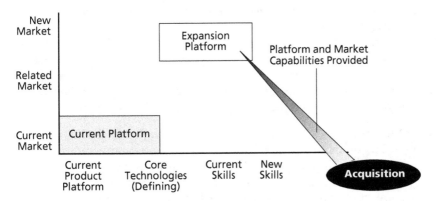

Figure 13-5 Type V acquisition: Acquire a company with a platform and market capability to diversify into a related market.

In another example, Healtheon merged with WebMD in 1999, even though the companies were in different (but related) markets. Healtheon provided business-to-business and consumer-to-business electronic commerce services that linked doctors and consumers with health care institutions. Its services simplified business and clinical health care processes and provided faster access to information. WebMD offered a comprehensive suite of Internet-based services and information for physicians, as well as health care information for consumers. In addition to each business's continuing focus on its own market, it was hoped that each would provide customer opportunities for the other in the merger. For example, if doctors used WebMD, they might be drawn to use Healtheon to automate their back-office services.

Sometimes, a company intends to do a Type I acquisition but ends up with a Type V. Even Cisco made this mistake when it acquired some new software platforms but did not have the needed channel of distribution. Cisco wasn't able to leverage sales of these products as it had expected, and the result was lower-than-anticipated sales after the acquisition took place.

Success in a Type V acquisition depends on the eventual value of the other reasons for the relationship, which is usually the basis for the premium paid for the acquisition.

Valuing Acquisitions

The subject of premiums brings up the question of valuation. How much is it worth to make an acquisition in order to get what is needed to execute a product strategy instead of developing the capability oneself? A simple make/buy analysis may provide an immediate answer, but this is usually oversimplified. Some companies are fortunate to be able to make acquisitions using their stock as inflated currency. This is much cheaper than paying real money to develop a needed capability themselves. Sometimes, though, an acquisition is the only way a company can get what it needs, since it can't develop that capability at any price. In other cases, a company may be able to develop the capability, but it may not have the time necessary to do it and to bring the new platform to market successfully.

Inflated Currency   This was the route Nortel took in March 2000, when it spent $1.4 billion to acquire CoreTek, a 120-person company that was a year away from shipping its first product. Far from being an aberration, acquisitions like these were becoming commonplace in late 1999 and early 2000. How could they make sense? CoreTek invested $26 million to develop its technology. Why couldn't Nortel, which invests almost $3 billion in R&D, develop the technology itself?

The answer is that acquiring technology in exchange for stock can sometimes be cheaper than developing it, especially with hyperinflated stock prices. Acquisitions that support product strategy can be worth a premium because they provide unique technology that can only be acquired. They can also provide technology much faster and enable the platform to be brought to market more quickly. But putting these reasons aside for a moment, it can also be cheaper to acquire a $26 million technology for $1 billion in stock.

> *Acquiring technology in exchange for stock can sometimes be cheaper than developing it.*

Here's why. At the time of the acquisition, Nortel's stock was trading for almost $130 per share, up from $25 a year earlier. At earnings from operations of $1.28 per share, the price was approximately 100 times earnings. It's important to note that investors focused on earnings from operations, effectively ignoring the cost of acquisitions. Assuming that Nortel could have developed the same technology for $26 million (which is not likely), the cost of this development would have reduced earnings by $18.7 million after taxes (at its 1999 tax rate of 28 percent). In theory, with a stock market capitalization of 100 times earnings, Nortel's market value would have gone down by $1.87 billion ($18.7 million times 100). By issuing stock worth $1.4 billion, Nortel held the dilution in its market value to under $1.87 billion.

The mathematics of the transaction depends, of course, on being able to pay for acquisitions with very highly valued stock. If Nortel had made this acquisition a year earlier, it would have paid five times more stock, and the deal could have been prohibitively expensive. At its previous valuation of 20 times earnings, the equivalent market value reduction would have been only $374 million ($18.7 million times 20). Instead of being "cheaper," the $1.4 billion acquisition of CoreTek would have been 3.5 times more expensive than the $26 million development cost, requiring much more justification.

In general, companies with stock prices valued at a very high multiple of earnings or revenues have a cheap currency to use in making acquisitions. They can pay relatively high prices for small companies such as CoreTek and acquire larger companies with lower multiples than theirs. However, this is a fast and high-risk game. To keep their stock price high in order to maintain cheap currency for acquisitions, high-multiple companies need a track record and continuing commitment to rapid growth. Thus product strategy for growth becomes even more important.

Acquiring Technology   Sometimes an acquisition may be the only way to get the technology needed to expand into a new market, as when a proprietary or patented technology cannot be duplicated or licensed. This may also be the case if a targeted acquisition dominates a market or channel. The acquisition may be the only way to penetrate the market. In these cases, valuation depends on what it will take to get into the market, but at some point the cost exceeds the potential value of expanding into a new market. Thus cost becomes a critical part of the product strategy decision.

One arresting case was the possibility that News Corp., along with the Liberty Media Group, would acquire General Motors just to get access to the satellite television platform in its Hughes Electronics business. General Motors' $250 billion auto business, an unwanted acquisition that came along with the satellite business, would most likely have been disposed of afterward.

Faster Access   It usually makes sense to pay a premium to get faster access to necessary technology, and frequently this is the justification for making an acquisition. If a new product platform can be brought to market faster, the increased revenue and competitive advantages can be great.

This was the reason behind two of the Type I acquisitions Microsoft made. Even with its enormous technical capabilities, Microsoft would have taken too much time to develop the platform it acquired from WebTV, and it would have missed the market. The same is true of its acquisition of Visio. In comparison, previously

> *It usually makes sense to pay a premium to get faster access to necessary technology, and frequently this is the justification for making an acquisition.*

Microsoft had attempted unsuccessfully to acquire Intuit, the leading competitor in the tax preparation software market. Microsoft then invested heavily to develop its own tax preparation software, only to conclude that it was too late to get into the market. The cost to develop and maintain the software was too high relative to the market share it was able to capture, and in March 2000 Microsoft decided to exit the market.

A company can actually estimate the value of an acquisition as it develops its product strategy by comparing the strategy for internal development to making the acquisition.

Other Business Relationships

We have focused so far on the five primary types of acquisitions to support product strategy. There are some additional strategies under the broad designation of business relationships that support product strategy. Since these are not as important, we cover them only briefly.

Joint Ventures   In a joint venture, two companies come together to form a third business owned jointly. The joint venture typically develops a new platform targeting a market that is new, but somewhat related to both companies. Without a shared platform, almost inevitably there will be a conflict over market opportunity. As in the expansion framework applied previously, a joint venture needs to combine sufficient market and channel capabilities with the necessary technology and technical skills from the two companies.

From a product strategy perspective, in a joint venture both parties must share a clear strategic vision and a common market platform strategy. All too often, companies forming a joint venture fail to do this because it's too rigorous and somewhat uncomfortable. However, in joint ventures a more rigorous process is even more critical than it is within a single company. Furthermore, in most successful joint ventures, both parties contribute equally. If they do not, and there are differences in their contributions to the joint venture and their benefits from it, inevitably there will be friction, even if the differences are more perceived than real.

> *Joint ventures are more fragile than acquisitions; for that reason, they're generally less successful.*

Joint ventures are more fragile than acquisitions; for that reason, they're generally less successful. In the early 1990s, Hewlett-Packard and Intel got together to design, manufacture, and market a new product platform: a 64-bit microprocessor (now called Itanium) aimed at powering computer servers. Originally, the two companies were 50/50 partners, but since that time, HP has become less involved and Intel has assumed more control. While Itanium is still under development, it's less powerful than originally expected[2] and coming to market later than anticipated.

There are several reasons for the troubles with this joint venture. It's very difficult for both partners to share a common vision. Each has its own vision and wants to use the joint venture to support it. It's unlikely that a common partnership vision will encompass each partner's vision sufficiently, and if it does, it's not likely to stay that way long enough, especially in rapidly changing technology industries.

Cultural differences also make joint ventures less successful. Cultural differences might include different decision-making styles, different attitudes on investment, different working practices and compensation programs, different product development processes, and so forth. Each partner has its own culture and is not likely to change it for the joint venture. The joint venture may be dominated by one partner's culture, or it may develop its own. In either case, it still has the problem of getting two or more cultures to work well together.

Other notable joint ventures that were less than successful include IBM, Motorola, and Apple working together to build the PowerPC microprocessor, and IBM and Sears partnering to create Prodigy.

Complex Multipurpose Mergers A complex multipurpose merger has a broad and vague rationalization. There are usually many potential opportunities for synergy, but they are not as clear or as straightforward as in the other types of acquisitions. For example, in the $350 billion merger of America Online with Time Warner, there appear to be hundreds of opportunities for synergy in the merged company, but it's difficult to see one or two that provide a significant strategic advantage.

The biggest potential advantage is likely to be AOL's ability to use Time Warner's cable network as a broadband distribution platform. There are also opportunities for cross-marketing; shared content such as CNN and Time Warner's music, magazine, and movie content; and distribution of AOL subscription CDs in Warner Bros. retail stores. Overall, however, the diverse strategic benefits tend to be more elusive.

A complex multipurpose merger is difficult to relate to product strategy because there are many reasons for the merger. Usually a number of acquisition types are buried in the deal, creating some problems. Right from the beginning, the two companies considering the merger get so immersed in a myriad of possibilities that it's often impossible to thoroughly evaluate them. The merger is based more on gut feel than on clear strategic analysis. During the merger process, it's difficult to focus strategically on building the new opportunities. They tend to get neglected. The operational issues in a large multipurpose merger can also become overwhelming. As a result of all these problems, these mergers tend to be disappointing.

Compaq Computer hoped that its January 1998 $8.4 billion merger with Digital Equipment would help it leapfrog into the higher-end corporate computing markets; instead, the merger almost killed it. By early 1999 Compaq's profits were down. In April the board fired CEO Eckhard Pfeiffer. Digital didn't provide anywhere near the benefits that Compaq had hoped for; instead, Compaq had to concentrate on solving problems in its newly acquired businesses.

Mergers like this are generally made for something closer to market price, so there is less of a premium that needs to be justified through some sort of strategic leverage. In the AOL and Time Warner merger, AOL did pay a premium of something like 60 to 70 percent (or about $20 billion) for Time Warner, so there was some need to justify strategic leverage.

Strategic Investments With a strategic investment, one company makes a noncontrolling investment in another in order to get preferred access to that company's market or technology. The idea is that the company making the investment gets the same return as other investors, but also gets other advantages. In order to get these other advantages, the company must make large strategic investments, frequently at more than the market price.

Some form of partnership or working relationship between the two companies usually comes along with the strategic investment. Generally, the working relationship will benefit both companies, but, in some ways, the investment works as a balancing factor if it doesn't. If the relationship generates more benefits to the company receiving the investment, the investing company is compensated by appreciation on its investment. If it benefits only the investing company, the other company at least received the investment at a premium price.

Microsoft jumped onto noncontrolling investments as a preferred method for forming strategic relationships. In 1998 it made about a dozen strategic investments, and in 1999, more than 30. At this writing, in early 2000, Microsoft had already made 20 strategic investments by the end of March. Some of Microsoft's strategic investments were:

- *August 1997:* Invested $150 million in Apple Computer. The two companies entered into a broad product and technology development agreement.

- *December 1998:* Invested $200 million in Qwest Communications. Qwest agreed to license a broad range of Microsoft products to build a new service offering based on the Microsoft Windows NT Server operating system.

- *May 1999:* Invested $5 billion in AT&T. AT&T agreed to increase its commitment to use Windows CE-based systems in an additional 2.5 to 5 million set-top devices.

- *May 1999:* Invested $600 million in Nextel Communications. Nextel agreed to give its customers access to the MSN network of Internet services.

- *September 1999:* Invested $15 million in Akamai Technologies. Akamai agreed to incorporate Microsoft Windows Media Technologies into its product and port its software to the Microsoft Windows Server operating system.

- *November 1999:* Invested $100 million in RadioShack.com. Radio Shack agreed to joint marketing of Microsoft products in its 7,000 stores.

- *December 1999:* Invested $200 million in Best Buy. The two companies agreed to a broad marketing alliance, including promotion of Microsoft products in Best Buy stores.

Strategic investments can also be a prelude to an acquisition. The two companies have the opportunity to become familiar with each other before making the acquisition commitment. Microsoft did this with WebTV Networks. It made a strategic investment in WebTV in September 1996 and agreed to collaborate on developing technologies for delivering Internet content through television sets. Less than a year later, it acquired WebTV for $425 million.

A strategic investment approach requires a lot of cash.

A strategic investment approach requires a lot of cash, something that Microsoft has. It can also be profitable if the investments are good. At the end of 1999, Microsoft had approximately $20 billion in investments, most of these strategic investments, which had increased from $14 billion six months earlier. Microsoft earned $1.2 billion over six months from its investments, and still had $18 billion more in cash to make future strategic investments.

Alliances and Partnering   Alliances and partnerships cover such a broad range of relationships that it's difficult to summarize how these support product strategy. Also, many alliances tend to be tactical, since they address alternative ways to implement a product strategy instead of shaping the strategy itself.

Forming Product Strategy with Acquisitions

Successful acquisition integration involves many processes, products, and people. In this chapter, we are concerned only with the integration of the acquired company into a unified product strategy, which, while obvious, is all too frequently overlooked. The acquiring company simply expects something to happen and seems surprised when nothing does.

We see two critical aspects of integrating an acquisition into a unified product strategy. The first is integration of the acquired business into the core strategic vision of the acquiring business. The second is development of a formal product strategy for the new product platform created by the acquisition.

1. *A common core strategic vision must be developed.*   It shouldn't be surprising that the acquired company and the acquiring company have different core strategic visions, since the reason for the acquisition in the first place is that the two companies are complementary, and very likely have different emphases. If the visions remain different, if there is disagree-

ment on where the industry is going, if there are different expectations of core technologies, if there is misunderstanding over roles, then it will be difficult to unify the product strategy.

A single core strategic vision must emerge. In most acquisitions, the acquired company's vision is subordinated to that of the acquiring company; however, the acquiring company's vision usually changes to integrate the acquisition. For joint ventures, a common core strategic vision becomes more problematic, since it's more difficult for joint venture partners to agree on a common vision.

The same is true for complex multipurpose mergers. Compaq and Digital had different visions. We look at both of these in detail in the case studies in Chapter 1. Digital, in particular, had been wandering without any strategic vision, and it was almost impossible for Compaq to revise its vision to integrate the Digital acquisition in the time frame necessary to get results.

The very first step following a major acquisition is to review the core strategic vision and see how it should change. When the review is done formally, inviting senior management of the acquired company to be part of the process, it's more likely that a unified vision will result.

2. *A market platform plan must be developed quickly to integrate product strategy.* If an acquisition is made for product strategy purposes, the development of that new strategy should not be left to chance. Don't expect that the two companies will eventually "get around" to developing a joint strategy. It doesn't happen naturally in a company without an acquisition, and it surely should not be expected to happen in the combination of two companies.

> *The very first step following a major acquisition is to review the core strategic vision and see how it should change.*

As soon as the acquisition is complete and the core strategic vision is revised, the company should form a joint team to develop a formal market platform plan for senior management approval. The team and senior management should follow a well-defined process so that logic rules over emotion; otherwise, the differences between the two companies can become disruptive. If necessary, this team should work offsite at a neutral location and get facilitation from experts in formulating product strategy. If the acquisition was worth a significant investment to make a product strategy feasible, it's also worth making sure that the acquisition actually gets integrated into the strategy.

With explicit development of a new market platform plan, the acquisition is integrated into a unified product strategy. Then emphasis can quickly shift to execution of this strategy. An added advantage is that the benefits of the acquisition are quickly quantified and verified.

Notes

1. Interview with John Chambers in "The Art of the Deal" by James Daly, *Business 2.0,* October 1999.

2. Russ Britt, "The Birth of a New Processor," *Electronic Business,* January 2000, pp. 62–68.

14

Growth through New Ventures

Some aspects of product strategy are even more important for new ventures than they are for well-established companies; too many entrepreneurs overlook product strategy in their eagerness to get going.

A new venture can be viewed as a product strategy to create a product platform with the expectation that it will lead to a complete business. The venture will succeed or fail on the quality of that product strategy. New ventures usually don't get a second chance.

Ironically, despite its importance, we find that many entrepreneurs fail to focus enough on product strategy. In their eagerness to get going, they start developing their initial product without thoroughly thinking it through. Frequently, their product strategies are flawed. The lucky ones discover the flaws in time to react; for others, the flaws in their product strategies prove to be fatal.

In this chapter, we apply the frameworks, concepts, and strategies discussed in earlier chapters that are most important to new ventures. As in all other businesses, a strong core strategic vision is the genesis of a new venture, and many of the product platform and product line concepts and frameworks described in this book are equally useful.

Establishing the Boundaries of a Core Strategic Vision

A new venture must be founded on a solid core strategic vision (CSV). As we describe in Chapter 1, a vision needs to answer the three questions:

- Where do we want the new venture to go?
- How will we get there?
- Why do we expect to be successful?

In some ways, these are more difficult questions for a new venture than for an existing company. A company with an ongoing business already has a vision and boundaries it is considering changing. The new venture is a clean sheet of paper and has little to leverage into a complete vision. The following example shows how the characteristics of a new venture's CSV differ from those of an established business. A new venture was created to develop an integrated set of Web-based application software products to automate product development management. This was the core strategic vision:

> To build a major business with long-term growth potential by becoming the leader in providing integrated application software for product development management. We will do this by developing a comprehensive application architecture that enables seamless integration of all product development information across all projects and functions, as well as with outside development partners. We expect to be successful because (1) customers will want an integrated system instead of individual products, (2) we will be the first to apply a proven management process architecture, and (3) we will leverage the intimate customer relationships of our consulting partner.

A few elements in this vision are typical of CSVs for new ventures. First, there is no reference to any current capabilities, other than those of a consulting partner, since the business is just starting. Second, the CSV states its intention to become a major business, implying an ambitious long-term strategy and a sizable market to support its products. Third, the emphasis on its product platform is more important than in some CSVs of current businesses. Finally, it refers to a business partner as a critical part of its strategy.

In the new Internet age, some entrepreneurs have a difficult time knowing where they want a new venture to go beyond its initial public offering (IPO).

Even the first CSV question presents some difficulty for some entrepreneurs. For many, it's difficult to look beyond an initial product to a long-term destination for the venture. In the new Internet age, some entrepreneurs have a difficult time knowing *where* they want the venture to go beyond its initial public offering (IPO).

On the other hand, most new ventures know *how* they will get there, even if they have a hard time knowing where they are going. The answer to this second question is usually articulated by describing the product or service they plan to develop.

Answering the third question is the most critical. A new venture needs to be able to explain *why* it thinks it can be successful against already entrenched competitors and possible threats from other new ventures. The answer to this question takes a new venture from simply a good idea into a real strategy. Seasoned venture capitalists will often say that the primary reason they don't invest in a new opportunity is

> *Seasoned venture capitalists will often say that the primary reason they don't invest in a new opportunity is that the entrepreneur's vision is disconnected from reality.*

not that the entrepreneur's vision isn't exciting, but that his or her vision is disconnected from reality. They don't think the venture can be successful.

We find that the CSV Boundary Framework described in Chapter 2 is very successful in evaluating the potential of a new venture, especially the *why*. The boundary conditions that constrain and enable the success of a core strategic vision serve the same purpose for a new venture. We recommend that all entrepreneurs go through the exercise of creating a CSV, fitting it with the boundary conditions. This is especially important in the early stages of a new venture, prior to first-round venture funding. Because of the fast-moving, dynamic nature of a new venture, it should be updated and reviewed regularly. Another important milestone for reviewing and updating the CSV is before the IPO, so the CEO of the venture can clearly articulate its vision to potential investors.

Not all the boundary conditions in the CSV Boundary Framework are the same for a new venture as for others.

Financial Plan (Economic Model)   The financial plan is the central focus of a new venture's business plan. It shows expected revenue and profit for this new product and the business around it. However, the financial model for a new venture must do more than that: It must define the economic model for the business in financial terms.

Each venture has an economic model that translates its business dynamics into financial terms. An existing business has a historic income statement that shows how it made (or lost) money. Its financial plan uses this as a baseline, with changes made from the baseline. A new venture has no baseline, so its financial plan brings its underlying economic model to life. In a way, the economic model is like the mathematical proof that the business concept can be translated into a profitable business: It incorporates a mathematical expression of how revenue and profit will be generated from the product. It defines the expected cost of acquiring new customers and how this is expected to change over time. It estimates the cost of developing and supporting new products.

Sometimes, the economic model for a new venture is fundamentally flawed. The business will never be profitable. Most experienced venture capitalists will be able to see the flaws and avoid making a bad investment.

The financial plan and economic model in the CSV Boundary Framework are reconciled with the CSV statement and other boundary conditions to create a consistent financial expression of the CSV and the expected result of the competitive strategy and product strategy. This exercise quantifies where the venture wants to go financially; for some new ventures, it alone proves enlightening.

Market Trends/Competitive Strategy   Usually, either a market or a technology trend is the basis of the opportunity for a new venture. When a market trend creates the opportunity, then this boundary condition is the one that primarily influences the CSV. The market trend can establish a new market segment that the venture will attack, instead of segments currently served by well-established competitors. As part of this boundary, it's necessary to estimate the potential size of that segment.

It's also essential to consider the venture's competitive strategy and its likelihood of capturing a sufficient share of that market segment. This analysis gets deeply into *why* the venture expects to be successful. We discuss some of the primary competitive strategy considerations later in this chapter.

A new venture may be pursuing an opportunity based on a new or emerging technology that is expected to create an entirely new market. The opportunity creates some unique product strategy challenges. Potential investors must be educated on the characteristics of this new market. Estimating the market potential before the market is even created requires some creativity, and early customers will be different from mainstream customers. Because this issue is so important to new ventures, we've addressed it in the last section of the chapter.

Technology Trends/Strategy   If the venture is created by a new technology trend, or new technology is developed by the venture, then this becomes a primary focus of the CSV. It's necessary to forecast the life of the new technology relative to other potential alternative technologies in order to carry the CSV into the future.

When investing in a technology-driven new venture, investors consult with experts in that technology as well as potential alternative technologies. Barriers to entry are based on the defensibility of the technology.

Product Strategy Product strategy enables the venture to achieve its CSV. It's the primary boundary condition for answering the question of *how* the venture will be successful. For existing companies, this boundary builds on current product platforms, extending them with the product strategy for new products. For a new venture, the focus is exclusively on the product strategy of creating a new product platform.

The product strategy should go beyond the initial product, if the CSV goes beyond the first product. In some cases, a new venture will express a CSV that has a long-term goal of dominating a new market or market segment, but the product strategy to support that vision is exclusively focused on the immediate, and thus is disconnected from the CSV.

However, a longer-term product strategy obviously can't be as specific and clear as the immediate strategy for the initial product. It's usually expressed in terms of a product roadmap or platform strategy that shows the direction and intent of longer-term product strategy to support the longer-term vision.

Business Charter The business charter boundary for the initial CSV of a new venture is completely unrestricted. The new venturers can create a CSV to do anything they want, so, in most cases, the charter of the business is established by the initial CSV. From that point on, however, this charter becomes a boundary constraint for the evolution of the venture.

If the CSV is too specific and too focused on the short-term, the resulting charter may be restrictive. One new venture fell into this

> *A new venture's core competencies are typically the skills and experiences of its founders.*

trap. It achieved its limited CSV very quickly, but then found it had to go through the painful process of reinventing itself in order to change to a more ambitious vision.

Core Competencies/Value Chain A new venture's core competencies are typically the skills and experiences of its founders. As the venture begins to grow, its core competencies expand through the addition of new management and technical talent. But institutional core competencies are generally limited in the early stages. As a result, the primary focus of this boundary is to expand to create the core competencies and the value-chain capabilities that the venture must develop in order to be successful.

Platform Strategy and Product Line Strategy in New Ventures

Every new venture eventually needs more than a single product. Most companies with only a single offering usually have limited success or are acquired by a larger multiproduct company. This does not mean a new venture must quickly add too many products or diversify into unrelated offerings. Rather, it means a new venture with a robust CSV should build a robust product platform with the ability to spawn multiple product offerings.

Some of the strategic concepts and frameworks introduced in Chapter 3 and Chapter 4 on platform management and product line strategy are essential for new ventures.

Platform Strategy   As we state in the introduction, a new venture is a strategy for a new product platform, a plan to create an entirely new product platform as the basis for a series of new product offerings. Too many new ventures fail to recognize the need for a formal platform strategy.

> *Too many new ventures fail to recognize the need for a formal platform strategy.*

In a new venture with limited resources, skipping over the platform strategy looks faster and easier because it's less restrictive. The common thinking goes: "Let's get an initial product to market first, and then we'll worry about a product platform for future products." A first-to-market strategy is generally behind the desire to take this shortcut.

While there may be some merit to focusing on getting a product to market rather than building a more sustainable platform, this approach should be consciously understood as a short-term versus a long-term strategic decision. Developing the first product of what will later be turned into a product platform is very different from developing a first product with little thought to subsequent products. In some cases, the first product may be inconsistent with a more robust platform that could support multiple product offerings. If this is the case, then the initial product will need to be replaced, potentially creating problems with customers.

A solid platform strategy leverages the resulting product offerings, enabling them to be deployed more rapidly and consistently. It leverages the cost of developing individual products and introduces a commonality that reduces costs. In Chapter 3, we use Amazon.com as an example of a product platform that has the following elements spread across all product offerings:

- Its one-click online ordering process makes placing an order convenient for its entire range of offerings.

- The capability to provide extensive online information is used in various offerings.

- Related customer services, such as wish lists, purchase circles, discussion boards, and the ability to browse by age or interest, provide additional value across all offerings.

- Its physical distribution network is purposely built to handle e-commerce for most of its offerings.

- Its Internet wireless ordering system is spread across all offerings.

- Its international Web site variations are spread across most offerings.

The importance of platform strategy depends on the original core strategic vision. Is the vision to create a single product or a sustainable platform of products? When you understand the Amazon product platform strategy more deeply, you see that it supports a vision that extends far beyond low-cost distribution of books.

> *A platform strategy approach in a new venture encourages a long-term view of product strategy.*

A platform strategy approach in a new venture encourages a long-term view of product strategy, even if the initial products demonstrate only a portion of the eventual strategy. Such an approach requires more discipline than simply developing a single product.

Earlier in this chapter, we use the example of a software venture with a robust vision of a number of integrated products for product development from a common Web-based software platform. While this platform strategy was very ambitious and very expensive to initiate, it had the potential of being a successful long-term strategy. In contrast, a number of other new ventures being explored at the same time were developing Web-based application software aimed at individual product development functions—sometimes referred to as "point products," because they are focused on a limited set of functions. While some of these ventures may have had aspirations to extend their businesses into other product development functions, the initial product offerings were not designed around a platform that would accommodate the integration of multiple products.

Market Platform Plan   This framework is a useful business model.While the MPP framework described in Chapter 5 is a useful business model in general, it's specifically applicable to new ventures because it focuses attention on the most critical product strategy issues. From a product strategy perspective, it forces a deeper characterization and prioritization of customer segments in the target market. New ventures, especially those creating a new market, frequently assume that the market is much more homogeneous than it really is. They learn from experience that the market is segmented into groups of customers, each with a different emphasis. The MPP framework reminds the new venture that there is a difference in market segments and that the basis of customer value and differentiation varies by segment. It sets the stage for prioritizing each customer segment and helps to shape the differences in product offerings for each segment.

Product line strategy results from this framework, giving the new venture a preliminary, time-phased plan for future product offerings. Collectively, these requirements define the building blocks of the new platform.

Platform Technology   A strategic understanding of the structure and elements of its platform technology is especially important for a new venture; otherwise, it lacks a deep understanding of what it really is as a business. The platform technology element framework illustrated in Chapter 5 (Figure 5-3) is very useful in building this strategic understanding.

> *For a new venture, the defining platform element is what makes it unique, and that is where attention and investment should be focused. The supporting platform elements are less important; in many cases, they're outsourced.*

For a new venture, the defining platform element is what makes it unique, and that is where attention and investment should be focused. The supporting platform elements are less important; in many cases, they're outsourced. The segmenting elements are unique to each product offering and can be delayed according to the priority for developing each offering.

New ventures usually have fewer resources to develop a new platform than larger companies and may need to build their product platform differently. They may need to stretch out product offerings over a longer period of time. They may need to develop some of the platform elements only partially in order to prove the business concept to investors. All this is part of the platform strategy for a new venture.

Viewing the Venture as an Expansion

By definition, a new venture is a strategy for expansion into a new market. Although this is very different from an existing company expanding into a new market, we find that the expansion framework introduced in Chapter 6 is a useful tool for a new venture.

Since this framework is based on the concept of leverage, the first—and overwhelming—message here is this: Most new ventures are at a disadvantage, since they have little or nothing to leverage. They need to start from scratch and build it all. The framework breaks this work into two dimensions.

> *Most new ventures are at a disadvantage, since they have little or nothing to leverage. They need to start from scratch and build it all.*

Product/Technology Dimension The strongest, easiest, and fastest form of leverage is to use an existing product platform to enter new markets, but a new venture doesn't have any platform to leverage. That's not much of a problem for a new venture creating a totally new product platform, since nobody else has that platform either. But a new venture can sometimes use an existing core technology to build a new product platform—for example, when someone else has developed the core technology and the new venture's product strategy is to take advantage of it to create a new market. The degree of leverage depends on the importance of the core technology to the new product platform. Defining technology provides the most leverage, while ancillary or supporting technology provides little advantage. In cases where the new venture acquires the exclusive license on a core defining technology to build a new product platform, the leverage can be great.

Unfortunately, too often, new ventures create a business based on a recently introduced core technology and make it their defining technology. While the product may be exciting, the problem is that there is nothing to keep other ventures from doing the same thing. This is the case with the thousands of new ventures created to use the Internet as the defining technology for e-commerce. Because there are so many competitors, the Internet has become simply a *supporting* technology, and most of these ventures have no real *defining* technology.

> *Unfortunately, too often, new ventures create a business based on a recently introduced core technology and make it their defining technology.... This was the case with the thousands of new ventures created to use the Internet as the defining technology for e-commerce.*

Unique technical skills form the third layer of technical leverage, but they need to be reasonably distinctive so that existing or potential competitors do not have the same, or possibly better, skills. Here again, skills related to the defining technology are the most successful.

Many successful new ventures are based on founders with unique technical skills. A venture still must build the necessary core technology and the resulting product platforms, but with truly unique skills, it will have the time to do that. If a new venture that is relying on technology must go out and acquire most of the critical technical skills it needs, its success is suspect.

Market Dimension   A new venture uses its understanding of customers and markets to design a new product, or it uses its experience in the channel of distribution to bring a product to the customer.

Frequently, a new venture is created on the basis of its founders' experience in the target market, which gives the venture an advantage in developing new products and services for that market. It can also give the new venture a competitive advantage in knowing how to sell to the market. The combined experience of knowing what these customers want and knowing how to sell to them can provide powerful leverage for a new venture.

There is a limit, however, to the leverage a new venture may realize. Even if it understands how to sell to a market, it needs to build its distribution channel. That takes a lot of time. When it starts, a business has no institutional brand-name recognition or reputation beyond the individual reputation of its founders. Many new ventures form strategic marketing alliances to overcome these problems.

Offensive Competitive Strategies

New ventures usually follow a primary strategy based on a vector of differentiation (described in detail in Chapter 7) and a secondary strategy based on being first to market. Generally, new ventures that follow a pricing strategy are not successful. It's difficult for a new venture to have the operational and scale advantages that are usually necessary for a primary strategy based on pricing.

> *Generally, new ventures that follow a pricing strategy are not successful.*

Vectors of Differentiation   Many new ventures use advances in technology to create a new vector of differentiation. They see an opportunity to achieve competitive advantage around a particular vector and build a company based on it. The executives of a new venture should understand the characteristics of a differentiation strategy. Of particular importance is how the strategy applies during the early stage of a market and how it changes in subsequent stages.

Since a new venture depends on the success of its differentiation strategy, it should be very aware of the risks of differentiation strategy and do what it can to minimize them. In the early stages, a new venture risks misunderstanding customer preferences. The new product may be a good idea, but will it appeal to a large enough segment of the market? New ventures usually don't have sufficient breadth and depth of contact in their target market to understand what the market really wants. They are dependent (often too dependent) on the influence of early customers.

In some cases, misunderstanding the market may manifest itself in too much unfocused differentiation. The new venture tries to do everything that early customers ask for and then loses any coherent vector of differentiation. As a result, the differentiation also may not have sufficient proximity to price.

New ventures are at risk of not being able to build a sufficient perception of the value of their differentiation. They may really have something unique, but they can't get far enough above the noise in the market to communicate it. They may not be able to get enough attention from enough customers. Indirect communication—getting industry analysts and the press to write about the product—usually requires a lot of time and money, both of which can be in short supply for the new venture.

First-to-Market Strategies   Being first to market is very important for new ventures, but it's also overrated. In Chapter 9, we examine the advantages of being the first to market with a new product. New ventures are rarely successful being followers. Even fast-follower strategies are limited for new ventures, unless the first to market fails to execute and leaves a big opening for followers to be successful. Despite this, some new ventures are "me too" followers and are generally not successful. Many of them did not intend to execute a follower strategy—they just got to market too slowly.

> *Being first to market is very important for new ventures, but it's also overrated.*

The first company to market with a new product can get an early market share advantage, especially when it creates a new market. With no similar products on the market, the new venture enjoys a period without competition. Since customers have no other choice, it's only a matter of convincing them to buy. As we discuss in the previous section, once the new venture comes under attack from competition, market share could possibly provide the basis for a defensive strategy.

The first company to market also gets a lead on cultivating market and technology experience. This is particularly helpful when a new venture has a sustainable vector of differentiation that enables it to get ahead and keep ahead of its competitors.

Defensive Competitive Strategies: Barriers to Entry

The biggest threat of failure for a new venture is that it doesn't have adequate barriers to entry. The story is all too familiar. A start-up company creates an innovative product that gives birth to an entirely new market, only to be surpassed by another, much larger company within a few years. The larger competitor takes notice of the new venture's success and executives say,

> *While defending preliminary success is a problem for all companies, new ventures are more susceptible to this threat.*

"Why can't we do that too?" They can, if there are minimal barriers to entry, particularly if they have more resources and other capabilities to leverage.

While defending preliminary success is a problem for all companies, new ventures are more susceptible to this threat. They usually don't have the resources—financial or otherwise—to fend off an attack by a larger competitor. New ventures tend to be surprised by these attacks and can't make the transition from playing offense to playing defense.

Creating barriers to entry is a defensive strategy. By nature, new ventures are more interested in offensive strategies than defensive strategies, and often they pay too little attention to critical defensive strategy. They might argue that they need to focus on being successful first before they can even think about how to defend that success. But when a competitor comes along later and beats them, they claim, "We wuz robbed!"

So the strategic question is: Should an entrepreneur start a new venture at all if he or she might not be able to defend its preliminary success? It's a way of asking the third CSV question—Why will we be successful?—but with an emphasis on long-term success, not just preliminary success.

Successful Defensive Strategies   A new venture can create barriers to entry in many ways, but some are more successful than others. Patent protection creates the best barrier to entry by competition. This was the traditional strategy of pioneers like Edison, Land at Polaroid, and companies like Xerox. Competitors can't do the same thing, at least in the same way. This defensive strategy depends on the product being original enough to meet patent requirements, something difficult for many ventures to achieve. Software companies are trying to use this defensive strategy. Although controversial, patents based on unique software algorithms have risen dramatically. Amazon.com, for example, has a patent on its one-click ordering process, which it defends vigorously.

A long and steep vector of differentiation creates a barrier to entry by making it difficult for competitors, even large competitors, to catch up. We discuss the characteristics of these vectors in Chapter 7 and use the example of SAP's vector of differentiation based on the integration of business information. As soon as competitors matched the capabilities of its product, SAP introduced a new version with even more functionality. New products, such as computer software, that seem to have a never-ending opportunity to increase functionality can use this defensive strategy.

Failed Defensive Strategies   Brand-name recognition can sometimes create a barrier to entry. The reasoning is, if a company has the most recognized brand name, customers will have a preference for its products. This approach fails on two counts. Not only isn't it a very good vector of differentiation; it's also not a very good defensive strategy. It's usually done out of desperation for lack of any other defense.

Early in the Internet gold rush, e-commerce companies relied on brand-name recognition as a defense from competition. One of the problems with this strategy is that only one competitor can have the best brand name; if many try to succeed at this strategy, most will fail. In the absence of anything especially unique, establishing a brand name takes time and money, and these are things that most new ventures are short of.

Get there first and discourage competition. Sometimes the mere presence of a company in a new market or market segment can discourage competitors. Likewise, a unique vector of differentiation may discourage others from pursuing the same one. To execute this defensive strategy, a new venture needs to convince competitors that they may not be able to overcome it.

Changing Venture Capital Investment Criteria   Historically, venture capitalists looked closely at a new venture's ability to establish barriers to entry and wouldn't invest in new ventures that couldn't sustain success over the longer term. The criteria changed in the late 1990s, as opportunities for initial public offerings (IPOs) grew rapidly. New ventures started going public much earlier. Preliminary success, sometimes only the possibility of preliminary success, was sufficient for a company to go public. This created an interesting phenomenon: A sustainable barrier to entry was no longer necessary for early venture capital investors to get a big return on their investments. Soon after the IPO, they were able to get their money out or distribute the shares to their investors. Barrier-to-entry risks were transferred to the public investors. Many of them lacked the experience to understand these risks when they purchased the stock.

Unique Challenges of Creating a New Market

Many new ventures seek to create an entirely new market. Their product strategy is to apply new technology—either their own or technology developed by others—to enable customers to do something entirely different. In these cases, it's more than just an improved product. It's a new market. Enabling consumers to purchase books online over the Internet is a new market, since it's very different from buying in bookstores. Enabling companies to automate their management process for product development creates a new market.

New ventures face three unique challenges in creating a new market.

1. *The market needs to be educated.*   A new market is undefined. Potential customers may not even know they are potential customers, let alone how the new product will benefit them. This is very different from more mature markets, in which customers already know the benefits and what products are expected to do, and they need only choose which product is best.

In a new market, the first company creating the market must educate the market. This includes not just potential customers, but also the market infrastructure, such as the press, industry analysts, and investors. The concepts that describe the market must be defined. For these reasons, creating a new market can be much slower and much more expensive than most new venturers expect.

> *Creating a new market can be much slower and much more expensive than most new venturers expect.*

2. *There is a lot of confusion in a new market.* Product standards are not yet defined, and customer expectations are not settled. In the early days of the automobile market, for example, Oldsmobile used tiller steering, while Cadillac and Ford used wheel steering (with the wheel on the right side). Early automobiles resembled carriages without any roof or covering. With several thousand companies building cars in the early stage of the market, there were just about as many designs.

The confusion in a new market makes it riskier. The standards that emerge may differ from the ones the venture was built on. This confusion also creates doubts among customers. They see different kinds of products from each competitor, and they hear different approaches, compounding the challenges of selling to them.

3. *Early-stage customers have distinct characteristics.* Most potential customers will decide to wait until there is some clarity in the market and products before committing to buy. The first customers in the early stages of a new market are unique. They tend to be pioneers and risk takers. They are attracted to the new, which might give them some benefit earlier than others. Successful new venturers understand the early market and don't get frustrated if many potential customers don't buy the product at this stage. They learn how to screen for those who are potential early customers.

Early-stage customers may also fall into a distinct market segment. For example, in application software, companies that are already developing an application on their own are the most likely early-stage customers. They have already decided to invest in the application; it's only a question of making it or buying it. Identifying this segment helps to locate early customers, but a note of caution: The segment may not be representative of the mainstream market segment, and optimizing the platform for it could make the product noncompetitive in larger segments.

15

Growth through Innovation

*Innovative companies are creative in seeing new possibilities
and persistent in pursuing them.*

All high-technology companies would like to be innovative. The issue is how. The goal of innovation strategy is to increase the likelihood of innovation by defining *how* companies should look for innovation opportunities. We classify innovation strategy into three groups: opportunity-driven, prediction-driven, and technology-driven.

Before examining each one, let's look at what we mean by innovation. In the context of product strategy, we use *innovation* to mean the act of creating something really new—developing a new type of product that creates an entirely new market. An improved or more competitive product may be new for a company, but it's not new in the sense that there was nothing like it before.

Innovation is not to be confused with *invention*, the discovery of a new device, method, or process through study and experimentation. Inventions can lead to innovations, but all innovations are not based on inventions. Nor are all innovations successful in the marketplace. History is full of innovations that, while seemingly clever and novel, never gained a foothold in the marketplace, or did so only after a long and tortuous journey.

What makes some innovations commercial successes and others only interesting novelties? Successful commercialization of an innovation requires a change in one of three components: the technology, the market context in which goods and services are delivered, or the business model.

> *Successful commercialization of an innovation requires a change in one of three components: the technology, the market context in which goods and services are delivered, or the business model.*

Nevertheless, changes in these three components do not necessarily result in an innovation. By and large, the changes are incremental and continuous. They are often predictable, and, in some cases, can be planned for.

For some innovations to take root, it's necessary for a discontinuous or disruptive change in one of these three components to occur, usually as rapidly emerging customer segments, technical capabilities, or organizational structures. Novel technologies that lack the proper business model to commercialize them, or that do not serve the demands of emerging customer needs, will not be successful innovations.

Governments, universities, and businesses have invested a lot to develop new technology that does not meet the emerging needs of customers and has no practical application. In this sense, the best technology doesn't always win, especially if it's not well suited to the new market. The Apple Newton personal assistance device is an example. It implemented novel handwriting recognition software with the goal of meeting a need for portable electronic data storage and retrieval. Previously a key limitation to the portability of such devices had been the data entry system. Workable keyboards made the devices too large, while smaller keyboards were too difficult to operate. The idea behind Newton was to enter data using a stylus and pad, enabled by a technology that could translate handwriting into computer text. The handwriting technology was not perfected, requiring a significant investment to "teach" the device to recognize a personal handwriting style, often with much proofreading and correction. More important, it did not really address the key needs of this emerging market, which were portability, connectivity, and ease of use. If the need to translate handwriting into electronic text and the ensuing freedom of data entry were the key drivers, the marketplace probably would have been more willing to invest in this technology and embrace future enhancements.

The PalmPilot, on the other hand, succeeded in meeting a similar market need by employing a different technology in a different market context. One key to its success was the decision to use a technology that did not recognize handwriting but, rather, required the user to employ simple graffiti or a digital keyboard to enter data. The user gave up the freedom of using standard handwriting to enter text for the speed, simplicity, and accuracy of the PalmPilot approach. Even though the PalmPilot technology was inferior to that of the Newton in handwriting recognition, it won out because it was able to meet the needs of this new market.

Ingredients of Innovation

Figure 15-1 illustrates the interplay of the three components needed to commercialize innovation: market context, the enterprise, and technology. Innovation using technologies that offer minor improvements does not require as much change in the market context or enterprise structure to be successfully commercialized. Truly discontinuous technologies require more dramatic changes. When polypropylene was introduced, for example, companies instantly found numerous applications for it, because it was

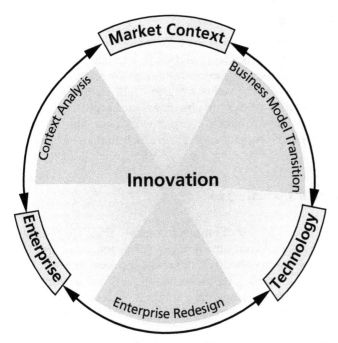

Figure 15-1 Three components are needed to commercialize innovation: market context, the enterprise, and technology.

more flexible and easier to use than preceding forms of plastic. Manufacturers incorporated these improvements into a wide variety of existing applications, such as roofing materials, pipes, and upholstery; components for dishwashers, clothes washers, and refrigerators; automotive parts; clothing; and consumer products, such as videocassettes.

The burden of innovation using mature technology shifts to creative inspiration on new ways to solve customer problems or generalize from a solution to specific applications.

Technology that emerges rapidly or offers a discontinuous advantage requires a larger response in the market context or enterprise structure of an organization. By the time a technology matures, most of its more obvious applications have been introduced. The burden of innovation using mature technology shifts to creative inspiration on new ways to solve customer problems or generalize from a solution to specific applications.

Opportunity-Driven Innovation Strategies

Opportunity-driven innovation strategies take the solution to a specific problem and generalize it to provide a solution to a broader set of problems. In this way, the solution addresses a market opportunity rather than a customer-specific fix. The two strategies differ by their sources. The two sources for such strategies are customers and problems. To create strategies from such opportunities, companies can organize to listen to specific customer needs and to generalize a solution for a specific problem.

Opportunities from Listening to Customer Needs

Customers are an obvious source of innovation ideas. They are the ones living with the problems that an innovation can solve, and they form the eventual market for the innovation. In some cases, a customer may challenge a company to solve a particular problem and, in doing so, force the company to come up with an innovative solution. Subsequently, there may be opportunities to generalize this solution to create an innovative product.

Such was the case with one of the major innovations of the twentieth century: the microprocessor. In 1969, a now defunct Japanese calculator manufacturer, Busicom, asked Intel to design a set of chips for a family of programmable calculators. The original design called for at least 12 custom chips, but Ted Hoff, the Intel engineer assigned to the project, thought the configuration was unduly complex. His solution was to develop a single-chip, general-purpose logic device that would retrieve its application instructions from semiconductor memory.

Hoff and Bob Noyce, a cofounder of Intel, realized that the trend toward custom-designed logic chips was increasing rapidly. The number of chips would soon exceed the number of circuit designers. Hoff's vision was transformed into silicon nine months later. The 4004 microprocessor consisted of 2,300 transistors and was 1/8-inch wide by 1/6-inch long. It had processing power equivalent to that of the first electronic computer, the ENIAC, which filled 3,000 cubic feet with 18,000 vacuum tubes when it was built in 1946. The 4004 could execute 60,000 operations in one second—primitive by later standards, but a major innovation at the time.

Intel had a problem with this innovation, though. Busicom owned the rights to it, having paid Intel $60,000 to design the chip set. Knowing that Busicom was in financial trouble and sensing the opportunity for the microprocessor as a generalized product, Intel offered to return the $60,000 to Busicom in return for exclusive rights to the product. Busicom accepted, and the rest is history.[1]

In many cases, a customer may specify exactly what is needed to solve a specific problem, and when development is completed may have no interest in generalizing the solution for others. This was the case in the late 1950s when IBM designed and built the first component insertion machine for printed circuit boards. After building and testing the design in house, IBM contracted with a local machine builder for eight machines according to its specifications. Perceiving that this was an innovation, the machine builder received permission from IBM in 1962 to market the X-Y table component insertion machine to others. This innovation was successful for the company, which became a leader in the market.[2]

> *Identifying innovation opportunities from listening to customers does not mean taking a poll or doing customer surveys.*

Identifying innovation opportunities from listening to customers does not mean taking a poll or doing customer surveys. Rarely does the average customer provide such insights. Instead, it's the customer in the forefront, solving emerging problems, who identifies these opportunities. The key is to identify these customers and invest time in listening to them.

Opportunities from Generalizing a Solution to a Specific Problem

The world is full of problems—big and small—and sometimes the solution to an individual problem can be generalized to solve similar problems, leading to the innovation of exciting new products. One of the most publicized cases of this kind of innovation occurred when Art Fry of 3M became frustrated with trying to mark his place in a hymnal when he was singing in the church choir. He used little scraps of paper to mark the pages for upcoming songs, but they usually fell out. Frustrated, he thought back to an earlier discussion with Dr. Spencer Silver, a 3M chemist who had mistakenly created a low-tack adhesive while trying to develop a super-strong one. "What I need," Fry thought to himself, "is a bookmark with Spence's adhesive along one edge. It would stay in place when I needed it to, but it wouldn't be so sticky as to damage the pages when I removed it."[3]

Solving this individual hymnal-marking problem eventually led to one of 3M's most famous products, the Post-it® Note, which has generated hundreds of millions of dollars in revenue for the company. The transition from the specific to the general is not always easy, and it wasn't with Post-it® Notes. Not everyone saw how they could be used. It took an all-out sampling campaign with some 3M offices and the town of Boise, Idaho, to show that there were more general applications for this innovation.

Prediction-Driven Innovation Strategies

Innovation strategies can also stem from projecting trends into the future, identifying a potential innovation before someone else does. While scientific breakthroughs are not predictable, the continued advance of emerging technology is. For example, when Gordon Moore of Intel projected the rate of improvement in computer memory chips in the early 1970s by looking at the historical rate of improvement, he forecast that capacity would double every two years (a progression from 1-K bit chips in 1971 to 1-MB chips in 1991). Moore's forecast continued to prove accurate. Many companies failed to apply his theory and missed opportunities to innovate new products, but others, such as Microsoft, jumped on these trends.

> *Innovation strategies can also stem from projecting trends into the future, identifying a potential innovation before someone else does. While scientific breakthroughs are not predictable, the continued advance of emerging technology is.*

Of course, emerging technology is also a source of opportunity for innovation. We'll examine three types of opportunities: those based on the declining cost of technology, those based on new applications of emerging technology, and those based on the intersections of multiple emerging technologies.

Opportunities Based on the Declining Cost of Technology

The declining cost of an emerging technology creates opportunities for new applications when the technology becomes more cost-effective, illustrated in Figure 15-2. The initial market for a new technology is small, focusing on select applications where the benefit is so high that cost does not matter. As cost declines, a secondary market provides a larger opportunity. Subsequent opportunities occur as each new market is larger than the preceding one.

Global-positioning technology is a good example of progressive opportunities created by declining costs. This technology was originally developed by the U.S. Department of Defense for military applications such as determining the location of a ship, airplane, or smart bomb. Using 24 satellites, global positioning can identify the location of a receiver within a few feet. Each satellite constantly transmits its position and time of

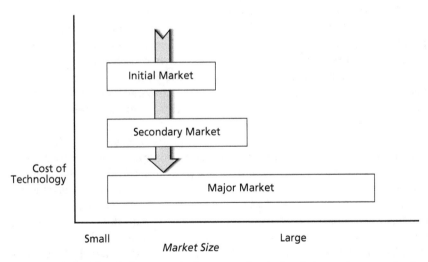

Figure 15-2 The declining cost of an emerging technology creates opportunities for new applications when the technology becomes more cost-effective.

transmission. By taking the readings from the three or four closest satellites, the receiver plots its longitude, latitude, and altitude.

Early global-positioning receivers were quite expensive, and the initial market for military applications was small. As costs declined, secondary markets became feasible with the application of global positioning as a navigational aid for commercial airlines, private airplanes, and recreational boating. By 1993, receiver prices were as low as $700 to $1,700, opening up opportunities for recreational uses, such as hiking and cross-country skiing as well as use in automobiles. Avis Rent-a-Car began testing global-positioning systems (GPS) in its fleet. By the late 1990s, GPS was an option in most luxury cars. It's likely to eventually become as ubiquitous as car phones.

Predictability is the key to this innovation strategy. The rate and extent of cost declines can be forecast by understanding the underlying technology. Then opportunities for innovation can be identified at each lower cost level.

Opportunities Based on New Applications for Emerging Technology

Incorporating new technology into an innovative product can create new markets. In some cases, the technology may be so innovative that no one is sure how it will be applied. The strategy here is to identify these opportunities and introduce an innovative product before anyone else does.

One example comes from identifying new opportunities for emerging genetic engineering technology. The market for fresh tomatoes exceeds $3 billion, and in recent years it changed only when biotechnology entered the picture, establishing a new market in the process—genetically engineered tomatoes. These new tomatoes—such as VineSweet and Calgene's Flavr Savr—have an improved taste and texture, a longer shelf life, and a year-round growing period.

Natural tomatoes have a built-in enzyme that accelerates rotting, and because of this, tomatoes are picked green and ripen during transport to the grocery shelves. Since a tomato is juicier when it's allowed to ripen on the vine, this early picking results in the lower quality that people observe in store-bought tomatoes. Calgene's Flavr Savr tomato resists rotting because it reverses the DNA sequence used to manufacture the rotting enzyme, giving the tomato a longer shelf life and improved taste and texture. The potential for this technology could be predicted, but the consumer backlash in 1999 was more difficult to predict.

Another example is the emergence of Internet technology, which has created almost unlimited opportunities for innovation. It has changed the way people shop by enabling e-commerce, and it has changed the way companies purchase materials from one another.

Opportunities at the Intersection of Multiple Emerging Technologies

The combination of two or more emerging technologies can create some exciting innovation opportunities. While each emerging technology can perform advanced functions, together they can do things that no one ever thought of before. Even more so than the others, this innovation strategy requires creativity.

The Wright Brothers applied two emerging technologies when they invented a workable airplane. The first was the gasoline engine designed in the mid-1880s to power automobiles. The second was advances in aerodynamics that were developed through experiments with gliders. Each of these emerging technologies was developed independently, but the Wright Brothers combined them innovatively.

The combination of emerging technologies in computing and communications provided numerous opportunities for innovation in high-speed switching systems and other new products. The PBX (private branch exchange), or switchboard, was created from the convergence of two technologies: telecommunications and computing. Combining these two technologies made it possible to automate and simplify the task of answering and switching telephone calls. Later, these technologies were combined with emerging technology to digitize voice to create voice-mail systems.

Internet technologies have given rise to many innovations by combining with other technologies. At the present time, there is much innovation arising from the combination of content and Internet-based delivery of that content.

To combine multiple technologies successfully requires understanding and applying the right combination of technologies to potential opportunities for doing things differently, and challenging existing products and processes to produce more innovative solutions.

Technology-Driven Innovation Strategies

Technology-driven strategies lead a company to find or discover a new technology and use it to invent new products. This strategy has been described as a technology in search of a product to validate it, but there are two approaches that can be successful.

Search for Solutions to Perceived Problems

Innovation can result from a deliberate search for a solution to a perceived opportunity or problem. This is the scientific approach to innovation.

DuPont used this approach to innovation when it developed nylon. Wallace Hume Carothers of DuPont investigated opportunities for making synthetic fibers through polymerization—building larger molecules out of smaller ones. Scientists had previously made new fibers, such as rayon, from cellulose, but had never synthesized them from simple chemicals.[4] After methodically trying different chemicals, DuPont eventually settled on amides—the same chemicals that form the protein in wool, silk, and other animal fibers. By carefully controlling the reaction, scientists built polyamides into strong, flexible fibers. This innovation led to nylon stockings, clothing, tires, parachutes, and many other products.

> *Innovation can result from a deliberate search for a solution to a perceived opportunity or problem. This is the scientific approach to innovation.*

Edison also used this strategy in creating artificial lighting using incandescent lamp bulbs. The problem was that no one had been able to make a strong, effective, high-resistance lighting element. After methodically trying numerous materials, Edison and his staff were able to find a material that worked. On top of this, Edison had to build electric generators, inexpensive transmission lines, methods for connecting the bulbs, and methods for installing wires into a house. This innovation by Edison was not a blinding flash of invention. It took years of work and trial and error.

Stumble over a Technology Breakthrough and Apply It

Many historic discoveries are found by someone "stumbling over" them. While this is a descriptive metaphor, the process isn't really based on luck. People can only stumble if they are going somewhere and there is something to stumble over, meaning they are involved in research of some type, *and* they recognize the importance of what they discover.

For example, Alexander Graham Bell stumbled over the breakthrough necessary for the telephone. On June 2, 1875, Bell was researching telegraph signals using magnetized steel reeds to transmit a fixed frequency signal when his assistant, Watson, accidentally made the reed vibrate. Much to Bell's surprise, the reed vibrated at his end and emitted a noise. The researchers determined that the vibration was transmitted by an electromagnetic current and caused a sound. Bell recognized the importance of what he "stumbled over" because of a theory that he had developed a year earlier for electrically reproducing speech. He had been trying then to figure out how to make an electric current change in proportion to the sound of the voice. This lucky accident solved his problem.

Kary Mullis discovered the process for polymerase chain reaction (PCR) one Friday night in 1983 as he was driving in northern California. PCR is a biological process for amplifying a particular molecule of DNA from a few to millions. Without amplification it's not possible to detect the presence of molecules in low concentration, but when they are amplified a million times, diagnostic instruments can detect the presence of any targeted molecule.

Mullis's discovery came while he was researching the identity of a nucleotide at a given position in a DNA molecule. Driving to Mendocino County late one night, he was thinking about his experiment when he realized a problem with it: The experiment would cause the number of DNA molecules to double. While this was a problem with the intended experiment, Mullis saw the possibility of progressive doubling to amplify the molecule to large numbers.[5]

PCR, and similar technologies such as strand displacement amplification, enabled major new innovations in diagnostic instruments. DNA identification allowed the diagnosis of diseases such as tuberculosis to be made in three hours, instead of the six weeks required using traditional bacterial culturing methods.

Sony developed its famous Walkman through a stumble. In 1978, engineers at Sony's tape recorder division were trying to develop a small portable tape recorder for journalists, called the Pressman. Unfortunately, they were unable to fit the recording mechanism into the required unit size, so they used it to listen to cassettes as they worked. Masaru Ibuka, Sony's honorary chairman, saw this incomplete tape recorder and admired the quality of its stereo sound. Remembering an unrelated project in which Sony engineers were working to develop lightweight portable headphones, he wondered about combining them. The combination would dramatically increase sound quality, and maybe it

Companies such as Sony that innovate through discovery have a common trait: They are continually pondering possibilities limited by current technology. When they see a way to remove the limitation, they recognize a solution.

could be a successful product without a recording capability. In 1979, the Walkman was introduced and became one of the most successful consumer products of the 1980s.[6]

People such as Bell and Mullis and companies such as Sony that innovate through discovery have a common trait: They are continually pondering possibilities limited by current technology. When they *see* a way to remove the limitation, they *recognize* a solution. They create environments that allow them to "stumble over" solutions. This innovation strategy depends on having creative people, and providing an environment for them to work on research with time to follow up on hunches or possibilities.

Barriers to Innovation

Innovation can't be planned or scheduled. It depends on a number of things coming together. Here we examine some of the barriers to innovation.

Lack of a Strategy for Innovation   Without an innovation strategy, a company shouldn't be surprised if it has little innovation. A company may have no innovation strategy simply because it never thought about having one. Perhaps it never expected to innovate. Sometimes companies don't have an innovation strategy because they do not understand innovation. They expect it to "just happen." In many cases, a company invests in innovation by allocating funds to research, but it doesn't have a systematic strategy for innovating and may be learning about and refining technologies without applying them.

Some companies have a strategy for innovation, but it's the wrong one. The innovation strategy needs to be appropriate for a company's market, core competencies, and vision. One company pursued a technology-based innovation strategy, investing heavily in finding new technical solutions for perceived opportunities, but its competitor pursued a more successful opportunity-based innovation strategy. The customer base was rich with ideas for innovative products. The former company didn't find innovations in the lab, while its competitor found them in the marketplace.

Failure to Implement   Innovation is work. While all product strategies require a lot of work to implement, innovation strategies suffer most from the misconception that "it will come to you." A study of innovation clearly shows that it doesn't happen that way, so once a strategy is chosen, work needs to be done.

Implementation begins by assigning responsibility. An individual or team needs to have the responsibility and resources to implement the innovation strategy. One company following a strategy of generalizing from customer needs, for example, assigns someone to visit customers to solicit new ideas. This is a one-year rotating assignment, which provides a fresh look at opportunities every year. The opportunities are reviewed by a cross-functional team that refines and prioritizes them, and the most promising opportunities are introduced into the company's review process for approval.

Innovation isn't just work; it's hard work. Too many companies that launch an innovation strategy start developing the first opportunity they come across. Why would they expect the first opportunity to be the best? Just lucky? The truth is, they just stop when they find *one*. Some people shop for a gift that way; they walk into a store and buy the first thing that

> *Too many companies that launch an innovation strategy start developing the first opportunity they come across.... Many opportunities should be identified and reviewed, and only the very best should be funded.*

seems appropriate. Others comb the aisles and go to many stores to find the "right" gift. Finding the right innovation to invest in is like finding the right gift. Many opportunities should be identified and reviewed, and only the very best should be funded.

Lack of Vision A core strategic vision is necessary to guide any innovation strategy. It indicates which opportunities fit the company's strategic direction and which do not.

An earlier example discusses a consumer electronics company that launched an innovation strategy for expansion, but because it didn't have a strategic vision, it pursued opportunities that were too far afield. It went into markets and technologies in which it had no experience and failed. At the same time, it overlooked some excellent opportunities within its own domain.

An outdated vision can also hinder innovation. One company making mainframe computer peripheral equipment had the opportunity and technical talent to develop local area networking systems for workstations and personal computers. Even though management saw the decline in mainframe sales, it couldn't bring itself to work on something that was not part of its strategic vision. As a result, by early 1994

> *An outdated vision can hinder innovation.*

the company was downsizing to 30 percent of its former size and still trying to squeeze out a profit following the decline of the mainframe market.

Inadequate Core Competencies As explained in Chapter 6, expansion into new markets requires the leverage of a strong base of core competencies. This is also true of expansion through innovation strategies.

Without sufficient core competencies, it's difficult for a company to identify innovations it can successfully pursue. If a company has limited core competencies, it needs to restrict its innovation strategy. In an extreme case, a company may need to strengthen its core competencies before it initiates any innovation or expansion strategy.

Market Resistance to Change   The biggest barrier to innovation is resistance to change. One fascinating historical example of resistance to change involves an improvement to the typewriter or computer keyboard. The current QWERTY keyboard used in typewriters and personal computers was invented by Christopher Latham Sholes in 1873 to reduce the chance of jamming the mechanism by having two typewriter keys rapidly struck in succession. The layout made it more difficult to type, and that reduced jamming. This design was so successful that it was used in all typewriters.

By 1932, typewriters were more mechanically efficient, and jamming was not a major problem. Professor August Dvorak designed a more efficient keyboard, arranging the keys so that the most frequently used keys were located in the most convenient places, and the load was distributed to the generally stronger right hand instead of the left hand. Dvorak's innovation, the Dvorak Simplified Keyboard (DSK), dramatically increased productivity. However, this innovation was never adopted by typewriter manufacturers. Nobody wanted to upset the way things were usually done and be incompatible with training or experience.[7]

Frequently, an innovation will require customers to do something different or new to benefit from the innovation. This can be a barrier to making the innovation successful, and market education may be necessary to achieve early acceptance.

Notes

1. Provided by Intel.
2. Eric A. von Hippel, "Has a Customer Already Developed Your Next Product?" *Sloan Management Review*, Winter 1977.
3. William E. DeGenaro, Director of Innovation Resources at 3M, "Encouraging Innovation," *Prism* (Arthur D. Little, Summer 1989).
4. "Inventors and Discoveries," *National Geographic*, 1988.
5. Kary B. Mullis, "The Unusual Origin of the Polymerase Chain Reaction," *Scientific American*, April 1990.
6. P. Ranganath and John M. Ketteringham, *Breakthroughs* (Pfeiffer & Company, 1994), pp. 115–136.
7. Stephen Jay Gould, "The Panda's Thinking of Technology," *Readings in the Management of Innovation*, edited by Michael L. Tishman and William L. Moore (Ballinger, 1988).

PART 4

The Process of Product Strategy

Product strategy ultimately comes down to reconciling priorities with resources. That successful reconciliation is otherwise known as strategic balance. While strategic vision defines an organization's goal with respect to product strategy and provides a framework for achieving it, that framework must be reconciled with the reality of available resources. Strategic balance reconciles a company's often unlimited product opportunities with its inevitably limited resources, and with its externally imposed opportunity constraints.

Part 4 examines the product strategy-setting process from the perspectives of available (and unavailable) resources, the push-pull of product focus versus product diversification, and the immediate versus delayed-gratification tension between short-term and long-term product development products. Part 4 also looks at the issue of how companies allocate R&D resources across business units, and, on a more fundamental note, how they allocate resources between the distinctly different activities of research and development. This part concludes by looking at how magnitudes of risk vary from project to project, and how those risks can be reconciled with their projected financial returns.

16

Strategic Balance and Portfolio Management

Eventually, product strategy comes down to setting priorities in line with resources.

Most high-technology companies have unlimited product opportunities. They can expand existing product lines, develop new product platforms, and create new vectors of differentiation. They can explore paths for expansion into new markets or even create entirely new markets. The problem is that they cannot do everything they would like to do. They have to make choices, set priorities, and allocate scarce resources. They must achieve a strategic balance among numerous opportunities for new products, which requires making trade-offs between short-term and long-term opportunities, between current platforms and new platforms, between diversification and focus, between expansion into new markets and increased competitiveness in current markets, and between research and development.

Portfolio management is the process of analyzing characteristics of products under development, and in some cases planned products, in order to align them with business and platform strategy priorities. Some companies use the term *portfolio management* to mean a bottom-up process for aggregating and displaying various criteria from project and product data. This is only half of the portfolio management process, however; the other half is aligning the analysis with a set of predetermined strategic objectives. To emphasize the importance of the second half of the process, we refer to it as *strategic balance.*

Strategic balance is an important concept in product strategy. If a company's product strategy for its newly developed platforms and product offerings is balanced, it is pursuing the proper mix of opportunities. If its product strategy gets out of balance, it may not achieve its overall vision, even if the individual strategies are appropriate. For example, a company could become preoccupied with short-term opportunities, while unknowingly sacrificing its future, or it could take on more high-risk projects than it realizes, coming up empty-handed on new products while revenue declines.

After we describe the strategic balance trade-offs, we discuss setting priorities to achieve this balance and the new application software for product development that can provide new tools and systems to make portfolio management and strategic balance much more effective. In the last section, we discuss how this new capability—a Web-enabled capability—will change portfolio management in the next generation of product de-velopment.

> ***Strategic vision defines the goal and provides a framework for achieving it.... Strategic balance reconciles a company's unlimited product opportunities to its limited resources.***

Let's be clear about the distinction between strategic vision and strategic balance, before continuing. Strategic *vision* defines the goal and provides a framework for achieving it. This vision has to be reconciled to reality—specifically, to fit the resources available. Strategic *balance* reconciles a company's unlimited product opportunities to its limited resources. This is done at a strategic level, above the level of individual products and below the level of portfolio management.

Strategic Balance Trade-offs

To achieve strategic balance, individual product development projects must be aligned in the right proportion to the strategic objectives. This requires making trade-off decisions among various strategic considerations or criteria. Some of these criteria are interdependent; a decision on one trade-off can affect another.

Companies classify new product projects in different ways. Wheelwright and Clark, for instance, introduced four primary classifica-

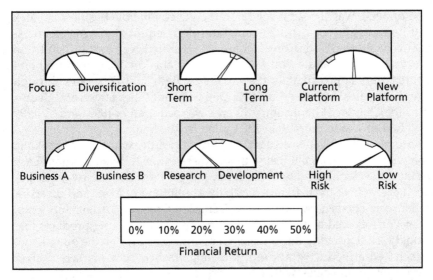

Figure 16-1   Periodically, every company needs to define the criteria for the mix in its product development portfolio.

tions based on the degree of change from one product to another: enhancements, next-generation platforms, radical breakthroughs, and advanced development. A structure like this helps clarify strategic thinking.[1]

Figure 16-1 illustrates the concept of strategic balance as an electronic dashboard. According to the readings on the dials, one of the six is in the acceptable range; five are outside the acceptable range; and the financial return is measuring 20 percent.

To achieve strategic balance, every company needs to define the criteria and mix characteristics it would like to achieve in its development portfolio. The following seven characteristics are typical of what a company needs to consider.

Focus versus Diversification

Focus means concentrating resources on a specific product platform or set of products to avoid diluting resources on other, less important, efforts, thereby increasing the chance of competitive success with a company's primary focus. Focus can be especially critical in rapidly emerging markets, as the following example shows.

Steve Hui founded Everex Systems in 1983, building the IBM PC clone maker to more than $425 million in revenue by 1991. But while its competitor, Dell, was focusing solely on the PC-compatible business, Everex lost its strategic focus and launched development of a new microprocessor, computerized drafting tables, a modified version of UNIX, a Macintosh clone, and a Sun Microsystems clone.[2] In 1989, both Dell and Everex were approximately the same size. Both sold PC clones through telephone sales. At the end of 1992, Dell was four times larger, and Everex filed for Chapter 11 bankruptcy. Everex was acquired in 1993, and by 1999 Dell had grown to more than $20 billion in revenue.

Although the Everex diversification was deadly, statistically speaking, companies can offset failures with successes through diversification. Each product development initiative will have its own risk and success factors. A good example of the extremes along the continuum of focus and diversification can be seen by comparing Centocor Corp. and Genzyme Corp. Centocor followed a strategy of focusing on one or two big products that would turn it instantly into a major company. Genzyme, on the other hand, established a product strategy of pursuing smaller niche markets using a variety of technologies with good odds for commercialization. The high expectations for Centocor's first big product, Centoxin, drove the market value of the company's stock to $2.2 billion, even though revenue was less than $100 million. When the FDA rejected the drug, the company's market value dropped by 85 percent. Then, on January 18, 1993, Centocor suspended additional clinical trials for Centoxin and ceased foreign sales of the product because of an excess mortality rate on patients treated with the drug. Centocor had gambled by putting most of its eggs into one basket and lost. Genzyme continued steady growth with a diversified product portfolio.

Both companies went on to be successful. Centocor achieved more than $400 million in revenue in 1999 and was acquired by Johnson & Johnson in 1999 for almost $5 billion. Genzyme grew to approximately $750 million by 1999.

Short Term versus Long Term

Current competitive pressures drive companies to emphasize short-term projects to achieve immediate gains. A new feature or performance improvement will quickly make a product more competitive and boost sales. With a short-term focus, however, a company sacrifices longer-term opportunities, often without considering the consequences. The result can be a vicious circle: One crisis follows another, because the company failed to invest enough in longer-term opportunities.

For example, one company making communications software products tied up most of its engineering resources in development of small projects. Major growth projects did not get any attention because marketing and sales, which were focused on quarterly quotas, constantly screamed at engineering to "be more responsive." The company's dilemma became critical when competitors introduced new generations of products. Marketing and sales then claimed that the company had inadequate technical capabilities.

A continuous short-term focus can be a sign of a troubled company. A company becomes reactive, rather than proactive, and if it does not break out of this cycle, it will eventually succumb to competition. Also, with an extreme short-term focus, too many prod-

> *A continuous short-term focus can be a sign of a troubled company.*

uct development resources are allocated to customer support to fix problems. In a sense, this is a backward investment, investing in product that is already sold.

Long-term opportunities are those that are anywhere from 3 to 10 years in the future, depending on product life cycles and development cycle time. Capitalizing on these opportunities requires development of a new product platform or even new technology. Companies that are competitively comfortable for the time being can pay more attention to longer-term opportunities. They can invest in future product platforms, expand core competencies to prepare for future expansion, or explore new markets.

Sometimes, at the other extreme, everything becomes strategic, and no projects are targeted for near-term return. This was the problem at a data communications company when a vice president observed during a phase review, "This is the fifth consecutive project where we are looking at a low return because it is strategic. What projects are going to make us any money?" Given that jarring observation, the senior management team realized that it needed to bring its short- and long-term perspectives into balance.

Too much investment in long-term opportunities can also cause competitive problems, particularly if most of these opportunities are also high risks. While a company is experimenting with long-range ideas and technologies that may not pay off, competitors can achieve immediate advantages that force a company to shift to a crisis mode. When this happens, the company never realizes the payoff of its longer-term investments.

Current Platforms versus New Platforms

As we discussed previously, all product platforms have a life cycle, and, at some point, a company needs to shift its emphasis and resources away from building on a current platform toward developing a new platform. The timing of this shift is an element of strategic balance. If a company shifts too soon, it fails to get as much as it should from its current platform. Competitors continue to improve their products and introduce new variations, while the company is distracted by developing its new platform. When introduced, the new platform may prematurely displace the previous one, reducing the return originally expected. Introducing a new platform too early may also frustrate customers, who are just getting used to the current platform. In some cases, developing a new platform too early could diminish the differences between it and the previous platform. The defining technology may not have advanced sufficiently, and customers may not see the difference, enabling competitors to leapfrog into the next generation.

> *At some point, a company needs to shift its emphasis and resources away from building on a current platform toward developing a new platform.*

But if a company waits too long before shifting its resources toward a new platform, it may not complete the platform in time to remain competitive. We saw that Data General had this problem. By taking too long to shift from its proprietary Eclipse platform to a UNIX-based platform, it did not develop competitive products in time. Revenue declined, and profits disappeared. What makes this shift difficult is the continued pull on resources to improve and expand products using the existing platform. If a company waits until the expected investment returns diminish on these opportunities, it can be too late. Ironically, some of the best investment returns are seen in the later stages of a platform's life cycle. Depending on the platform life cycle and the investment required, a company might need to increase its overall investment or divert resources from other areas to achieve the proper shift.

> *If a company waits too long before shifting its resources toward a new platform, it may not complete the platform in time to remain competitive.*

One Business Unit versus Another

Many companies allocate R&D resources across business units, such as divisions or product lines, without assigning priorities or distinguishing among differences in opportunity. They provide every unit with equal access to R&D resources or allow each to spend an equivalent amount of revenue on R&D, even if the opportunities vary. This practice takes away one of the advantages of a multidivisional business, which is the ability to shift the allocation of resources to business units with better opportunities. Instead, the company tends to subsidize lower-opportunity businesses by letting them invest as much as higher-opportunity businesses.

To achieve strategic balance, a multidivisional business needs to establish priorities for allocating R&D to each business. Theoretically, this makes sense, but in practice it is difficult. The R&D staff resides in individual divisions and is not readily redeployed. In addition, it is not easy to measure the differences in various opportunities across divisions. For these reasons, strategic balance across divisions is usually phased in over time. A company may also choose to retain a portion of its development resources at the corporate level to fund selected expansion opportunities, which might span multiple divisions or occur in a division with high-growth opportunities.

Research versus Development

Investments in product development are very different from investments in research. The end result of a product development investment is a new product. The goal is clear, and the path followed to get there is reasonably well defined. Investments in research, on the other hand, are aimed at creating, acquiring, or improving core competencies that will be used in future products. The result of research efforts could be a new material, a new process, a new base chemistry, or a new electronic module, which is then applied to establish innovative product differences or a new product platform.

> *As part of achieving strategic balance, a company must decide how to divide its resources between research and development.*

As part of achieving strategic balance, a company must decide how to divide its resources between research and development. This split varies, depending on a company's objectives. If it focuses entirely on development with no investment in research, its core competencies may atrophy. Large companies allocate funds for research in part by establishing corporate centers for pure research, such as the Palo Alto Research Center of Xerox, Becton Dickinson's Research Center, and Bell Labs at AT&T.

High Risk versus Low Risk

All product development efforts are risky, but the magnitude of risk varies from product to product. While some companies are comfortable at higher levels of risk, others may prefer a more moderate risk profile.

Managing a company's risk profile is an important part of strategic balance.

Different types of risks prevent a company from turning what is perceived as a good opportunity into a successful product:

- *Market risks.* These are the risks of bringing the wrong product to market. The product may not be what the customers really want. It could be priced wrong or insufficiently differentiated. It could be inferior to other competitive products. In any case, the market was misjudged.

- *Technical risks.* Running into technical difficulties reduces the success of a product. It may not meet performance expectations. It may cost too much to make it do what was expected. In the worst case, the product may not work at all.

- *Manufacturing risks.* Perhaps a company cannot manufacture a product properly, or maybe it faces higher than planned manufacturing costs, problems in making the quantity required, or delays in starting manufacturing.

- *Market introduction risks.* Problems can occur with the launch of a complex or innovative product into the marketplace, especially a worldwide launch. Efforts include using promotion to educate the customer on the product's benefits, training the sales force, preparing the indirect sales channels, supporting value-added resellers, and setting up the service process. Shortcomings in these areas can doom an outstanding product to mediocre sales.

- *Managerial risks.* Managerial risks are primarily failures in execution. The product is right, but the company just cannot complete the necessary development as planned. The failure could be in the quality of the product or in completion to schedule.

Typically, a company uses some form of weighting scheme to compute the aggregate risk level from the different risk categories.

Financial Return

Most companies use a financial measure, such as return on investment (ROI), to judge success. Many companies set some level of "hurdle rate" that each opportunity needs to achieve before it is approved. This hurdle rate establishes criteria for allocating resources and achieving strategic balance. A single rate for all opportunities ignores the importance of other criteria and turns product strategy into a capital budgeting exercise—"as long as the return on investment is higher than the cost of capital." This approach has led some high-technology companies into decline. For a new product opportunity, ROI is an *approximate* estimate that combines numerous projections—unit sales, pricing, costs, and so on.[3] Despite this, ROI is frequently used as the ultimate decision criterion.

One company, for example, used a 15 percent ROI hurdle rate for all new product projects. New product proposals consistently projected an ROI of 15 to 20 percent in order to surpass the hurdle rate and get funding. Some, of course, failed to achieve the projections. A portion never came to market. None was more successful than anticipated. Overall, the company did not get a very good return on its investment in R&D.

This poor return could have been mathematically determined in advance. The company set diminished expectations for product development investments by automatically approving everything that met an adequate financial return. Inadvertently, it incorporated financial mediocrity into its strategic balance.

Overall, the portfolio of new products developed must increase profit. Each opportunity, with a few possible exceptions, needs to contribute to that profit—some more than others. In fact, some opportunities, particularly those not being pursued for other reasons, should require a much higher return than others.

Setting Priorities

Portfolio management and strategic balance help companies not only analyze their product development, but also make decisions for the future. These decisions require setting priorities. Project A should be deferred to give priority to project D; the scope of project L should be changed to reduce its risk; and so on. Conceptually, setting these priorities is viewed as a top-down and bottom-up alignment.

Strategic balance is a top-down process. It defines a strategic profile of how a company chooses to balance its new product investments. It estab-

The key is aligning the top-down strategic targeted mix with the bottom-up actual mix.

lishes the criteria for the preferred mix of opportunities that fits a company's strategy. This requires making the trade-offs discussed earlier, and specifying the desired balance: long term versus short term, high risk versus low risk, and so on. The result is usually summarized in a table defining the targeted criteria.

The bottom-up process involves collecting actual information from product development projects. Usually, this is done manually as a recurrent project, but increasingly it is being automated by product development management systems (discussed in the next section of this chapter). The information is then summarized and presented in various charts for management analysis.

The key is aligning the top-down *strategic targeted* mix with the bottom-up *actual* mix. Where certain criteria are not aligned, a company needs to decide what actions to take. It can realign projects in the development pipeline to better balance the target criteria. It can bias the criteria for approving new projects in order to bring the mix into alignment. It can also choose to ignore the alignment problems and decide that the targeted mix is not important.

In practice, this rebalancing is much more difficult than it appears. For example, changing the portfolio mix to reduce risk may cause the short-term/long-term mix to go out of balance. The portfolio mix also needs to be balanced with another constraint: the resources available to complete the projects in the portfolio as planned. Rebalancing the mix will some-times initiate replanning of some of the projects in the portfolio, which can, in turn, change the balance again.

Currently, many of those responsible for managing this complex process do not have sophisticated tools, so it can take a lot of time and effort. For this reason, many companies attempt to do it only periodically, when there is a need to step back and reevaluate their portfolio and devel-opment pipeline. Now, integration of this process as a regular activity in the product development process is becoming feasible with the availabil-ity of enterprise software for product development and more advanced tools for portfolio management.

Beyond Portfolio Management

In many ways, portfolio management and strategic balance have simply been surrogates for the information that has not been available to man-agers until now. New Web-based enterprise software for the product development process has recently given com-panies the opportunity to go beyond portfolio management to achieve

> *In many ways, portfolio manage-ment and strategic balance have simply been surrogates for the in-formation that has not been avail-able to managers until now.*

a whole new level of performance, by integrating all the information in product development projects and product strategy. This integration will change the way companies do product strategy and integrate it into prod-uct development.

In many ways, this change is very similar to the change that took place in the 1970s when MRP (materials requirements planning) replaced the inventory management practices used up until then. Before then, inventory was planned according to mathematical formulas for reorder points: Companies determined when to reorder an item to replenish inventory on the basis of historical usage patterns. There was a lot of debate over the best formulas, but none was very accurate if the future need was unlike that of the past need, which was often the case.

Large-scale computer technology and MRP software enabled companies to integrate information distributed throughout manufacturing. Companies were able to take a forecast of what they expected to sell and extrapolate that into subassemblies and components to determine gross requirements. Material in process or on hand was subtracted from these gross requirements to determine net requirements. These, in turn, could be time-phased and compared with what was already on order to suggest when purchase orders needed to be placed. This was the information that manufacturing really needed. The resulting improvement in manufacturing performance was remarkable.

Large-scale, Web-based technology and product development enterprise software are enabling a similar change in product development management in the following ways.

1. *Consolidated revenue and profit forecasts will replace portfolio analysis.* Portfolio analysis and strategic balance guidelines provide a useful test to see if the current pipeline of products under development fit with the goals for strategic balance. But this is not what senior management really wants to know. What it wants to know is the forecasted revenue and profit for all products under development. A distribution of expected ROI on products in development is interesting, but what management really wants is some assurance that the investment in product development will enable the company to grow and be profitable for the next several years.

The problem is that this information is not easily available. Individual project teams have revenue and profit forecasts for their products, but these are usually buried in spreadsheets or presentations, using different formats, time horizons, and levels of detail. Consolidating this information manually is a major task. Someone needs to get the information from each project team and then consolidate it on a spreadsheet. Even then, the results may be unreliable because of the variation in the way teams prepare the data.

Since enterprise software for product development automates this data consistently for all products under development, the consolidation across projects is a by-product (just as the inventory on hand for MRP was a by-product of stockroom automation). This automatic consolidation will provide management with new insights into product development, such as the following:

- Consolidated revenue and profit forecasts to show if products under development will achieve growth expectations.
- Consolidated breakdown of revenue by channel, product category, or geography to see if any unusual shift can be anticipated.
- Consolidated forecasts of expected cost of goods sold, marketing and sales expense, and so forth to compare against high-level forecasts.
- Consolidated schedule of product release dates to show the sales force a profile of what is expected.
- Consolidated summary of resource requirements to complete all products under development.
- Consolidated summary of capital requirements assumed in approved product development plans.

Since the information comes from actual project data, it's available on demand and in real time. Changes at the individual project level are immediately reflected in the consolidated information.

2. *Product strategy and product development will be integrated.* Portfolio analysis suffers from this major assumption: Since the analysis includes only current development projects, it assumes that no new projects will be started. This, of course, is an invalid assumption, and calls into question the validity of the analysis beyond the short term.

Enterprise software will automate product strategy information and integrate it with product development to provide a comprehensive view with capabilities such as the following:

- Preparation, management, and communication of product line and product platform plans.
- Rough estimate of critical characteristics (forecasted revenue and profit, estimated resource requirements, etc.) for planned products.
- Consolidations similar to those described in the previous sections, with planned products included.
- Platform element analysis.
- Technology roadmaps.
- Platform life cycle management.

The ability to integrate rough-cut information from planned products with the information on products under development will provide management with the comprehensive information it needs to make the decisions that will grow the business.

3. *Product strategy will be balanced with development capacity.* The integration of product strategy with resource management will finally enable

those developing product strategy to take resource capacity into consideration. Previously, educated guesses about available capacity were about the best that could be hoped for in developing platform and product line plans. A product line plan was a time-phased conditional plan modified as resources became available to actually begin development.

Once a product line and new platform plans are translated into rough-cut capacity requirements, resource requirements can be estimated. This can be integrated with estimates of expected capacity availability in order to adjust the sequence and timing for release of product offerings and new product platform development. The capability will enable companies to put into development more realistic product strategy and development plans.

4. *Simulation of alternatives will enable an optimized product strategy.* With the ability to consider capacity in formulating product strategy, the obvious next step is to ask "what if" questions. What if we canceled the development of product K and product L to provide capacity to develop product M? Will this produce more revenue and profit over the next three years? Answers to questions like these will enable companies to increase the impact of product strategy decisions beyond portfolio analysis.

And the analysis can be taken even further with more complex questions. What if we delay products K and L and accelerate development of product M? Answering this question requires multilevel plans and forecasts for all products in development. This is the capability eventually expected of advanced product strategy application software. In some ways, it is like the simulation capabilities of supply chain software.

5. *Product development forecasts will be integrated with financial plans.* Consolidation capabilities will enable companies to integrate quantitative product strategy forecasts (including both planned products and development projects) with financial plans. Until these enterprise software systems became available, these could not be aligned. Product development projects were individually approved based on their own forecasts. Forecasted revenue from new products was one of the most critical elements of financial plans, but this forecast was rarely based on what was currently in development, since the information was simply too difficult to get and usually inconsistent.

Strategic Balance in Action

This case study illustrates how a multidivision company approached strategic balance. The company has six divisions, each developing related but different products (Figure 16-2). In this case, the company used PRTM's R&D Effectiveness Index as an overall strategic metric for R&D. The R&D Effectiveness Index compares the profit from new products

	New Product Revenue %	Profit % of New Products	Investment in R&D	Effectiveness Index
Division A	30%	25%	9%	1.13
Division B	15%	18%	7%	0.54
Division C	20%	10%	8%	0.45
Division D	30%	10%	9%	0.63
Division E	10%	10%	6%	0.27
Division F	5%	12%	7%	0.14

Figure 16-2   A hypothetical example shows how a company can manage its "R&D effectiveness."

with the investment in new product development, using a formula. As a simple interpretation, the index computes the ratio of increased profits from new products, divided by the investment in product development. When the index is above 1.0, the return from new product development is running at a rate greater than the investment.[4]

The CEO was not satisfied with the results of the new product development efforts. He believed intuitively that the company was not getting enough in return for its research and development investments. "Our growth has been less than 10 percent per year," he said, "while the industry has been growing at 25 percent. Our profit margins are shrinking every year, and we don't seem to have as many new products as our competitors."

He didn't know what to do. "The directors think I should cut R&D spending. They also believe that we shouldn't be investing the same relative percentage of R&D in each division, but they don't have any specific suggestions on how to shift it. Marketing and engineering, of course, say that we are not spending enough. Lately, I've begun to wonder if we have fundamental problems in our product strategy."

The CEO didn't have a way to measure the performance of product development, and as a result he didn't know how to fix it. The R&D Effectiveness Index provided him with the measure of performance he needed. Overall, the company had an R&D Effectiveness Index of 0.5. Approximately 20 percent of its revenue came from new products, and the profit on these products was 12 percent. The company invested 8 percent of revenue in R&D (computation: $[20\% \times (12\% + 8\%)] / 8\%$). The index varied widely by division, as seen in Figure 16-2.

Even though it invested more in new product development, Division A had the highest index, owing to a higher percentage of new products and a higher rate of profitability. Divisions C and D also invested heavily in R&D, but their index was lower because the profitability of their new products was less. Divisions B, E, and F had a low percentage of new products in their revenue and, as a result, had a low R&D Effectiveness Index.

No one, including the CEO, knew why each division invested what it did in R&D. A budget of 6 to 9 percent seemed to be acceptable within the company, and the R&D budget just continued from year to year, increasing at about the same rate that the divisions grew. The differences in the R&D Effectiveness Index across divisions were not easily explained. Perhaps some had better markets than others. Division A, for example, was in a hot market, while division F was in a mature market.

The CEO set an ambitious goal for improvement. Using the R&D Effectiveness Index as the overall metric, he set a goal of improving effectiveness from 0.5 to 1.4 over the next five years. Underlying goals were to improve the new product content of revenue from 20 to 40 percent, increase the profitability for new products from 12 to 15 percent, and reduce R&D investment from 8 to 6 percent. This would result in an index of 1.4 ([40% × (15% + 6%)] / 6%). These underlying goals, as well as the R&D Effectiveness Index, were set by year. They were composite goals for the company as a whole; each division had its own individual goals.

The company implemented a two-pronged program to increase its Effectiveness Index. One focused on improving the product development process within each division. The second was aimed at changing the company's strategic balance and deploying its R&D resources differently.

Until that point, the divisions had not set any criteria for deploying their resources. They assigned resources on a project-by-project basis without reflecting on the overall mix. There was no strategic balance to their product strategy; any balance or imbalance was the result of individual tactical decisions. The resulting profile of their current portfolio is characterized in the Current Criteria column in Figure 16-3.

The CEO set out to achieve a strategic balance. The short-term emphasis on product development would be more evenly balanced with long-term opportunities. Half of these long-term opportunities would involve new product platforms to replace the current platforms. More emphasis would be placed on diversification, particularly opportunities for growth by expanding into related markets.

The criteria for financial return were segmented into three levels. Most (60 percent) of the projects would require an ROI of 30 percent or greater. Some would be permitted an ROI of 20 to 30 percent, but these opportunities would need to be prioritized using other criteria, since only 30 percent of all projects would be funded at this level of return. A smaller num-

	Current Criteria	Target Criteria
Short Term vs. Long Term	Short Term: 80% Long Term: 20%	50/50% Split Between Short and Long Term
Current vs. New Platform	Current Platforms: 95% New Platforms: 5%	Invest at Least 25% in New Platforms
Focus vs. Diversification	Focus: 99% Diversification: 1%	Selectively Invest Between 10% and 20% in Diversification
Low vs. High Risk	Low Risk: 90% High Risk: 10%	Allow High-Risk Projects to Be as Much as 25% of Total
Financial Return	Hurdle Rate of 15% ROI	60% of Projects: 30% ROI 30% of Projects: 15% – 30% ROI 10% Strategic: No ROI
Investment by Division	6 – 9% of Revenue in Each Division	Reduce R&D in Divisions E and F by Half Allocate 10% of R&D for Company-Wide Opportunities
Innovation vs. Development	Innovation: 0% Development: 100%	Innovation: 10% Development: 90%

Figure 16-3   This hypothetical example shows the gap between current and target criteria for a product portfolio that has not been strategically balanced yet.

ber (10 percent) of projects would be considered strategic, and no ROI would need to be estimated. Most of these were expected to be innovation or research projects.

The balance across divisions was also being changed. R&D in divisions E and F would be reduced by half. R&D investment in other divisions would be adjusted to fit their R&D Effectiveness Index targets. Finally, 10 percent of all R&D would be allocated companywide instead of by division, a move that would fund some of the diversification efforts. The CEO expected it would take three years to achieve this targeted strategic balance.

Although the work was just beginning, the CEO felt in control, having set a clear direction. "We certainly have our work cut out for us, but we know what we need to do and how we are going to get there. The R&D Effectiveness Index is our overall guide. There is no magic to the goal of 1.4. Perhaps we could do even better. However, I do know that an improvement of that magnitude is both achievable and badly needed."

Notes

1. Steven C. Wheelwright and Kim B. Clark, *Revolutionizing Product Development* (The Free Press, 1992).

2. Julie Pitta, *Business Week,* February 1, 1993, p. 75.

3. ROI is frequently calculated improperly, and the result is wrong. Despite this, it is still used to make decisions.

4. For additional information on the R&D Effectiveness Index, see *PRTM Insight,* Summer 1998.

17

The Process
Elements

Companies with a better product strategy process create better product strategy. Why, then, do so many companies fail to recognize the importance of product strategy as a process?

It is hoped that by this point, we've established the importance of product strategy in determining the destiny of high-technology companies. For some, the thinking in this book may provoke a call to action to improve product strategy in their company. Where should they start? Our underlying belief is that product strategy is a *management process,* and the results are only as good as the process of getting there. In the

> **Product strategy is a management process, and the results are only as good as the process of getting there.**

six years since the original edition of this book, PRTM has helped many high-technology companies improve their product strategy by implementing a management process for product strategy. Almost without exception, every one of these companies changed its strategic direction, aligned all its related strategies, and began executing a new product strategy with a reinvigorated confidence.

Some companies appear to instinctively excel at product strategy, because they have an individual leader with the right instincts and sufficient influence at the right time. While this is one way for a company to develop a successful product strategy, throughout this book we've seen examples of companies that failed when leadership changed or when their leaders' instincts were wrong "the next time around." A sustainable product strategy goes beyond dependence on the instincts of any single leader; it requires that product strategy become an *institutional* proficiency. This gets us back to the importance of a product strategy process.

We began this book with a discussion of strategic vision; both the various types of visions, and the importance of a core strategic vision (CSV): Where are we going? How will we get there? Why will we succeed? A CSV is thus both a map and a compass. It's the seminal tool not simply for conceiving and shaping a product strategy, but for shaping all other organizational strategies and incorporating them en masse into a unified, purposeful, and practicable context. The point we're most emphasizing is that a product strategy is only one outcome of a CSV.

Just as the CSV shapes product strategy at the overall business level, the market platform plan (MPP) shapes it at the operational level. The MPP serves as the market-level "translation" of the CSV, especially for companies that serve multiple markets or market segments. It determines how best to configure new products from the standpoint of the organization's intended customers, and the best time, from a market standpoint, to introduce new products. Market platform planning, when done properly, keeps high-technology companies from becoming exclusively "product-centric," to the detriment of customer pathway planning. A good product strategy is focused on market opportunities, by way of specific product platforms and product lines.

> *Market platform planning keeps high-technology companies from becoming exclusively "product-centric," to the detriment of customer pathway planning.*

Then, there's the matter of strategic boundaries: the limits, both imposed and chosen, within which product strategy must fit. We've discussed boundary conditions in the context of an organization's core strategic vision. Boundaries may or may not be malleable. The technological evolution and competitive trends in a particular industry are apt to be very difficult boundary conditions to change, but goals for short-term financial growth can be altered to accommodate a product strategy with the greatest ultimate potential. Investments in new areas of technology can change a company's product strategy boundaries, but such investments need to make sense in the context of an organization's overall business strategy.

Many of the companies we've worked with have what is sometimes referred to as a "fuzzy front end" when it comes to product strategy. They have a lot of individual product ideas, which, as often as not, are not connected in any discernible way. Needless to say, these companies have a lot to learn about overall business planning and strategy, not to mention project pipeline management and product platform strategy. They haven't begun to look at all the consequences of their often impulsive decisions to develop this or that product. Their strategies, by necessity, are oriented toward business units and functions, but they must also be integrated with other strategies being executed within their organizations.

Fortunately, more and more high-technology companies are realizing that they need not only better product strategies, but also much tighter links among all their strategies. At the highest level, they need to develop the ability to translate intentions into actions, even under the stresses of complexity and uncertainty that are a fact of life in high-technology industries. And they need to develop the ability to adapt to change at the accelerating pace of change. Those skills amount to what we call strategic integration.

Strategic Integration

Product strategy is not an island unto itself. It is one component of a company's overall business strategy. While it's almost a fact of life that organizational structures create disconnections among organizational strategies, the aim of strategic integration is to close those disconnections. Product strategy must be integrated with, and thus compatible with, other strategies, and the product strategy process must be integrated with other strategic processes. These include manufacturing and supply chain strategies, customer relationship management strategies (marketing, sales, channel management, and customer service/support), and a company's overall business planning, including its annual budget planning and long-range strategic planning.

Strategic integration, in its ultimate form, is a cross-functional strategic planning process that's focused on organizational context setting. Beginning with the core strategic vision, it determines the organization's overall direction, focusing on the "vital few" long-term initiatives that are critical to business success, and allocating the organization's resources accordingly. The CSV also aligns investments with strategic investment targets. At the market platform planning (MPP) level, strategic integration entails the development of realistic, sustainable, and winning plans for attacking specific business opportunities. The MPP level of strategic integration also enables trade-offs to be made among investments in various specific product opportunities.

Another development that has made strategic integration increasingly important is that many high-technology companies are, in a sense, the victims of their own gains in executing individual processes and activities. Inevitably, their process execution skills start to outpace their strategy-setting capabilities. In other words, their ability to *do* begins to outstrip their ability to figure out *what* to do next. And, as previously mentioned, the convergence of complexity and uncertainty in the high-tech sphere

> *Among its other functions, strategic integration keeps the horse in front of the cart; it ensures that strategy precedes execution, whatever pressures and distractions an organization happens to be facing.*

only compounds the problem. A lot of companies are much more complex than they used to be, and the competitive environments in which they operate have become a great deal more unstable. Among its other functions, strategic integration keeps the horse in front of the cart; it ensures that strategy precedes execution, whatever pressures and distractions an organization happens to be facing. Again, it also keeps the company's purpose—its core strategic vision—from breaking up under stress into a jumble of disjointed purposes.

Process Architecture

A thorough description of the product strategy process is well beyond the scope of this book, but we'd like to provide an overview here. How does a company actually *do* product strategy? *Who* does what? *When* do people do it? *What* skills do they need to do it well? How do the individual activities *fit* together? The answers to these questions define product strategy as a management process. Fundamentally, it's a series of actions, activities, and decisions to bring about a result: a successful product strategy.

The process of product strategy is unique for every company, since each has its own organization, different types of products, distinct culture, and unique management style. We've found in our experience, however, that there is enough commonality to enable the product strategy process to be described at a high level.

Figure 17-1 shows how the frameworks and strategies previously described (referred to here, in a process context, as *elements*) work together. This can be used essentially as a "blueprint" for the product strategy process. Any management process defines structure, timing, responsibilities, and skills. *Structure* defines what goes where. *Timing* delineates what elements precede others and how frequently each element of the process is executed. A management process also needs a clear definition of who is

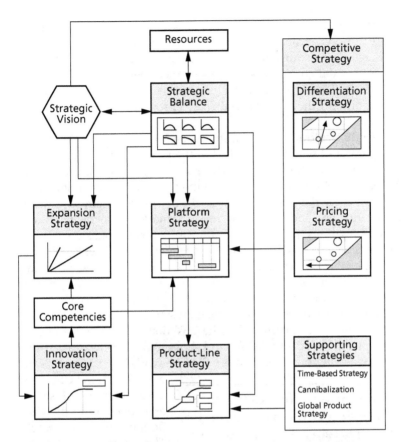

Figure 17-1   Product strategy is a management process, and, like any such process, it defines structure, timing, responsibilities, and skills.

responsible for each element of the process. Without a clear definition of responsibility, a process tends to founder and lose momentum while waiting for somebody to do something. Furthermore, conflict can occur when different people end up doing the same task, or tasks fall through the cracks because everyone assumes someone else will take care of things. Finally, in product strategy, *skill* is a necessary ingredient.

Fitting the Six Elements of the Process Together

The product strategy process has six structural elements. The first three—strategic vision, platform strategy, and product line strategy—are basic. As we discuss in Chapter 5, all product strategy flows either explicitly or implicitly through these three levels. Expansion strategy and innovation strategy are optional structural elements. A company needs them only if it wants to invest in expansion or growth. Strategic balance and portfolio management regulate the other elements to keep them within the mix of objectives. Each of these elements is discussed earlier in some detail; the focus here is on how they work together as a process.

Core Strategic Vision. The core strategic vision gives direction to the entire company, and within the context of the product strategy process it provides the direction for product platform strategy. If the current platform strategy is not adequate to achieve the strategic vision, a new platform strategy is needed. In some cases, a new platform strategy alone may not be sufficient, and expansion into new markets may be necessary. Strategic vision guides the extent and direction of this expansion.

Strategic vision also sets the tone for competitive strategy. It suggests the general direction for vectors of differentiation (see Chapter 7) by indicating how products can succeed. It implies the importance of price in product strategy and may indicate the need for *supporting strategies*. Strategic vision also guides strategic balance and portfolio management. Strategic vision can be arrived at within a company, using the CSV Boundary Framework outlined in Chapter 2. We've found CSV workshops to be extremely successful in formally reviewing or developing a CSV. The workshop is usually conducted with the CEO and a small group of senior executives using the CSV Boundary Framework. The process of applying the boundary conditions of financial plan/economic model, market trends, technology trends/strategy, product strategy, business charter, and core competencies/value chain as a group helps achieve consensus around not only the CSV but also the strategic actions necessary to implement it.

> *Platform strategy first articulates the strategic vision as a specific product strategy. Failure to recognize this next step in the process inhibits implementation of the vision.*

Platform Strategy. Platform strategy first articulates the strategic vision as a specific product strategy. Failure to recognize this next step in the process inhibits implementation of the vision. It's this specific relationship to platform strategy that puts the core strategic vision into action. The software company CEO we discuss in Chapter 1, who out of frustration distributed a 53-page vision memo to all employees, did not understand how these process elements were linked. He didn't have a process view of product strategy; he thought it somehow "just happened."

Since the result of expansion strategy is usually a new product platform, it can initiate platform strategy. Competitive strategy is implemented primarily at the platform strategy level. This is where the vector of differentiation is created and the cost structure established. It is also where a strategy based on a first-to-market or fast-follower approach is considered, as well as one based on a global product or cannibalization. The strength of core competencies limits platform strategy.

Platform strategy is a critical part of the market platform plan described in Chapter 5. Developing the MPP is primary in any product strategy process.

Product Line Strategy. Product line strategy is a subset of product platform strategy, since the individual products within a product line generally stem from a common platform. Like platform strategy, product line strategy is regulated by the strategic balance element to maintain the appropriate mix of investments. Product line strategy is also driven by the elements of competitive strategy, but it is constrained by what was done at the platform level.

Product line strategy is typically included in the development of the MPP, since it is so highly dependent on platform strategy.

Expansion Strategy. Expansion strategy exists somewhat outside the basic product strategy process structure. It's optional and not pursued by some companies. Since its focus is much broader than platform strategy, it's only loosely coupled to strategic vision and strategic balance, which guide its extent and direction. Expansion strategy requires leveraging core competencies—whether they are available, must be developed, or need to be acquired. It's a multistep process. The first step is to consider the need for an expansion strategy. When the product strategy boundary in the CSV is insufficient to achieve the vision, this need is identified. The next step is to evaluate the possible opportunities along various expansion paths in order to develop a prioritized list of potential new product platforms that could enable a company to grow. Finally, one or two of these potential new platform opportunities is evaluated as part of an MPP process.

Innovation Strategy. Expansion opportunities and innovation are closely linked. Innovation can be guided by the desired direction of expansion and may create the core competencies needed for expansion. Innovation is not driven by strategic balance, but is limited by the funding allocated to the pursuit or nurturing of innovations. Because innovation strategy is a set of changes to organizational practices and philosophies to stimulate innovation, the results are not as clear as those of the other structural elements.

Strategic Balance and Portfolio Management. The priorities established by the objectives of strategic balance serve to allocate resources and provide direction to platform strategy, expansion opportunities, product line strategy, and innovation. This is generally a rough-cut allocation providing strategic guidance only. Specific resources are assigned to individual projects in product development through a phase review process in which it's most likely that the portfolio will be considered.

Strategic balance initially reconciles the strategic vision and the resources available. Resources, particularly those related to product development investment, may need to be regularly adjusted to achieve the core strategic vision.

Synchronizing the Six Elements

Each element of the product strategy process is on a different schedule, making it more challenging than other management processes, since the scheduling of each element needs to be synchronized. The following is an overview of the timing for the various elements.

A CSV tends to be relatively stable, changing only when a company needs to alter its direction. In high-technology companies, strategic vision changes more frequently than in other companies, but, even here, it ordinarily changes only every three to seven years. Most companies formally review their CSV annually as a prelude to a formal strategy cycle. Using the CSV Boundary Framework for this review is excellent discipline for identifying which strategic issues need to be considered. When a company needs to consider changing its CSV, senior management, especially the CEO, must allocate more time to this process.

A company should confirm its strategic balance at least once a year, and periodically evaluate the strategic balance of its actual project portfolio to its preferred mix. This comparison is also referred to at most major product development phase reviews. The preferred mix of strategic balance is not changed very often, since it usually takes a while to make the shift. Most major changes in this balance occur when a company needs to make a strategic adjustment.

Product platform strategy is related to the life cycle of the individual product platforms, so significant changes are not very frequent. However, in the most effective product strategy processes, the MPP is reviewed annually as a part of the strategic planning cycle. Product line strategy is included in the MPP and subsequently reviewed and revised throughout the year as new products begin development.

Expansion strategy generally depends on resource availability, making allocation of sufficient resources very important. There is an exception, however. The more aggressive companies will regularly try to identify potential expansion paths as part of an aggressive growth strategy.

Innovation strategy cannot be put on a set schedule. Innovation happens when the conditions are right and the opportunities arise. All a company can do is to create the best conditions for cultivating innovation.

Figure 17-2 illustrates these cycle and timing differences over a 14-year period for a prototypical company. Its original CSV was prepared in 1990 and not revised until 1998. It also determined its strategic balance (SB) in 1990 and then revised it three times over the following 13 years. The company prepared a plan for platform A in 1990, and the platform lasted for six years, until 1996, when it was replaced by platform B, which was replaced by platform C.

The company also expanded into a new market with platform X, which was replaced by platform Y. This opportunity was identified as a result of an expansion planning effort (Exp-1) during 1996 and 1997. The company

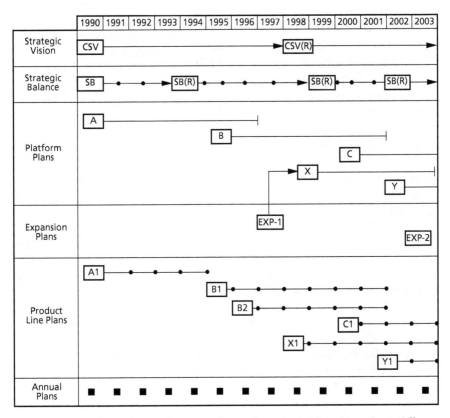

Figure 17-2 The different elements of a product strategy structure have different timing cycles.

initiated another effort (Exp-2) with expected completion in 2003. Product line plans (A1, B1, etc.) were initiated at the same time that the related platforms were completed. Platform B launched two product lines (B1 and B2). The company did annual planning at the end of each year, updating product line plans and comparing its product development portfolio with its strategic balance criteria as part of that process.

Delineating Clear Responsibility for Each Element

One of the fundamental causes of failure in product strategy is lack of clear responsibility, which varies even more than timing among companies. In some companies, the responsibilities and authorities for product strategy are not clearly defined. They are not part of someone's job, or they may be at the wrong level of authority and therefore not effectively implemented. Besides organizational and product differences, companies have differences in ability. Some executives are good at product strategy, while others are not. Nonetheless, several guidelines can be suggested for assigning responsibility.

> *A strategic vision is not formed by consensus, which leads to a diluted or unnecessarily complex vision. The CEO listens to others, evaluates alternate visions, crafts the final vision, and then preaches it to everyone.*

Role of the CEO. It's the CEO's responsibility to develop the CSV. This doesn't mean preparing it alone or in a vacuum. A wide range of views is important in forming a vision. But don't be misled. A strategic vision is not formed by consensus, which leads to a diluted or unnecessarily complex vision. The CEO listens to others, evaluates alternate visions, crafts the final vision, and then preaches it to everyone.

The CSV workshop we discussed earlier is a very effective way for the CEO to lead other members of the senior management team in shaping the CSV. Since this is a thorough, structured process, it helps keep the group focused collectively and disallows individual political issues in order to achieve a common vision.

The CEO may review the CSV with the board of directors and solicit their input. In some cases, members of the board may even attend the CSV workshop. In the end, though, it's up to the CEO to determine the vision. The responsibility of the board of directors is to replace the CEO with one who is capable of creating and implementing a CSV, if the current CEO cannot do it.

Role of Executive Management. The executive management or senior management team, as just discussed, has a role in assisting the CEO to develop a CSV, but its responsibility goes beyond that. Senior managers are responsible for approving the platform and product line strategies as part of the MPP, including competitive strategy for these products. They do this as a group, not as individual executives with specific functional responsibilities.

In PRTM's PACE[1] process for product development, the senior management group responsible for approving individual products is referred to as the PAC (product approval committee). In that context, the senior or executive management group responsible for approving MPPs is sometimes referred to as the S/PAC (strategy PAC). The makeup of an S/PAC varies, but it includes those responsible for the overall product strategy of the company. The CEO is a member and frequently the chairman of this group.

In addition to approving the MPPs, the senior management team as a group also initiates investigation of opportunities for expansion into new markets, and works on an MPP for this expansion. Senior executives in a company are responsible for setting the strategic balance criteria, selecting the expansion paths to be evaluated, and approving platform strategy. This is the responsibility of the senior executives who have the authority to set product strategy for the company.

Role of Market Attack Teams. An MPP is prepared by a small cross-functional team, formed by the executive management group and empowered to develop the MPP, working to a very specific process and schedule (typically two to three months) for completion of the MPP. Usually, the team members are managers with the breadth of experience and necessary skills to develop the MPP in addition to their other responsibilities. They are sometimes referred to as market attack teams (MATs) to emphasize proactive product strategy.

At the completion of the MPP, these teams recommend a comprehensive platform and product line strategy to the S/PAC for approval. Small teams guided by senior executives, which can also be chartered as market attack teams, then evaluate specific expansion paths and define potential innovation opportunities for individual projects.

Integrating Product Strategy with Product and Technology Development

The product strategy process does not exist in a vacuum. It is tightly integrated with other management processes, particularly product development and technology development. This integration is depicted in Figure 17-3.

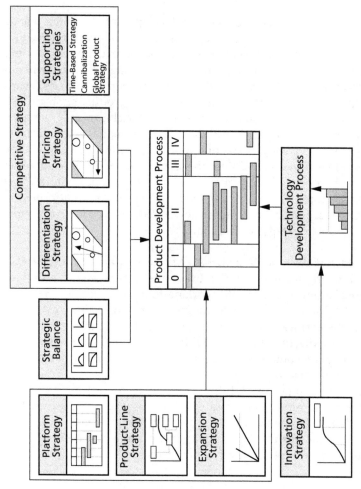

Figure 17-3 The product strategy process is tightly integrated with product and technology development.

Product strategy and product development are integrated in two principal ways. First, the product strategy process, through product platform strategy, product line strategy, and expansion strategy, creates the specific opportunities for new product development. These opportunities are clarified and reviewed as part of the concept evaluation phase (Phase 0) of product development. If they pass the review, opportunities become projects and proceed through development, usually through a phase review process.

In the two initial phases of the review process, a new product opportunity is evaluated for its strategic fit and its chance of competitive success. This is where competitive strategy is integrated. The general basis for competing was established in the CSV, but it is applied specifically at this point. The success of competitive strategy is considered before the opportunity progresses to later phases of development.

The product approval committee typically considers strategic balance and portfolio management as it approves individual projects. Sometimes it makes adjustments to the product line plan if needed.

The product strategy process is also integrated with the technology development process. The CSV sets the direction for technology strategy, as it does for product strategy. Specific technology development is integrated in preparing an MPP. Innovation strategy sets the tone and agenda for technology strategy and development.

Using Core Competencies to Leverage or Restrict Product Strategy

As we previously discussed, core competencies can leverage or restrict product strategy. Core competencies in technology and marketing are directly applied to product platforms and individual products. There is also another type of core competency that is not directly applied to a product; instead, it enables a particular product strategy. For example, a company with a core competency that enables it to develop products faster than competitors can implement strategies based on timing that competitors cannot match because they do not have this competency.

> *Without any particular technical core competency, a high-technology company is hard-pressed to establish a vector of differentiation beyond a temporary, easily copied feature or function.*

Technical Core Competencies. Technical core competencies help companies achieve sustainable vectors of differentiation. By developing, improving, or applying a technology better than that of competitors, a high-technology company can establish a vector for differentiating its product in a way that achieves competitive advantage. Without any particular technical core competency, a high-technology company is hard-pressed to establish a vector of differentiation beyond a temporary, easily copied feature or function.

Expansion strategies that employ product/technology leverage depend on technical core competencies. If a company has technical core competencies that are robust and rapidly improving, it should have many potential expansion paths. Microsoft was in this position and took advantage of its technical core competencies in its expansion strategies. If a company's technical core competencies have atrophied or become obsolete, it has very little leverage to expand in the product/technology direction.

Marketing Core Competencies. Marketing core competencies are usually related to unique advantages in the marketplace, particularly channels of distribution or close relationships with customers. A superior position in an important channel of distribution is a core competency that can exploit expansion paths in this direction.

Although more difficult to establish and sustain than other core competencies, a close relationship with customers may also provide a core competency for understanding the market, which, in turn, can be used to identify a vector of differentiation not seen by competitors.

Time-Based Strategy and Product Development Competency. Chapter 9 explains why successful time-based strategy requires a core competency in product development. If a company has a better product development process than its competitors, it can pursue an exciting range of timing strategies. It can be first to market, or it can be a fast follower. However, if it does not have a core competency in managing its product development process, its timing strategy options are severely limited. It can be first to market only by starting way ahead of its competitors, and even then it needs to worry about eventually being passed by faster competitors.

Pricing Strategy and Manufacturing Supply Chain Competencies. Manufacturing supply chain competencies refer collectively to the integrated processes of order fulfillment through manufacturing to supplier management. Companies need to have a quick, low-cost supply chain to compete successfully using a pricing strategy offense. Chapter 6 explains that a company needs to be the best at managing its product costs, or it will simply lose money by competing this way. Managing product costs means managing the entire supply chain, not just one link, such as production costs.

Pricing Strategy and Product Development Competency.   Pricing strategy may also require a management core competency in the product development process for a company to be a low-cost competitor. There are two reasons for this requirement. First, design for cost and the discipline to develop low-cost platforms need to be an integral part of the product development process. Second, in cases where development is a significant cost element, the product development process itself needs to be highly productive.

Global Product Strategy and Global Operations Competencies. Chapter 10 shows how global product strategy is closely linked with a company's global operations capabilities, including its international manufacturing and its worldwide product development process. Without a core competency in these processes, execution of a global product strategy will be inefficient, although it may not be competitively threatened unless competitors can execute a global product strategy well enough to achieve an economic advantage.

Differentiation Strategy and Product Development Competency. A differentiation strategy also may depend on a core competency in product development, since clearly defining and implementing a vector of differentiation is not always easy. It frequently requires a disciplined and rigorous product development process that emphasizes differentiation throughout the phases of development.

Product Strategy Proficiency

Why was Microsoft able to grow from a $125 million software company in 1984 to a $21.9 billion powerhouse in 15 years, while other software companies of that era, such as Lotus and WordPerfect, were left behind? Why did companies like Wang fail? Why did Compaq and Dell succeed in the 1990s while many other PC companies went out of business? How could Amazon.com build a major e-commerce business while others failed? Why did Apple Computer have so many ups and downs?

Success versus failure. Excellence versus mediocrity. Growth versus stagnation. For most high-technology companies, the difference comes down to a good product strategy versus a bad one or a sustainable strategy versus getting it right one time. Successful high-technology companies are proficient at product strategy.

Product strategy proficiency requires raising product strategy from a fortuitous, periodic event to a core competency, and this doesn't happen by chance. It requires a product strategy process and the integration of that process with other strategies and other management processes. The product strategy process is no different from other management processes, such as the supply chain process or the product development process. It needs to be designed, developed, and successfully implemented before it can be expected to yield results.

> *Product strategy proficiency requires raising product strategy from a fortuitous, periodic event to a core competency, and this does not happen by chance.*

Designing a product strategy process is complex for several reasons. First, most companies lack a common understanding of the conceptual terminology necessary for understanding and communicating product strategy. While crisp, concise communication is important in developing a product strategy, key terms such as *product platforms* and *defining technology* have widely different meanings throughout a company. Second, some of the concepts and frameworks we describe may need to be introduced throughout the company, necessitating a broad education program for the management team. Finally, the process itself needs to be designed. This includes a definition of the process elements, their interaction with each other, and the way they integrate with other processes.

Developing the details of the product strategy process involves taking the design down to the next level. Frameworks must be introduced, such as the core strategic vision and the market platform plan, as well as new techniques. Typically, this requires some significant training and facilitation.

Finally, changing any management process is always difficult, and the product strategy process is no exception. In fact, because of the critical impact it has on the company and because of multiple strategic perspectives, it's usually even more difficult to implement. Implementation starts with an advocate within the company who envisions the opportunity to improve product strategy proficiency. With the backing of senior management, this advocate undertakes the effort to build or rebuild a product strategy process. A change is usually seen immediately as the company shifts its strategic direction as a result of the new process.

Product strategy proficiency requires a commitment to a product strategy process. There is no other way to achieve consistent success.

Note

1. PACE® (Product And Cycle-time Excellence®) is the product development process framework developed by PRTM and used by more than 350 companies.

Index

About the Author

Michael E. McGrath is a cofounder and managing director of Pittiglio Rabin Todd & McGrath (PRTM), a leader in helping technology-based companies develop agile, robust management processes and methodologies. In over two decades of management consulting, he has worked with more than 100 companies in the United States, Europe, and Asia. McGrath initiated PACE® (Product And Cycle-time Excellence®), PRTM's product-development consulting practice, and has directed many of PRTM's projects in reducing time-to-market in a variety of high-technology companies. He coauthored the books *Product Development* and *Setting the PACE in Product Development*, and has published numerous articles on international manufacturing, product development, and trends in the high-technology industry.